# Aspects of Teaching Secondary Mathematics

The Open University *Flexible*
Postgraduate Certificate of Education

The readers and the companion volumes in the *flexible* PGCE series are:

*Aspects of Teaching and Learning in Secondary Schools: Perspectives on practice*

*Teaching, Learning and the Curriculum in Secondary Schools: A reader*

*Aspects of Teaching Secondary Mathematics: Perspectives on practice*

*Teaching Mathematics in Secondary Schools: A reader*

*Aspects of Teaching Secondary Science: Perspectives on practice*

*Teaching Science in Secondary Schools: A reader*

*Aspects of Teaching Secondary Modern Foreign Languages: Perspectives on practice*

*Teaching Modern Foreign Languages in Secondary Schools: A reader*

*Aspects of Teaching Secondary Geography: Perspectives on practice*

*Teaching Geography in Secondary Schools: A reader*

*Aspects of Teaching Secondary Design and Technology: Perspectives on practice*

*Teaching Design and Technology in Secondary Schools: A reader*

*Aspects of Teaching Secondary Music: Perspectives on practice*

*Teaching Music in Secondary Schools: A reader*

All of these subjects are part of the Open University's initial teacher education course, the *flexible* PGCE, and constitute part of an integrated course designed to develop critical understanding. The set books, reflecting a wide range of perspectives, and discussing the complex issues that surround teaching and learning in the twenty-first century, will appeal to both beginning and experienced teachers, to mentors, tutors, advisers and other teacher educators.

If you would like to receive a *flexible* PGCE prospectus please write to the Course Reservations Centre at The Call Centre, The Open University, Milton Keynes MK7 6ZS. Other information about programmes of professional development in education is available from the same address.

# Aspects of Teaching Secondary Mathematics

Perspectives on practice

Edited by Linda Haggarty

London and New York

First published 2002
by RoutledgeFalmer
11 New Fetter Lane, London EC4P 4EE

Simultaneously published in the USA and Canada
by RoutledgeFalmer
29 West 35th Street, New York, NY 10001

*RoutledgeFalmer is an imprint of the Taylor & Francis Group*

© 2002 Compilation, original and editorial matter,
The Open University

Typeset in Bembo by Bookcraft Ltd, Stroud, Gloucestershire
Printed and bound in Great Britain by Bell & Bain Ltd, Glasgow

*British Library Cataloguing in Publication Data*
A catalogue record for this book is available from the British Library

*Library of Congress Cataloging in Publication Data*
A catalog record has been requested

ISBN 0–415–26641–6

# Contents

List of figures                                                                          vii
List of tables                                                                           viii
List of abbreviations                                                                    ix
Foreword                                                                                 xi
Introduction                                                                             xiii

**PART 1  The Mathematics classroom**

1   The changing primary mathematics classroom: the challenge of the
    National Numeracy Strategy                                                           3
    MIKE ASKEW

2   Mathematics 11–16                                                                    18
    STEPHANIE PRESTAGE

3   Examining some changes in mathematics post-16                                        33
    DOUG FRENCH

4   Mathematics for post-16 vocational courses                                          52
    SUSAN MOLYNEUX-HODGSON AND ROSAMUND SUTHERLAND

**PART 2  The Mathematics curriculum**

5   School mathematics and mathematical proof                                            71
    MELISSA RODD AND JOHN MONAGHAN

6   Issues in the teaching and learning of arithmetic                                    91
    PETER HUCKSTEP

7   Generalisation and algebra: exploiting children's powers                            105
    JOHN MASON

8   Issues in the teaching and learning of geometry                                     121
    KEITH JONES

9   Probability and randomness                                                          140
    DAVE PRATT

**PART 3  Pedagogical issues**

10  Teaching for understanding                                                          153
    ANNE WATSON

11  Progression in mathematics                                             164
    PAT PERKS

12  Language issues in mathematics                                         179
    TIM ROWLAND

13  Differentiation                                                        191
    LINDA HAGGARTY

14  Developing thinking in mathematics                                     203
    MARIA GOULDING

15  Mental mathematics                                                     217
    CHRIS BILLS

16  Making the most of your textbook                                       228
    LAURINDA BROWN

17  Minding your Qs and Rs: effective questioning and responding
    in the mathematics classroom                                           248
    JOHN MASON

18  Coursework and its assessment                                         259
    CANDIA MORGAN

19  Formative assessment in mathematics                                    273
    DYLAN WILIAM

Index                                                                      285

# Figures

| 2.1 | Mathematics related to prime factor decomposition | 22 |
|-----|---------------------------------------------------|-----|
| 2.2 | Perimeter of a hexagon | 27 |
| 4.1 | The specification for the coursework portfolio | 57 |
| 8.1 | The likely learning sequence of functions of mathematical proof | 132 |
| 9.1 | Graphs generated from 1400 trials | 146 |
| 9.2 | Charts generated from various numbers of trials | 147 |
| 11.1 | Denvir's possible hierarchy of strategies for division | 167 |
| 11.2 | 'Splurge' diagram for 'percentages of …' | 170 |
| 11.3 | 'Splurge' diagram for solving equations | 171 |
| 11.4 | 'Splurge' diagram for equations and formulae | 173 |
| 11.5 | More 'splurge' on percentages | 177 |
| 13.1 | Variables in the learning process | 198 |
| 13.2 | Flowchart for a Mastery Learning unit of work | 200 |
| 16.1 | 'Making everyone understand' | 238 |
| 16.2 | Assessment sheet from Key Maths Teacher File | 239 |
| 18.1 | A one-dimensional table | 265 |
| 18.2 | A two-way table | 265 |
| 19.1 | Two items from the Third International Mathematics and Science Study | 274 |

# Tables

| | | |
|---|---|---|
| 2.1 | The mathematics areas for the programmes of study | 20 |
| 2.2 | Expected attainment during the Key Stages | 25 |
| 2.3 | Page 1/30, The National Numeracy Strategy | 29 |
| 2.4 | Page 3/6 extract from the Teaching programme for Year 7 | 29 |
| 3.1 | Comparison of students taking A level in mathematics and English | 35 |
| 11.1 | Extracts from the National Numeracy Strategy | 169 |
| 11.2 | Starting points for equations | 174 |
| 19.1 | Ego- and task-related attributions | 279 |
| 19.2 | Developing students' self-assessment skills | 283 |

# Abbreviations

| | |
|---|---|
| ATM | Association of Teachers of Mathematics |
| BTEC | Business and Technology Education Council |
| CAME | Cognitive Acceleration in Mathematics Education |
| CASE | Cognitive Acceleration in Science Education |
| DES | Department of Education and Science |
| DfEE | Department for Education and Employment (now Department for Education and Skills) |
| FSMU | Free-standing mathematics units |
| GCSE | General Certificate of Secondary Education |
| GNVQ | General National Vocational Qualification |
| HMI | Her Majesty's Inspector |
| ICT | Information and Communications Technology |
| ITT | Initial Teacher Training |
| JMC | Joint Mathematical Council |
| KS | Key Stage |
| MA | Mathematical Association |
| MEI | Mathematics in Education and Industry |
| NC | National Curriculum |
| NCC | National Curriculum Council |
| NNS | National Numeracy Strategy |
| NS | National Strategy |
| NVQ | National Vocational Qualification |
| PGCE | Postgraduate Certificate of Education |
| QCA | Qualifications and Curriculum Authority |
| SAT | Standard Assessment Test |
| SMP | School Mathematics Project |
| TIMSS | Third International Mathematics and Science Study |

# Sources

Where a chapter in this book is based on or is a reprint or revision of material previously published elsewhere, details are given below, with grateful acknowledgements to the original publishers. In some cases chapter titles have been changed from the original; in such cases the original chapter title is given below.

*Chapter 19* This is an edited version of three articles: 'Formative Assessment in Mathematics Part 1: Close Questioning' originally published in *Equals* 5(2), 1999; 'Formative Assessment in Mathematics Part 2: Feedback' in *Equals* 5(3), 1999; 'Formative Assessment in Mathematics Part 3: The Learner's Role' in *Equals* 6(1), 2000.

# Foreword

The nature and form of initial teacher education and training are issues that lie at the heart of the teaching profession. They are inextricably linked to the standing and identity that society attributes to teachers and are seen as being one of the main planks in the push to raise standards in schools and to improve the quality of education in them. The initial teacher education curriculum therefore requires careful definition. How can it best contribute to the development of the range of skills, knowledge and understanding that makes up the complex, multi-faceted, multi-skilled and people-centred process of teaching?

There are, of course, external, government-defined requirements for initial teacher training courses. These specify, amongst other things, the length of time a student spends in school, the subject knowledge requirements beginning teachers are expected to demonstrate or the ICT skills that are needed. These requirements, however, do not in themselves constitute the initial training curriculum. They are only one of the many, if sometimes competing, components that make up the broad spectrum of a teacher's professional knowledge that underpin initial teacher education courses.

Certainly today's teachers need to be highly skilled in literacy, numeracy and ICT, in classroom methods and management. In addition, however, they also need to be well grounded in the critical dialogue of teaching. They need to be encouraged to be creative and innovative and to appreciate that teaching is a complex and problematic activity. This is a view of teaching that is shared with partner schools within the Open University Training Schools Network. As such it has informed the planning and development of the Open University's initial teacher training programme and the *flexible* PGCE.

All of the *flexible* PGCE courses have a series of connected and complementary readers. The *Teaching in Secondary Schools* series pulls together a range of new thinking about teaching and learning in particular subjects. Key debates and differing perspectives are presented, and evidence from research and practice is explored, inviting the reader to question the accepted orthodoxy, suggesting ways of enriching the present curriculum and offering new thoughts on classroom learning. These readers are accompanied by the series *Perspectives on practice*. Here, the focus is on the application of these developments to educational/subject policy and the classroom, and on the illustration of teaching skills, knowledge and understanding in a variety of school contexts. Both series include newly commissioned work.

This series from RoutledgeFalmer, in supporting the Open University's *flexible* PGCE, also includes two key texts that explore the wider educational background. These companion publications, *Teaching and Learning and the Curriculum in Secondary Schools: A reader* and *Aspects of Teaching and Learning in Secondary Schools: Perspectives on practice,* explore a contemporary view of developments in secondary education with the aim of providing analysis and insights for those participating in initial teacher training education courses.

Hilary Bourdillon – Director ITT Strategy
Steven Hutchinson – Director ITT Secondary
The Open University
September 2001

# Introduction

Mathematics teaching is both exciting and intellectually challenging. It is exciting to be involved with young people's learning of the subject, particularly when that learning has taken place as a result, partly, of our own efforts. It is also intellectually challenging because there are so many complex decisions to be made, not only in advance of each lesson but also during each lesson.

Mathematics teachers have an important responsibility as they try to inspire learners with the power and elegance of mathematics at the same time as they help them to become successful mathematicians (as measured in a much narrower sense in national tests and examinations). Indeed, attending to both of these simultaneously is in itself a demanding task for any teacher.

Intellectually challenging tasks are unlikely to be accomplished successfully through decision-making based simply on common sense, naive ideas. Rather, teachers need to be educated about the powerful ideas already available in relation to mathematics and the teaching and learning of mathematics. Providing a richer, informed set of ideas about each of these helps teachers to extend the boundaries within which they make their decisions. It also allows teachers to make choices – and be aware of the nature, purpose and likely consequences of those choices – as they teach and as they reflect on their teaching.

This book is concerned with examining some aspects of mathematics teaching and learning which are of direct relevance to teachers. Each chapter provides background information, insight and analysis in relation to mathematics teachers' practical concerns. It is aimed particularly at those who are learning to become mathematics teachers and at those experienced mathematics teachers who are interested in further developing their thinking and practice through the re-examination of a range of classroom-related issues.

It is divided into three sections to help the reader structure their own reading and thinking as they go along. However, there are overlaps between ideas and sections so that many chapters may inform thinking for other sections as well as those in which they are placed.

Part 1 is concerned with the changing mathematics classroom. There are changes taking place for all mathematics teachers, whether they teach at primary, secondary or tertiary level. What are those changes? What kinds of practical challenges do those changes raise? What kinds of opportunities and concerns have been identified in relation to those changes? Mike Askew (Chapter 1) looks at the changing Primary classroom and, in particular, how current research about the ways in which pupils learn can be understood alongside the requirements of the National Numeracy Strategy. Stephanie Prestage (Chapter 2) takes a similarly broad perspective in relation to mathematics 11–16, looking at both the National Curriculum and the National Strategy requirements and exploring how each of these might be used by teachers as they continue to develop their practice. In Chapter 3, Doug French examines the changing demands of mathematics post-16, particularly for those pupils choosing to study mathematics as an academic discipline, and identifies practical strategies for improving teaching and learning at this level. Complementing this, Susan Molyneux-Hodgson and Rosamund Sutherland provide an overview in Chapter 4 of changes in post-16 vocational provision in relation to mathematics, identifying important issues which teachers need to be aware of and consider as they plan, teach and assess at this level.

Part 2 is concerned with important elements of the mathematics curriculum. There have been changes in emphasis given to elements of the school curriculum as well as a change in the language used to describe some of that curriculum. This section therefore returns to some familiar roots in mathematics and examines how those roots have developed. Each chapter adopts a reflective approach and also includes practical ideas which can be used in the classroom. In Chapter 5, Melissa Rodd and John Monaghan examine the notion of proof and reflect on its importance – and its re-emergence – in school mathematics. Peter Huckstep (Chapter 6) explores arithmetic and, historically, its perceived importance. He reflects on the ways in which 'numeracy' has replaced 'arithmetic' in the language of prescribed curricula in school mathematics. John Mason presents powerful ideas about algebra in Chapter 7, arguing that the learning of algebra is enhanced through pupils being encouraged to experience and explore generality in their own mathematics. Keith Jones presents equally powerful arguments in favour of the importance of geometry, examining its nature and purpose, issues to do with the learning of geometry, and practical ideas and suggestions for its teaching. The section ends with a chapter by Dave Pratt who looks at the teaching and learning of probability and randomness. By presenting and exploring classroom situations and analysing them in relation to available research, he offers suggestions and ways in which these ideas can be successfully taught.

The first two parts can be thought of as the warp and weft of what is currently defined as school mathematics. The third part examines some pedagogical issues which emerge in the resulting fabric of school mathematics. The pedagogical issues examined in the chapters here are rooted in classroom concerns, and each offers theoretical ideas within which practical solutions are identified and offered.

Anne Watson (Chapter 10) offers ideas on how to teach in order to develop pupil understanding. What is particularly interesting is the way she clarifies for the reader the types of understanding for which teachers might be aiming.

Pat Perks (Chapter 11) examines progression within mathematics and suggests a way of working when preparing to teach a topic in mathematics which helps teachers (and subsequently their learners) make useful progress and establish connections within mathematics.

Tim Rowland (Chapter 12) looks at language issues in mathematics. In a particularly thoughtful chapter, Tim provides an overview of some basic ideas which beginning teachers will find useful as they develop their thinking about this important issue.

Linda Haggarty and Maria Goulding (in Chapters 13 and 14) each explore ways of extending pupil thinking. Linda argues for the need for teachers to attend to differentiation and explores strategies for doing this. In particular she offers a practical strategy for differentiation which has proved successful for teachers in busy classrooms. Maria looks at similar issues from a different perspective. Her attention is focussed on strategies for cognitive acceleration and she identifies ways in which teachers can work with learners in the classroom to achieve this.

Interest in mental mathematics has grown significantly, particularly since its encouragement within the National Numeracy Strategy. Chris Bills (Chapter 15) examines what it is, what its claims are and how it can be used as an effective strategy in the classroom.

An important resource for very many teachers is their textbook: it helps them to plan, order, teach – and provides practice for – elements of the curriculum. But even a cursory glance through the textbooks that are available tells any mathematics teacher that they need to control its use, rather than allowing the textbook to make pedagogical decisions for them. In Chapter 16, Laurinda Brown offers ideas on how to make the most of available textbooks.

In Chapter 17, John Mason explores the way teachers very often use questioning (for example, as a means of control) in their classroom and from this starting point, develops a strategy for using questioning techniques more effectively for learning mathematics. He also offers ideas on how teachers can encourage learners to question, and how they might subsequently respond.

The final two chapters are concerned with assessment in mathematics and both offer practical and accessible ideas based on extensive research. Candia Morgan (Chapter 18) raises important questions about the assessment of coursework which provide a framework within which to reflect on possibilities and potential pitfalls of this kind of assessment. Dylan Wiliam (Chapter 19) offers practical and manageable strategies for using formative assessment – and hence improving learning – in mathematics classrooms.

Learning and developing as a mathematics teacher requires more than 'training' in a diverse set of skills or techniques. Learning and developing as a mathematics teacher requires engagement in, and reflection on, powerful ideas in mathematics education. Through engagement and reflection, mathematics teachers can locate themselves and their endeavours in an intellectually stimulating and challenging setting which recognises (as teachers recognise themselves) that learning and teaching are demanding activities which deserve the best efforts of informed, educated and thoughtful professionals. This book represents a stimulus for thinking and intelligent action.

I would like to thank all the contributors to this book who, without exception, are as keen as I am to make powerful ideas available and accessible to everyone in the mathematics education community. I would also like to thank Sue Dutton, whose guidance, help, support and friendship helped to make this book a reality.

Linda Haggarty

# 1 The Mathematics classroom

# 1 The changing primary mathematics classroom
## The challenge of the National Numeracy Strategy
Mike Askew

## Introduction

Up until the introduction of the National Curriculum (NC), primary school teachers were largely free to choose both the content of and approaches to teaching mathematics. While the widespread use of commercial mathematics schemes meant that variation between schools may not have been as great as this freedom might suggest, with the introduction of the National Curriculum a greater degree of equality of opportunity for pupils was expected. Central to the design of the National Curriculum was the setting of attainment targets.

Helping children achieve these levels of attainment was to be accomplished through ensuring everyone had access to the mathematics curriculum through the programmes of study. Teachers were expected to use the programmes of study flexibly so that pupils' different needs could be met through appropriate differentiated provision; teachers were:

> free to determine the detail of what should be taught in order to ensure that pupils achieve appropriate levels of attainment. How teaching is organised and the teaching approaches used will be also for schools to determine.
>
> (Department of Education and Science & Welsh Office, 1987, p. 11)

So entitlement was defined in terms of an intended curriculum with the specifics of what and how still in the hands of the teachers. While the needs of the state were beginning to be catered for, in the policy documents at least the flavour was still of education primarily serving the needs of the individual. The NC 'Policy to Practice' document sent out to all schools emphasised the need for pupil access to 'a broad and balanced curriculum, relevant to his or her needs' (Department of Education and Science, 1989).

As Willan (1998) remarks 'The National Curriculum had a deeply egalitarian rhetoric: a curriculum regardless of location, status or background' (p. 274). But this was an egalitarian curriculum in the sense of opportunity of access and as the above quotes illustrate, two key principles were embodied in the spirit of the NC:

- that the needs of individual pupils had to be provided for;
- that the actual teaching approaches that would meet these needs should be determined by teachers.

However, with the introduction of the National Numeracy Strategy (NNS) there has been a marked shift in these principles with moves:

- away from the needs of the individual towards collective targets;
- towards increasing specification of teaching approaches.

While the only aspect of the NNS that is statutory is the requirement of primary schools to teach a daily mathematics lesson, it is clear that schools are attempting to deal with such changes. In this chapter I examine these changes in emphasis and consider some of the possible implications for teaching primary mathematics arising from them. Before looking at these in detail, I want to set the scene in terms of theories of learning and what we know about effective teaching.

## Learning: acquisition or participation?

Sfard (1998) points out that theories of learning can be divided broadly along the lines of whether they rest upon the metaphor of 'learning as acquisition' or 'learning as participation'. 'Learning as acquisition' theories can be regarded broadly as mentalist in their orientation, with the emphasis on the individual building up cognitive structures (Alexander, 1991; Baroody and Ginsburg, 1990; Carpenter *et al.*, 1982; Kieran, 1990; Peterson *et al.*, 1984). In contrast, 'learning as participation' theories attend to the sociocultural contexts within which learners can take part (Brown *et al.*, 1989; Lave and Wenger, 1991; Rogoff, 1990).

While some writers argue for the need for a paradigm shift away from (or even rejecting) acquisition perspectives in favour of participation, I agree with Sfard in the suggestion that the metaphors are not alternatives but that both are necessary and each provides different insights into the nature of teaching and learning. However, I would argue that whether one's initial attention is on acquisition or participation can greatly alter the teaching approaches adopted.

One pertinent implication of viewing learning as 'acquisition' is the way that such a view separates the learner from what is to be learnt. If learning is coming to acquire knowledge, then there are overtones of consumers and commodities. Mathematical knowledge is a set of skills, facts and concepts that somehow have to be 'transferred' over to the learner, the teacher becoming some sort of shopkeeper who has access to the 'goods' and can, metaphorically, hand them over to the pupils. A further implication of this metaphor for learning is the separation of responsibilities in the classroom: teachers teach and pupils learn. If the pupils fail to learn then it is either because the teacher has 'failed to deliver the goods' or that pupils have not managed to 'hold onto' them. To change the metaphor, knowledge as a liquid commodity can come in jugs and either teachers fail to pour it out carefully enough or pupils are 'leaky vessels' (Shuard, 1986) so the knowledge soon dribbles out.

In contrast to this view, regarding knowledge as arising from participation emphasises the social nature of coming to understand. Rather than knowledge being something that exists independently of learners just waiting to be 'passed on', knowledge is seen as being the result of social agreement and taking part in social practices that induct the learner into such agreements. An example should help illustrate what I mean. Have a look at the diagram below and jot down what fraction you think it represents.

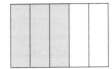

Most people will respond that the diagram represents ³/₅ or perhaps ²/₅. But 'read' in a particular way then it can also be seen as representing ²/₃, 1½ , 1²/₃ or 2½ (for example, if you 'read' the shaded part as the unit then the whole is 1²/₃ ). There is nothing inherent in the diagram itself that makes ³/₅ the 'right' answer. And, I suggest, people do not come to read this as ³/₅ through individual activity that they have carried out by folding paper, shading in and so on. Such activities simply provide a context within which they come to learn that the 'accepted' (i.e. socially agreed) way of interpreting the diagram is ³/₅. They come to read it as ³/₅ because that is how others – teachers, textbook writers, peers – all read it. The learner has become part of the 'community of practice' (Rogoff, 1995) that reads fractions in this way.

The idea of classrooms as 'communities of practice' embodies the perspective on learning as participation. Working together as a community suggests that the clear demarcation between teaching and learning suggested by the 'acquisition' metaphor becomes blurred. In a community of practice the teacher is a learner as well and the pupils can also teach each other. Furthermore, the responsibility for success or failure becomes a joint one. I have a copy of child's answer to a test question on coordinates. The context is one of a ship moving over a coordinate grid and the question requires the pupil to write down 'what to tell the ship' in order to get it to move between two points. This particular child wrote down 'ready, steady, go!' The question this raises for me is who actually got it wrong? As teachers and test writers we are all well inducted into the (bizarre) world of mathematical questions where ships can be sentient. But the child has drawn upon a different community of practice, one possibly more familiar, one that involves giving instructions to others to get them to move. The answer tells us nothing about whether or not the child could give mathematical instructions, had the distinction between the different communities been made clear. (See Cooper, 2001, Chapter 13 in the companion volume *Teaching Mathematics in Secondary Schools: A reader* for more ideas on this.)

The element of joint responsibility for success or failure came through clearly in the 'raising attainment in numeracy project' (Askew *et al.*, 1997a) where close observation of teacher and pupil interactions revealed how each interpreted the other's actions and words in ways that led to misunderstandings. For example, many of the low-attaining Year 3 pupils in the study over-relied on counting strategies. When asked to count out a collection of objects and then soon after asked how many there were they would recount the collection. When we talked this through with the teachers, they explained that clearly the children had not yet reached the stage of being able to 'conserve' quantities and that allowing them to recount would provide the experience they needed in order to come to be able to conserve. However, once we suggested to the teachers that they might stop the children when they started to count and ask them if they really needed to, it became clear that the children knew perfectly well how many there were. However, from the children's perspective they appeared to be used to a practice that meant that whenever a teacher said, 'How many are there?' it indicated they had to count.

I do not want to suggest that it is a question of participation being 'right' and acquisition being 'wrong'. Clearly children do acquire mathematical knowledge. But I do want to suggest that how they acquire mathematical knowledge, and what they have participated in, will affect the nature of that knowledge. For example, the child who only learns multiplication facts through the rote memorisation of tables will have a different understanding of the nature of multiplication from the child who learns multiplication facts through participating in a range of activities that links multiplication to problem-solving and highlights the relationship with division. So while a child might be able to answer 3 × 8 quickly they could not make the link to answering 24 ÷ 8.

## Orientations towards teaching

In the King's College study of 'Effective Teachers of Numeracy' (Askew *et al.*, 1997b) the 90 teachers in the study could not be distinguished as effective (as measured by pupils' gains on a test of numeracy) on measures such as amount of whole-class teaching, pupil grouping or qualifications. However, through analysis of case studies of 18 of the teachers, three clusters of beliefs or 'orientations' characterising beliefs and understandings of the relationship between teaching and learning emerged. We dubbed these three orientations *connectionist*, *discovery* and *transmission*. Of the three, having a *connectionist* orientation was positively associated with pupil learning gains, while the learning gains of pupils with teachers demonstrating *discovery* or *transmission* orientations were lower.

Before briefly examining some of the characteristics of a *connectionist* orientation from a perspective of participation I propose the following simple model: that within a mathematics lesson there is a triadic relationship between teacher, pupils and mathematics.

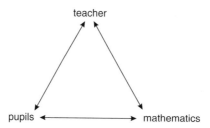

From our analysis what seemed to distinguish some highly effective teachers from the others was a consistent and coherent set of beliefs about how best to teach mathematics whilst taking into account children's learning. These teachers also had a clear understanding of mathematics as an interrelated set of ideas. In particular, the theme of 'connections' was one that particularly stood out in our observations of and interviews with these teachers. We came to refer to such teachers as having a *connectionist* orientation to teaching and learning numeracy. What distinguished these teachers was the way they attended to all three bonds on the triadic model. Other orientations that we identified tended to focus more on one or other of the triadic bonds. So teachers who displayed a *discovery* orientation paid particular attention to the pupils–mathematics link, with the role of the teacher being somewhat backgrounded. In contrast, *transmission* oriented teachers put more store on the teacher–mathematics link, with the role of the pupil being less important. To set the scene for examining some of the implications of the NNS in terms of this triad, I discuss in a little more detail the characteristics of a *connectionist* orientation.

## Connectionist orientation and the teacher–pupils link

Teachers displaying characteristics of this orientation worked at making connections with children's methods and understanding. Pupils in their lessons spent time explaining to each other, in pairs or small groups or to the whole class. But while the teachers were interested in and valued children's thinking they did not accept these uncritically. They would discuss with children the strengths and weaknesses of the various methods and, when appropriate, also share their own methods when these were more effective. Misunderstandings that children displayed were seen as important parts of lessons, needing to be explicitly identified and worked with in order to improve understanding. *Connectionist* oriented teachers held the belief that children come to lessons already in possession of mental mathematics strategies but that the teacher has responsibility for intervening, working with the children on becoming more efficient.

In practice this meant that, for the *connectionist* orientation, teaching mathematics was based on dialogue between teacher and children, so that teachers better understood the children's thinking and children gained access to the teachers' mathematical knowledge through the talk.

Also associated with the *connectionist* orientation was a belief that most children are able to learn mathematics, given appropriate teaching which explicitly introduces the links between different aspects of mathematics.

## Connectionist orientation and the teacher–mathematics link

The lessons that we observed of the *connectionist* oriented teachers displayed a high level of presenting ideas so that the connections between different aspects of mathematics were made clear. For example, addition and subtraction would be taught together, or fractions, decimals and percentages treated as one topic. Making these connections clearly rested on the teachers themselves having a deep understanding of the mathematical connections. However, such understandings were not predicted on the basis of levels of formal mathematics qualifications: 'more' was not necessarily 'better' in terms of helping the pupils understand the connections. Rather it was the fact that these teachers appeared to have a good understanding of the structure of the number system and the multifaceted nature of meanings and applications of mathematics operations and notation (for example, that the mathematical operation of subtraction can be used to calculate a variety of situations including finding the difference, taking away, counting on).

In lessons this understanding of the mathematical connections became evident through the extensive use of different representations of mathematics: moving between symbols, words, diagrams and objects, and making explicit the connections between these. (See also Perks, Chapter 11, in this volume.)

## Connectionist orientation and the pupils–mathematics link

The *connectionist* orientation included the belief that being numerate involves being both efficient and effective. For example, while 2016 – 1999 can be effectively calculated using a paper and pencil algorithm, it is more efficient to work it out mentally. Being numerate, for the *connectionist* orientated teacher, meant that pupils needed to develop an awareness of different methods of calculation and the ability to choose an *appropriate* method.

As indicated, a *connectionist* orientation means emphasising the links between different aspects of the mathematics curriculum. The application of number to new situations is important to the *connectionist* orientation, with children drawing on their mathematical understandings to solve realistic problems. The *connectionist* orientation also places a strong emphasis on developing reasoning and justification, leading to the proof aspects of Using and Applying Mathematics.

The 'Effective Teachers of Numeracy' research was carried out prior to the introduction of the National Numeracy Strategy. So is it still possible to be *connectionist* in one's orientation towards teaching mathematics within the frameworks advocated by the NNS? I shall examine this question by looking at each of the links in the teacher–pupils–mathematics triad in the light of current policy recommendations.

## The teacher–pupil relationship in the light of current policy recommendations

It's a popular aphorism that if you ask what a secondary school mathematics teacher teaches they will reply 'mathematics' while a primary school teacher will say 'children'. The tradition of primary education with one teacher taking every subject and being a 'generalist', lends itself to attending to the needs of children rather than the demands of the subjects, a view that over the years has been endorsed by policy documents.

In line with a shift away from a focus on the individual to a focus on the collective, the reports of the Numeracy Task Force recommend styles of teaching that fit, with some subtle but important shifts of emphasis, between the preliminary and final reports.

In the preliminary report one of the recommendations was that more time should be spent in mathematics lessons with the teacher involved in 'direct communication with pupils ... particularly by teaching the whole class together, using good questioning techniques'. In the final report this means has become an end in itself. The first recommendation is for a daily mathematics lesson and that:

teachers should teach the whole class together for a high proportion of the lesson.

(DfEE, 1999, p. 2)

This shift in emphasis is mirrored by a subtle change in the advice given on differentiation. The main sense of the report is that standards need to be improved for all, based on the fact that international studies:

comparing England's performance in mathematics with other countries show this country to be performing relatively poorly in comparison with others.

(op. cit. p. 8)

While the National Target is to get 75 per cent of 11-year-olds to level 4 in the National Tests for mathematics by 2002, this does not preclude 'those achieving level 4 to reach their full potential, which may be well above the level 4 threshold' (op. cit. p. 8).

The preliminary report warns that providing too many different levels of work can result in the teacher 'trouble shooting', but that 'differentiated work can be provided when pupils are working on their own in groups, divided according to attainment' (p. 21). While the final report acknowledges that there may be a certain amount of differentiation in group work, there is more emphasis on the need to narrow the overall range of attainment:

Perhaps the most important consideration is our aspiration for the gap in attainment between pupils to become smaller over time, particularly for underachieving pupils to improve their standards of achievement, as our strategy makes an impact.

(op. cit. p. 55)

The report immediately goes on to draw teachers into agreeing with this and gives clear guidance on the role of setting:

We know that teachers share this aspiration, and they should remember that it means that over time, setting may need to be used less as the range of attainment narrows.

(op. cit. p. 55)

That teachers 'share this aspiration' is, I suggest, still open to empirical verification. In talking to groups of teachers I do not get a sense that this is a widely shared view and on several occasions have been taken to task for possibly suggesting that it was no longer the remit of primary teachers to 'help all pupils reach their full potential'.

Central to this debate is the model of learning that teaching is based upon. Markedly lacking from either the preliminary or final reports of the Numeracy Task Force is any discussion of the model of learning that the recommendations are based upon. Indeed at the launch of the National Numeracy Project, Chris Woodhead, then Chief HMI, talked about the over attention that had been paid to differentiation and implied that more emphasis needed to be placed on 'instruction'. When asked what model of learning this was based upon, he replied to the effect that he did not have a model of learning, only a model of teaching.

I suggest that any model of teaching has to be based on some model of learning, however tacit that model is.

Returning to the models of learning as either acquisition or participation leads to different perceptions of what might be meant by 'potential'. The dominant model in schools would appear to be based on an acquisition view of learning, with potential being some sort of 'capacity' and the mind as some sort of container. Some pupils have larger containers than others and so have more 'potential' in that they can be filled more.

Taking a participation stance towards learning leads to a different perspective on potential. Rather than children having innately different capacities, differences in attainment may be the result of what they have had the opportunity to participate in before. For example, research has shown that the answer to the question 'How many books do you have at home?' is a powerful predictor of children's success at school (Beaton et al., 1996), suggesting that a home environment which places value on learning may be a determinant of 'potential'. To take another metaphor, if two identical eggs are rolled down a hillside, the one that starts higher up the hill will roll further, because its starting position gives it greater potential energy rather than there being any difference within the egg itself.

So, if the National Numeracy Strategy is to raise the majority of pupils to a minimum level of attainment this may mean a shift in teachers' perceptions of the idea of ability from something fixed to something changeable. As Anne, one of our *connectionist* teachers, pointed out, this means keeping an open mind on what pupils may or may not be able to achieve.

> But I have the same expectations for the children, I always think about it as not so much what the children are doing as what they have the potential to do. So even if I have children like Mary in the classroom who are tremendously able, I am really just as excited with the children who are having that nice slow start, because, who knows, tomorrow they may fly – you just don't know.

Given that ideas of 'ability' run deeply through the way we talk about children, rather than changing beliefs, the challenge presented to teachers may be one of changing practice and acting 'as if'. As Hart (1998) points out, it is not a matter of whether or not people innately have more or less 'ability' but the consequences of acting as though they do. For example, acting in this way raises questions about organising pupil grouping. If you act as though different levels of attainment in mathematics are a consequence of innate pupil differences, then it is reasonable to put pupils into attainment groups as their 'needs' may be different from each other. On the other hand, acting as though all pupils can potentially succeed in mathematics but starting at different points, then working with mixed ability groups would seem a reasonable way of those children with more advantage supporting their peers. Such an approach is supported by research findings demonstrating that groups with some spread of attainment (but not too wide a spread) lead to better learning outcomes than groups with a narrow spread of attainment (Askew and Wiliam, 1995).

In summary, the 'connectionist' teacher is likely to be attending to two things in relation to the teacher–pupil relationship. Firstly, paying close attention to listening to pupils' explanations in order to learn about the children's thinking. Secondly, working with the children's understandings but not being limited by them. For example, if a child is using an ineffective strategy such as making tally marks to count on from one number to another, the 'connectionist' teacher would spend time talking to the child to establish their method (children are very good at 'hiding' such approaches on pieces of scrap paper) and then would work with the child on a more efficient method, say by counting on to the next multiple of ten.

## The pupil–mathematics relationship in the light of current policy recommendations

Here is a classroom snapshot: children with small boards on their laps, writing solutions to a problem that the teacher has put on the board. Sounds like a Victorian lesson, but this is a scene from a classroom observed in 2001. Instead of blackboards and chalk the children were using individual whiteboards and markers. So has the NNS meant a return to Victorian styles of teaching? Definitely not, but there are some differences in the resources teachers and children are using in mathematics lessons, compared with what might have been in evidence a few years ago.

When one visited a primary classroom not so many years ago, there was likely to be a great deal of practical activity: interlocking cubes for counting in early years and, later, the use of base ten blocks (structured as ones, sticks of ten, squares of 100 and cubes of 1000) to model addition and subtraction. One of the key changes that is being brought about by the NNS is a shift in emphasis on the way we teach number, particularly place value and addition and subtraction. There is a move away from attending to the cardinal (that is, size of a collection) to attending to the ordinal aspects of number (that is, position on a number line). While there are many strengths to this change in emphasis, I argue that we need to take care not to 'throw the baby out with the bathwater'.

Research (Gray, 1991) has shown that by the time children reach the top end of primary school they have largely fallen into two groups – those who are confident in number work and those who are having difficulty. What seems to distinguish these groups is the extent to which they rely on strategic or procedural methods to solve calculations.

Children who are operating strategically appear to have two things at their disposal. Firstly they have committed some number facts to memory and secondly, they have a number of strategies that they can mentally draw upon (Askew and Wiliam, 1995). These two aspects are not independent of each other: each supports and helps develop the other. For example, a child who knows that $6 + 6 = 12$ may be able to 'figure out' that $6 + 7 = 13$. This eventually becomes a 'known fact' that can be used as the basis of other 'derived facts', for example, $60 + 70 = 130$. Hence their knowledge and understanding continue to develop.

On the other hand, children who are operating in a procedural fashion have a more limited range of known facts and strategies at their disposal and, in particular, rely on counting strategies. Until recently, while this might have slowed children down, when the expectation was that calculations with numbers above 20 should be done using a written algorithm, these children only needed to be able to operate on single-digit numbers and so their limited understandings were less obvious. The change in emphasis towards working mentally whenever that is appropriate exposes the limitations of such children's strategies and understandings. For example, a child who does not have a sound understanding of place value and different ways to partition numbers may end up using inefficient strategies such as tallying for finding the difference between two numbers.

It may be that such children have not been weaned off using either physical objects or fingers to support their counting, and so come to see mathematical calculation as a physical activity rather than something to be done mentally (Askew et al., 1996). The work of the Realistic Mathematics Education Group at the Freudenthal Institute has shown what a powerful tool the 'empty' number line can be in helping children move away from counting methods and develop strategic methods for addition and subtraction (Beishuizen, 1995).

Number lines that you often find in UK classrooms have divisions for every single number. While these provide some support for children, they can allow them to continue to count in single steps to carry out calculations. Simply drawing an empty line to support working out, say, 28 + 17, discourages using 17 steps to count on from 28 and provides a tool for sharing different methods, such as counting on 2 to 30 and then making a jump of 15 to 45 or making a jump of 10 to 38, counting on 2 to 40 and then adding on another 5.

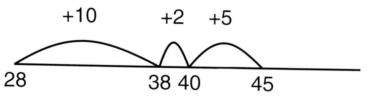

As Gravemeijer (1997) puts it, the empty number line is both a model of and a model for the calculation. The demonstration on the board of the different mental strategies through the empty number line is a model of what some people seem to do in their heads. And by working with the empty number line children begin to internalise and use such methods without the support of the line. Hence it becomes a model for carrying out calculations. In contrast, while base 10 blocks are a model of how place value works, they are not a particularly good model for carrying out mental calculations.

Everyone working together as a whole class, sometimes on the same activity, marks another of the major shifts in mathematics lessons advocated by the NNS. But while children might all be working towards the same end, the methods that they use will vary. For example, take a problem like this:

Three cars, four bicycles and two six-wheeled lorries went past the school gate. How many wheels went past?

The most confident children may do most of the working-out in their heads, only jotting down intermediate steps on paper or individual whiteboards. Others may need to record multiplications and additions that they carried out, while the least confident may be most comfortable drawing pictures to help them find the answer. During the time that the others are working out the answer, the more confident children can be getting ready to explain to the class their methods of solution, or devising similar problems for the class to work on. Using individual whiteboards helps both the teacher and the pupils. The public nature of the recording helps the teacher make rapid assessments of children's thinking as shown by their working. The transient nature of the recording gives the children confidence to try things out without worrying about 'getting it right'.

This emphasis on mental calculations has led to the development of other resources to support whole-class feedback. Many classrooms are now equipped with sets of digit cards for children to hold up to show answers to calculations, or number fans where the digits are linked together, avoiding time wasted looking for missing cards. Place value cards (sets with hundred, tens and units separate so that they can be stacked on top of each other to display a number) have advantages over digit cards for showing answers as they make explicit the structure of our place value system. Traditionally we talked about 35 as being 'three tens and five units'. Now it seems that children's understanding is better served by thinking of it as thirty and five, so that the ordinal aspect of 35, that is, its position on the number line is made clear – it is five more than thirty. In contrast the statement three tens and five units concentrates on the cardinal aspect of number, that is the size of a collection. By stacking and unstacking place value cards this structure is made clear. Extending the cards into decimal places means that decimal fractions can be seen to be part of our place value system rather than a whole new idea.

Place value charts – ten columns with each row showing units, multiples of ten, multiples of 100 and so on – help children learn to read numbers through tapping out entries in each row. These charts are also a powerful tool in helping teach the effects of multiplying and dividing by ten, by examining the relationship between the numbers in adjacent rows. Later this can be extended into looking at multiplying and dividing by 100 or 1000 by skipping over rows.

So, with the increased emphasis on working with the symbolic, is there no longer any place for the use of 'manipulatives' in mathematics lessons? I suggest there is. As part of the Leverhulme Numeracy Research Programme, a five-year longitudinal study of children's learning in number and calculations, we interviewed some Year 6 children about their calculating strategies. Sam was asked if he knew what 37 multiplied by 10 was. Three hundred and seventy was the rapid reply. 'How did you know that so quickly?' 'Well everything moves up a place so the thirty becomes three hundred and the seven seventy. I used to just say "you add a nought" but you're not allowed to say that any more.' When I asked Sam why not, he replied, 'I don't really know, it's just that's what my teacher likes us to say now'.

If you have a clear image that multiplying by ten scales everything up by a factor of ten, then the reason why the digits all move up a column is clear. On the other hand, concentrating too much on the movement of the digits may not give you the insight into why that happens. Base 10 blocks do provide a powerful image for this. Modelling multiplying by ten by exchanging individual unit cubes for ten sticks, ten sticks for 100 squares and 100 squares for 1000 cubes clearly demonstrates why the digits move up a place when we multiply by ten. Without this image the 'move up a place' rule is likely to be just as meaningless as the 'add a nought' rule.

> In summary, the 'connectionist' teacher will be thinking about how class-room materials and symbols help children understand the underlying mathematics rather than simply provide them with the means of finding answers to calculations.

## The teacher–mathematics relationship in the light of current policy recommendations

As I have indicated, a main difference between primary mathematics classes now and not so many years ago is the increased emphasis on the teacher as the mediator of mathematical knowledge, rather than this being done through commercial texts. To act as an effective mediator in children's learning means having a sound knowledge of both the mathematics itself and 'pedagogical content knowledge' (Shulman, 1986), that is, how to present subject knowledge in ways that help learners understand it.

Research in mathematics education is beginning to help us understand the pedagogic models for certain aspects of the primary mathematics curriculum. For example, the American work on 'Cognitively Guided Instruction' (Carpenter and Peterson, 1988) has shown how detailed understanding of the strategies children use to solve addition and subtraction calculations can inform the construction of teaching and learning experiences. This work complements the work of the Freudenthal Institute mentioned above. Although the NNS Framework for Teaching Mathematics (DfEE, 1999) does not explicitly set out to provide teaching models for every aspect of the curriculum, many of the ideas arising from such research can be detected in the range of examples of learning outcomes.

However, our knowledge of pedagogic models for other aspects of the number curriculum, for example, multiplication and division and fractions and decimals, is rather less well developed. In these cases, more demands are placed on the teachers' subject knowledge and how this can be translated into examples that are meaningful to children.

For example, at Year 6, children are expected to be able to answer questions like $3 \div 0.75$. One way to approach this is to use the fact that $3 \div 4 = 0.75$ and deduce, using the relationship between multiplication and division, that $3 \div 0.75$ must be 4. While this provides you with the correct answer, it does not give you much insight into why the answer is 4. Such insight requires one to 'read' $3 \div 0.75$ in a particular way. Often the division symbol is only 'read' in one way – shared – possibly because of the use of the sharing model for division with practical materials in the early years of schooling.

One way of helping children develop insight into calculations is to place them into the context of a problem. But what sense does it make to try to construct a situation around 3 'shared by' 0.75? However, sharing is not the only model for division: repeated subtraction is the other model. It is the difference between

THE CHANGING PRIMARY MATHEMATICS CLASSROOM 15

I have 42 apples and share them among 6 people. How many apples do they each get?

and

I have 42 apples and put them into bags of 6. How many bags can I fill?

While each of these can be answered by the calculation $42 \div 6$, the underlying situations are very different, as are the answers: 6 people getting 7 apples each is not the same as 7 bags of 6.

Reading $3 \div 0.75$ as a repeated subtraction – how many times can I subtract 0.75 from 3 – can lead to insight as well as appropriate problem contexts:

I have three metres of fabric, how many lengths of 0.75 metres can I cut from it?

Note how this also provides some insight into why, in this case, division 'makes bigger'. The answer is not 4 units, but 4 lots of 0.75: the division has not miraculously turned 3 into 4!

> So the 'connectionist' teacher will have a broad understanding of the principles of the number system and the different sort of situations that might give rise to various calculations to be able to help children develop insight into the reasons behind answers, rather than simply attending to getting the answers.

## Conclusion

This is a time of great change in the teaching of primary mathematics. Many of our previous assumptions are being challenged and there is no doubt that many of the changes will have a positive impact on children's learning. But we must also continue to learn as teachers, to question what we do and look carefully at its impact. While the National Numeracy Strategy and the Framework for Teaching Mathematics provide considerable detail to inform the teaching of primary mathematics, the day-to-day decision-making of teachers in providing children with access to this mathematics is still the most crucial element. Listening to pupils, understanding their reasons and being able to place these within a broad understanding of mathematics as a discipline places considerable demands on teachers' own knowledge. As the NNS unfolds over the coming years it will be interesting to see how teachers' knowledge develops.

## References

Alexander, P.A. (1991) 'A cognitive perspective on mathematics: issues of perception, instruction and assessment', in *Proceedings of NATO Advanced Research Workshop: information technologies & mathematical problem solving research conference*, Oporto, Portugal.

Askew, M., Bibby, T. and Brown, M. (1996) 'Numeracy Recovery – exploring practices through group observation', in *Proceedings of British Educational Research Association Conference*, University of Lancaster, September 1996.

Askew, M., Bibby, T. and Brown, M. (1997a) *Raising Attainment in Numeracy: final report to Nuffield Foundation*, King's College, University of London.

Askew, M., Brown, M., Rhodes, V., Wiliam, D. and Johnson, D. (1997b) *Effective Teachers of Numeracy: report of a study carried out for the Teacher Training Agency*, King's College, University of London.

Askew, M. and Wiliam, D. (1995) 'Recent research in mathematics education 5–16', *Ofsted Reviews of Research*, London: HMSO.

Baroody, A.J. and Ginsburg, H.P. (1990) 'Children's mathematical learning: a cognitive view', in R.B. Davis, C.A. Maher and N. Noddings (eds) *Constructivist Views on the Teaching and Learning of Mathematics*, Reston, VA: National Council of Teachers of Mathematics.

Beaton, A.E., Mullis, I.V.S., Martin, M.O., *et al.* (1996) *Mathematics Achievement in the Middle School Years. IEA's third international mathematics and science study,* Centre for the Study of Testing, Evaluation and Educational Policy, Boston, MA: Boston College.

Beishuizen, M. (1995) 'New research into mental arithmetic strategies with two-digit numbers up to 100', in *Proceedings of European Conference on Educational Research*, University of Bath, September 1995.

Brown, J.S., Collins, A. and Duguid, P. (1989) 'Situated cognition and the culture of learning', *Educational Researcher,* 18(1): 32–42.

Carpenter, T.P., Moser, J.M. and Romberg, T.A (1982) *Addition and Subtraction: a cognitive perspective*, Hillsdale, NJ: Lawrence Erlbaum Associates.

Carpenter, T.P. and Peterson, P.L. (1988) 'Learning through instruction: the study of students' thinking during instruction in mathematics', *Educational Psychologist*, 23(2): 79–85.

Cooper, B. (2001) 'Culture, class and "realistic" mathematics tests', in L. Haggarty (ed.) *Teaching Mathematics in Secondary Schools: a reader*, London: RoutledgeFalmer.

Department for Education and Employment (DfEE) (1999) *The National Numeracy Strategy: framework for teaching mathematics from Reception to Year 6*, London: DfEE.

Department of Education and Science (DES) (1989) *From Policy to Practice*, London: HMSO.

Department of Education and Science and Welsh Office (1987) *The National Curriculum 5–16: a consultation document*, London: DES.

Gravemeijer, K. (1997) 'Instructional design for reform in mathematics education', in M. Beishuizen, K. Gravemeijer and E.C.D.M. Van Lieshout (eds) *The Role of Contexts and Models in the Development of Mathematical Strategies and Procedures*, Utrecht: Freudenthal Institute.

Gray, E.M. (1991) 'An analysis of diverging approaches to simple arithmetic: preference and its consequences', *Educational Studies in Mathematics*, 22(6): 551–74.

Hart, S. (1998) 'A sorry tail: ability, pedagogy and educational reform', *British Journal of Educational Studies*, 46(2): 153–68.

Kieran, C. (1990) 'Cognitive processes involved in learning school algebra', in P. Nesher and J. Kilpatrick (eds) *Mathematics and Cognition: a research synthesis by the international group for the psychology of mathematics education (ICMI Study Series)*, Cambridge: Cambridge University Press: 96–112.

Lave, J. and Wenger, E. (1991) *Situated Learning: legitimate peripheral participation*, Cambridge: Cambridge University Press.

Ma, L. (1999) *Knowing and Teaching Elementary Mathematics: teachers' understanding of fundamental mathematics in China and the United States*, Mahwah, NJ: Lawrence Erlbaum Associates.

Peterson, P.L., Swing, S.R., Stark, K.D. and Waas, G.A. (1984) 'Students' cognitions and time on task during mathematics instruction', *American Educational Research Journal*, 21(3): 487–515.

Rogoff, B. (1990) *Apprenticeship in Thinking: cognitive development in social context*, New York: Oxford University Press.

Rogoff, B. (1995) 'Evaluating development in the process of participation: theory, methods, and practice building on each other', in E. Amsel and A. Renninger (eds) *Change and Development: issues of theory, application and method*, Hillsdale, NJ: Lawrence Erlbaum Associates.

Sfard, A. (1998) 'On two metaphors for learning and the dangers of choosing just one', *Educational Researcher*, 27(2): 4–13.

Shuard, H. (1986) *Primary Mathematics Today and Tomorrow*, London: Longman for SCDC.

Shulman, L.S. (1986) 'Those who understand: knowledge growth in teaching' *Educational Researcher*, 15: 4–14.

Willan, P.T. (1998) 'Whatever happened to entitlement in the National Curriculum?' *The Curriculum Journal*, 9(3): 269–83.

# 2 Mathematics 11–16
## Stephanie Prestage

## Introduction

If you teach mathematics in a state secondary school in England and Wales then you are bound by certain government policies and professional traditions in relation to the curriculum. There is a National Curriculum and a National Strategy for Key Stage 3, as well as the GCSE syllabuses and external examination structures. In this chapter I will talk about the first two. I suggest that you have a copy of the National Curriculum (NC) with you as you read this chapter. You can download a copy from www.nc.uk.net or you can buy a copy from an HMSO bookshop (DfEE, 1999). Copies of the National Strategy for Key Stage 3 can be obtained from DfEE Publications (DfEE, 2001).

In England and Wales there is a National Curriculum for all the main subjects through the primary and secondary schools. It is a statutory document that has been passed through Parliament and sets out the legal requirements for all state schools. Take a deep breath and read the general aims of the National Curriculum.

> The school curriculum should aim to promote pupils' spiritual, moral, social and cultural development and prepare all pupils for the opportunities, responsibilities and experiences of life.

Quite a responsibility! The four main purposes of the National Curriculum are:

> *To establish an entitlement* The National Curriculum secures for all pupils, irrespective of social background, culture, race, gender, differences in ability and disabilities, an entitlement to a number of areas of learning, and to develop knowledge, understanding, skills and attitudes necessary for their self-fulfilment and development as active and responsible citizens.
>
> *To establish standards* The National Curriculum makes expectations for learning and attainment explicit to pupils, parents, teachers, governors, employers and the public, and establishes national standards for the performance of all pupils in the subjects it includes. These standards can be used to set targets for improvement, measure progress towards those targets, and monitor and compare performance between individuals, groups and schools.
>
> *To promote continuity and coherence* The National Curriculum contributes to a coherent national framework that promotes curriculum continuity and is sufficiently flexible to ensure progression in pupils' learning. It facilitates the

transition of pupils between schools and phases of education and provides a foundation for lifelong learning.

*To promote public understanding* The National Curriculum increases public understanding of, and confidence in, the work of schools and in the learning and achievements resulting from compulsory education. It provides a common basis for discussion of educational issues among lay and professional groups, including pupils, parents, teachers, governors and employers.

(taken from the National Curriculum website under 'About the Curriculum')

Writing about the shape and meaning of mathematics in the National Curriculum is a little daunting. It keeps changing! How the current document has evolved is a long story (see Brown, 1996 for an explanation of the first six years) but you should know that the first proposals appeared before Parliament in 1989 and became the first Order in the September of that same year. Its fourth revision (great-grandchild) became the current legal requirement in September 2000. Whilst the framework has changed over the years (challenging the idea of continuity and coherence) the content in fact has altered very little.

I will start by explaining the framework for the current mathematics Order and consider some of the issues arising through working with the document for planning for the teaching and learning of mathematics. Throughout this chapter I will consider some of the tensions created by these government policies, including such things as entitlement, standards, continuity and public understanding. You might like to keep these in mind as the structure and content of the document are revealed.

## The National Curriculum – the Mathematics Order

The Mathematics Order, like many of the National Curriculum documents, provides information to help schools implement mathematics in their school and consists of Attainment Targets and a Programme of Study for each grouping of school years known as Key Stages. If you have your NC documents in front of you it contains the mathematics curriculum for pupils of ages 5–16: Key Stage 1 is for 5- to 7-year-olds; Key Stage 2 for 7- to 11-year-olds; Key Stage 3 for 11- to 14-year-olds; and Key Stage 4 for 14- to 16-year-olds. The front part of the book contains the Programmes of Study (what is to be taught), and at the back of the book (each as a three-page fold) are the Attainment Targets (how the pupils are to be assessed). Stay calm. You cannot learn the whole of the document but you must know your way around it, where to find the mathematics and how to use it in your planning and for your assessment of pupils.

The Education Reform Act 1988 defines Attainment Targets as the knowledge, skills and understanding which pupils of different abilities and maturities are expected to have by the end of a Key Stage. This is the definition still used in the current document. In mathematics there are four Attainment Targets:

- Ma1 – Using and Applying Mathematics
- Ma2 – Number and Algebra
- Ma3 – Shape, Space and Measures
- Ma4 – Handling Data

**Table 2.1** The mathematics areas for the programmes of study

| Key Stage 1 | Key Stage 2 | Key Stage 3 | Key Stage 4 |
|---|---|---|---|
| (school Years 1 and 2) | (school Years 3, 4, 5 and 6) | (school Years 7, 8 and 9) | foundation and higher (school Years 10 and 11) |
| • Ma2: number<br>• Ma3: shape, space and measures | • Ma2: number<br>• Ma3: shape, space and measures<br>• Ma4: handling data | • Ma2: number and algebra<br>• Ma3: shape, space and measures<br>• Ma4: handling data | • Ma2: number and algebra<br>• Ma3: shape, space and measures<br>• Ma4: handling data |

(The Attainment Targets are labelled as Ma when referring to particular mathematics Attainment Targets. En is used for English, Sc for science and so on.) Pages 86 to 93 of the document contain the attainment targets. You need to know the labelling of the attainment targets to make sense of the Programmes of Study but it is the Programmes of Study that I will first consider in depth.

## The Programmes of Study

The Programme of Study sets out what pupils should be taught in each subject at each Key Stage (KS) and provides the basis for planning schemes of work. It sets out the 'essential ground to be covered to enable pupils to meet the Attainment Targets at the ranges of levels for each Key Stage' (p. 6). The areas of mathematics for each Key Stage are given in Table 2.1.

There are also requirements for Ma1, Using and Applying Mathematics, defined within each of the content sections Ma2, Ma3 and Ma4. (This used to be a separate area but in the 2000 document it has been integrated within the content areas.) Ma1 is discussed later in the chapter.

To give a flavour of the Programme of Study, here is an extract from the Key Stage 3 Programme of Study from Number and Algebra relating to the number system and in particular to integers. Turn to page 30 of the document and look at the top paragraph. The direction to the teacher is that 'Pupils should be taught to':

> … use their previous understanding of integers and place value to deal with arbitrarily large positive numbers and round them to a given power of 10; understand and use negative numbers, both as positions and translations on a number line; order integers; use the concepts and vocabulary of factor (divisor), multiple, common factor, highest common factor, least common multiple, prime number and prime factor decomposition.
>
> (p. 30)

The NC is full of such statements and it would be worthwhile browsing through pages 30 and 31 (and the rest eventually) to get some sense of how the document is assembled. It is full of itemised lists of bits of mathematics, more a syllabus list, detailed and disconnected, an end point to arrive at rather than a route through the mathematics. Take, for example, prime factor decomposition, the last item mentioned in the paragraph above. First of all remind yourself about the mathematics. Do you remember doing this at school? Take any number and express it as a product of prime numbers, for example:

$$24 = 2^3 \times 3$$
$$100 = 2^2 \times 5^2$$
$$102 = 2 \times 3 \times 17$$

(You might remember meeting this in its abstract form in your undergraduate course as the Fundamental Theorem of Arithmetic though you might need to dig around in your notes to rediscover to what it was fundamental). Anyway, back to the document. Having decided that you know about the mathematics itself what does the document say you have to teach? On page 30 the document suggests that pupils should be taught to 'use the concepts and vocabulary of ... prime factor decomposition', then on page 31 in the top paragraph you will read, under calculations that pupils should be taught, to 'find prime factor decomposition'. So on page 30 you are teaching the pupils to use it and on page 31 you are teaching the pupils to find it. Clearly this distinction between using and finding might not be sensible for teaching or for learning. The National Curriculum tells you what to teach but it does not tell you how to teach, nor does it indicate a teaching sequence that will create learning opportunities for that which is to be learned. You will have to decide about the mathematics. You will have to connect the mathematics that will lead to pupils knowing about prime factor decomposition. You will decide teaching sequences that will connect the mathematics together having an understanding of what prior knowledge is needed by the pupils and how this new piece of knowledge then connects to the rest of the curriculum and your teaching aims.

Pause for a moment and think about all the mathematics involved with prime factor decomposition. I find a good way to do this is actually to do the mathematics and then analyse what was involved in what I actually did. A lot of mathematics comes into play. My first thoughts are in Figure 2.1 (overleaf).

You also need to think how prime factor decomposition might go beyond technique, just finding the factors, and become a useful piece of knowledge. What kind of mathematics starting point might need a proof using prime factor knowledge? You might like to explore the relationship between the number of factors and the prime factors. How does knowing about prime factors help with knowing about factors? Is there a number with exactly five factors but only two prime factors? How does knowing about prime factors help to know about common factors between numbers? In terms of the structure of the number system and the development of number theory why is the uniqueness of the factorisation important?

This brief detour into thinking about a particular piece of mathematics offers an indication of the difference between knowing your mathematics to pass examinations and knowing about the mathematics for teaching. The latter requires a rich and deep understanding of the subject, its connections and relations in order to respond to all aspects of pupils' needs. The more that you teach the more opportunity there is to practise connecting the mathematics.

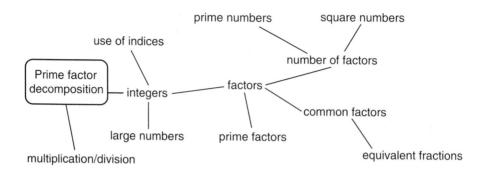

**Figure 2.1**    *Mathematics related to prime factor decomposition*

Let's take another aspect of mathematics, place value. An understanding of place value lies at the heart of all number work. When you know about the number ten and its symbolic form 10 you are beginning to know about place value. Add in the four operations and decimals and you are coming to know more about place value, add in rounding and approximations and standard form and you are coming to know more and more about place value. Each of the levels 3, 4 and 5 of the Ma2 (the number Attainment Target) begins 'Pupils show an understanding of place value to ... ' but in the Programme of Study place value is never explicitly mentioned. You have to work at connecting the mathematics within the curriculum to obtain a holistic view of mathematics for progression and assessment.

Information and Communications Technology (ICT) permeates the Programmes of Study and offers an integral resource for the learning of mathematics (though not part of the formal assessment arrangements). General software mentioned includes spreadsheets, databases, geometry and graph packages. Each of these offers a new range of alternatives for teaching and for learning and for thinking about mathematics.

The good thing for a new reader accessing the information in the document is that much of the Key Stage 4 Programme of Study is a repetition of the Key Stage 3. The paragraph under 'integers' on page 58 is a direct copy from page 30. If you are teaching across the 11–16 age group then it would be worth going through Key Stage 4 Programme of Study, crossing out what is old to reveal the new. You might also think about what this repetition tells you about the 'essential ground to be covered ... ' (p. 6).

Wherever a statement is taken from, the Programme of Study or an Attainment Target, the learning needs of pupils will require the teacher to make many decisions about how to use it in a classroom context. Discussion with other teachers about possible meanings is imperative, for without it the document has little or no meaning. Talk to the teachers in the school department you are working within to get a wide range of views and ideas.

## Attainment Targets and level descriptions

Attainment Targets consist of eight level descriptions intended to be of increasing difficulty, plus a description for exceptional performance above level 8. They are defined for the first three Key Stages only. At Key Stage 4, GCSE examinations are used to assess performance. Each level description describes the types and range of performance that pupils working at that level should characteristically demonstrate. For example, here is the level description for level 5 in Ma2:

> Pupils use their understanding of place value to multiply and divide whole numbers and decimals by 10, 100 and 1000. They order, add and subtract negative numbers in context. They use all four operations with decimals to two places. They reduce a fraction to its simplest form by cancelling common factors and solve simple problems involving ratio and direct proportion. They calculate fractional or percentage parts of quantities and measurements using a calculator where appropriate. Pupils understand and use and appropriate non-calculator method for solving problems that involve multiplying and dividing any three-digit number by any two-digit number. They check their solutions by applying inverse operations or estimating using approximations. They construct, express in symbolic form, and use simple formulae involving one or two operations. They use brackets appropriately. Pupils use and interpret coordinates in all four quadrants.
>
> (p. 89)

Interestingly, I cannot find mention of prime factor decomposition anywhere in the level descriptions (have I missed it?). Have a look through the Attainment Target for Ma2 and see in which level you think that this piece of mathematics has been subsumed.

The level descriptions provide the basis for making judgements about pupils' performance at the end of Key Stages and, of course, cannot include every part of the Programme of Study. Which mathematics from the Programme of Study is explicitly in the level descriptions? Why do you think that these have been chosen? Fortunately when you begin to work in a school, the mathematics department will already have made decisions about teaching programmes, resources and assessment practices. But it is interesting to note which aspects of the Programme of Study are to the fore.

Level descriptions provide the basis for making judgements about pupils' performance at the end of Key Stages 1, 2 and 3. Advice is given as follows:

> *Assessing attainment at the end of a key stage using the level descriptions*
> In deciding on a pupil's level of attainment at the end of a key stage, teachers should judge which description best fits the pupil's performance. When doing so, each description should be considered alongside descriptions for adjacent levels.
> (taken from the National Curriculum web site under 'About the Curriculum')

Best fit is a wonderfully ambiguous statement and allows the teacher to make judgements on the collective evidence that a pupil creates over a period of time. You might imagine however a few complications for those who are literally minded.

- I have a pupil who is definitely beyond level 4 with some of level 5 and a little bit of level 6 …
- I have pupils with several bits of level 4 missing but who has most of level 5 …

The problems of mismatch and interpretation arise from the fact that a teacher has to make judgements on all pupils in Key Stage 3 in the May of Year 9, a level has to be awarded at the end of the Key Stage for all pupils. How does this affect continuity and coherence? What if a teacher could declare that a pupil had completed level 5 at the time when level 5 had actually been completed, would this be more sensible? Add to any complication of the teacher determining a level the fact that the external tests at the end of a Key Stage are marked as percentage scores and yet reported as a level. How does the next teacher know what a pupil knows? A declared level 5 from the Standard Assessment Test (SATs) score could mean all sorts of things about a pupil's knowledge of mathematics, as could a declared level 5 from the previous teacher. Imagine pupils arriving to your class in Year 7 each with a level 5 from their SATs score (a percentage score from their SATs paper). How much can you assume that they know when they arrive? How much did they need to know to get an overall percentage equivalent to a level 5? What might they have forgotten over the summer holidays? How would you find out? What revision might they need?

Fortunately, working in a secondary school there will be many teachers in this predicament. Find out how your department deals with these issues.

The NC gives the expected range of levels for pupils working in a Key Stage as well as the expected attainment for the majority of pupils at the end of the Key Stage. Earlier NC documents had this as the level expected for an average pupil at the end of a Key Stage. This is quite a significant jump in expectations. Maybe the shift has come from mixing up the mathematical use of the word 'expected', related to average, with the colloquial use of the word. There are external tests for pupils at the end of the first three Key Stages, Standard Assessment Tests (SATs). At Key Stage 3 pupils sit a couple of written test papers in the May of their Year 9, with questions set across different levels. Percentage scores are used to award a level. You must be aware of how hyped the media get at results' time, publishing league tables of different schools' performances. What is missed if performance is the main measure used to judge a school? What is missed from the assessment of mathematics attainment if a written test is the major evidence of attainment (whence ICT)?

At Key Stage 4 there are two Programmes of Study, foundation and higher. Pupils who attain level 5 or above are expected to follow the higher Programme of Study. See Table 2.2 for this summary. Again, however, there is a lot of repetition in the two Programmes of Study and it would be worth your while looking for similarities and differences to make the curriculum content more manageable.

Now if the majority of the pupils at the end of Key Stage 3 are expected to be between levels 5 and 6 (and what does 'between' mean?) then the majority of pupils at Key Stage 4 will follow the higher Programme of Study. (The use of the word 'higher' here conflicts with the current use of the word 'higher' in GCSE which is a syllabus that about 25 per cent of pupils follow.) Perhaps this labelling will not matter in the long term.

**Table 2.2** Expected attainment during the Key Stages

| | KS1 | KS2 | KS3 | KS4 | |
|---|---|---|---|---|---|
| Range of levels during the KS | 1–3 | 2–5 | 3–7 | foundation<br><br>for pupils < level 5 at KS3 | higher<br><br>for pupils ≥ level 5 at KS3 |
| Expected attainment for the majority at the end of the KS | 2 | 4 | 5–6 | national qualifications<br><br>GCSE | national qualifications<br><br>GCSE |

The spirit of NC assessment, however, is evident in the following two statements taken from the 'About the Curriculum' on the web site (my emphasis):

> The level descriptions are not designed to assess individual pieces of work. They list aspects of attainment, based on the programmes of study, which teachers need to assess to build up a picture of a pupil's performance over time in a range of contexts.

> Teachers are required to report annually to parents on pupils' progress. Although not designed to be used at the end of each year across the key stage, the level descriptions can be used as a basis to describe pupils' progress.

These bring good news. During each Key Stage teachers are required to teach the Programme of Study, with a view to pupils achieving levels of attainment within the ranges specified for each key stage. The expectation is that the attainment of most pupils is likely to lie close to the middle of the ranges, so an average pupil might be expected to progress through a level every two years. (I have included this to give some indication of the type of statement you will find within the Order. It does not mean that all pupils travel in the same straight line at the same rate in each target – see Chapter 11 on progression). Realising this 'speed' of movement through the levels is quite important. To test pupils regularly and explicitly against the levels through Years 7, 8 and 9 might be highly demotivating since a pupil's learning might lie within level 5 over a couple of years. It might seem as though their learning is 'standing still'. This would be a challenging thing to explain at a parents' evening.

The Qualifications and Curriculum Authority (QCA), against the advice in the National Curriculum, have recently published interim SATs papers for the end of Years 7 and 8. What are the pros and cons of a school using these tests? Further tensions in the use and definition of levels will emerge as schools take on the National Strategy for Key Stage 3 (see below). This has targeted the teaching in Year 7 as revision of level 4, but mainly level 5 and included the failure language of 'catch-up' for those pupils who have not yet achieved level 4.

## Ma1 and its permeation within Ma2–4

There is now no separate section of the Programme of Study for Ma1, the first Attainment Target, using and applying mathematics. Teaching requirements relating to this Attainment Target are included within the other sections of the Programme of Study. Ma2 to 4 refer mainly to mathematical content and have recognisable labels – number, algebra, shape and space, and handling data. Most of the statements you read will seem familiar. Ma1 is found at the beginning of each area in the Programme of Study. For example, on page 29 in the document you will find the following labels:

- problem solving
- communicating
- reasoning.

These are the headings for Ma1 'using and applying mathematics'. Under these headings you will find details of mathematical processes (mainly verbs) which you may not remember working on when you were learning mathematics. It is not immediately obvious what Ma1 is about nor how the role of the teacher in planning for pupils to experience and improve in Ma1 is to be defined. It is all very well having the document but what will you carry around in your head? For this reason Ma1 will require particular attention when planning and also for assessing pupil outcomes (Ma1 has eight level descriptions). It lies at the heart of all mathematics.

It might be useful to develop an overview of each of these three strands, possible meanings for each of them, before using the statements within the Order to plan with and to assess pupils. (NCC, 1992 document has a very helpful analysis of Ma1.) Starting in reverse order:

- *The reasoning strand* is about pupils finding solutions and giving justification. It involves pupils of all ages developing the ideas of generalisation, argument and proof. Finding solutions includes aiming for a generalisation or a conclusion. Giving justifications includes convincing yourself and others that your solutions are correct. The reasoning strand should be thought of in terms of the breadth of possibilities of finding solutions and giving justifications – from 'most pupils in our class walk to school' to 'the interior angles in a triangle add to 180°' to '$\sqrt{2}$ is an irrational number'.
- *The mathematical communication strand* is about pupils formulating, discussing, interpreting data, recording and presenting findings for a variety of purposes in a variety of ways. Mathematical communication arises out of different purposes including expressing your own ideas, making sense of what others say and write and clarifying your own ideas.
- *The problem-solving strand* is about pupils making decisions about problems and methods and monitoring their decision-making. It includes pupils selecting the mathematics, materials and resources to use, planning methods, checking the information and reviewing progress.

The problem-solving strand is the trickiest to get an overview of since you might imagine (quite correctly) that pupils were solving problems all the time in mathe-

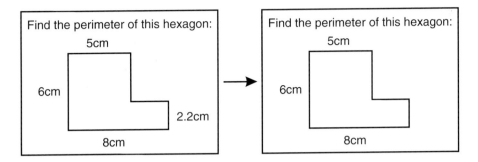

**Figure 2.2** *Perimeter of a hexagon*

matics lessons. True. But if you look at some of the sections in the Programme of Study about problem-solving in Ma1 it moves to pupils working on problems more independently over time and then accounting to others for their decisions and solutions. Thinking about this strand in terms of making and monitoring decisions enables it to be planned for in many, if not all, of your mathematics lessons.

You might like to think about some mathematics that you have done recently or some mathematics that you have observed pupils doing. Whilst you are recalling the task, try to identify some of the decisions that were made or decisions that the task required the solver to make. How did you communicate your ideas or justify your solution? Or have a go at this mathematics question which I came across recently. It is apparently a typical homework problem for Year 7 pupils in Hungary. Monitor what you are doing and see how it matches to the three strands in Ma1.

How many isosceles triangles can be found if their areas must be 9 cm² and each of the three vertices lies on a grid point, one of which must be (3,1)?

Any mathematics that you plan can include some aspect of Ma1. One route into this is to consider the choices that the pupils are being asked to make in any task that you set. If the pupils are allowed to make choices and are then expected to monitor and justify those choices they will be working on aspects of Ma1. You sometimes have to create the opportunity to make choices. The diagram on the left of Figure 2.2 shows a typical perimeter problem. The pupil needs to work out the lengths of the unlabelled sides and to calculate the perimeter. The change on the right is to remove one of the given lengths.

A consequence of removing one of the lengths is that the question no longer has one solution in terms of the calculation. The pupil has to decide on a missing length and calculate the perimeter. However the pupil can be encouraged to make different decisions about the missing length and to collect a number of special cases. At one level the perimeter calculation can be made many times (the provision of practice). At another level, it is possible to challenge the pupil to move from the special cases to the generalisation that the perimeter is always the same! The pupils could then be encouraged to offer a justification for this result. The practice of finding the perimeter of compound shapes is still as strong, but the focus is no longer on the special case but the general result and the implications for this to the pupils' understanding of perimeter. The task allows for differentiation, offering practice for those that need it yet having sufficient breadth for your mathematically able pupils.

Here is another example. The question on the left offers no choices to the pupils whereas, with slight amendment as in the question on the right, there is plenty of choice.

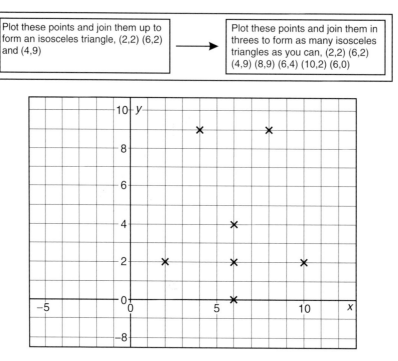

| Plot these points and join them up to form an isosceles triangle, (2,2) (6,2) and (4,9) | ⟶ | Plot these points and join them in threes to form as many isosceles triangles as you can, (2,2) (6,2) (4,9) (8,9) (6,4) (10,2) (6,0) |

However, it is for you to make the decision about the extent to which the pupils are to be offered choices. Depending on the focus for the lesson you can decide to extend or limit the choices. In this way Ma1 can begin to permeate the other aspects of the mathematics curriculum described in Ma2–4.

## The National Strategy for Key Stage 3 mathematics

September 2001 also saw the advent of the National Strategy (NS) for KS3 (DfEE, 2001). The National Curriculum offers a syllabus and level descriptions; the GCSE boards offer syllabuses and examination papers. The NS is no different and offers a syllabus ('pupils should be taught to …') and exemplar questions ('as outcomes pupils should …'). It is intended to be a working document for teachers, providing yearly teaching programmes to help secondary schools set appropriate expectations for their pupils. It also outlines some teaching methods. The guidance is not statutory, but it sets out a very clear and precise strategy which schools are expected to follow.

The NS gives examples of medium-term planning charts, suggesting how 'units of work' might be constructed. Here is the planning chart for the autumn term in year 7 which assumes 36 hours of mathematics teaching time, and which includes revision of level 4 mathematics from the NC but works mainly with level 5 mathematics from the NC. It is called a medium-term plan but in fact is not a plan at all. Like many schemes and textbooks it is a list of topics to be covered.

Beside the chart is the reminder that 'Using and applying mathematics to solve problems should be integrated into each unit'.

**Table 2.3** Page 1/48, The National Strategy Key Stage 3, example planning chart and possible units for Year 7 (DfEE, 2001)

| Strand | Unit desription | Hours |
|---|---|---|
| Number 1 | Place value<br>Integers<br>Calculations | 6 |
| Algebra 1 | Sequences and functions | 6 |
| Shape, space and measures 1 | Mensuration (perimeter and area) | 4 |
| Number 2 | FDPRP (fractions, decimals, percentages, ratio and proportion) | 6 |
| Algebra 2 | Equations and formulae | 5 |
| Handling data 1 | Handling data, including probability | 6 |
| Shape, space and measures 2 | Coordinates<br>Geometrical reasoning: lines, angles and shapes | 3 |

The 6 directly under 'hours' in the table indicates about two weeks of mathematics lessons on the topics in the first section. Quite how to understand what is in each topic remains unclear however since, for example, place value occurs in the spring and summer terms of Year 7 too. Integers, on the other hand, only appears explicitly in the autumn term of Year 7 so we now turn to p 3/6 to find that in the teaching programme for Year 7 under 'numbers and the number system' we have:

**Table 2.4** Page 3/6 extract from the teaching programme for Year 7 (DfEE, 2001)

| 48–59 | Integers, powers and roots |
|---|---|
| 48–51 | Understand negative numbers as positions on a number line; order, add and subtract positive and negative integers in context. |
| 52–55 | Recognise and use multiples, factors (divisors), common factor, highest common factor and lowest common multiple in simple cases, and primes (less than 100); use simple tests of divisibility. |
| 56–59 | Recognise the first few triangle numbers, squares of numbers to at least 12 x 12 and the corresponding roots |

In Table 2.4, the bold heading is meant to represent a 'key objective' and the numbers down the side are the page references for the supplement of examples whose purpose is to 'illustrate the level of difficulty of each teaching objective' (p. 1/ 4). These key objectives are a new dimension in the NS and are defined as 'central to all pupils' achievement in relation to NC levels'. It is interesting to look through these to see if you can find where the 'key objective' of 'integers, powers and roots' appears.

Key objectives relating to number and algebra (Ma2) Year 7

- Simplify fractions by cancelling all common factors; identify equivalent fractions.
- Recognise the equivalence of percentages, fractions and decimals.
- Extend mental methods of calculation to include decimals, fractions and percentages.
- Multiply and divide three-digit by two-digit whole numbers; extend to multiplying and dividing decimals with one or two places by single-digit whole numbers.
- Break a complex calculation into simpler steps, choosing and using appropriate and efficient operations and methods.
- Check a result by considering whether it is of the right order of magnitude.
- Use letter symbols to represent unknown numbers or variables.
- Know and use the order of operations and understand that algebraic operations follow the same conventions and order as arithmetic operations.
- Plot the graphs of simple linear functions.

(DfEE, 2001, p. 2/ 3)

You now might like to look back at the NC level description for Ma2 level 5 (page 89 in your document). The level description in the NC for level 5 and possible part of level 4 should match these key objectives in the NS. It is irritatingly similar but not quite the same. Presumably school mathematics departments will be doing this matching in order to account for coverage. Can you account for the particular emphases in the key objectives? I wonder where prime factor decomposition fits into any of this?

## The teacher, the pupil and the curriculum

Most teachers use schemes of work and use them to account for the coverage of the curriculum. Most teachers have been doing this for ever – reading the scheme or syl-labus, looking at what is expected in the examination or test and then planning activi-ties accordingly with or without a textbook. The NC offers a syllabus ('pupils should be taught to …') and level descriptions ('the type and range of performance of a pupil working at that level …'). The NS offers a syllabus ('pupils should be taught to …') and exemplar questions ('as outcomes pupils should …'), just like the GCSE boards offer syllabuses and examination papers. There is no advice on how to move from the teaching aim to the learning outcome other than by inference. There is little advice on what you have to teach the pupils in order that they can be assessed using a particular assessment item. Practising the assessment item alone is not good teaching – though I suppose it might provide good assessment results in the short term. Progression through the mathematics needs to be determined – and quite rightly so, this is the job of the skilled professional.

Planning with any syllabus, the NC, the NS or a GCSE syllabus you might consider:

- the practice of key skills and their use in as wide a range of contexts as possible;
- organising the topics across the whole time period to integrate the different strands of mathematics;
- what needs repeated practice, what concepts are brand new, what aspects need to be rehearsed in advance of new work;
- the mathematical progression through the topics;
- that different learners need different approaches;
- that having taught something, you then take every opportunity to re-present it;
- that variety is the spice of life!

From the discussion in the earlier sections it follows that the Mathematics Order is not a scheme of work and its presentation as four separate targets disguises the nature of the subject. Some revisiting is already built into the NS to allow for development through the topic over time. Mathematics is not made up of separate elements which can be taught in isolation from one another. Lots of things come into play as concepts build and reform and new ideas emerge.

Additionally, when thinking about planning for learning, the mathematical development of each pupil is different and difficult to predict. At any point in time a pupil will have achieved a wide variety of levels across the Attainment Targets. In a class, therefore, different pupils will be at different places in their learning. Further to this, research shows that pupils develop their own particular routes to learning mathematical concepts. There is nothing new in these ideas, they have always existed and remain a central challenge for all teachers. But these issues need to be considered when planning for pupils' learning.

The National Curriculum document, therefore, requires careful interpretation by the teacher into sequences of classroom activities that weave the many strands together and that take account of pupils' responses and experiences and needs. It is sensible for any lesson to be about a range of statements taken from the Programme of Study. (In many secondary schools some of these decisions are part of the departmental policies and practice. The department in which you work will offer advice on the way that they are using the NC in their particular school context for their pupils' needs.)

Working with ideas across a whole Key Stage might help. Pupils need opportunities to consolidate material at earlier levels, to link with ideas met more recently, as well as beginning to develop the seeds of new ideas which will eventually lead to attainment at later levels. For example, working on $\pi$ (Ma3, KS3 and KS4, p. 39 and p. 68), you might offer early ideas on irrational numbers (Ma2, in the level description for exceptional performance, p. 89), whilst practising using simple formulae expressed in words (Ma2, KS3, p. 47) or exploring number patterns relating to diameter and circumference using a spreadsheet (Ma2, KS3 p. 34), whilst working on all three strands of Ma1 with the reasoning strand leading to a generalisation about the relationship between the diameter and circumference of all circles. There are many such scenarios.

But what will you keep in your head? What are the long-term aims for your pupils in Key Stage 3? At the beginning of each Key Stage Programme of Study in the National Curriculum document there is a lovely summary statement about the long-term aims for the Key Stage. Unlike the itemised bits of mathematics in the Programme of Study and in the NS it offers coherence and an attention to the learner that you might find useful. Here is the statement for Key Stage 3; it is in grey on the right hand side of page 29. And when you think that there are three years to work on these things, life as a teacher seems a whole lot calmer.

> During Key Stage 3 pupils take increasing responsibility for planning and execut-ing their work. They extend their calculating skills to fractions, percentages and decimals, and begin to understand the importance of proportional reasoning. They are beginning to use algebraic techniques and symbols with confidence. They generate and solve simple equations and study linear functions and their corresponding graphs. They begin to use deduction to manipulate algebraic ex-pressions. Pupils progress from a simple understanding of the features of shape and space to using definitions and reasoning to understand geometrical objects. As they encounter simple algebraic and geometric proofs, they begin to understand reasoned arguments. They communicate mathematics in speech and a variety of written forms, explaining their reasoning to others. They study handling data through practical activities and are introduced to a quantitative approach to prob-ability. Pupils work with increasing confidence and flexibility to solve unfamiliar problems. They develop positive attitudes towards mathematics and increasingly make connections between different aspects of mathematics.
>
> (p. 29)

I find that paragraph quite soothing in its summary ambitions for the Key Stage 3 pupil.

I would like to finish with a challenge. What would your National Curriculum model look like? A 3-D pop-up model of a plate of spaghetti? A maze with many routes to the centre? What would it contain? Whatever you picture, it is important not to perceive the National Curriculum as a straitjacket. It is meant to guide, not to restrict, and should not limit your imagination and creativity when planning for the learning of your pupils.

## References

Brown, M (1996) 'The context for the research – the evolution of the National Curriculum for mathematics', in D. Johnson and A. Millett (eds) *Implementing the Mathematics National Curriculum: policy, politics and practice*, London: New BERA Dialogues, PCP.

DfEE (1999) *Mathematics: the National Curriculum for England and Wales*, London: HMSO.

DfEE (2001) *Key Stage 3 National Strategy: framework for teaching Mathematics Years 7, 8 and 9*, London: DfEE Publications.

NCC (1992) *Using and Applying Mathematics Book A: notes for teachers at Key Stages 1–4*, York: National Curriculum Council.

# 3 Examining some changes in mathematics post-16

Doug French

## Post-16 education

In recent years there has been a lot of debate about mathematics in the post-16 sector of education. This has been related particularly to issues linked to A level, but has taken in concerns about a wider range of courses at different levels and continuing concerns about the breadth of the curriculum. Governmental response to some of the issues raised by the report of Lord Dearing (Dearing, 1996) has resulted in substantial changes to the structure of courses and assessment post-16, for AS and A level and also more vocationally-oriented courses.

In the past, post-16 education in schools was largely equated with A level courses, with some provision for students to retake O level examinations that they had previously failed. Vocational education was seen as the province of colleges of further education. The situation has changed dramatically over the last twenty years or so with many more vocational courses finding a place in schools, a substantial development of sixth form and tertiary colleges extending the role of further education colleges into what used to be seen as the province of the school sixth form, and a proliferation of examinations and courses. Throughout there has been a concern about the need to broaden the educational experience of students post-16 and to raise the status of vocational qualifications. It is also important to remember that independent schools have a substantial input into the post-16 sector, contributing a very large number of A level candidates.

## Changes in mathematics post-16

In many respects both the content of A level mathematics and teaching approaches have changed little in the post-war period. A comparison between typical textbooks of the 1950s and many textbooks widely used today will reveal considerable similarity in both content and style, although the contrast between examination papers may be greater. In the late 1980s several curriculum development projects, most notably The School Mathematics Project (SMP) 16–19 and Mathematics in Education and Industry (MEI), set out to produce new A level courses which aimed to extend the range of teaching styles and encourage the use of technology (see, for example, SMP, 1991; Hanrahan et al., 1994). Both continue to be influential. The Mathematical Association (MA) and The Association of Teachers of Mathematics (ATM) have also produced innovative and interesting material aimed for A level teachers and their students (see, for example, ATM, 1988; Drape and Stripp, 2000). Further information about these four organisations will be found on their websites.[1]

## Some statistical data

The number of students taking mathematics at higher levels has long been a matter of concern. There have been three notable declines over the past twenty years:

- the decline in the proportion of the eligible population taking mathematics at A level;
- the decline in the number of students taking science A levels alongside A level mathematics;
- the decline in the number of students taking 'double maths' at A level – mathematics and further mathematics.

The first of these is illustrated in Table 3.1 using some data to compare the number of students taking A level in mathematics and English since 1990. The second column shows the number of candidates entered for A level each year. The third column shows the number of GCSE candidates with grade C and above in the examinations taken two years before. The fourth column gives the number of A level candidates as a percentage of the group with GCSE grade C and above – those who can be considered eligible to take the subject to A level.

The number of A level entries in mathematics has declined very significantly over this period. Over most of this period the number of 18-year-olds has been falling – the demographic dip – and in fact the numbers taking mathematics have been roughly proportional to the size of the 18-year-old population and have increased since 1998 as the population has increased. However, during the same period the numbers taking A level English have increased dramatically despite the fall in the population.

In both subjects the numbers achieving GCSE grade C and above has increased significantly again despite the downward trend in the population of 16-year-olds over the period. The numbers for English are higher than for mathematics, a disparity that has been in evidence over a much longer period with GCE O level, which was replaced by GCSE in 1988. The majority of A level candidates come from this group and so the percentages in the final column gives a fair picture of the proportions of those eligible who choose to continue studying the respective subjects. The percentages for English are fairly steady over the period, but the decline in mathematics is substantial. The number of students continuing their education post-16 has increased considerably over the period and, with the increasing proportions achieving suitable GCSE grades, this has resulted in a substantial increase in the popularity of A level in English and a number of other subjects, but a decline in mathematics. Up to 1990 mathematics was the most popular subject at A level, but since then it has been displaced quite convincingly from its top position by English.

This must surely be a matter of the greatest concern to all who value and enjoy mathematics and, together with corresponding declines in the popularity of the physical sciences, has obvious implications for the country's future supply of mathematicians, scientists and engineers.

**Table 3.1** Comparison of the number of students taking A level in mathematics and English since 1990

| Maths Year | AL entries | GCSE A*ABC | % AL |
|---|---|---|---|
| 1990 | 79 747 | 237 299 | 33.6 |
| 1991 | 74 972 | 248 393 | 30.2 |
| 1992 | 72 384 | 243 866 | 29.7 |
| 1993 | 66 340 | 247 190 | 26.8 |
| 1994 | 64 919 | 252 514 | 25.7 |
| 1995 | 62 188 | 255 360 | 24.4 |
| 1996 | 67 442 | 296 240 | 22.8 |
| 1997 | 68 880 | 298 555 | 23.1 |
| 1998 | 70 554 | 320 676 | 22.0 |
| 1999 | 69 945 | 322 238 | 21.7 |
| 2000 | 67 036 | 314 966 | 21.3 |

| English Year | AL entries | GCSE A*ABC | % AL |
|---|---|---|---|
| 1990 | 74 182 | 282 277 | 26.3 |
| 1991 | 79 187 | 315 142 | 25.1 |
| 1992 | 86 779 | 345 518 | 25.1 |
| 1993 | 89 238 | 345 243 | 25.8 |
| 1994 | 88 214 | 354 991 | 24.8 |
| 1995 | 86 382 | 361 040 | 23.9 |
| 1996 | 86 627 | 346 992 | 25.0 |
| 1997 | 95 223 | 367 836 | 25.9 |
| 1998 | 94 099 | 376 589 | 25.0 |
| 1999 | 90 340 | 363 753 | 24.8 |
| 2000 | 86 428 | 360 328 | 24.0 |

Note
Data based on annual tables of examination results published by QCA

## Task 3.1

- What reasons can you suggest for the relative decline in popularity of mathematics as an A level subject?
- Does it matter that a smaller proportion of eligible students are taking mathematics at A level?
- What can be done to increase the popularity of A level mathematics?

## Post-16 qualifications

### AS and A level

Provision for mathematics beyond Key Stage 4 is provided through courses at AS and A level (with specifications, formerly referred to as syllabuses, that have to satisfy subject criteria laid down by QCA), repeat GCSE courses, free-standing mathematics units (FSMUs), and a variety of vocational courses leading to qualifications such as NVQ and GNVQ. All post-16 provision is required to incorporate the key skills of communication, application of number and application of ICT. (See Chapter 4 by Molyneux-Hodgson and Sutherland for a detailed discussion of all these issues.)

The reforms in post-16 qualifications which took effect from September 2000, leading to the first AS level examinations on new specifications in the summer of 2001 and A level examinations in 2002, arose from recommendations made in Lord Dearing's report (Dearing, 1996) which were designed to broaden study in the sixth form whilst maintaining the depth which is characteristic of A level courses.

The main features of the requirements as they affect mathematics are summarised as follows:

- Revised specifications (syllabuses) come into effect for examinations taken in 2001 (AS) and 2002 (A level).
- Specifications are based on subject criteria agreed by QCA.
- Students should take five subjects, three at A level and two at AS.
- Modular A levels all have six modules (three for AS) with modules at two levels: AS and A2. At least three A2 modules are required for A level.
- Examinations only take place twice a year, in January and June.
- Some element of synoptic assessment is required, relating to the understanding of the subject as a whole.
- For at least 25 per cent of the overall award only a 'scientific' calculator may be used.
- No more than 20 per cent of the overall award may be based on coursework.
- Certain formulae, specified in the subject criteria, may not appear on sheets of formulae available during examinations.

Further details of the subject criteria will be found on the QCA website.[2] The number of awarding bodies and the number of syllabuses have been drastically reduced. The three English awarding bodies, listed below, offer either one or two specifications for mathematics and full details will be found on their websites[3]

- Edexcel (London and BTEC)
- OCR (Oxford, Cambridge and RSA)
- AQA (NEAB, SEG, AEB and City and Guilds)

Wales and Northern Ireland have their own awarding bodies. Scotland has its own examination system which is completely different to the rest of the UK.[4]

All specifications have a similar module structure leading to different awards. AQA and OCR both offer two specifications (A and B), linked to SMP 16–19 and to MEI respectively. As an example, the modules and awards offered by the single specification of Edexcel are as follows.

| Modules | Awards |
| --- | --- |
| Pure Maths: P1 to P6 | AS Maths: P1, P2 + 1 applied module |
| Mechanics: M1 to M6 | A Maths: P1, P2, P3 + 3 applied |
| Statistics: S1 to S6 | AS Further Maths: P4 + 2 others |
| Discrete Maths: D1 to D2 | A Further Maths: P4, P5 + 4 others |

## Other post-16 qualifications

Post-16 qualifications have been categorised under five NVQ levels with broad equivalences as given below.

- Level 1  Four GCSEs at grades D–G or Foundation GNVQ
- Level 2  Four GCSEs grades A*–C or Intermediate GNVQ
- Level 3  Two A levels or Advanced GNVQ
- Level 4  First degree
- Level 5  Higher degree

All post-16 students are required to demonstrate competence in the three key skills of communication, application of number and ICT, and other key skills include working with others, improving own learning and performance, and problem solving. Students will have to provide portfolio evidence for achievement in the first three areas and this may be taken partly from work done as part of AS, A and GNVQ courses together with some external assessment.

GNVQs are available in a number of vocational areas and may be taken alongside AS and A levels. There is no GNVQ qualification in mathematics as such, but competence in mathematics relevant to the topic area is incorporated where appropriate. Concern about the mathematical element of GNVQs is one factor which has lead to the development by the QCA of 'free-standing mathematics units', referred to as FSMUs, which are available at levels 1 to 3 (foundation, intermediate and advanced) in topics such as managing money, handling and interpreting data and working with algebraic and graphical techniques. Further details can be found on the QCA's website given in the endnotes.

The intention is that FSMUs can be taken alongside AS and A levels and GNVQs and that they might be a more useful and congenial alternative to repeating GCSE in mathematics. Previous attempts to provide alternatives to repeating GCSE to achieve at least a grade C or, in the past, repeating O level, have never been successful because the dominant qualification is the one that is recognised and expected by employers and is therefore demanded by students and their parents. This makes it difficult to provide a course at this level that is interesting and valuable rather than being a repeat in a similar style to what the student has already encountered without achieving much success. Teachers commonly find 'repeat GCSE' classes particularly difficult to motivate and as a result success is often limited.

---

### Task 3.2

- Why is it so important for all students to achieve a GCSE at grade C or above?
- How can this apparently vital goal be attained by more students post-16?
- How can alternatives to GCSE be made more attractive to students?

---

## Curriculum and assessment issues

### Teaching styles

> The teacher presents a topic on the blackboard, works through an example and while the students carry out exercises based on the topic the teacher helps individuals.
>
> (HMI, 1982)

> It is very easy for A level teaching in mathematics to depend too much on exposition by the teacher and for students to adopt passive styles of learning.
>
> (Cockcroft, 1982)

The experiences of many A level mathematics students today is commonly very similar to that described in the two quotations above, written around twenty years ago. Cockcroft's comment criticises the style that HMI noted as being the norm.

Some recent research (Taverner, 1997) looked at students' assessment of the frequency of 'perceived learning activities' in their A level subjects. These included items such as 'presentation of a topic by the teacher', 'exercises (working examples)', 'having notes dictated to you', 'class discussions led by the teacher', 'discussion in groups', 'making use of IT' and 'working in pairs'. The first three items featured largely in the experience of all mathematics students, but interesting differences emerged with students following the SMP 16–19 course, indicating much higher frequencies than others in the last four items; the same was true to a lesser extent of the MEI course on the discussion and pairs items. On the other hand, Taverner does point out that the assessment demands of modular courses may lead to 'an increasingly didactic, compartmentalised style of teaching and learning', an observation that may be particularly significant now that all A level mathematics courses in England are modular.

Serious criticisms of the mathematical competence of undergraduates have appeared in the report *Tackling the Mathematics Problem* (LMS, 1995) and in a report from the Engineering Council (Sutherland and Pozzi, 1995), which have focused particularly on lack of fluency in algebraic skills and weak performance in using mathematics to solve problems presented in an unstructured format. The problem-solving issue is highlighted in LMS (1995) by a problem which involved calculating the shaded area in the figure below, leaving the answer in terms of $\pi$. This was solved successfully by only five per cent of 55 honours mathematics students (12 with grade A at A level) entering an English university in October 1994.

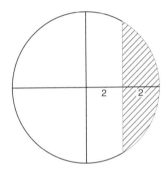

No doubt many more of the students would have solved the problem successfully if it had been presented in a structured form, because the mathematics involved in the individual steps does not go beyond higher level GCSE. The difficulty lies in deciding what steps are needed to arrive at a solution. If students are to become good problem solvers they have to be given actual problems to solve themselves, without being told what to do at each step, and they require an understanding and fluency with a range of appropriate algebraic and other skills. Askew and Wiliam (1995) have noted that 'success in problem-solving requires both specific content knowledge and general skills' and have made a useful comparison with numerical competence which requires 'a blend of *knowing that* and *figuring out*'.

The predominant didactic teaching style which is oriented towards developing and practising techniques, and then applying them to structured standard problems, may be successful in enabling students to obtain the examination grades they require. However, it seems to be much less effective in developing both the understanding and fluency and the thought and persistence that are needed for successful problem-solving. If that is the case the short-term aim of getting good grades is prevailing over the longer one of developing the broader mathematical skills needed for higher education and in the wider world of employment.

Students constantly need to be challenged to think for themselves through encountering a wide variety of problems that use and extend the skills and ideas they have been learning. Discussion is an important element in developing problem-solving skills – alternative approaches need to be considered, including how to recognise false starts and blind alleys, and what to do when you are stuck. Whilst employing a wider range of teaching styles may only be a partial answer to the problem, it is something that lies within the control of the individual teacher. More-over it has a considerable influence on students' attitudes and enthusiasm, as well as their attainment, without in any way detracting from examination success, as another quote from HMI emphasises.

> Lessons observed over the years in a number of sixth forms show that teaching for broader interest and teaching to excite the pupils' imagination are com-pletely compatible with examination success.
>
> (HMI, 1982)

---

### Task 3.3

- Is it reasonable to expect all students with A level mathematics to be able to solve an unstructured problem like that discussed above?
- How do you learn to solve problems whose solution requires familiar mathematics without being given detailed step-by-step instructions?
- What factors inhibit the development of students' problem-solving capabilities?

---

### The problem of proof

The idea of proof is a vital part of mathematics: it is important to show that new results follow logically from accepted results and to clarify the conditions under which they hold true. Besides serving as verification, proof also has an explaining role in the sense of providing insight and understanding. Understanding where a result comes from, why it is true and its connections with other results adds greatly to our ability to use it successfully in a variety of contexts, besides being one of the major sources of the fascination that mathematics can provide.

In the past proof had a substantial role in the teaching of geometry, at least to those students from whom the A level population was drawn, so that by the time they entered the sixth form there was an understanding of the role of proofs and some of the forms they can take. More recently, changes in the way geometry has been presented have resulted in students acquiring less sense of what is involved in math-ematical proof. This has been exacerbated by the tendency, often under the guise of 'investigations', to accept results uncritically, having established that they work in a few particular cases, and also by giving little emphasis to the derivation of formulae and other results. (See also Chapter 5 by Rodd and Monaghan, and Chapter 18 by Morgan.)

Concern about the demise of proof in school mathematics has resulted in it being given explicit mention in the new version of the National Curriculum (DfEE/QCA, 1999) which came into operation in September 2000. At the same time the core content for AS and A level (QCA, 1997) now makes explicit mention of proof (the third section applies only to A level, not AS):

- Construction and presentation of mathematical arguments through appropriate use of logical deduction and precise statements involving correct use of symbols and appropriate connecting language.
- Correct understanding and use of mathematical language and grammar in respect of terms such as 'equals', identically equals', 'therefore', 'because', 'implies', 'is implied by', 'necessary', 'sufficient', and notation such as $\Rightarrow$, $\Leftarrow$ and $\Leftrightarrow$.
- Methods of proof, including proof by contradiction and disproof by counter example.

(QCA, 1997)

Two examples involving proof illustrate some of the requirements implied by these core statements and suggest ways in which students might be encouraged to think about them.

- Show that $n(n + 1)(2n + 1)$ is divisible by 6 for all integer values of $n$, whereas $n(n + 1)(2n - 1)$ is not.

Substituting values of $n$ from 1 to 5 into $n(n + 1)(2n + 1)$ gives 6, 24, 84, 180 and 330, all of which are divisible by 6. So, the first result looks plausible, but we have not proved it because we cannot check it for all numbers! We need to show why it is always divisible by 6.

A key insight is that a number has to be divisible by both 2 and 3 to be divisible by 6. Since $n$ and $n + 1$ are consecutive numbers one of them must be even and so $n(n + 1)(2n + 1)$ is certainly divisible by 2.

We now have to show why it is divisible by 3. If either $n$ or $n + 1$ is a multiple of 3 there is no difficulty, but, if not, we have to show that $2n + 1$ is a multiple of 3. What we do know in this case, by thinking about consecutive numbers, is that both $n + 2$ and $n - 1$ will be multiples of 3. It then follows that $n(n + 1)(2n + 1)$ is a multiple of 3 because $2n + 1$ is equal to their sum, $(n + 2) + (n - 1)$.

In the case of $n(n + 1)(2n - 1)$, a counter-example is found easily by substituting $n = 1$ to give 2, which is not a multiple of 6. It also should be evident, following on from the previous argument, that $(2n - 1)$ is not a multiple of 3 when $(2n + 1)$ is, because they differ by 2.

It is relatively easy to present such arguments to students, but much more difficult to get them to produce their own. When an example like this is being discussed they should be asked to make suggestions, to explain the reasons for statements that have been made and to consider alternative approaches and related questions.

- Investigate the truth of $\dfrac{\sin\theta}{1+\cos\theta} = \dfrac{1-\cos\theta}{\sin\theta}$

The presence of fractions in this identity should prompt us to realise that the expressions will not be defined (and therefore are not true) for certain values of θ. So, a first step is to note that θ cannot be an integer multiple of π.

A common error in attempting a proof is to argue that the truth of the final statement below proves that the initial statement is true.

$$\frac{\sin\theta}{1+\cos\theta} = \frac{1-\cos\theta}{\sin\theta} \Rightarrow \sin^2\theta = 1-\cos^2\theta \Rightarrow \cos^2\theta+\sin^2\theta = 1$$

This is incorrect because we have started by assuming that what we are trying to prove is true. It is like arguing that $1 = 2$ because we know that $0 = 0$ and we can say $1 = 2 \Rightarrow 0\times1 = 0\times2 \Rightarrow 0 = 0$. However, unlike the attempt to prove $1 = 2$, we can legitimately reverse the steps of the argument to prove the trigonometrical identity:

$$\cos^2\theta+\sin^2\theta = 1 \Rightarrow \sin^2\theta = 1-\cos^2\theta \Rightarrow \frac{\sin\theta}{1+\cos\theta} = \frac{1-\cos\theta}{\sin\theta}$$

In order to appreciate the nature of mathematical reasoning and proof, students need to encounter and discuss faulty reasoning just as much as they need to see correct arguments. A useful resource for teachers on the subject of proof is The Mathematical Association's publication *Are You Sure? Learning about Proof* (French and Stripp, 1999).

---

## Task 3.4

- How can we help students to appreciate and understand proofs and to produce proofs of their own?
- What is the difference between an equation and an identity?
- How can the diagram be used to prove that

$$\frac{\sin\theta}{1+\cos\theta} = \frac{1-\cos\theta}{\sin\theta} \quad ?$$

Hint: Angles BAD and CBD are both equal to ½θ. We can then say that, in triangle BAD, $\tan\frac{1}{2}\theta = \dfrac{\sin\theta}{1+\cos\theta}$ and, in triangle CBD, $\tan\frac{1}{2}\theta = \dfrac{1-\cos\theta}{\sin\theta}$. This shows that the two expressions in the identity are equal, although the following diagram may be less helpful for θ > 90°!

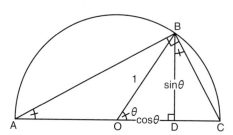

- Show that the sum of the cubes of three consecutive numbers is a multiple of 9.

Hint: If $n - 1$, $n$, $n + 1$ are three consecutive numbers, then the sum of their cubes can be expressed as:

$$(n-1)^3 + n^3 + (n+1)^3 = 3n^3 + 6n = 3n(n^2 + 2)$$

To show that this is a multiple of 9 we need to show that $n(n^2 + 2)$ is a multiple of 3. When $n$ is a multiple of 3 there is no problem, so we have to consider what happens when $n$ is not a multiple of 3. In that case $n$ can be expressed as either $3m + 1$ or $3m - 1$ where $m$ is an integer. Substituting and simplifying shows that $n^2 + 2$ is a multiple of 3:

$$n^2 + 2 = (3m \pm 1)^2 + 2 = 9m^2 \pm 6m + 3$$

- Investigate the truth of $\frac{1}{2}(a+b) \geq \sqrt{ab}$ (the arithmetic and geometric means inequality).

A detailed discussion about proving this result can be found on pages 46 to 50 of 'Are You Sure? Learning about Proof' (French and Stripp, 1999).

## Formulae for AS and A Level Mathematics

The subject criteria for mathematics (QCA, 1997) include a list of formulae which candidates are expected to remember and which may not be included in formulae booklets for AS and A level examinations. Copies of this can be found on the QCA's website and also in the specifications of the awarding bodies. The decision to specify formulae in this way has arisen in part because of students' perceived lack of fluency with results that are considered 'basic' in the sense that having them 'at your finger tips' is essential in solving problems.

To many who have been brought up to expect that a book of formulae will always be available, the prospect of requiring students to 'remember all those formulae' may seem formidable. However, remembering is related to the way in which you have used and come to understand particular formulae and the extent to which you see links and connections between different ideas.

Trigonometric identities are often considered difficult to remember and they are often not linked to the pictures from which they can be derived. The right-angled triangle with unit hypotenuse, shown in the diagram overleaf, not only provides a simple picture giving meaning to $\cos \theta$ and $\sin \theta$, but it also reminds you of $\cos^2 \theta + \sin^2 \theta = 1$ linked to Pythagoras' Theorem, and the connection between $\tan \theta$ and the gradient of the slope reminds you that $\tan \theta = \dfrac{\sin \theta}{\cos \theta}$

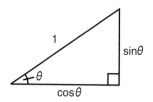

Often a simple example which can be worked out from first principles aids recall of a formula. If you want the tenth term of an arithmetic sequence which starts at 4 and has a common difference of 7, you can work it out mentally as $4 + 9 \times 7$. This can serve to remind you of the formula for the $n$th term as $a + (n - 1)d$, which you might need for a more complicated problem. Similarly, thinking of the sum of an arithmetic series as the mean term multiplied by the number of terms and realising that the formula for the $n$th triangular number is a special case, both give greater sense to the general formula for the sum and help the memory.

---

## Task 3.5

- Why is it important to remember formulae?
- How is it that you can remember some formulae easily?
- What methods can you devise to make it easier to understand and recall some of the formulae on the QCA's list?

---

### Information and communications technology

Computers are an increasingly dominant feature of everyday life and substantial claims are made for the impact that they can and will have in education. Bibby (1991) speaks of 'microtechnology driving a wedge between mathematical content and the associated traditional mathematical skills' with the resulting problem of how much emphasis teachers should give to carrying out algorithms manually. Computers and calculators have been used in some mathematics classrooms over a long period of time, but even with A level classes their use is far from universal and their potential as teaching tools often remains unexploited. This may in part be due to resource limitations and lack of teacher expertise, but it is also because many A level text books (with some notable exceptions, such as SMP 16–19 and MEI) and the usual forms of assessment do little to encourage ICT use.

Graphical calculators are a particularly valuable tool and, because of their relative cheapness, portability and obvious usefulness, many students are willing to buy their own. Projecting a calculator display onto an overhead screen is much cheaper and simpler than projecting a computer screen and is an excellent way of providing a focus for discussion of the properties of graphs and for considering a range of other mathematical ideas. Some examples will illustrate the possibilities.

The following figure shows stretches in the $y$ and $x$ directions of the function $f(x) = \sin(x)$. Whilst the former is usually readily recognised by students, the latter is far less obvious and often comes as a surprise. Such graphs offer a useful way of reinforcing results concerning derivatives: in this case, the fact that if $f(x) = \sin(2x)$, then we have $f'(x) = 2\cos(2x)$.

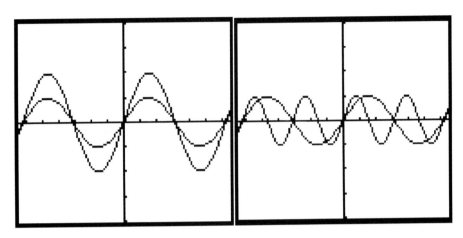

The Newton-Raphson formula involves generating a sequence of values converging on a root of an equation. The calculations can be done with a scientific calculator, but it is much simpler and clearer to display them on the large screen of a graphical calculator, using the ANS facility.

The formula $x_{n+1} = x_n - \dfrac{f(x_n)}{f'(x_n)}$ produces successive approximations to the equation

$f(x) = 0$. On the screen image shown below it has been used to approximate the cube root of 5 by taking $f(x) = x^3 - 5$ and with $x = 2$ as a first estimate.

```
2
                                  2
Ans-(Ans^3-5)/3/Ans^2
                              1.75
                       1.710884354
                       1.709976429
                       1.709975947
```

A spreadsheet could be used as an alternative for this type of example and for other examples where it is instructive to look at sets of numerical values. Spreadsheets have a variety of other uses, particularly for statistical work where it is possible to make use of large data sets and probability where simulation is a useful tool.

Dynamic geometry software such as Geometer's Sketchpad and Cabri Géomètre[5] also offers a lot of scope for exploring geometrical ideas through the challenge of constructing a correct diagram and then being able to manipulate it by moving points on the screen. The following diagram shows the locus of a point on an up-and-over garage door. The curve appears to be part of an ellipse and proving this involves a useful application of trigonometry and parametric equations.

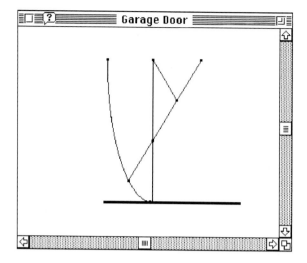

Advanced calculators like the Texas Instruments TI-89 and TI-92, and the computer algebra system, Derive, on which they are based, offer another interesting and potentially valuable classroom tool. Their ability to carry out symbolic manipulation poses a significant challenge to how algebra and calculus might be learnt and used in the future.

The screen from a TI-92 (above) shows the factors of a sequence of related expressions. Such results have the potential to prompt all sorts of interesting questions which demand a greater understanding than that required simply to do the manipulations.

- Why is $x - 1$ a factor each time?
- How do you explain the result for $x^3 - 1$?
- Why does $x^4 - 1$ not seem to fit the pattern?
- What are the factors of $x^6 - 1$ going to be?
- What is the link with geometric series?

The range of operations that such a calculator can perform is very impressive. The major questions that it raises are what skills and understanding are needed in order to use it intelligently, and to what extent A level mathematics will need to change as a consequence. It will be interesting to see how that challenge is met when such calculators are cheap and widely available to A level students. Useful references on these questions are a report by the National Council for Educational Technology (now BECTa) (NCET, 1995), the interesting review by Berry and Monaghan (1997), and Taylor (1995), for some thoughts on implications for examinations.

---

## Task 3.6

- What role should ICT play in an A level mathematics course?
- What do you need to know about graphs and functions in order to use a graphical calculator intelligently?
- How might the availability of calculators which can do symbolic algebra influence the content and teaching of A level mathematics in the future?

---

## Applications: mechanics and statistics

All A level specifications must include applications of mathematics in some form which embraces the idea of mathematical modelling. Traditionally courses have offered either a choice between mechanics and statistics or some elements of both. Discrete or decision mathematics has been available as another option. All the current modular schemes include this same range of choice.

Over the last twenty years or so mechanics has become much less popular as an option. In response to that the Mechanics in Action Project has set out to improve the quality of mechanics teaching and make the subject more appealing and accessible, particularly by encouraging the use of practical work of all kinds. In the same way the teaching of statistics has been enhanced by the work of the Royal Statistical Society's Centre for Statistical Education with an emphasis on using real data, a process that is greatly aided by the availability of powerful computers with access to the internet.[6]

---

## Task 3.7

- What are the arguments for and against all A level mathematics students doing some elements of both statistics and mechanics?
- Why do you think mechanics has become less popular in recent years as an option? Does it matter?
- Is there a case for an A level in pure mathematics?

---

## Subject knowledge for student teachers

It seems a good general principle that any teacher should have studied their subject beyond the level at which they are required to teach. Thus all secondary mathematics teachers are expected to have studied mathematics in some form as part of their degree courses. Most secondary PGCE courses are aimed at those who intend teaching across the whole 11 to 18 age range. Although many will in fact teach in 11 to 16 schools, reviewing the subject knowledge required for A level can ensure a clearer sense of what will be involved in the next stage for abler pupils and provide an important perspective, particularly for teaching the higher tier of a GCSE course.

The Initial Teacher Training National Curriculum for Secondary Mathematics (TTA, 1998) sets out requirements, described as 'advisory only', which are needed 'to teach mathematics post-16 effectively'. They require a confidence in subject knowledge, including knowledge of applications such as mechanics or statistics, 'at a level which goes beyond the A level core' and specify particularly:

- the nature and methods of proof;
- techniques of algebra and calculus;
- coordinate and vector geometry;
- the analysis of discrete and continuous limiting processes;
- infinity and infinite processes.

Reading around and beyond the immediate requirements of day-to-day A level teaching is an important continuing source of enrichment and ideas for every teacher. Many of the suggestions in the next section are as pertinent to the teacher as to the student!

## Preparing for Higher Education

### Extending the abler students

Those who are very able in mathematics and particularly those who are likely to study it beyond school, either by doing a mathematics degree course or as an important component in a degree, particularly in the physical sciences or engineering, should have the opportunity to take their mathematics further than the requirements of the single A level course. There are two things that can be offered to them – one is to let them take the new Advanced Extension Papers which replace what used to be called special papers. These have more demanding questions than the single A level, but are based on the same material.

The other possibility is to offer further mathematics either at AS or A level so that students do what is referred to as 'double maths' or in the case of AS 'maths and a half'. Current modular schemes and the encouragement to do five subjects with three at A level and two at AS increase the flexibility for students to do either AS or A level mathematics, which in the latter case would normally be a fourth A level. Schools with small sixth forms often find it difficult to offer further mathematics because the number of students involved is very small. Two recent developments are aimed at encouraging more schools to offer further mathematics to their able students. The Mathematical Association has a leaflet that gives advice about the practicalities of offering A level courses in further mathematics and also has a panel of experienced teachers who can offer advice. Details of both will be found on the Association's website given in the endnotes. MEI has established an online course in

A level further mathematics which will be backed by individual tutorial support. Details will be found at www.mei-distance.com.

In teaching at any level it is very easy to focus attention on the short-term aim of the next assessment hurdle, whether it be GCSE or A level, and pay insufficient attention to the needs of the next stage or to promoting a broader interest in the subject. At both GCSE level and at A level there will be students who will not take mathematics further and it is important that their course provides a coherent end point. It is unhelpful, when such students ask what the purpose of studying a particular topic, to tell them that it is needed for the next stage. Students should see meaning and purpose in what they are doing throughout a course. That may come from the intrinsic interest that can be generated in a topic or it may come through pointing to ways in which the ideas are linked to aspects of the wider world. For all students the need is to stimulate their interest, to extend their thinking powers and to help them to become autonomous learners. All students will benefit from seeing that mathematics lessons are concerned with more than ensuring examination success, important though that is.

Mathematics teachers have an understandable tendency to 'spoon-feed' students too much, with the unfortunate effect that many find it difficult to maintain their interest and success when faced with the greater mathematical demands of a degree course and the requirement to work independently. For those who aspire to take mathematics at university, there is an obvious need to extend their mathematical knowledge and understanding as far as possible and to challenge them constantly with demanding problems. They need both to be given some insight into what to expect in a university course and to develop an ability to use books (see below for some suggestions) and other resources, such as the internet, both to stimulate and broaden their interests in the subject and to extend their knowledge and understanding.

---

**Task 3.8**

- How could you have been better prepared for your degree course?
- What advice would you offer to a student intending to do a degree course in mathematics?
- What mathematical reading have you found valuable?

---

## Some books for A level mathematics students and their teachers

Baylis, J. and Haggarty, L. (1988) *Alice in Numberland*, London: Macmillan.
Davis, P.J. and Hersh, R. (1983) *The Mathematical Experience*, Harmondsworth: Penguin.
Gardner, M. (1986) *Knotted Doughnuts and Other Mathematical Entertainments*, New York: W.H. Freeman (and many other titles).

Hardy, G.H. (1967) *A Mathematician's Apology*, Cambridge: Cambridge University Press.
Kaplan, R. (1999) *The Nothing That Is: a natural history of zero*, Harmondsworth: Penguin.
Maor, E. (1998) *Trigonometric Delights*, New Jersey: Princeton University Press.
Mason, J. (1988) *Learning and Doing Mathematics*, London: Macmillan.
Stewart, I. (1987) *The Problems of Mathematics*, Oxford: Oxford University Press (and many other titles).

## Notes

1   SMP: www.smpmaths.org.uk
    MEI: www.meioffice.freeserve.co.uk
    Association of Teachers of Mathematics: www.atm.org.uk
    The Mathematical Association: www.m-a.org.uk
2   QCA: www.qca.org.uk
3   Edexcel (London and BTEC): www.edexcel.org.uk
    OCR (Oxford, Cambridge and RSA): www.ocr.org.uk
    AQA (NEAB, SEG, AEB and City and Guilds): www.aqa.org.uk
4   Wales: www.wjec.co.uk
5   *Geometer's Sketchpad* is obtainable in the UK from Capedia Ltd, Harford Centre, Hall Road, Norwich, NR4 6DG and a demonstration may be viewed on the website of Key Curriculum Press at www.keypress.com
    *Cabri Géomètre* and *Derive*, and a wide range of calculators including the *Texas Instruments TI-89 and TI-92* are obtainable from Oxford Educational Supplies at www.oxford-educational.co.uk or Chartwell-Yorke at www.chartwellyorke.com. You can find out more about *Cabri Géomètre* from www.cabri.imag.fr.
6   Mechanics in Action: www.man.ac.uk/CME/MAP/
    Centre for Statistical Education: www.science.ntu.ac.uk/rsscse

## References

Askew, M. and Wiliam, D. (1995) *Ofsted Reviews of Recent Research: recent research in mathematics education 5–16*, London: HMSO.
ATM (1988) *Whatever Next? Ideas for use on A level mathematics courses*, Derby: Association of Teachers of Mathematics.
Berry, J. and Monaghan, J. (eds) (1997) *The State of Computer Algebra in Mathematics Education*, Bromley: Chartwell Bratt.
Bibby, N. (1991) 'Wherefore "plug-and-chug"?' *The Mathematical Gazette*, 75(471): 40–8.
Cockcroft, W.H. (1982) *Mathematics Counts*, London: HMSO.
Dearing, R. (1996) *Review of Qualifications for 16–19-year-olds: summary report*, London: SCAA.
DfEE/QCA (1999) *Mathematics: the National Curriculum for England*, DfEE/QCA.
Drape, S. and Stripp, C. (2000) *Problem Pages*, Leicester: The Mathematical Association.
French, D. and Stripp, C. (1999) *Are You Sure? Learning about proof*, Leicester: The Mathematical Association.

Hanrahan, V., Porkess, R. and Secker, P. (1994) *MEI Structured Mathematics: pure mathematics 1*, London: Hodder and Stoughton.

HMI (1982) *Mathematics and the Sixth Form*, London: HMSO.

LMS/IMA/RSS (1995) *Tackling the Mathematics Problem*, London: London Mathematical Society/Institute for Mathematics and its Applications/Royal Statistical Society.

National Council for Educational Technology (1995) *Algebra at A level: how the curriculum might change with computer algebra systems*, Derby: ATM.

QCA (1997) *GCE Advanced and Advanced Subsidiary Examinations: subject cores for mathematics*, London: QCA (available from the QCA website).

SMP (1991) *16–19 Mathematics: foundations*, Cambridge: Cambridge University Press.

Sutherland, R. and Pozzi, S. (1995) *The Changing Mathematical Background of Undergraduate Engineers*, London: The Engineering Council.

Taverner, S. (1997) 'Modular courses – a drip feed approach to teaching and learning?', *Teaching Mathematics and its Applications*, 16(4): 196–9.

Taylor, M. (1995) 'Calculators and computer algebra systems – their use in mathematics examinations', *The Mathematical Gazette*, 79(484): 40–8.

TTA (1998) *Initial Teacher Training National Curriculum for Secondary Mathematics (Annex G of DfEE Circular 4/98)*, London: Teacher Training Agency.

# 4 Mathematics for post-16 vocational courses

Susan Molyneux-Hodgson and
Rosamund Sutherland

## What counts as mathematics?

The aim of this chapter is to raise awareness of the points of view of students in post-16 education who are required to learn mathematics, or deal with mathematical ideas, whilst studying other subjects. These students are likely to be following vocational courses, such as the General National Vocational Qualifications (GNVQs), the National Vocational Qualifications (NVQs), the Modern Apprenticeship scheme or BTEC. Many of the ideas and issues raised in this chapter could also be of relevance to teaching on more academic courses.

What could count as mathematics in different areas of the workplace or everyday life? Consider the case of an architect, for example, would she be using mathematics when she scales up from a model to a real building? Is a nurse working mathematically when he works out the timing for drug administration to patients? Does a school science technician use mathematics when she makes up a specific concentration of sulphuric acid?

---

**Task 4.1**

Think for a while about these questions and generate some more questions which relate to your own experience.

---

## 'Mathematising' the world and mathematics in practice

Within this chapter we want to distinguish between the activity of 'mathematising' the world and the activity of using mathematics as a resource within ongoing work. We would argue that there are subtle yet important differences between these two activities which relate to the purposes or goals of the people carrying out the activity.

The work of applied mathematicians is concerned with 'mathematising' the world. They build mathematical models which enable them to explain and predict phenomena, for example a mathematical model of the weather, of the spread of a disease or of the behaviour of a building in an earthquake. Mathematical modelling is an important part of the school mathematics curriculum and it is arguably important for all citizens to learn about the potential and constraints of mathematical modelling. Without this understanding people may hold naive beliefs regarding the power of mathematical models and may not understand why, for example, a mathematical model of the Thames millennium bridge did not predict that it would wobble when people walked over it.

Whilst mathematical modelling is an important aspect of much vocational activity, it does not get to the heart of what people are doing when they 'appear' to be using mathematics as part of their vocational practice at work or on vocational courses. So, although it might be possible for a mathematician to 'mathematise' a *practice*, this does not mean that the person carrying out the practice is overtly or even implicitly using mathematics. Paul Dowling (1991) used the example of a spider spinning a web to ask the question, 'Is the spider doing mathematics?' There is a long history in mathematics education of teachers 'seeing the mathematics in a practice' and making the leap to saying that those carrying out the practice are doing mathematics. This could be called a maths-centric perspective, seeing the world from the eyes of a mathematician, and there is much interesting literature about the inappropriateness of this view in many situations (see, for example, Lave, 1988; Seely Brown *et al.*, 1989). This literature also questions the concept of 'transfer' as a useful one relating to learning. The idea of transfer implies that what is learnt in one situation can be (unproblematically) applied to other situations; for example, that having learnt about *x*–*y* graphs in a mathematics class, students would have little difficulty producing and using graphs in science.

Students on vocational courses of study will be engaged in, for example, becoming engineering technicians, becoming health care assistants or becoming graphic designers. They will not be involved in the practice of becoming a mathematician. In teaching these vocational students then, it will be important for you to understand the perspectives from which these students themselves are viewing their activity. Understanding their perspective is only a first step in thinking about teaching these vocational students, because, as we shall see later in this chapter, there are still many unresolved issues about how we can best go about teaching mathematics for vocational practice.

---

## Task 4.2

*Can you think of an example when you have seen mathematics in a practice or activity, and have subsequently become aware that the person engaged in the practice is not seeing the world in a mathematical way?*

## Mathematics qualifications post-16

Having framed the relationship between mathematics and vocational practices in this way, we now describe aspects of the current curriculum and examination framework for post-16 students. Although the focus of this chapter is on vocational education the qualification framework is the same for both academic and vocational students. The two main qualifications we will discuss are the Key Skills Qualification (which includes Application of Number) and Free-standing Mathematics Units. Although different in many ways, there are some similarities. For example, both qualifications can be studied at various levels and fit into the National Framework of Qualifications, and both qualifications can be studied by students following any other course of study. They can also be taught in similar ways and are both assessed using a combination of external testing and portfolio compilation.

### Key skills

The notion of Key Skills (originally known as 'core skills') emerged from the industrial sector and this sector's concerns regarding new employees' capabilities in a number of areas considered crucial to the success of business and the ability of the UK to compete in a world market economy (CBI, 1989). The concerns of industry were subsequently echoed in education policy statements (HMI, 1989) and a set of six areas of 'desirable competencies' emerged (NCC, 1990), later disseminated as the six 'core skills'. These areas have remained largely unchanged and are currently known as the six Key Skills, shown in the table below.

| Main Key Skills | Wider Key Skills |
| --- | --- |
| Application of Number | Working with Others |
| Communication | Improving Own Learning and Performance |
| Information Technology | Problem Solving |

The Key Skill of interest in this chapter is Application of Number. As mentioned above, Key Skills can be studied at different levels and it is possible to study an individual Key Skill at a level that is different from the subject qualification a student is studying. For example, it is possible for someone to study a GNVQ at level 3 (Advanced Level) and Application of Number at level 2 (Intermediate Level), but all three of the main Key Skills must be gained, at some level, in order to gain the Key Skills Qualification. The qualification consists of three Units (Application of Number, Communication and IT), a student either passes or fails (there are no grades) and the assessment is via portfolio evidence and external tests (one test for each Key Skill). It is possible to gain exemption from some of the Key Skill assessments, for example, a grade A–E in AS or A level mathematics exempts students from the external tests for level 3 Application of Number.

Key Skills were initially an integral aspect of vocational qualifications, and gaining criteria in each Key Skill element was necessary to passing the subject qualification.

# Part B

## WHAT YOU MUST DO

*You must:*

### N1.1

Interpret straightforward information from **two** different sources.
At least **one** source should be a table, chart, diagram or line graph.

*Evidence must show you can:*

- obtain the information you need to meet the purpose of your task; and
- identify suitable calculations to get the results you need.

### N1.2

Carry out straightforward calculations to do with:

   a. amounts and sizes;

   b. scales and proportion;

   c. handling statistics.

- carry out calculations to the levels of accuracy you have been given; and
- check your results make sense.

### N1.3

Interpret the results of your calculations and present your findings. You must use **one** chart and **one** diagram.

- choose suitable ways to present your findings;
- present your findings clearly; and
- describe how the results of your calculations meet the purpose of your task.

Since September 2000, the passing of vocational qualifications has been decoupled from the Key Skill requirements although all students studying for vocational qualifications will be strongly encouraged to take the Key Skills Qualification, at an appropriate level. This separate qualification also means that students following non-vocational qualifications – such as AS and A levels – are more likely to work towards gaining Key Skills certification.

The QCA specifies what students need to know and what evidence students must provide in order to achieve a Key Skill at a particular level. They also provide guidance on the kinds of activities students might engage with in order to demonstrate competence in any Key Skill component. The example above is taken from the QCA website and provides the specification for level 3 Application of Number.

This Application of Number specification is a statement of what a student 'must do'. It does not specify the context of learning or how students will produce evidence of learning. This is where teachers and students need to interpret what has been provided by the curriculum authorities and find ways of fulfilling what is required. As a result schools and colleges can choose to organise the 'provision' of Key Skills in a number of ways, ranging from taught input from mathematics teachers, to no separate mathematics teaching at all. Many people believe that it is better for students to learn the mathematics they need 'just-in-time' within the context of their vocational course because in this way they will appreciate the need for mathematics and are more likely to be motivated to learn. Later in this chapter we shall discuss why we believe that it is far from straightforward for students to learn Application of Number in this way.

## Free-standing Mathematics Units

Free-standing Mathematics Units (FSMUs) are a new type of qualification aimed at encouraging students to include appropriate mathematics into their post-16 Programme of Study. They have been developed for both A level and vocational students and are available at Foundation, Intermediate and Advanced level. The aim of the FSMU programme is to increase participation in post-16 mathematics learning and they offer students an opportunity to develop their understanding of a specific aspect of mathematics, without having to take a full-scale qualification in the subject. Each unit requires about 60 hours of study and is equivalent to one sixth of an A level or one third of an AS level. Units at the Foundation Level are: Managing money, Working in two and three dimensions, Making sense of data. Units at the Intermediate Level are: Calculating finances, Solving problems in shape and space, Handling and interpreting data, Making connections in mathematics, Using algebra, functions and graphs. Units at Advanced Level are: Understanding mathematical thinking, Using and applying statistics, Working with algebraic and graphical techniques, Modelling with calculus.

The assessment uses both a continuous assessment approach through portfolio work and an externally set and marked examination. The examination also places an emphasis on examining the mathematics that have been applied to a situation. The focus throughout is on *applying* mathematics and the intention is that the portfolio work should be situated within an 'application' context. Each unit is accompanied by suggestions about which groups of students for which the unit is likely to be valuable. For example, 'Handling and interpreting graphs' is likely to appeal to vocational students in the areas of science, technology, business, economics, leisure and tourism, geography, social sciences and health.

Free-standing Mathematics Units specify what a student needs to learn and the contents for the coursework portfolio which the student needs to develop. This is illustrated in Figure 4.1 by the specification for the coursework portfolio for the Intermediate unit 'Using algebra, functions and graphs'.

This specification indicates that evidence must be produced within the context of 'using and applying' mathematics. The guidance for the teacher which accompanies this unit states that:

> It is essential that the areas of mathematical content that are associated with this unit are brought together in a way that is meaningful to candidates so that they can

| 7.3    Coursework Portfolio | Your Coursework Portfolio should include the evidence set out below. This should be set in situations from your studies, work towards other qualifications, work or interests (hobbies). | |

| What you need to produce: | You must: |
|---|---|
| Reports of at least two investigations you carry out into situations in which you show your use of: | Your reports should include written evidence of all mathematical analysis and computation showing your working in full, especially when you have used a calculator. |
| a  graphs, | |
| b  linear, proportional and non-linear models, | |
| c  algebra. | |
| You should show evidence that in places you have used both estimation and checking to ensure that your work is accurate. | |
| In the totality of your reports you should: | |

| a  use graphs and graphical techniques to: | ensure that your graphs are: |
|---|---|
| • plot<br>  (i)   data<br>  (ii)  at least one linear model<br>  (iii) at least one other non-<br>       linear model<br>  where at least one is plotted<br>  by hand and at least one is<br>  plotted using either a graphic<br>  calculator or computer<br>  software. | (i)   correctly and<br>       appropriately scaled<br>(ii)  fully labelled<br>(iii) accurately plotted |
| • explain how each graph relates to what is happening in the real world situation(s) you investigated by identifying and calculating any appropriate key features of the graphs including<br>  (i)   intercepts with axes<br>  (ii)  gradients<br>  (iii) areas under graphs | • show that you can link the key features of your graphs to the real situations you are investigating<br><br>• indicate clearly on your graphs how you have used them to find data |
| • predict what will happen for cases for which you have no data | • quote values resulting from graphs to an appropriate level of accuracy |
| • solve problems involving<br>  (i)   linear, and<br>  (ii)  non-linear<br>  functions | • explain (without carrying out calculations)  how inaccuracies and errors in your data may have affected your interpretation of your graphs |

**Figure 4.1**  The specification for the coursework portfolio for the Intermediate unit 'Using algebra, functions and graphs' (continued on next page)

b   find:
- one linear or proportional function to model data (using values you have found for the gradient of the line and its intercept on the vertical axis), and
- one non-linear function to model data

- identify yourself the appropriate type of function to fit to data
- find an appropriate function to fit your data

c   solutions to problems arising from algebraic expressions used to model real world situations involving techniques that include:
- simplifying expressions
- changing the subject of formulae
- solving equations
- using simultaneous linear equations

- use understandable algebraic notation
- show clearly the stages of your working

**Figure 4.1**  (continued from previous page)

investigate real world situations from their other areas of study, work or interests. Data should be real, identified and collected by the student wherever possible.

(QCA, 2000, p. 15)

The use of ICT is explicitly specified within each unit. For example,

Candidates are required to use either a graphic calculator or function plotting software on computer when completing their work for their Coursework Portfolio. The use of a standard scientific calculator will be expected in the written examination.

(AQA, 2000, p. 5)

It is claimed that:

The work that a candidates produces for a Free-standing Mathematics Unit will allow them to gather evidence toward the Key Skill in Application of Number, although the two qualifications are substantially different. FSMUs allow candidates to develop a branch of mathematics to some depth while Application of Number is concerned with developing a wide range of underpinning number skills.

(AQA, 2000, p. 26)

Schools and colleges are using FSMUs to give post-16 students a fresh start in mathematics.

It gives students who have previously experienced failure a different approach. They like learning through the use of computers and they like portfolio work.

(quote from lecturer in FE college, Winter *et al.*, 2000)

## Approaches to teaching Mathematics to vocational students

Within this section of the chapter we raise issues about the practice of teaching mathematics to vocational students. Traditionally, mathematics for vocational students has been taught as a separate subject, possibly with examples drawn from their vocational practice. However, this approach is not very satisfactory because students find it difficult to link the mathematics learned as a separate subject to the mathematics they need within their vocational practice, and thus are not likely to be very motivated to learn mathematics being taught in such a way. Teaching mathematics as what is often called a 'service subject' is also notoriously difficult and unrewarding, which may also be linked to the fact that it is often considered to be relatively 'low status' work within Further Education Colleges (in comparison, say, with teaching A level mathematics).

Both the Key Skills and FSMU qualifications offer the opportunity to integrate mathematical work and vocational work in more meaningful ways. However, practices vary considerably between educational institutions. For example, during the piloting of the Key Skills Qualification (1997–1999) provision of mathematical input was found to vary widely. Some institutions offered timetabled teaching sessions in Application of Number, others 'drop-in' workshops, and yet others no separate teaching input at all – all Application of Number work was dealt with within the contact hours for vocational study. Stand-alone mathematics teaching has the advantage of allowing a focus on becoming competent with mathematical ideas, but raises the issue of how students apply what they have learnt into new contexts (the 'transfer' issue). Drop-in sessions can focus on students' individual needs but can require teachers to work in an ad hoc way with individual students. Relying on vocational subject tutors to deal with mathematics requires a multitude of people to become 'mathematics teachers' and creates a tension between learning of subject matter and attending to mathematical demands at the same time.

It is likely that schools and colleges will continue to take different approaches to the provision of both Key Skills and FSMU, and decisions are often dominated by resourcing issues rather than a consideration of the 'best' educational situation for vocational students to learn mathematics.

On the one hand, QCA guidance suggests that separate mathematical input can be provided:

> Students' Key Skills will be developed across a range of learning activities that may include direct teaching of the skills to be practised elsewhere within the students' learning programmes.

(QCA, 2000)

That is, teachers will teach the mathematical skills to students and the students then would use these skills within their vocational studies. However, at the same time, the idea that mathematical work should be embedded in vocational contexts is also strong:

Key skills should be made explicit, and learnt, practised and assessed within contexts that are relevant to individuals

(ibid.)

which could be achieved by either a mathematics teacher, vocational subject teacher, or a combination of both.

As well as the mode of provision varying between educational institutions, the nature of classroom interactions between teacher and students also varies between institutions. In a study of FSMU work in schools and colleges, a range of teaching and learning strategies were employed by tutors, including whole-class work, small groups and individual work. Classes often took place in well-resourced rooms which allowed for easy integration of ICT into teaching. This study also found that teachers did not view FSMUs as material that should be taught in traditional ways and they all espoused the desire for their students to work and learn independently. This of course also ties into the rhetoric of Key Skills and vocational provision in general. Whatever the strategy for teaching, it is apparent that issues regarding the application of mathematical ideas, transfer of mathematical learning between different vocational contexts and how all this can be taught and assessed are critical.

As a teacher of mathematics to vocational students you need to be aware of the structural constraints within the educational institution in which you practise on what and how you can teach. These will relate to management decisions which possibly derive from views about how best to 'deliver' Key Skills or FSMUs. You may also want to question and understand the dominant ideologies within the educational institution related to teaching and learning mathematics for vocational practice.

We end this section with an example of GNVQ Science students learning mathematics within the context of their vocational science course (NCVQ, 1996). The group of students being studied had no mathematics teaching other than what their science tutors chose to provide, or emphasise, in the course of their science teaching. We present here an excerpt of an interaction that took place between a student and teacher within the context of studying the properties of materials with a view to designing a new kettle (Molyneux-Hodgson and Sutherland, 1998).

Two GNVQ Science students were evaluating some properties of a wire (trying to work out strain, which is extension ÷ original length). They had recorded extension and original length in different units (millimetres and metres respectively), and so needed to carry out a conversion.

Cathy wrote on paper: $\text{strain} = \dfrac{0.7 \text{ mm}}{1.725 \text{ m}}$

She converted 0.7 mm into metres quickly in her head, stating out loud, '0 point 0 0 7' (which is an incorrect conversion – out by a factor of 10). The science tutor joined the group to 'guide them' through the start of the analysis. He asked if Cathy was sure of her answer, which unsettled her.

The tutor's approach was to work incrementally, using what could be termed a 'unitary approach' i.e. he wrote 1 mm on paper and asked what that was in metres, then 0.1 mm, etc. He also made use of a metre ruler which was to hand.

Together they arrived at the conversion sum $\frac{0.0007}{1.725}$. The tutor then suggested that, having converted to metres, the students should also try to convert the measurements to millimetres, and when these were done, decide which they thought was the simpler approach. They chose to carry out the calculation in mm, i.e. $\frac{0.7}{1725}$.

The tutor's intervention focused on a more formal approach to the conversion. He did this by leading them, by question and answer, through the 'unitary' method rather than presenting a formula or using a calculator. This raises the issue of how students will make sense of this particular method if they usually use other approaches.

The tutor made use of physical props to support his teaching, bringing in a metre rule to provide additional 'visual' support for the students. This teaching episode was contingent with the student's ongoing activity, that is, he did not set out to teach this idea, but it became appropriate within the session. Here, the teaching of conversion ideas was brought about by the situation and had not been originally planned.

**Task 4.3**

Do you think the science tutor intervened and taught the mathematical ideas appropriately? How might you have dealt with teaching conversions to these students?

## Questioning the idea of teaching mathematics within a vocational context

Inherent to the notion of Application of Number or applying mathematics, is the idea that mathematical work can be *embedded* in vocational contexts.

The Key Skills units aim to develop and recognise candidates' ability to apply these skills in ways that are appropriate to different contexts in order to improve the quality of learning and performance.

(QCA, 2000)

So the emphasis is on 'applying' and 'applying appropriately' across contexts. According to the early Key Skills rhetoric:

> … the core skills movement is based on beliefs about transfer. It assumes that it is possible to identify generic skills that are transferable across education and work contexts …

> (ED, 1993)

As mentioned earlier in this chapter, however, there are serious questions being raised about what it means to 'mathematise' situations and whether 'transfer' is a useful notion. There is a huge debate over whether there are such things as 'key' or 'core' skills, and indeed over the educational use of the concept of 'skill' (Hyland and Johnson, 1998).

> Core (key) skills are defined as those skills, or cognitive processes, which are common and fundamental to performance in a wide range of activities in employment and life in general. Because they are common to many activities, their acquisition in one context facilitates their transfer to many others.

> (NCVQ, 1995)

We would argue that the rhetoric of Key Skills and the metaphor of transfer do not capture the complexity of what is happening when we make use of mathematical ideas in vocational contexts. There are a number of reasons for this. Firstly, as the example which follows illustrates, at least in some vocational subjects knowledge of the subject is inextricably linked to mathematical knowledge, and so even such an apparently straightforward idea as converting between units becomes 'something else' when it is embedded within a scientific context. Secondly, the approaches which a practitioner might actually use when working on what might appear to be a Key Skill within a vocational context (for example, converting between units, fitting a graph to experimental data) are likely to be very different from what might be *taught* as a transferable 'key skill'. In other words, practitioners develop ways of dealing with 'bits of mathematics' that vary between vocational practices and relate to the epistemology of the practice rather than the abstract mathematical idea.

The following example describes the activity of an 18-year-old student following an Advanced GNVQ Science course. Again, the institution in which she studied made no separate provision for mathematical input, all of the work towards fulfilling the Key Skill of Application of Number was contained within her vocational science study. We want to describe part of this student's experience for three reasons:

1   to provide a description of what your potential students may engage in during vocational study;
2   to demonstrate how mathematics can be deeply embedded within ongoing vocational study, leading to problems for assessment and
3   to highlight how the nature of the student's experience means she may not be developing the mathematical competencies which are required by the qualification or desired for successful vocational activity.

## Learning chemistry and using maths

Whilst studying a GNVQ Science unit titled 'Control Reactions', students worked on a series of questions, on a photocopied handout, based around the topic of 'equilibrium constant', which led them through calculations they had to carry out on data they had already collected from laboratory experiments.

Working on the last question, the tutor posed questions to orient the students to the science of the situation, for example, 'What is the titration doing?' He wrote on a board the words,

Amount of NaOH =
reacted (mol)

He asked students, 'How do we work out how many moles of NaOH have been reacted?' One student called out, 'Divide one by the other' to which the tutor replied, 'No'. No one else answered so he continued to write, completing the expression, and asked students to 'Work this out'.

$$\text{Amount of NaOH} = \frac{\text{vol. soln}}{1000} \times \text{conc}^n \ (\text{mol dm}^{-3})$$
reacted (mol)

This formal expression provided by the tutor contained an implicit conversion from $cm^3$ (cubic centimetres) to $dm^3$ (decimetres) signified by the division by 1000. The expression was written on the board, in its entirety, with no accompanying explanation. The students substituted in the values given in the problem statement, calculating a value for 'Amount of NaOH'. As the students had not responded to the tutor's question, 'How do we work out how many moles of NaOH have been reacted?' he provided the students with the expression they needed, asking them just to carry out the arithmetic. Thus an emphasis was placed on the arithmetic (Application of Number) rather than the structure (scientific meaning) of the formal expression – including the implicit conversion.

The assessed written work that followed on from this involved students in calculating an 'equilibrium constant' using their own experimental data. One student's work, described below, demonstrates a consequence of not paying attention to the meaning and structure of the expression taught in the class.

Heidi worked through the series of calculations. She had correctly recorded the expression to find 'concentration' (concentration = $\frac{\text{amount}}{\text{volume}}$)

continued on next page

which had involved rearranging the expression used earlier. She correctly recorded the right units of measurement for each quantity (e.g. dm$^3$). However, when carrying out the calculation (the arithmetic) she did not take into account the fact that her experimental value for 'volume' was measured in cm$^3$ and dm$^3$. Consequently she calculated a series of concentration values that were incorrect by three orders of magnitude. For example,

$$7. \text{ work out concentration}$$

$$\text{concn.} /\text{mol dm}^{-3} = \frac{\text{amt of substance}}{\text{volume of solution} /\text{dm}^3}$$

$$\text{ethanol,} \quad \frac{0.0822}{10} = 8.22 \times 10^{-3}$$

$$= 8.22 \times 10^{-3} \text{ mol dm}^{-3}$$

whereas the correct concentration was 8.22 mol dm$^{-3}$. Heidi had used the correct expression, substituted the values for 'amount' and 'volume' but had neglected the conversion aspect of the problem. The complexity of the chemistry situation was such that it would have been difficult for her to keep track of all aspects of the problem. This would be particularly difficult given the implicit use of the conversion calculation in class.

Heidi was successful in some situations and not in others. This may be unsurprising. We need to ask what it was that Heidi was learning about converting, whether she had demonstrated 'Application of Number' competence and whether she was likely to succeed in other situations, either during her course or at work.

### Task 4.4

Are Heidi and her fellow students learning mathematics which is 'good enough' for application within a vocational context? Or are they finding alternative ways of succeeding, or coping with the mathematical demands of their studies?

We have used some examples from GNVQ Science to illustrate how mathematics for vocational students operates in practice. Whilst these allow us to highlight some of the issues around the use of mathematics in vocational domains, we need to consider whether science is a special case or if there are wider-ranging issues at stake. The range of post-16 vocational courses available for study is large and includes GNVQs in Travel and Tourism, Business Studies, Health and Social Care, Manufacturing, Art and Design. Some of these may immediately strike you as being domains in which mathematics could be applied, the others less so.

For example, if you were providing teaching input to a GNVQ Art and Design course, how would you go about finding authentic opportunities for students to:

> carry out multi-stage calculations … and rearrangement of formulae.
> (Application of Number specification, Level 3)

Whilst it is not hard to imagine learners, irrespective of their subject of study, being able to:

> read and synthesise information
> (Communication specification, Level 3)

or:

> plan and use different sources and appropriate techniques to search for and select information
> (Information Technology specification, Level 3)

the criteria which apply to number work seem more difficult for some vocational areas to fulfil than others.

What does it mean, for example, for learners to know how to work out missing angles and sides in right-angled triangles in GNVQ Travel and Tourism, and in GNVQ Engineering? What about 'rearranging formulae' in GNVQ Art and Design and GNVQ Science? Are the activities the same? Could you teach rearranging formulae in a class containing students from a range of GNVQ courses? This in turn leads to the more general question:

> To what extent can learners' mathematical work be 'authentic' or truly integrated with the vocational subject matter?

## Questioning the idea of assessing Mathematics within a vocational context

The forms of assessment for both Key Skills and FSMU involve external tests and the generation of a portfolio of evidence by the student. The portfolios demonstrate that students have collected evidence to show what they have applied. As mentioned above, to what extent is producing a piece of 'evidence' confirmation of what a student 'knows'? An assumption is being made that appropriate demonstration of a mathematical idea in a vocational context implies that the student has a) learnt the mathematics and b) can apply mathematics. We believe this assumption should be open to question.

The issue of who are the most appropriate people to assess mathematics within vocational work is also open to question.

> Don't assume that a mathematics, IT or English specialist will automatically be competent to assess the Key Skills in Application of Number, IT or communication.

(QCA, 2000)

The above quote signals that the Key Skill Qualification, at least, is somehow different from other maths-related qualifications. Whereas a PGCE prepares a newly-qualified teacher to assess what they have taught in a National Curriculum subject, the link between teaching and assessment is not so straightforward in the case of Key Skills. So, as well as Application of Number potentially being taught by non-mathematics specialists, there is a view that mathematics specialists are not necessarily best placed to assess what has been learned by students. The case of Heidi, which we presented earlier, exemplifies the complexity of the work that would have to be assessed for Key Skill achievement and raises the question of who can make sense of the vocational context to a sufficient extent to assess how the mathematics is being used in practice?

## Concluding remarks

Within this chapter we have raised issues related to:

- mathematics and its use and application in a vocational context;
- teaching and learning mathematics for vocational practice.

We suggest that whilst it may not be appropriate to 'mathematise' activity just for the sake of it, or possibly even for pedagogical purposes, there will be many situations where the capacity to draw on mathematics will enable someone to perform more efficiently or effectively. In this sense mathematics becomes a *resource* which is harnessed within a vocational practice, for example, to carry out essential computations which are inextricably linked to the vocational practice, or to develop mathematical models which enable people to predict and explain some aspect of the practice.

Good learning will only occur if it is orchestrated by good interactive teaching. As we have discussed throughout this chapter mathematics-in-practice is not mathematics, it will have been transformed by the practice into a form that is unrecognisable as mathematics to students. This implies that teaching has to emphasise this transformation and the relationship between mathematics and mathematics-in-practice. It also raises issues about who should do the teaching and how it should be organised. Whereas it is not sufficient for students to learn mathematics as a separate subject in order for them to use it in a vocational context it may be necessary for them to be confident and competent with a range of mathematical ideas before they can be expected to learn how to apply mathematics to a vocational practice. You need to be aware of all the past histories of failure that students may bring to classes but it is worth remembering that students who might resist offering explanations, or talking at all, in what they view as a mathematics lesson, could be articulate and vociferous in another context which enthuses them.

Whether you teach vocational students who are studying mathematics for a Key Skill Qualification or a Free-standing Mathematics Unit or some other purpose, the 'mathematical' experiences of your students will be paramount. You may be faced with groups of students who do not want to be learning mathematics, do not see why they need to learn mathematics and are resentful of the time that they have to spend in these classes. So in order to make these classes pleasurable for you and the students you are going to have to come up with creative ways of getting started as a teacher. Drawing on the powers, expertise and knowledge of the students is a potential way forward which has some chance of success. This means that you have to value and be interested in what the students know. The students will be the ones who intimately know about their vocational practices and who can bring to a discussion rich examples for the whole group to think about and work on. If they themselves ask questions and make decisions about the mathematics they need to know and carry out 'thought experiments' into their future working lives it is quite likely that the whole class will develop their own curriculum which closely resembles any prescribed curriculum.

Within the chapter we have drawn upon examples taken from our work with GNVQ Science students because this has enabled us to look closely at what it might mean to use, learn, teach and assess mathematics within the context of a vocational practice. We suggest that when you set out to teach mathematics to vocational students you could similarly look closely at what it might mean to use, learn, teach and assess mathematics within the vocational practices from which your students are drawn.

## References

AQA (2000) 'Using algebra functions and graphs, free-standing maths units', www.aqa.org.uk/qual/pdf/AQA6988WSP.pdf

CBI (1989) 'Towards a skills revolution', *Report of the Vocational Education and Training Task Force*, London: Confederation of British Industry.

Dearing, R. (1996) *The Review of Qualifications for 16–19 Year Olds*, summary report, London: SCAA Publications.

Dowling, P. C. (1991) 'Contextualising Mathematics: towards a theoretical map', in M. Harris (ed.) *School, Mathematics and Work*, Basingstoke: Falmer Press: 93–120.

Employment Department (ED) (1993) *Development of Transferable Skills in Learners*, Sheffield: Employment Department Methods Strategy Unit.

Her Majesty's Inspectorate (HMI) (1989) *Post-16 Education and Training: core skills*, an HMI Paper, London: HMSO.

Hyland, T. and Johnson, S. (1998) 'Of cabbages and Key Skills: exploding the mythology of core transferable skills in post-school education', *Journal of Further and Higher Education*, 22(2): 163–72.

Lave, J. (1988) *Cognition in Practice: mind, mathematics and culture in everyday life*, Cambridge: Cambridge University Press.

Molyneux-Hodgson, S. and Sutherland, R. (1998) *Mathematical Competencies of GNVQ Science Students: the role of computers*, final report to The Leverhulme Trust, University of Bristol.

National Curriculum Council (NCC) (1990) *Core Skills, 16–19*, York: NCC.

NCVQ (1995) *GNVQ Briefing: information on the form, development and implementation of GNVQs*, London: NCVQ.

NCVQ (1996) *Mandatory Units and Test Specifications for Advanced Science*, London: NCVQ.

QCA (2000) www.qca.org.uk

Seely Brown, J., Collins, A. and Duguid, P. (1989) 'Situated cognition and the culture of learning', *Educational Researcher*, 18: 32–41.

Winter, J., Molyneux-Hodgson, S. and Sutherland, R. (2000) *Evaluating Free-standing Mathematics Units in the Classroom*, final report to the Nuffield Foundation, University of Bristol.

# 2 The Mathematics curriculum

# 5 School mathematics and mathematical proof

Melissa Rodd and John Monaghan

> If a student has gone through his mathematics classes without having really understood a few proofs like the [angle sum of a triangle is half a turn], he is entitled to address a scorching reproach to his school and to his teachers … If the student failed to get acquainted with this or that geometric fact, he did not miss so much; he may have little use for such facts in later life. But if he failed to get acquainted with geometric proofs, he missed the best and simplest examples of true evidence and he missed the best opportunity to acquire the idea of strict reasoning. Without this idea, he lacks a true standard with which to compare alleged evidence of all sorts aimed at him in modern life.
>
> (Pólya, 1945, p. 217)

## Introduction

This chapter is designed to help you deepen your understanding of mathematical proof and how it is linked with other forms of reasoning and ways of understanding in school mathematics. It is also intended to show that learning to prove in a mathematically acceptable way is difficult for pupils (at school) and even students (in Higher Education). Principal forms of mathematical proof relevant for school mathematics are introduced within the text through discussion of a related mathematics education or a curricular issue.[1] We aim to prompt your ideas about how to teach mathematics in a manner such that proof is natural, integral and vital. To start with we give one curriculum's outline of progression in proof as this will establish a working vocabulary for the various aspects of mathematical proof in school mathematics.

## Progression in proving – from the mathematics National Curriculum for England

As for every other aspect of the curriculum, pupils progress in their knowledge, skills and understanding of mathematical proof. Communication of an explanation is considered a foundation for reasoning and proof (note for Key Stage 1 Ma2 1i). So infants, in Key Stage 1, are encouraged to explain their methods in their number work. For example, one child explains that $5 + 6 = 11$ because $5 + 5 = 10$ and as $5 + 1 = 6$ there is one more, so the answer's 11, and another explains that he has counted on six more from five. The Key Stage 2 Programme of Study links this requirement for pupils to explain their reasoning with the admonishment to 'develop logical thinking' (Ma2 1k), though the NC leaves what would count as 'logical thinking' at this stage to our judgement. In Key Stage 3, more formal requirements are specified in the Programme of Study with the introduction of some key terms: in the Ma2 'reasoning' section we find the following terms, some of which will be discussed in context within this chapter: 'generalisation', 'conjecture', 'counter-example', 'step-by-step deduction', 'practical demonstration', 'proof', 'assumptions'. Throughout the mathematics NC[2] there is an emphasis that 'practical demonstration' should be distinguished from a 'proof'. In Ma3 the word 'justify' is used as a refinement of mere explanation (which was all that was required in Primary Key Stages) and 'definitions' are distinguished from 'facts', conventions' and 'derived properties'. The Key Stage 4 Foundation programme is altogether very similar to that of Key Stage 3 – suggesting, perhaps, that the new work on proof is to be considered above level 5. In the Key Stage 4 higher programme, Key Stage 3 proof-concepts are further developed by requiring that pupils can do 'short chains of deductive reasoning' (Ma2 1l) and 'understand necessary and sufficient conditions' (Ma3 1j).

Understanding progression is an important aspect of learning to teach, as the Initial Teacher Training (ITT) NC for England and Wales specifies in its section A. In this section of the ITT curriculum, mention is made of aspects of proof. However, the terms used in the ITT NC are in some instances slightly different from those used in the NC 2000; the ITT NC is due to be revised around 2002, so we will base our use in this chapter in the terms developed in the pupils' NC.

Throughout this chapter we incorporate ways to get pupils involved with proving mathematical results as we describe curricular issues relevant for new secondary mathematics teachers. There are three main sections:

1   Emotion – getting pupils involved with mathematical proofs;
2   Challenge – when can we be sure of a mathematical result?
3   Purpose – seeing is not enough! Developing a need for mathematical proof.

We draw in information about different proof structures and ideas for teaching as we discuss these issues. We start with a brief orientation to mathematical proof.

## What is proof?

'Proof' is a grand word. Like 'right' and 'true' it has a worthy ring. It is good to prove or offer proof in law, in life and in mathematics. Proof that little brother ate the biscuits and denied elder sister her share could be attempted by pointing to biscuit remnants on him. It is not an absolute proof, the crumbs and chocolate smears could have been planted. Such a 'proof' is a confirmation of a conjecture on the basis of observation: a rudimentary scientific approach.

In many western legal practices, forms of admissible argument, with items of observational evidence, are presented to jurors whose burden it is to decide whether prosecution or defence have presented a sound proof of their case. Proof in mathematics is not much like science or the law. Or is it?

---

**Task 5.1**

Think of similarities and differences between what you understand as mathematical proof compared with scientific or legal proofs.

---

Logic is at the heart of mathematical proof. And there are different logical structures which are used within mathematical proofs. We shall look at: *step-by-step deduction*, *proof by contradiction* and *counter-example*.

## Emotion: catching interest and nurturing involvement

How to get pupils involved with mathematical proof – that's a hard task! But like most things the trick is to find a way to their minds though their emotions. Before looking at a mathematical task that might do this, we review how the notion of counter-example has become important in mathematics education. In the following section, another classroom task is suggested to nurture pupils' 'need to prove'.

---

### Counter-example and investigations in school mathematics

Counter-example is a powerful tool in both science and mathematics. The philosopher Karl Popper's characterisation of scientific advance is that hypotheses are subject to falsification. (If little brother has chocolate round his mouth, prompting the conjecture that he has eaten some biscuits from the newly-purchased packet and then the packet is found unopened, this observation has falsified the conjecture.) Reasoning in this fashion of falsifying hypotheses has a logical structure:

$p \Rightarrow q \ \& \sim q$ then $\sim p$  (in words, if p implies q and not q, then not p).[3]

Mathematics uses this argument structure too through using a counter-example to refute a conjecture about a generality. This type of proof is characteristic of the 'quasi-empirical' aspect of mathematics which was investigated by Imre Lakatos, one of Popper's students in the late 1950s. Lakatos's idea that mathematical discovery requires a 'bottom up' logic (where ideas for what might be mathematically true are developed and changed as a result of investigation of the truth of particular cases) has been very influential in mathematics education.

### Investigations

One strand of influence was the incorporation of 'investigations' in mathematics which had its heyday in the mid-1980s after the publication of the

Cockcroft Report. Investigations provide an opportunity for pupils to experiment and this leads to conjecture-forming. A problem that emerged with pupils and their mathematical investigations was that children too easily accepted that the pattern that they spotted within their investigation was a generally true result: 'This holds for all the cases I've tried, so it is correct'. As mentioned above, the programmes of study in the National Curriculum in England throughout Key Stages 3 and 4 specify that pupils 'understand the difference between a practical demonstration and a proof' and that they 'understand the importance of a counter-example' (in the 'reasoning section' in Ma2 (number and algebra)). Positive aspects of investigating in mathematics are part of the 'problem solving' sections of the National Curriculum. One of the purposes for introducing 'investigations' into the mathematics curriculum[4] was as a vehicle for pupils to express themselves within their mathematics. It is emotionally satisfying for pupils and their teacher when a child discovers a mathematical something and is excited and happy. (See Chapter 6 by Mary Barnes in the companion volume 'Teaching Mathematics in Secondary Schools: A reader' for further discussion of this.) Nothing is as motivating as pleasure and this opportunity for pupils to experience pleasure within mathematics was considered crucially important if more people were to pursue mathematics to a higher level. This argument does not appear to have succeeded and investigations, per se, are now recognised not to be sufficient bait. Mathematics alone rarely speaks to the pupils, the teacher is the conductor and mediator within much of pupils' mathematical learning. Many mathematics teachers did not have confidence in the process or the product of investigations. Furthermore, for investigations to be 'integral' to the curriculum they had to be assessed. So exam boards set clear grade descriptions resulting in 'investigating' becoming ossified and unimaginative. The fact is that a real open-ended mathematical quest does not fit nicely into lesson-allotted time spans of 35 or 50 minutes, let alone an examination.

The mathematics curriculum in England has undergone many changes[5] and the introduction of investigations is but one. In the 1970s and 1980s deductive proof was considered to have been too hard for most pupils, so it was taken out of GCSE (and by default out of the lower secondary curriculum). In the NC 2000 all pupils at Key Stages 3 and 4 are entitled to learn about proof, deductions and 'geometrical reasoning' (Ma3). So what has changed? Answer: the emphasis on pedagogy. In previous eras when geometry of a formal type was taught it was largely taught by teacher demonstration and pupil imitation. This method did not work well enough, although obviously a few did catch on. Not enough pupils could muster the proofs at examination time and many of those who did merely reproduced the teacher's poem, rather than use the ideas and methods to express our own conviction of the result. Now, the emphasis is on pupils producing a justification themselves, owning the result because they have struggled with it, and becoming emotionally involved in, whether or not it is true. And, unlike the 1980s emphasis on the pupil doing this alone, nowadays the teacher is recognised as a key mover in developing a pupil's mathematical character.

When emotions are involved in learning the results are more profound than when the pupil is just going through the motions. This can work against engagement in mathematics, as is well known[6]. As mentioned above, real mathematical investigation can be highly pleasurable. What we turn to here is a situation where logic and emotion may become entwined. This is not a bad thing at all; it is a place where a teacher's pedagogical craft may be developed.

Let us take a well-known mathematical problem which serves to highlight some logical and emotional aspects of mathematical investigating.

Take a circle, put n points round the circumference, join each point to every other point: how many regions have been (in the sense of 'can be') created within the circle? (This example is also discussed by Ronnie Goldstein in the companion volume 'Teaching Mathematics in the Secondary School: A reader'.)

Let's start this problem by looking at small numbers of points on a circle.

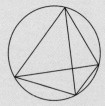

n = 2 forms 2 regions, n = 3 forms 4 regions, n = 4 forms 8 regions.

What's happening? A pattern is emerging here! (Isn't it a pleasant experience to feel that you have come to something that's 'out there', there's a sense of satisfaction emerging as the doubling is noticed.) Check out n = 5: 16 regions, hooray! Has a conjecture formed? – how could you help the conjecture forming?! Now try n = 6. It is getting tricky to draw clearly and count the regions accurately. The number of regions seems to be 31 – that can't be right! The answer should be 32. Try another diagram with a sharper pencil. Still 31. This is annoying, there had been a 'high' feeling, a sense that a general pattern had been discovered. It may take many pencil sharpenings and carefully-drawn diagrams to dislodge from a person's mind the conjecture that the number of regions doubles as the number of points increases by 1. In the classroom, pupils will want to see how other people are getting on and look at other people's diagrams. It can also be fun to take a vote, while most of the class are drawing diagrams representing n < 6 cases, on whether the pattern is 'doubling'. Invariably, the class is unanimous. But they'll soon appreciate that what is true in mathematics cannot be decided by a vote! Eventually, by individual or collective effort, the idea that the theorem: given n points on a circle, the number of regions formed is $2^{n-1}$ is, sadly, false. The conjecture has to be rejected. Now that stage of the problem is finished: there is no point in pursuing that idea any further.[7]

This sense of finality – when a counter-example has been accepted – is a very mathematical feeling: there is an absolute answer to this one small problem; it is most satisfying to be certain – and independently certain – not having to rely on teacher's information or friends' opinions. Part of the teacher's challenge is to help the pupils want to prove things for themselves, to elicit in the pupils the mental and emotional requirement that only proof will do. Counter-examples are useful devices to ignite this emotional need.

---

### Nurturing the need to prove while developing the skill of symbolising

Another good way to stimulate pupils' involvement and need to prove is through number puzzles. Here is another 'tried and tested' starter. It is ideal for pupils working at around level 6 or 7 but suitable for a full attainment range class from level 3 upwards.[8]

---

Take a three-digit number, reverse the digits – is the reversed three-digit number different from the original? If not choose again. Subtract the smaller number from the larger. Reverse the digits of this answer and add it to its reversed digit counterpart. What's the final answer?

---

Amazing! Everyone (almost!) in class has exactly the same answer even though they all started with their own individual choice!

Don't you just need to know why?! How to find out why? More examples? That would just be like being in a bigger class. This activity shows well how observation can stimulate the personal need to seek after the structure within numbers and their representation. It is also an opportunity to encourage symbolisation (useful notation) and algebraic manipulation of these symbols.

Here is a possible classroom approach: several pupils write up their numerical solutions on the board and the common features of the process are discussed. Explicitly:

> we notice that we always have to do an exchange when we start with subtracting in the units column (the standard subtraction algorithm is assumed implicitly). Why? This gives the opportunity to symbolise – if the original three-digit number is represented as $abc$ and is larger than its reverse $cba$, this implies that $a > c$ which is equivalent to $c < a$, so when we 'take away' the units we are trying to subtract $a$ from $c$ which 'doesn't go' so one of the tens has to be exchanged for ten units. This next action of symbolically crossing through the $b$ and writing $b - 1$ would have been done in each of the particular cases that the pupils wrote up on the board and are there for them to relate to the algebraic version.

---

**Task 5.2**

*In painstaking detail continue to relate each stage of the calculation of the symbolic representation of the general problem to specific (preferably pupil-calculated) examples. If you can visualise yourself explaining to pupils how each stage of their calculation can be represented in terms of symbols, this might help you slow down and unpick the structure of the numbers.*

---

In this problem, exposing the structure of the problem not only explains why it works but also proves that *when a three digit number and the number formed by reversing its digits are not the same, then subtracting these two numbers and then adding that answer with its reverse always gives 1089.* In this case the explanation also serves as the justification, as will be discussed in the next section.

## Challenge: when can we be sure?

Hearing someone else's explanation of why the answer is 1089 doesn't need to convince us. But there are occasions when it is appropriate to accept another person's reasoning. We'll use the NC terms of 'explanation' and 'justification' to point to the intrinsic persuasiveness of a mathematical proof.

### Explanations and justifications

From first starting school, children are encouraged to express their reasoning through their *explanations*. Such explanations are subjective, informal and, sometimes, wrong!

*Teacher*   Explain why you put 23.4 × 10 = 23.40
*Pupil*     Because when I multiply by 10 I add a nought.

Pupils' explanations of this sort, which expose misconceptions, are a gift to teachers who can then work with these pupils on overcoming their conceptual errors. If pupils are able to present their reasons for their ideas publicly, then as they develop, these explanations can come under increasing scrutiny without undermining their confidence. The teacher will be in a position to help the pupil develop the logical structure of their explanations. Mathematical explanations with a transparent, accurate logical structure, starting with sound assumptions, are mathematical arguments or *justifications*: they tell those who can follow about the truth or falsity of the mathematical statement in question. For example, consider the mathematical statement 'the angle sum of a triangle is half a turn'. Explanations could include:

- measuring angles of various triangles;
- lining up the torn-off corners against a ruler;
- constructing a line parallel to one side of the triangle through the other vertex, observing alternate angles at this vertex and deducing that the angle sum of the triangle is equal to the sum of the angles along a line – which is half a turn.

Our reading of the NC sense of 'justify' is that the last of these three 'explanations' could serve as a proper mathematical justification of the truth of this statement.

## What is a theorem?

'Theorem', like 'proof', is a grand word. It connotes status and, in mathematics, status is only claimed securely when there is a proof. While mathematicians use the word 'theorem' in conjunction with expectation of a proof, sometimes a proof takes a long while to emerge – take the example of 'Fermat's last theorem' which awaited 300 years for a proof! So, strictly speaking, Fermat's last theorem was not a theorem until recently! In Appendix 2 we state that a 'lemma' is a result that is needed to prove the main result. A lemma has lower status than a theorem but there is no real difference between a lemma and a theorem.

The most famous theorem in secondary school mathematics is known as Pythagoras' theorem. Do you agree? We expect you to know this theorem but we will state it precisely because a precise statement is needed for a precise proof.[9]

If $ABC$ is a plane triangle with $B$ a right angle, then $AC^2 = AB^2 + BC^2$.

Note that a diagram is not strictly necessary, though it is highly likely to help.

---

### Task 5.3

Prove Pythagoras' theorem.

---

Go on, have a go without referring to any books and without turning to Appendix 1 which provides a proof.

Done it? OK, now look at our proof in Appendix 1. This is an algebraic proof based on similar triangles. There are many proofs of Pythagoras' theorem. Yours does not need to look like ours. You can find a wealth of proofs at www.cut-the-knot.com/pythagoras/index.html.[10] Li and Du (1987, p. 61) show a dissection based on sixth-century Chinese mathematics.

Pythagoras' theorem is not immediately obvious but the proof is not too difficult (it may not be 'easy' but it is accessible to pupils). Sometimes the opposite is the case: a theorem is 'obvious' but the proof is difficult. This is the case for what is called the 'intermediate value theorem'. A broad statement of this theorem is, 'a continuous function which starts with a negative value and ends with a positive value is 0 somewhere between'. Visualise this. However, the proof is so hard that we refer you to Chapter 7 (Three Hard Theorems) of Spivak (1967, pp. 106–7, p. 113) for details. One reason why the proof is hard is the 'rigour' mathematicians employ in such proofs. Another reason is that it makes essential use of the *completeness axiom* of the real numbers.

## Axioms and assumptions

This leads us into a formidable mathematical domain: the territory of axioms. An 'axiom' is an assumption, taken as true, from which other mathematical truths are derived. Is all of mathematics in a land that is governed by axioms and their associated rules of inference? The mathematician's answer would probably be 'yes'. However, for a schoolteacher, the issues are less clear cut. As children grow their intuitions about numbers build up from counting small numbers of objects but the mathematicians' axiomatic approach to the real numbers often takes a top down approach.[11] Undergraduate mathematicians find this switch from the bottom up approach of their school experience to the formal routine required by mathematics from the late-nineteenth century a really difficult step. How can we help these talented students prepare for mathematics in Higher Education through our teaching in school?

A possibility is to introduce some formalities when working with numbers. The standard number line represents the 'real numbers': every number has its place, every point represents a real number of some sort – rational or irrational, fraction, integer, transcendental. Irrational numbers are not mad but precisely those numbers that cannot be written as a ratio (i.e. cannot be written as a fraction) and they are real numbers. These real numbers are 'captured' by fourteen axioms[12] which include properties like distribution, commutativity and the existence of inverses. Mathematically inclined school pupils can enjoy the challenge of deducing known properties of numbers from the axioms.[13]

---

### Task 5.4

Starting from the real numbers' axioms of closure, additive associativity, additive identity, additive inverse and distribution, prove that 'a minus times a minus is a plus'. A proof of the lemma 'multiplication by zero always gives zero' is in Appendix 2.

---

Does the process of producing this proof satisfy you or irritate you? How could you adapt this proving experience for pupils so that they are motivated to be precise and logical rather than turned off by the pernickety pedanticism of it all?

Axioms have a famous place in geometry because of the role of the 'parallel postulate' axiom of Euclid:

> Given a straight line, *l*, and a point, *P*, not on *l*, then there is one and only one straight line through *P* parallel to *l*.

Different geometrical systems can be obtained if this axiom is replaced by different assumptions. For example, on a sphere – where the equivalent of a straight line is a great circle – there are no lines parallel to a given line as all great circles meet at poles.

Like axioms for a whole system of number or geometry, assumptions for a given problem are also important in developing the ideas of proof. Doug French has illus-

## 'Theorem' – all triangles are isosceles

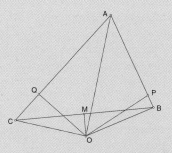

Given a triangle ABC construct the angle bisector at A and the perpendicular bisector of BC. Let O be the point at which these two lines meet. Construct perpendiculars from O to meet AB and AC at P and Q respectively.

The proof is based on the idea of congruent triangles: triangles which are the same shape and size. What ensures that one triangle is exactly the same as another? Clearly if all the corresponding sides are the same length, then we have the same triangle! In this case we use the abbreviation 'SSS' ('side, side, side'). Other conditions for congruence are: 'SAS' (for 'side, angle, side'), 'AAS' (for 'angle, angle, side') and 'RHS'[14] (for 'right angle, hypotenuse, side'). The symbol ≡ is used to denote the congruence of two triangles.

To show: AB = AC

Proof

Firstly, let us show AP = AQ by proving △APO ≡ △AQO:

We have ∠BAO = ∠CAO (by construction of the angle bisector at A)

And we have ∠P = 90° and ∠Q = 90° (by construction of the perpendiculars from O to AB and AC, respectively)

AO is the common line

therefore: △APO ≡ △AQO (AAS) and so AP = AQ

It is left as an exercise for you to show in a similar vein that:

(1) △MBO ≡ △MCO (SAS) and (2) △BPO ≡ △CQO (RHS). From (2) we have PB = QC.

Using (i) AP = AQ and (ii) PB = QC and AB = AP + PB and AC = AQ + QC, we (surely?) can deduce AB = AC and so this (and any!) triangle is isosceles.

Find the false assumption!

The hint is to draw your own diagram as accurately as you can – get the compasses out! – and don't be seduced by what you can see! The lack of rigour was not in the deductive steps, but on reliance on a misrepresentative diagram.

trated this in Chapter 3 on post-16 mathematics. In the trigonometyry problem a nonsense answer is obtained if an expression is divided by zero and so it is essential to assume that the denominator is $\neq 0$ before the manipulation is done. This is the basis of the 'false proof' that $1 = 2$ (or any other distinct numbers). It is fun to go through 'false proofs' with a class because they are challenged to track the argument and to point out where the false step has been made. On page 80 is another 'false proof', in this case it is geometric. Where was the false assumption?

## Intuitions, rigour and argument

Nevertheless, it isn't easy to say exactly what 'rigour' is, in general. We tend to resort to analogies or metaphors like 'the argument was watertight'. One way of viewing rigour in mathematics is that every single case is encompassed. Yet this can't be what we mean in mathematics! Coming back to the angle sum of a triangle, we teach children that the sum is half a turn or 180°. We want them to understand that this is so for every single triangle. But there are an infinite number of triangles, so we cannot demonstrate this physically. This suggests that 'cases' have to be represented as types. What is another type of triangle? By asking yourself the 'what if …?' question: 'What if I drew my triangle on a sphere and measured the angles?', this should give insight into a different type of triangle from our intuitively-experienced triangles in a plane. As mentioned above, spherical triangles are governed by a different axiom system from the planar Euclidean type and as a consequence have different angle sum.

Much contemporary teaching works from children's intuitions. Pupils are led from their comfort zones to interesting and new experiences. Perhaps this is why mathematics is so hard. There are discontinuities in conceptual development and it is not comfortable to take on radically new ideas which must dislodge notions that have become intuitive. Take the idea that there are decimals which cannot be written as fractions – isn't this unintuitive?[15]

To show that there are indeed numbers which cannot be written as fractions, pupils may be shown that the number $\sqrt{2}$ cannot be written as a fraction. By this stage pupils are likely to have become familiar with square roots and the $\sqrt{\phantom{x}}$ symbol. There is a 'standard proof' of this result which may be found in almost every textbook that touches upon the subject. (The proof is 'standard' in that the structure is the same, though the details may be expressed differently.) We will use the version in an A level text (Bostock *et al.*, 1982) in order to locate aspects of this standard proof which are difficult to accept as 'convincing' from the pupil's point of view (another, more discursive version is in Appendix 3, for you to compare):

*To prove that $\sqrt{2}$ is irrational*

The negation of $\sqrt{2}$ is irrational is $\sqrt{2}$ is rational.

Now $\sqrt{2}$ is rational $\Rightarrow \sqrt{2} = \dfrac{a}{b}$ where $a$ and $b$ are integers with no common factor

$$\Rightarrow 2 = \frac{a^2}{b^2} \Rightarrow 2b^2 = a^2 \Rightarrow a^2 \text{ is even} \Rightarrow a \text{ is even} \Rightarrow a = 2c, \text{ where } c \text{ is an integer}$$

$$\Rightarrow 2b^2 = 4c^2 \Rightarrow b^2 = 2c^2 \Rightarrow b^2 \text{ is even} \Rightarrow b \text{ is even} \Rightarrow b = 2d$$

Hence we have:

($\sqrt{2}$ is rational) $\Rightarrow$ ($\sqrt{2} = \dfrac{a}{b}$ where $a$ and $b$ are integers with no common factors and $a = 2c$ and $b = 2d$)

which contains a contradiction. As the conclusion of this implication is false, the hypothesis that $\sqrt{2}$ is rational is also false.

i.e. $\sqrt{2}$ is irrational.

(ibid. p. 169)

Let us now suggest inherent difficulties in this standard proof. Firstly, this is an example of a *reductio ad absurdum* proof, or proof by contradiction. Such proofs start by assuming the opposite to that which is intended to be proved and showing that a contradiction results.[16] A further – and probably the most severe – difficulty in understanding this proof is the fact that the assumption which gives rise to the contradiction is not that $\sqrt{2}$ can be expressed as a fraction but that $\sqrt{2}$ is expressed as a fraction in lowest form and it is the 'lowest form' bit of the assumption that results in a contradiction. (It is well to muse for a minute and convince yourself that stipulating that it is in its lowest form is a reasonable thing to do.) Another reason for it being difficult is that steps in the proof may appear as unconnected statements: how would you know to square the expression squared in the second line? This tempts a student to learn 'that' rather than 'why'.

## Purpose: step-by-step to seeing the point of proving

Indeed, such a proof can be learnt 'off by heart' and reproduced for examination purposes. However, we'd like to see the purpose of proof in school mathematics shift from production of proofs for exams to development of the pupils' desire to use proof to be sure themselves and to have the confidence and competence to convince others of the truth of a mathematical statement using a mathematical proof. This is most salient when the ideas, such as showing that $\sqrt{2}$ is a real number which is not a fraction, go beyond our intuitions and real-life experiences. That mathematics goes beyond our intuitions is one reason why mathematicians demand 'rigour' in the reasoning of proofs.

The proof that $\sqrt{2}$ is irrational proceeded 'step-by-step'. Despite the dodgy premise, the 'all triangles are isosceles' proof also exemplified a step-by-step deduction. Learning how to construct this type of argument is in the 'reasoning' section of Ma3 in the NC Programmes of Study. The new National Curriculum for England specifies this explicitly and many people teaching and starting to teach mathematics will not have had much practice in this type of 'formal' reasoning. As we mentioned, Euclidean geometry was a traditional part of the selective schools' curriculum in the first two thirds of the twentieth century, though previously considered too difficult for all pupils. Those updating the NC for 2000 seem to have recognised that the perspicuous arguments possible in elementary Euclidean geometry are very good models[17] for logical reasoning more generally. The challenge is for teachers to motivate their pupils to use these reasoning techniques and to skill their pupils in the techniques. In France, Euclidean geometry was not abandoned as it was in anglophone countries and the pressure was on to make the topic more accessible to French pupils.

## Seeing is believing, proving is knowing

This pressure stimulated the development of Cabri Géomètre, a piece of dynamic geometry[18] software which demonstrated the generality of geometric conjectures by 'dragging' points or lines within constructed figures. (There are other dynamic geometry packages which do similar things.) For example, the medians of a triangle can be constructed and a vertex of the triangle dragged around the screen, and *voila!* they remain concurrent. This sort of software seems to be giving a sense of 'that' – so does it serve as a justification? It doesn't look much like a mathematical proof! And no, a Cabri demonstration is not a mathematical justification, even though it may give the pupil a sense of 'that'.

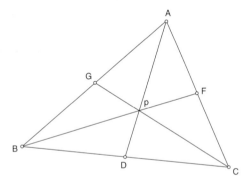

How can using dynamic geometry help pupils to learn to solve geometric problems by step-by-step deduction? Michael De Villiers' suggestion is that pupils could be asked to 'explain' the result they have seen rather than argue for its truth, as a justification suggests. By explaining in terms of the constructions used to create the figure, a step-by-step argument emerges, which formally establishes the 'that'. The point is that the pupil is motivated by the desire to communicate structural features of the geometric problem. By expressing their understanding of *what follows from what* the skill of step-by-step deduction is developed.

For example, an equilateral triangle can be constructed as follows:

- create a circle and then a point, *A*, on its circumference;
- construct another circle using the point on the circumference as the centre and the original circle's centre, *B*, as defining the radius;
- mark a point of intersection, *C*, of the two circles and join *ABC*.

If this figure is 'dragged' the triangle remains equilateral. This does not need to be further proved for pupils to believe that it is true: the visual stimulus is so convincing it seems silly to pretend not to know that the triangle will always be equilateral. A proof of the fact of the matter does not seem to be needed. So our job as teachers is to motivate the pupils to produce the text of a proof, even though they feel they already know the answer. They have to learn the structure so that it can be applied with confidence in situations where the truth of the proposition is not so obvious, as in the intermediate value theorem. As teachers we want to mould the pupils' explanations into nice little deductive proofs. Let's look at how an explanation of 'the triangle produced by the construction (given above) is equilateral' can be shaped to make an acceptable proof:

*Teacher*    Why is the triangle equilateral?
*Pupils*    The sides are all the same.
*Teacher*    Yes, the line segments[19] AB, AC and BC are all the same length. Why are they the same length?
*Pupil 1*    Because the circles are the same size.
*Teacher*    How do you know that?
*Pupil 2*    AB is … for both …
*Teacher*    Yes, AB is a radius for both circles …
*Pupil 3*    So it's the same as BC and the same as AC as well!
*Teacher*    That's the idea! AB is the same length as BC and the same length as AC. Now how can we write this in a very clear, logical fashion?
*Pupil 4*    Start by saying what we are trying to show …
*Teacher*    Which is?
*Pupil 5*    ABC is equilateral …
*Teacher*    Who'll come and write it up while the others suggest what to put …

In this case, as in the 1089 example, the pupils' ideas are moulded publicly by the teacher with the continued negotiation with the class. The proof is not alien but a refinement of what has been reasoned instinctively, given the powerful visual stimulus. In this case the belief in the truth of the proposition did not come from the proof; the belief that the construction always made an equilateral triangle came from the visual–dynamic sense data. However, the dynamic geometry experience provided a comfortable environment for developing a short deduction and, implicitly and importantly, what constitutes such a deduction. While this process was motivated by 'explanation' it actually teaches 'justification' processes. The structure of the justification here is of the form

$$p \Rightarrow q \ \& \ p \text{ then } q.^{20}$$

## On individually necessary and jointly sufficient conditions

Dynamic geometry can also be used to help teach pupils about necessary and sufficient conditions (as in Ma3 'reasoning'). It is clearer to refer to conditions being 'individually necessary and jointly sufficient' to emphasise that several conditions are needed and if we've got all those then we have the result for sure: there are features that are all necessary in my construction of a figure if I want it to drag and keep the shape; if I use those features, then the shape is retained when dragged. For example, pupils may 'construct' a parallelogram by creating a point, $A$, and a (distinct) line segment, $BC$, then constructing a ray[21] parallel to $BC$ through the point $A$. The line segment $AB$ is constructed and a point, $D$, on the ray through $A$, is marked so that $AB$ appears parallel to $CD$. The final construction of the segment $CD$ makes $ABCD$ look like a parallelogram – until one of the points $A$, $B$ or $C$ is dragged. This (real!) case can be used to help pupils understand *which* conditions are important: which are individually necessary. In particular, here, we have the reinforcement that parallelograms must be constructed with *two* sets of parallel lines; both are necessary. And two sets of parallel lines and their corresponding intersection points are jointly sufficient.

## Visualisation

For sighted people, what we see dominates how we make sense of the world. However, mathematics abstracts from the world of the senses and does not rely on information from the sense of sight for its truth. There have been blind geometers, for example, the Russian mathematician, Pontryagin. For most of us, however, our sight sense supports our being able to imagine abstractions. Take parallel lines: having the experience of seeing railway tracks converge on the horizon does not force us to assert that they meet. An adult understanding of the invariance of the train width overcomes the 'converged' sense datum, yet the 'train track' visual stimulus creates meaning for the whole 'parallel' concept. It is how proof and visualisation relate that we turn to now.

The visual sense is convincing but we see only particulars, only concrete instances. That means that when things are changed – like the 'parallelogram' being dragged – the general, abstract features that were anticipated, do not remain – the 'parallelogram' is revealed as the trapezium it really is! This is why the seductive sense of sight has not been a traditional route to mathematical knowledge: looking at something might give some good ideas, might be an explanation for something, but does not serve as a justification. However, professional mathematicians as well as novice students may be convinced of the truth of something through some visualisations; if such a visualisation can be interrogated – exposing the abstract or general features of the configuration in question – might it not serve as a proof? In the secondary National Curriculum 'visualisation' is hardly mentioned, except under 'properties of transformations' in Ma3 and certainly the emphasis in the new revised version is that formalities are to be taught. The emphasis is on precision and communication rather than imaginative insight. Let us anticipate the next rewriting of the National Curriculum by looking at the delicate interplay between proof and visual imagination. Again let's use a very well-known mathematical example to draw out issues about proving, sense making and visualising: the question posed to the young Gauss which has gained mythical status in maths education was something like: 'What is the sum of all the numbers from 1 to 1000?'[22] This sum can be visualised as the number of blocks in a stepped triangular array and in school mathematics the '$n^{th}$ triangular number' is just the sum of the first $n$ natural numbers. A visualisation of the proof of the formula is shown on the next page.

**Task 5.5**

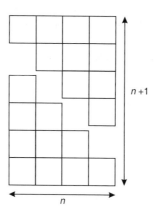

$n+1$

$n$

Work out a way of using the diagram shown above to help pupils with the symbolism of the formula for the general case.[23] The pedagogical point is in mediating between a visualisation and the symbolic manipulation.

Contrast this visualisation of the proof with the following 'formal' proof by induction, with comments which might occur to a student.

Firstly, establish that the result holds for 1: this means plug in $n = 1$ to the formula:

$$\sum_1^1 r = \frac{1}{2}(1 + 1) = \frac{1}{2} \times 2 = 1$$

Now use the 'induction hypothesis': this means write out the formula for $n = k$, add on $(k + 1)$ and manipulate the symbols to get the formula with $k + 1$ plugged in:

$$\sum_1^{k+1} r = \sum_1^k r + (k+1) = \frac{k}{2}(k+1) + (k+1) = (k+1)\left(\frac{k}{2}+\frac{2}{2}\right) = \frac{k+1}{2}((k+1)+1),$$

as required. QED.[24]

It is useful for mathematics teachers to be aware of many 'types' of proof[25] but it is essential that they be aware of the ways pupils might interact with proofs. From a teaching and learning standpoint, induction – as for all 'types' of proof – has some disadvantages: the result must be stated first; the result may not be intuitively convincing due to the formal logic employed; the proof may not be insightful in the sense that it may not show why a result holds.

## When proof makes it obvious

Seeing why something which is not immediately obvious as 'obvious' is a thrill to experience and, for the teacher, to observe in pupils. There is an old story of a university professor who writes a statement on the board and says, 'This is obvious'. He (well it is an old story) steps back and looks puzzled. He disappears for 20 minutes and returns claiming, 'It is obvious'. The proof gave him security that what he had asserted was true. We'd like our pupils to be able to rely on mathematical proofs too.

## Notes

1    While most detailed examples are from the National Curriculum for England, we refer to various curricula from different parts of the British Isles.

2    In mathematics education the term 'demonstration' can be used for a proof – this is confusing! It has occurred because the French word 'demonstration' has the connotation of 'explicit showing of why' something is true, i.e. a proof, and, of course the English word is spelt in the same way.

3    This argument form is called *modus tollens*, see Glymour, C. (1992). *Thinking Things Through.* p. 56. In our example we have: $p$ (the chocolate mouth comes from eating the biscuits) $\Rightarrow q$ (biscuits are missing) & $\sim q$ (biscuits are NOT missing) then $\sim p$ (the chocolate mouth did NOT come from eating those biscuits). Logic demands rejection of the conjecture. But does that mean that little brother is wholly innocent?

4    Banwell, C., *et al.* (1972) *Starting Points* is an inspiring early text on pupils interestedly doing mathematics.

5    Howson, G. (1982) *A History of Mathematics Education in England* gives as many details as you could wish for!

6    Buxton, L. (1981) *Do You Panic About Maths?* was a seminal work on the negative power of emotion on mathematical attainment.

7    Hopefully, you will want to find out the true relationship between points and regions! Hint: the number of regions is a polynomial function of $n$.

8    Pupils with exceptional mathematical talents, after solving the three-digit problem, could be encouraged to deepen their understanding of the number system by formulating analogous problems using more digits.

9    Theorems evolve and rarely, if ever, start life as precise statements. Lakatos, (1976). pp. 142–54 discusses the evolution of a theorem.

10   Correct at time of writing. If this does not work for you now, then do a search on 'Pythagoras'. You are bound to find a site with proofs.

11   This analogy is used in ibid. p. 98.

12   Ibid. p. 99 and p. 102.

13   The pioneering mathematics educator, Efraim Fischbein in his (1987) *Intuition in Science and Mathematics,* p. 102 concurs with this idea: 'the chapter of negative numbers has to be treated formally from the beginning. … this is the first opportunity offered to a pupil to consider mathematical concepts from a formal deductive point of view.'

14   Why is 'ASS' not a sufficient condition for congruence?

15   And there are many more of these numbers than fractions – unintuitive or what?!

16   The logic of this reasoning is of *modus tollens* (see Glymour, 1992, p. 56) type and is not often used in everyday situations. (Could you prove little brother ate the biscuits by assuming that he didn't and obtaining a contradiction?!)

17   See the moral development section in *Mathematics, the National Curriculum for England* (DfEE, 1999, p. ix).

18   In 'dynamic geometry' packages the user constructs geometric figures on the screen using basic 'building blocks' of points, lines or circles. The constructed figures can be moved by 'dragging' one of the basic building blocks. Invariants of the construction are demonstrated by the figure exhibiting these same properties throughout the dragging.

19   Straker, A. *Talking Points in Mathematics* illustrates how mathematical concepts can be developed by reinforcing correct mathematical terms within teacher questioning and pupil–teacher dialogue. See the section in the chapter on 'negotiating meaning'.

20   This form is called *modus ponens* (Glymour, 1992, p. 55). In this case we have, given a triangle, $p$ (each edge of the triangle is a radius of circles which are congruent) $\Rightarrow q$ (all three edges are congruent) & $p$ is true by construction then we can conclude that $q$ is

true. We need to note that $q$ (all three edges of a triangle are congruent) is the definition of an equilateral triangle.

21   A line emanating from a point.

22   Gauss's answer was to represent the sum twice: $1 + 2 + 3 \dots + 1000$ and then $1000 + 999 + \dots + 2 + 1$ so twice the sum was 1000 times $(1000 + 1)$.

23   Nitsa Movshovitz-Hadar has developed ideas to help pupils justify the proposition that the sum of the cubes of the first $n$ numbers is equal to the sum of the first $n$ numbers squared in the same spirit. See Rodd, M. M. (1998) 'Proof and Proving: Why, When and How?' *Mathematics in School*, November, pp. 44–6, for this and some other proof issues.

24   *Quod erat demonstrandum*, Latin for 'which was to be proved'.

25   We haven't discussed 'proof by exhaustion', i.e. considering every possible case. It isn't exhausting, but it is a little tedious at times!

## References

Banwell, C., Saunders, K. and Tahta, D. (1972) *Starting Points*, Oxford: Oxford University Press.

Barnes, M. (2001) '"Magical" moments in mathematics: insights into the process of coming to know', in L. Haggarty (ed.) *Teaching Mathematics in the Secondary School: a reader*, London: RoutledgeFalmer.

Baylis, J. and Haggarty, R. (1988) *Alice in Numberland*, London: Macmillan Educational.

Bostock, L., Chandler, S. and Rourke, C. (1982) *Further Pure Mathematics*, Cheltenham: Stanley Thornes.

Buxton, L. (1981) *Do You Panic About Maths?* London: Heinemann.

De Villiers, M. (1996) 'Why proof in dynamic geometry?' in M. De Villiers (ed.) *Proof and Providing: why, when and how?* Centrahil, South Africa: Association for Mathematics Education of South Africa: 24–42.

DfEE (1999) *Mathematics, the National Curriculum for England*, London: HMSO.

Fischbein, E. (1987) *Intuition in Science and Mathematics*, Dordrecht: Reidel.

Glymour, C. (1992) *Thinking Things Through*, Cambridge, MA: MIT Press.

Goldstein, R. (2001) 'Integrating computers into the teaching of mathematics', in L. Haggarty (ed.) *Teaching Mathematics in the Secondary School: a reader*, London: RoutledgeFalmer.

Howson, G. (1982) *A History of Mathematics Education in England*, Cambridge: Cambridge University Press.

Lakatos, I. (1976) *Proofs and Refutations*, Cambridge: Cambridge University Press.

Li Yan and Du Shiran (1987) Crossley, J.N. and Lun, A.W-C. (trans) *Chinese Mathematics: a concise history*, Oxford: Clarendon Press.

Polya, G. (1945) *How to Solve It*, London: Penguin.

Rodd, M.M. (1998) 'Proof and proving: why, when and how?' *Mathematics in School*, 27(4): 44–6.

Spivak, M. (1967) *Calculus*, Menlo Park, CA: W.A. Benjamin.

Straker, A. (1993) *Talking Points in Mathematics*, Cambridge: Cambridge University Press.

## Appendices

### Appendix 1

*Pythagoras' theorem*

If $ABC$ is a plane triangle with $B$ a right angle, then $AC^2 = AB^2 + BC^2$

The first line of the proof below requires that the point $D$ lies between $A$ and $C$. The following lemma proves this.

Lemma

If $ABC$ is a plane triangle with $B$ a right angle and $D$ is a point on $AC$ produced such that $BD$ is perpendicular to $AC$, then $D$ lies between $A$ and $C$.

Proof

Suppose that $D$ does not lie between $A$ and $C$. Then either $A$ lies between $D$ and $C$ or $C$ lies between $A$ and $D$. Suppose that $A$ lies between $D$ and $C$. Then $\angle CBD > 90°$ and so $DA$ produced could not pass through $C$. Suppose then that $C$ lies between $A$ and $D$. Then $\angle ABD > 90°$ and so $DC$ produced could not pass through $A$. Since either alternative produces a contradiction it may be concluded that $D$ lies between $A$ and $C$.

*Proof of Pythagoras' theorem*

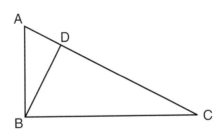

Drop a perpendicular $BD$ on to $AC$ produced. By the above lemma $D$ lies between $A$ and $C$.

$\nabla ABC$, $\nabla ADB$ and $\nabla BDC$ are similar triangles ★

This gives $\dfrac{AD}{AB} = \dfrac{AB}{AC}$  i.e. $AB^2 = AD \cdot AC$

Also $\dfrac{BC}{AC} = \dfrac{DC}{BC}$  i.e. $BC^2 = AC \cdot DC$

Adding gives $AB^2 + BC^2$

$$= AD \cdot AC + AC \cdot DC = AC(AD + DC)$$

$$= AC^2 \quad QED$$

Pythagoras' theorem has a 'converse', i.e. it holds the other way around. Can you show that: if $ABC$ is a triangle with $AC^2 = AB^2 + BC^2$, then is $B$ a right angle? [★ This statement requires a proof. We leave this as an exercise for you.]

## Appendix 2

A lemma is a result that is needed to prove the main result. Here we show that multiplying by zero gives zero, from the axioms:

*To show:* $\forall\, x \in R,\ x \times 0 = 0$

1   $0 + 0 = 0$ (adding the additive identity, 0, to the identity $0 = 0$)
2   $x \times (0 + 0) = x \times 0$ (multiplying both sides by $x$)
3   $x \times 0 + x \times 0 = x \times 0$ (using distribution)
4   $-x \times 0 + (x \times 0 + x \times 0) = -x \times 0 + x \times 0$ (additive inverse is added to both sides)
5   $(-x \times 0 + x \times 0) + x \times 0 = -x \times 0 + x \times 0$ (additive associativity used)
6   $0 + x \times 0 = 0$ (using the additive inverse on both sides)
7   Therefore $x \times 0 = 0$ (using additive identity again)

## Appendix 3

1   Assume $\sqrt{2} = \dfrac{a}{b}$ where $a$ and $b$ are whole numbers and the fraction is in its lowest form: $a$ and $b$ have no factors in common.

2   Square both sides of the equation we get $2 = \dfrac{a^2}{b^2}$.

$\therefore 2 = \dfrac{a^2}{b^2} \Rightarrow 2b^2 = a^2 \Rightarrow a$ is even, i.e. of the form $2c$.

$\therefore 2b^2 = (2c)^2 = 4c^2 \Rightarrow b$ is even

This is a contradiction. $\therefore \sqrt{2}$ cannot be in the form $\dfrac{a}{b}$.

3   Deduce from this that $a^2$ must be even (as it is twice $b^2$) and that $a$ must be even (because an odd times an odd is odd and an even times an even is even).
4   Rewrite $a$ as $2c$, for some whole number $c$: $a = 2c$.
5   Substitute this expression into $2b^2 = a^2$ to get $2b^2 = (2c^2) = 4c^2$.
6   Divide both sides of the equation by 2: this gives $b^2 = 2c^2$.
7   Deduce that $b$ must be even (as well as $a$) by repeating step 3 of the argument, using the equation in step 6.
8   Deduce a contradiction: step 3 showed that $a$ was even, step 7 showed that $b$ was even, but step 1 assumed that $\dfrac{a}{b}$ was in its lowest form, i.e. $a$ and $b$ had no common factor.

# 6 Issues in the teaching and learning of arithmetic

### Peter Huckstep

## Arithmetic and numeracy

Any inquiry into *arithmetic* in contemporary mathematics education seems to be at once undercut by the terms used in the content of statutory and non-statutory government policy documents, since it is these that are inevitably most used by teachers. Scarcely any mention of 'arithmetic' is made in either the National Curriculum for England (DfEE/QCA, 1999) or in The National Numeracy Strategy (DfEE, 1998) (which is concerned with raising levels of achievement in primary school pupils, and is currently being extended into Key Stage 3 (DfEE, 2000)). The key words in these documents are either 'number' or 'numeracy'.

Unlike 'arithmetic' the term 'numeracy' has only a short history, yet a connection between them can be found in the grammatical variant, 'numerate', which one dictionary defines as 'the ability to perform basic arithmetic operations'. This definition was extended by a major government report *Mathematics Counts* (Cockcroft, 1982) usually referred to as 'The Cockcroft Report'. The report's final definition of 'numerate' included not just the ability to *perform* arithmetical operations but also the ability to *make use of* these operations ' … with confidence in practical everyday situations'. Further, it required 'the ability to have some *appreciation and understanding* of information which is presented in mathematical terms … ' (pp. 10–11, my italics). The report's overriding commitment to the usefulness of mathematics as a 'powerful', 'concise' and 'unambiguous' means of communication was clearly evident in this revision.

In one of the National Numeracy Strategy policy documents the definition of 'numeracy' is extended further still to include the 'number system', 'measures' and 'an *inclination* and ability to solve number problems in a *variety* of contexts' (DfEE, 1998, p. 11, my italics). It is described there as a '*proficiency* that is promoted through giving a sharper focus to the relevant aspects of the National Curriculum Programmes of Study for mathematics' (p. 11, my italics). Additional remarks about numeracy in a training video present it not as a subject in its own right, but rather as a by-product, something that is produced when mathematics is taught well!

Despite the fact that 'arithmetic' is scarcely mentioned in the National Curriculum or The National Numeracy Strategy, it remains fossilised as one of 'The Three Rs' – reading, (w)riting and (a)rithmetic – a notion that runs deep in the public, and hence the political, consciousness. It is pre-reflectively regarded as a *basic skill*, and whilst it is tempting to suppose that the more wholesome term 'numeracy' can take on this role we have already seen that this functions largely as an evaluation.

Nevertheless, as we have also seen, being numerate does at least include performance in 'arithmetical operations' even if it does not end there. Yet the reason 'arithmetic' has fallen into disuse in contemporary educational discourse is almost certainly because of its perceived narrowness as it stands. It has come to have connotations of practice and drill in routines, the value of which conflict with more enlightened views of pupils' thinking, changes in the needs of the work place and the integrity of mathematics. If we are to continue to think of mathematics as partly, but importantly, involving arithmetic then it is necessary to look at ways that draw out its breadth in an individual's education. A helpful point to begin such a revised view is through a consideration of the supposed purposes of learning the subject.

## The value of arithmetic

Despite the fact that a numerate individual is supposed to be able (and inclined) to *make use* of arithmetical operations, educationists have often questioned whether the value of learning arithmetic lies in such practical utility[1] (Hardy, 1967; Whitcombe, 1988; Wells, 1989; Davis, 1995; Andrews, 1998). These writers usually seek some kind of *intrinsic* value in arithmetic as a form of entertainment, or as means to aesthetic satisfaction or, again, as leading to the acquisition of self-knowledge of a kind usually associated with the arts or social sciences. Others, still, have regarded mathematics primarily as a vehicle for providing 'mental-training' of some kind. (Huckstep, 2000). Despite what some purists may want to argue, a thoroughgoing denial of the practical usefulness of arithmetic is impossible to sustain. Much depends upon whether we mean potential or actual usefulness, but one thing is clear: the *sole* value of mathematics does not lie in its usefulness.[2]

The intrinsic value of arithmetic can be traced back to antiquity, where personal flourishing was especially associated with the life of contemplation rather than purposive activity. Pythagoras, for example, was characterised as saying that the world is essentially number. He seems to have been so impressed by observing that musical notes are a function of the ratio between the lengths of vibrating strings that he made a bold generalisation. He argued that numbers are revealed in everything, which bestows on them a godlike character and, thus, implies that contemplating them purifies the soul.

What was essentially the Pythagorean doctrine influenced Plato and persisted through the Middle Ages in such thinkers as St Augustine for whom all beautiful forms – both of nature and of artefacts – were made intelligible in terms of numbers (Augustine, 1993, edn. pp. 60–1). In some respects this metaphysical notion of what is basic inhibited the growth of a mathematics curriculum that addressed practical issues. Yeldham (1936) in *The Teaching of Arithmetic through Four Hundred Years* observes that the view that ' ... number is the *basis* of all things ... stood for eight hundred years ... as the recommendation of a *theoretical* arithmetic which was largely a discussion of factors, ratio and proportion ... ' (p. 9, my italics). It was not until much later that the practical art of calculation with written algorithms of Hindu-Arabic origins was firmly established and finally replaced the less efficient use of abaci and Roman numerals.

Education often teeters between the conflicting demands of 'practical' and 'theoretical' knowledge – between following particular rules and understanding general principles, between knowing how and knowing why. The distinction is not trivial. It has come to represent not just kinds of cognition but levels of life. In Ancient Greece Aristotle illustrated this by the respective defining characteristic of the craftsman and the designer. Whilst the craftsman must meticulously carry out instructions, the designer must understand the *rationale* for those instructions. In the context of arithmetic we might say that it distinguishes accountant from number theorist. The quest for understanding has come to be one of the hallmarks of a liberal (rather than a vocational) education. We have, as one mathematics educator has remarked recently, ' ... repeatedly demonstrated ourselves to be poor predictors of the sort of competencies that will be needed even a few years hence' (Davis, 1995, p. 6). Valuable as practical education often is, theoretical knowledge can provide freedom from the devastating consequences of finding that one's particular skills are obsolete.

In the nineteenth century the chief reason for learning arithmetic was often its value as a form of 'mental training'. One writer who carefully elaborated upon this view was Sir Joshua Fitch, an inspector of teacher training colleges. In his *Lectures on Teaching* Fitch categorises arithmetic both as an 'art' and a 'science'. Whilst broadly accepting that the routines of arithmetic-as-an-art can help the individual to solve pressing problems of daily life[3] Fitch argued that arithmetic-as-a-science involves an investigation of the principles upon which its rules are based. He, like many of his contemporaries, thought that this approach to arithmetic had a special indirect role in 'calling out the reasoning faculty'. Arithmetic taught in this way, Fitch claimed, provides ' ... a certain kind of mental exercise, of unquestioned service in connexion with *all conceivable subjects of thought* ... ' (Fitch, 1902, p. 342, my italics).[4]

It is highly questionable whether mathematical reasoning can have such universal scope. Indeed, Thomas Tate (1854) writing some fifty years earlier had flatly denied this, pointing out that mathematics ' ... only exercises the mind in appreciating one kind of evidence', namely, *mathematical evidence*. All the same, Tate, himself, upheld a similar, but more modest view of his own, acknowledging that the 'mathematical sciences' are ' ... one of the best *initiatory* trainings of the reasoning powers ... ' (p. 90, my italics). His idea was, in essence, that the clarity of arithmetical evidence, equally open to teacher and pupil, allows pupils to respond to 'why' questions with suitable 'because' answers, thereby providing an introduction to the *modus operandi* of rational discourse.[5] Of course, whether or not this more modest form of mental training results in diminishing returns, when the 'initiatory training' is secured and other 'subjects of thought' get a footing, is a nice point and one on which I have discussed elsewhere (Huckstep, 2000).

The National Curriculum acknowledges some of this diversity of value in learning mathematics. In a brief rationale, which prefaces the Programmes of Study, entitled 'The importance of mathematics', the practical value is drawn out by referring to mathematics as a 'tool', and some of the more intrinsic features by referring to it as a 'creative discipline'[6] which can 'stimulate moments of wonder'. Further aesthetic goals are implicit in the rationale when reference is made to a pupils' discovery of an 'elegant solution' in problem solving.

Despite repeated scepticism the mental-training view, too, is endorsed to some extent in policy documents during the last twenty years or so, though this is often rather muted in tone (DES, 1979, pp. 4–5; Cockcroft, 1982, p. 2). Often mathematics is given no special pride of place for mental training and success in achieving this goal is supposed to be dependent upon the way that the subject is taught. Yet when the rationale from the current National Curriculum asserts that the tools that mathematics include are ' ... logical reasoning, problem solving skills, and the ability to think in abstract ways ... ' it shows that this view dies hard.[7]

It should be clear that in order to realise the diverse value claimed for arithmetic attention must be paid to the way in which it is conceived and taught. Neither the extremes of the metaphysical view held by the ancients, nor the impoverished view, with its almost exclusive emphasis on practice and drill in routines, can be wholeheartedly accepted. The pursuit of either theoretical or practical arithmetic can be taken to excess. Both aspects have a part to play in contemporary mathematics education even though historically there has always been an uneasy symbiosis between them (Howson, 1982, pp. 1–5).

It is now necessary to outline some of the issues that have a bearing on the way arithmetic is conceived and taught in order that some of its supposed value might be best enjoyed. It has already been remarked that arithmetic is usually regarded as something that is basic to education. Nowadays we no longer view this in the metaphysical sense mentioned earlier. It is more in the sense of a basic *skill*. So it is worth dwelling a little on this fundamental aspect of arithmetic.

## A basic need to quantify

If, as one distinguished philosopher has put it, we are 'prone to talk and think about objects' (Quine, 1969, p. 1), rather than persisting in regarding the world as only stuff, then we are also prone to keep tabs on some of these objects. In other words, we have a fairly basic need to *quantify*. Interestingly, the most basic means of quantification can still be found amongst the most highly developed aspects of our civilisation. The simple tallies, \\\, \\, \, seen as we approach a junction on the motorway are an effective way to answer the question 'how far?' since there is a one-to-one correspondence, or pairing, between each of these marks and a unit of road. The answer to the question 'how far?' is answered not by a single number but by the production of a set of marks equivalent to the set of road units. Of course, instead of producing the written tallies an equally effective answer to the same question would be to utter a sound for each unit of road. For example, 'slash', 'slash slash', or 'slash slash slash' would suffice. Provided the pairing between sounds and units of road has been made, the verbal answer is effective.

Counting is a highly sophisticated development of this verbal method. By pairing distinguishable and ordered names it becomes sufficient to give only the final name used in the pairing as the answer to the question 'how many?' The complete set of sounds used in a pairing may in principle be recovered, but in practice this is unnecessary, so counting is not only an effective way of answering the question 'how many?' it is also economical and efficient. But with counting, unlike 'tallying', only one sound comes to represent many objects. This is difficult for young children who initially persist in repeating back the set of names used. As we shall see, an analogous difficulty arises when numerical statements are applied to extra-numerical situations.

This simple illustration allows an important pedagogical issue to arise. The fact that counting is based upon a mapping, typically on kinds of things, suggests that the activities of sorting/classifying and comparing should be taught *first*. During the 1970s and until recently what we can, for brevity, call a 'set-theoretic' approach, became the orthodoxy of early arithmetic. But as one writer reminds us 'the most fundamental concepts of a subject, from the point of view of explanation, are not likely to be the most familiar'.[8] A sequence of lessons may be determined by a variety of principles. An analysis of the basic mathematical principles is invaluable in planning, but our judgements must always be open to revision by other considerations. Even in a young child's life the *social* phenomena of linguistic entities contend with physical objects in terms of familiarity. Young children enjoy the number rhymes that they learn by heart at their carer's knee. So, whilst each whole number has the dual function of denoting either the size of a set or of a relative position within the number system, the *cardinality* implicit in sorting and mapping activities has recently been somewhat displaced by an emphasis on *ordinality* (Thompson, 1997; Tahta, 1998). Apart from forcing us to acknowledge that learning mathematics is, in important respects, similar to learning a *language*, another consequence of this observation is the widespread use of models such as number lines and number squares.

## 'Only connect'

It is worth emphasising the importance of paying attention to the ordinal aspect of numbers throughout the teaching of arithmetic. Beyond the simple quantification of sets of objects there is a tendency for some teachers and pupils to persist in articulating arithmetical operations in terms of certain actions on those sets. In such cases, addition is not only *exemplified* as the total of combined sets of objects, it also comes to *mean* this. Similarly, subtraction, multiplication and division come to mean 'taking away', 'repeated addition' and 'sharing', respectively. In primary schools, there are good reasons to associate number statements, initially, with simple actions but these notions need to be extended to meet the *versatility* of arithmetical statements. The same subtraction statement that can be applied to a 'take-away' situation can also be applied to a comparison.

In secondary school the problem is particularly acute when dealing with negative integers and fractions. The familiar rule 'two minuses make a plus' is meaningless if we think of subtraction of negative integers in terms of 'taking away' a negative number of objects. But $7 - (-3)$ viewed ordinally as a comparison, in other words, *the difference between* 7 and $(-3)$ on the number line as 10 is illuminating. Other statements, for example $(-3) - (-7)$, are not so straightforward. But the general inverse property of subtraction, easily demonstrated on the positive integers, can help. Thus, the question 'What must be added to $(-7)$ to make $(-3)$?' immediately yields the answer 4. Of course contextualised models like debts, temperatures and lifts are even more helpful, in the initial stages, but once again these stress the ordinal rather than the cardinal aspects of number.

With fractions we come up against situations that appear paradoxical. Recently, a booklet from the Teacher Training Agency (undated) offering 'needs assessment material' for newly-qualified teachers asks whether a half is always, sometimes or never greater than a third. The commentary in the 'diagnostic feedback' points out that this is 'sometimes' true depending upon whether we are concerned with 'numbers' or with the 'operations'. Once this distinction is made, a conclusive example is provided to show that a half is only *sometimes* the greater fraction, namely, 'a half of 12 is 6, whereas a third of 30 is 10' (p. 15). Clearly the ordinal aspect of fractions guarantees that a half is *always* greater than a third. It is to see these entities as rational numbers occupying a place on the number line alongside the positive integers. It is to view fractions in a nominal way rather than adjectivally. No fewer than five different meanings can be attached to a simple fraction like three-fifths that can relate to sub-region, a subset of discrete objects, a point on a number line, the result of a division or a ratio (Dixon *et al.*, 1984). The versatility of arithmetical statements provides economy, but as so often this is achieved at a cost in the learning stage.

Nevertheless, one of the most profound discrepancies in pupils' attainment in arithmetic lies in overlooking pupils' understanding of arithmetical principles situated in contexts outside the classroom (Nunes *et al.*, 1993). The same pupils who can solve problems in games and commerce are often those who fail to succeed with school mathematics even though both rest on strikingly similar principles. It is not simply proficiency in disembodied principles that count as mathematics, 'situated' mathematics counts too. Here we find ourselves up against some of the narrowness referred to earlier. What is required is a realisation that school mathematics provides *models* for extra-mathematical situations and a connection between the two must be made. The supplanting of one for the other is insufficient.

Teaching that both reveals the autonomy of the operations of arithmetic and allows pupils to make connections between various extra-numerical states-of-affairs is central to mathematical understanding. A useful teaching strategy to adopt is to regularly invite pupils to provide suitable situations for bare statements in mathematics. Even pupils who can recall simple facts such as $6 \times 3 = 18$, sometimes have difficulties in suggesting a short problem for which this statement would be the appropriate arithmetical statement. The responses are often illuminating and provide the teacher with a useful assessment task (McIntosh, 1979).

The reader is invited to write a simple story for the following: $\frac{2}{3} \div \frac{1}{4}$. Student teachers, when invited to do this task, usually respond at first with the 'story' of a pizza two-thirds of which remains and is to be *shared* equally amongst four people. They are at first baffled when they realise that since $\frac{2}{3} \div \frac{1}{4} = \frac{8}{3}$ this appears to be more than a whole pizza! Of course this sharing story is appropriate for $\frac{2}{3} \times \frac{1}{4} = \frac{1}{4} \times \frac{2}{3}$ which may be thought of $\frac{1}{4}$ 'of' $\frac{2}{3} = \frac{1}{6}$, yet it is instructive to see how the erroneous connection with 'shared' and '÷' is so easily made. Division on the integers can be interpreted not only as (equal) sharing but also (equal) grouping or *repeated subtraction*. So that just as $12 \div 4$ can be thought of as 'how many 4s can be subtracted from 12?' $\frac{2}{3} \div \frac{1}{4}$ can be similarly thought of as how many $\frac{1}{4}$ (pizzas), can be subtracted from $\frac{2}{3}$ (pizza). The answer of $\frac{8}{3}$ then begins to make sense (Rowland, 1997).

In order to have a rich understanding of arithmetic not only must pupils be able to make connections between bare mathematical statements and operations and contexts to which they may applied, but also to make connections *within* mathematics. It is, for example, necessary to be able to see links between fractions, decimal, percentage and ratio. Recently, a so-called 'connectionist' orientation has been identified as a central characteristic of effective teaching of numeracy (see Chapter 1 by Mike

Askew, as well as Askew *et al.,* 1997). Its learning gains exceed those where pupils are taught by a teacher with either a 'discoverist' or 'transmissionist' orientation.

Teachers whose beliefs about the learning of arithmetic have a 'discoverist' complexion regulate their teaching rather too exclusively upon such notions as pupil 'readiness'. The danger here is that the rate of learning and its development tends to be delimited by what the pupil can find out for herself or himself, and by a persisting tolerance towards methods of calculation that produce correct results in an over-elaborate way.

The necessity for refining pupils' thinking harks back to the example given earlier where primitive means of quantification were outlined. There it was pointed out how the sophistication of counting is an example of both an effective and efficient method. Yet for reasons of efficiency even counting methods must, at some stage, give way to other methods. To continue to calculate $7 \times 8$, for example, by repeatedly adding eight (or seven) is to use only an effective solution. In the next section this qualitative distinction in pupils' methods of calculation will be discussed in more detail.

Teachers of the second kind – those who have a 'transmissionist' orientation – are inclined to view arithmetic narrowly as rules and routines to be learnt in isolation and independently of the pupils' responses. The shortfall of this teaching is in the other direction. Typically, a 'transmissionist' is one who teaches a refined method with insufficient regard for pupils' initial need for the transparency of a more naive method. The predominance of a style of teaching of this kind once again has a bearing on the earlier reasons given for the disappearance of 'arithmetic' in current educational discourse.

According to the research findings (ibid.), effective teachers are typically *connectionists*: maintaining a synthesis between the other two orientations by combining the best of the pupil-centred and teacher-centred considerations found in each of them. Thus, a connectionist teacher values, amongst other things, dialogue between pupil and teacher and the development of efficient methods by building upon pupils' errors and their effective methods of calculation.

## Calculation – the three Es: Effectiveness, Efficiency and Economy

For all the importance of understanding the relationship between the symbolic and the extra-symbolic form of mathematical activity, our mathematical preoccupations are not only or always spent at this interface. There are sufficient occasions in our lives when the arithmetical operation is either given or self-evident. A total, a ration or percentage is required perhaps, and the attention must be almost exclusively directed towards a *calculation* of some kind. But here a different issue breaks out.

The progression from mere effectiveness in getting a task done towards the added value of getting it done more economically or efficiently is of current concern particularly in the teaching of calculation. It has rightly become a distinguishing character of quality and progression in pupils' work. But the supposition that the solution is simply to introduce pupils to highly-refined standard algorithms is fraught with difficulties.

Plunkett (1979) in a penetrating and often cited analysis describes the standard written algorithms as 'cognitively passive' by which he means that they can be selected and carried out with little or no deliberation since such algorithms are of general application. But whilst calculations can indeed be carried out in this way with automaticity, *economy of effort* is not always forthcoming. Clearly, standard written algorithms can be used effectively, though tortuously, to solve the following: $1002 - 13$; $17.5\%$ of 60; and $4.99 \times 36$. Yet a moment's pause is sufficient to make us realise that each of these can be carried out with much less effort in the head by an ad hoc mental method. $1002 - 13$ can be carried out simply by, say, counting back 11 from 1000. Successively halving $10\%$ of 60 provides us with $5\%$ and $2.5\%$ of 60 so a simple sum is all that is then required. Again, treating the 4.99 in the third example as £5 and making the necessary adjustment to 180 is all that is required. So whilst the absence of deliberation per se can provide efficiency in one way, cognitive passivity at a time when *selectivity* is required can take it away. For this reason, pupils need to acquire what Anghileri (2000) has called 'number sense'. This facility underlies the National Curriculum requirement that pupils should be able to *select* and use ' … *appropriate* and efficient techniques and strategies to solve numerical problems'.

## Mental mathematics as a first resort

Valuable as the selective use of standard written methods may be, the importance of mental calculation *as a first resort* can hardly be gainsaid.[9] We have seen that it is economy of effort that immediately justifies this plea, but there are other advantages in advancing the development of mental methods of calculation. Without the constraint of recording a calculation in a uniform way we can flout the usual rules. In particular the right to left direction typical of many written methods can be replaced by combining the 'significant' digits first so that an early approximation is achieved. The partitioning involved in such a method extends to multiplication where conscious use of the distributive property allows ingenious methods to arise, e.g. $25 \times 39$ as $(25 \times 40) - 25$. Alternatively, it may suit a pupil to keep the first number of a calculation intact and add to or subtract from it in convenient increments. For example, to find the sum of 27.8 and 38.6 a pupil might begin with 38.6 and count on 48.6, 58.6, 65.6, 66, 66.4. The choice here is partly a matter of convenience. The above examples show that the numbers involved in any given calculation guide us in our selection, but the particular mental method that a pupil selects need not be simply a matter of convenience. It goes hand in hand with an understanding of the properties of numbers and their operations. In this respect, pupils can both 'invent' their own ad hoc methods and can also learn from the methods of others.

But to allow pupils to flourish in this way requires a particular classroom ethos: one that is characterised by tolerance and encouraging pupil–teacher and pupil–pupil interaction drawn out by a degree of sensitive 'open' questioning. Indeed, it is within these interchanges that the modest view of 'mental training', outlined earlier, can get a purchase. Reasoning in arithmetic is an ideal vehicle to initiate pupils into the *modus operandi* of rational discourse, provided the quality of pupil–pupil and pupil–teacher dialogue is grounded in reasons that are sufficiently intelligible to the pupils.

Pupils will, of course, need a stock of number facts that can be quickly recalled and which will increase as 'derived facts' are figured out from mental methods. In addition, pupils must be given opportunities to explore a range of relationships that exist between numbers. To be sceptical about pupils' ability and willingness to construct their own methods in this way is to be unaware of how pupils' minds can be stimulated by sensitive teaching. Also, whilst it may seem far-fetched to suppose that the primary importance of mathematics lies partly in its being 'a creative discipline' (DfEE / QCA, 1999), it remains true that there is room for inventiveness in calculations at all stages of learning.

There are obvious limitations on the scope of mental methods. They are clearly not suitable for calculations beyond certain magnitudes, though once again much will depend upon the particular numbers involved and also the extent to which jottings are used to support them. Herein lies part of the value of written algorithms. Yet it is sometimes supposed that there is a straightforward progression from mental methods towards standard written algorithms. If this simply means that mental methods should be *temporally* prior then this much is implied in the phrase 'mental methods as a first resort'. But progression can imply that (standard) written methods should be a formalisation of mental methods and this needs to be reconciled with a continued emphasis on flexibility. However, standard written algorithms can be taught as an *alternative* to mental algorithms, but is important to ensure that pupils are clear about which approach has been adopted by the teacher. Written methods need not necessarily be shown to *evolve* from mental methods, merely that in carrying them out quick recall of number facts, or facts derived from the application of mental strategies, provides expedience in following the standardised rules. Of course, reasons for the rules upon which standard methods are based ought to be understood by pupils. Moreover, pupils ought to be able to recover those reasons when, for example, errors are occurring which remain after checking has taken place. But to continue to direct one's attention to the rationale for a routine with every episode of its use would deprive the algorithm of its purpose.

## Sensible use of calculators

Written calculations have their limitations, too. Not all calculations can and ought to be carried out either in the head or on paper. There are occasions when it is necessary to use an electronic calculator. However, with the advent of this tool a controversy has broken out, inside and outside education, which is reminiscent of that between the 'abacist' and the 'algorist' of earlier times. The calculator (unlike the computer) has been thought by its many opponents to threaten the well-being of the mind. One response to this concern is to indicate how the *sensible* use of calculators not only preserves one's autonomy, but can also have added benefits.

An analogy should make this clear. Just as we might drive a car to a leisure centre that would be otherwise out of reach, in order to exercise the body, so a calculator can allow us to work with numbers outside the reasonable scope of alternative means. In this way it can allow us, on the one hand, to work with the awkward numbers of 'real-life' data and on the other to facilitate arithmetical *investigations* by speeding up what would otherwise be tedious routines of the activity. But although the calculator is an efficient machine, its efficient use is relative to the choice of functions made by its user. Also, the display must be interpreted correctly. Success in both of these is grounded in relevant understanding.

If any method of calculation is to have an authentic practical purpose it is important to ensure that the extra-mathematical applications that are made of arithmetic are varied and relevant to pupils wherever possible. Much arithmetic teaching is supported by the use of textbooks, the examples and exercises of which are not always of this kind. The material in mathematics textbooks needs to be regularly supplemented or replaced by novel ideas as they arise. A familiar shopping catalogue (often free of charge) can provide numerous ways of applying arithmetic that link to pupils' interests outside school. Here the creative teacher can provide opportunities for totalling, approximation and decimals at the very least.[10]

## Investigations

Another way to avoid the narrow connotations of arithmetic is to preserve the integrity of mathematics. Mathematics is developed by the endeavours of those who do more than seek results by calculation. We have already seen that pupils can be inventive in their arithmetic and in this way can have some control over their learning. The implicit justification for this, so far, has been largely a matter of its expedience. But there are more intrinsic reasons for providing other opportunities of this kind that have a degree of open-endedness. The expression 'How many different ways are there for doing x?' is a classic invitation for a pupil to *investigate* and behave more like a mathematician than a technician.

A comprehensive definition of a mathematical investigation is difficult to find. Sometimes it is equivalent to 'problem solving'. Others, however, have suggested that whilst investigations are truly open-ended, problem-solving is more strictly open-'*beginninged*'. Yet one important characteristic of both is the degree to which pupils are free, so to speak, to put their own mark on their work. Clearly, wherever the mathematical starting point, if it is to be an open activity, pupils must be given *some* freedom to make their own choices about diverse matters within that mathematical activity. This might concern materials used, forms of recording, the mathematical techniques selected, the avenues that are taken and so on and so forth. It is important that we stress the necessity for this freedom since it is quite possible to present 'an investigation' in a mannered way, where the expectation follows a strict routine – try a few cases, find a rule, justify the rule, extend the investigation. For many pupils this can provide a helpful structure. But it is important as a teacher to be conscious of how much freedom one is really giving to pupils. At the top of page 101 is a classic example of a starting point that quickly leads to some rich but accessible mathematical enquiry.

Clearly, the pursuit of this investigation leads towards generalisations of a kind that can be helpfully described and developed further by the use of algebra. Pointing this out to pupils too soon removes much of the pleasure from this kind of activity. But for this discussion it illustrates how algebra is, in one sense at least, *generalised arithmetic*. It is also a reminder of how progress in algebra is partly dependent upon proficiency and broad understanding in arithmetic.

---

**Polite numbers.**

A number is polite if it is the sum of a string of consecutive positive integers. For example, since 2 + 3 + 4 = 9, 9 is a polite number. Similarly, 30 is polite since it is the sum of 6 + 7 + 8 + 9. Again, 21 + 22 + 23 + 24 + 25 = 115 showing that 115 is also polite. Interesting questions arise from this definition of polite numbers, such as:

- Are there any non-polite numbers? If so, what are they?
- Are there any quick ways of determining the string for any given polite number?
- Which polite numbers can be made from more than one string?
- How can the investigation be extended by replacing the defining rules with others?

---

## Summary and conclusion

The issues selected for discussion in this chapter arise from the tendency to view arithmetic rather too narrowly. Historically, the theoretical and practical elements of arithmetic have both been significant. Yet an over-zealous preoccupation with either of these elements can place arithmetic in a poor light for those who learn it and expect to value it. Even if little else is achieved by assimilating arithmetic into 'numeracy', it draws our attention to what might be missing in some of the current interpretations of this area of mathematics. It is important to make regular connections between the operations of arithmetic and those extra-arithmetical contexts to which they may be readily applied. There are sound educational reasons, too, for using arithmetical skills for exploring the fascinating patterns and properties that exist within the number system. The scope for inventiveness and elegance in pupils' calculation reveals further essential aspects of arithmetic. Finally, we can add that arithmetic, taught appropriately, can go some way towards exemplifying rationality, and thus has general application of a different order. As we assemble these reminders much of the scepticism about the current nature of what we call arithmetic begins to disappear.

## Notes

1   Indeed, Andrews has recently suggested that the justification of mathematics on the basis of its usefulness is a *myth*. For a short critique of Andrews' claim see Huckstep (1999).

2   The author of the Perry Report famously insisted at the beginning of the twentieth-century that 'The study of mathematics began because it was useful, continues because it is useful, and is valuable to the world because of the usefulness of its results, while the mathematicians, who determine what the teacher shall do, hold that the subject should be studied for its own sake.' (Griffiths and Howson, 1974, p. 17).

3    It may surprise the reader to learn that Fitch wrote: 'For all practical purposes, whatever I may have learned at school of fractions, or proportions, or decimals, is, unless I happen to be in business, far less frequently available to me in life than a knowledge, say, of the history of my own country, or of the elementary truths of physics.' (Fitch, 1902, p. 291).

4    In some respects Fitch anticipates the British mathematics educationist R.R. Skemp (1976) who distinguished between what he called 'instrumental' and 'relational' understanding.

5    Writers more recently have pointed how the procedures of mathematics are essentially non-authoritarian (Sawyer, 1964, p. 82; Skemp, 1971, p. 110).

6    Couched in such terms the notion of mathematics as a 'creative discipline' is innocuous enough. However in the hands of over-zealous educationists some implausible claims have been made. See Huckstep, P. and Rowland, T. (in press).

7    Indeed, Geoffrey Howson writing about the Lower Secondary National Curriculum in France writes: ' ... mathematics teaching is seen to have two aspects: one concerns the way that mathematics is derived from and met in many disciplines, the other the way that, in return, mathematical knowledge and methods can contribute to various specialities. In a manner which hints at 'old-fashioned' faculty psychology but which, nevertheless, must still have some justification, it is pointed out that mathematics education should assist the intellectual development of the pupil through: developing reasoning powers – observation, analysis, deductive thought; stimulating the imagination; promoting the habit of clear expression, both written and oral; stressing the qualities of proceeding methodically and with care.' (Howson, 1991, pp. 73–4).

8    As one writer has put it: 'Even if there is *a* sense in which someone could not be said *fully* to understand arithmetic without understanding set theory, this is only in the sense in which it might be said that someone could not fully understand the movement of billiard balls without understanding the principles of sub-atomic physics ...' (Hamlyn, 1967, p. 200).

9    But the temporal precedence of mental over written mathematics is not a new idea. Once again we can refer to Tate who a century and a half ago wrote: 'Young children should be practised, for some time, in mental calculation, before they are taught anything relative to the symbols and notation of numbers'. (Tate, 1854, p. 140)
Moreover, he seemed to be concerned with the ownership of method, too, when he insisted that: 'All tricks and clap-traps of mental calculation should be conscientiously avoided. The boy called upon to give the answer should give the process of investigation.' (Tate, 1854, p. 140)

10   Nevertheless, we must also be careful not to suppose that commercial contexts are the most important models for mathematical contexts. Indeed, recently much emphasis has been placed on the value of mathematics lessons to provide education in moral/political contexts such as human rights. For example, see *The Maths and Human Rights Resource Book: Bringing Human Rights into the Secondary Mathematics Classroom* Peter Wright (ed.) which can be obtained from The Education Office, Amnesty International UK, 99-119 Roseberry Avenue, London, EC1 4RE.

## References

Andrews, P. (1998) 'Peddling the myth', *Mathematics in School*, 27(2): 2–4.
Anghileri, J. (2000) *Teaching Number Sense*, London: Continuum.
Askew, M., Brown, M., Rhodes, V., Wiliam, D. and Johnson, D. (1997) *Effective Teachers of Numeracy: report of a study carried out for the Teacher Training Agency*, King's College, University of London.

Augustine, St. (1993 edn) *On Free Choice of the Will*, Indianapolis, IN: Hackett.

Cockcroft, W.H. (1982) *Mathematics Counts*, London: HMSO.

Davis, B. (1995) 'Why teach mathematics?' *Mathematical Education and Enactivist Theory for the Learning of Mathematics*, 15(2).

DES (1979) *Mathematics 5 to 11. A handbook of suggestions*, London: HMSO.

DfEE (1998) *The Implementation of the National Numeracy Strategy: the final report of the Task Force*, London: HMSO.

DfEE/QCA (1999) *Mathematics: the National Curriculum for England*, DfEE/QCA.

DfEE (2000) *The National Numeracy Strategy Framework for Teaching Mathematics: Year 7*, London: HMSO.

Dickson, L., Brown, M. and Gibson, O. (1984) *Children Learning Mathematics*, Eastbourne: Holt Education.

Fitch, J. (1902) *Lectures on Teaching*, Cambridge: Cambridge University Press.

Hamlyn, D.W. (1967) 'The logical and psychological aspects of learning', in R.S. Peters (ed.) *The Concept of Education*, London: Routledge and Kegan Paul.

Hardy, G.H. (1967) *A Mathematician's Apology*, Cambridge: Cambridge University Press.

Howson, A.G. (1982) *A History of Mathematics Education in England*, Cambridge: Cambridge University Press.

Howson, G. (1991) *National Curricula in Mathematics*, Leicester: The Mathematics Association.

Huckstep, P. (1999) 'How can mathematics be useful?', *Mathematics in School*.

Huckstep, P. (2000) 'Mathematics as a vehicle for "mental training"', in J. White and S. Bramall (eds) *Why learn maths?*, London: Bedford Way Papers, University of London.

Huckstep, P. and Rowland, T. (2000) 'Creative mathematics: real or rhetoric', *Educational Studies in Mathematics*, 42(1): 81–100.

McIntosh, A. (1979) 'Some children and some multiplication', *Mathematics Teaching*, 87: 14–15.

Nunes, T., Schliemann, A.D. and Carraher, D.W. (1993) *Street Mathematics and School Mathematics*, Cambridge: Cambridge University Press.

Plunkett, S. (1979) 'Decomposition and all that rot', *Mathematics in School*, 8(3): 2–7.

Quine, W.V. (1969) 'Speaking of objects', in *Ontological Relativity & Other Essays*, NY: Columbia University Press.

Rowland, T. (1997) 'Dividing by three-quarters: what Suzie saw', *Mathematics Teaching*, 160: 30–3.

Sawyer, W.W. (1964) *Vision in Elementary Mathematics*, Harmondsworth: Penguin.

Skemp, R.R. (1971) *The Psychology of Learning Mathematics*, Harmondsworth: Penguin.

Skemp, R.R. (1976) 'Relational understanding and instrumental understanding', *Mathematics Teaching*, 77: 20–6.

Tahta, D. (1998) 'Counting counts', *Mathematics Teaching*, 163: 4–11.

Tate, T. (1854) *The Philosophy of Education*, Longman, Brown, Green and Longmans.

Teacher Training Agency (Undated) *Assessing your Needs in Mathematics: needs assessment materials for Key Stage 2 teachers*, London: Teacher Training Agency.

Thompson, I. (ed.) (1997) *Teaching and Learning Early Number*, Milton Keynes: Open University.

Wells, D. (1989) 'Why do Mathematics?' *Mathematics Teaching*: 127: 34–7.

Whitcombe, A. (1988) 'Mathematics: creativity imagination beauty', *Mathematics in School*, 17(2): 13–5.
Yeldham, F.A. (1936) *The Teaching of Arithmetic through Four Hundred Years*, London: George G. Harrap.

# 7 Generalisation and algebra
## Exploiting children's powers

John Mason

## Introduction

A car hire firm needs a pricing policy to enable it to cope with unusual requests from customers; a distribution company has to make sure that each customer has the product they want, when they want it, where they want it. In each case, the customer wants something particular – a price, or delivery, of a particular product – but the entrepreneur needs some way of dealing with and responding to the range of customer requests. The customer wants a particular, but the entrepreneur needs the general: a general formula or general principles on which to base decisions. The customer needs arithmetic, but the entrepreneur needs algebra.

Now consider very young children being taught to count: an adult points to a succession of similar objects and utters a curious 'poem' of apparently arbitrary sounds 'one, two, three, …'. From a large number of such experiences, the child 'learns to count', so that on encountering completely new and unfamiliar objects in a new setting, counting can still take place. The child is generalising. Those generalisations (numbers) can then be manipulated. But no one would try to expose children to all possible three-digit subtractions, still less would they expect them to memorise all the possibilities. Rather, children are expected to use their powers to work out *how* to do three-digit subtractions, using a collection of rules or procedures for dealing with particular situations (larger from smaller, zeros in the larger number, … ). Again they are expected to generalise, to reconstruct for themselves from what they are exposed to and instructed in, a procedure for dealing with all possible cases.

Now consider an economically active adolescent-adult. Companies are constantly imploring them to buy clothes, to obtain and use credit cards, to take out insurance, to invest money, to gamble; in short, to buy a range of goods and services from a number of competing sources. As a voter, they are harangued from all sides by general assertions about the economy, about social issues, about ecological and technical issues. In every case what they hear are generalities, sometimes accompanied by particular examples. As a functioning member of society, it is vital to be disposed and inclined to test generalities against particulars, to recognise false, biased, or incomplete generalisations, and to be sufficiently articulate to be able to challenge those assertions, and the basis for implied or hidden calculations or assumptions.

Algebra is, in one sense, the language of generalisation of quantity. It provides experience of, and a language for, expressing generality, manipulating generality, and reasoning about generality.

In this chapter I touch briefly on some of the roots of algebra, and indicate some routes towards algebra (Mason *et al.*, 1985). I also put forward a number of conjectures which are summarised at the end. The conjectures cannot be *proved*, only validated through personal experimentation in working with oneself, with colleagues, and with children.

## Algebra as the language of generalisation

The word algebra itself derives from the title of a treatise of the ninth century, written by Mohammud ibn Musa, from Khwarizm (now Khiva in the Uzbek Republic). In it he summarised and extended the work of earlier writers on solving equations. The title of his treatise included the words *al-jabr* and *al-muqabalah* meaning literally the science of performing on both sides, adding the same thing (*al-jabr*) and subtracting the same thing (*al-muqabalah*). Typically, one untranslated word in the title eventually came to stand for the whole, but we might easily have been teaching Almukaba rather than Algebra!

The notion of 'doing the same thing to both sides' is already a generalisation of a method of approach to a class of problems in which scholars used a symbol such as $x$ to stand for an unknown quantity in order to express a fact or calculation, which in turn produces an equation which then needed to be solved. Al Khwarizmi's treatise records these methods.

### The role of examples

We want students to recognise the type of problem they encounter, especially on a test. To do this we show them how to solve some 'worked examples', and then expect them to reconstruct for themselves a method for doing 'all such problems'. There is a significant issue however: when someone is showing you an example, are you attending to the generality, or to the particularities of the 'example'? In other words, what for you is the example an 'example of'? The teacher, aware of a generality, can stress generic aspects and downplay particulars when 'doing an example'. For example:

> Find the arithmetic mean of the following shoe sizes for a class of children:
> 4, 4, 4, 4, 4, 4, 4, 4, 4, 5, 5, 5, 5, 5, 5, 5, 5, 5, 5, 5, 5, 5, 5, 5, 6, 6, 6, 6, 6

Working through this with a class, you are likely to point out that there are ten 4s, fifteen 5s and five 6s, so an easy way to do the adding is to multiply 10 by 4, add 15 times 5, add 5 times 6, and divide by 10 + 15 + 5. No doubt you would make general remarks about 'this is what you do', and 'you multiply the frequency of a value by that value', because you are aware of the generality. But your students may be transfixed by the long list, they may be frightened of having to do a lot of adding, they may find it difficult to concentrate mentally to count correctly the 4s and the 5s without getting lost, and they may not connect 'frequency' with 'the number of repetitions of a value'.

Worse, doing a particular calculation may obscure the general technique, may even attract students' attention to details that are not what the teacher wants them to attend to.

## Roots of algebra in children's powers

Children enter school already having displayed immense powers of imagining and expressing (using language to describing what they see or imagine, displaying using their bodies, depicting), generalising and specialising (in picking up and using language), and conjecturing and reasoning (detecting patterns in language so as to be able to make up their own sentences to express themselves). Exercising, developing and extending one's powers are sources of pleasure and self-confidence. Failure to use those powers is at best throwing away an opportunity and, at worst, turns students off mathematics and off school.

So as a teacher I am faced with the question, 'Am I stimulating my students to use their powers, or am I trying to do the work for them?' In this section I review those powers briefly, in preparation for subsequent sections which look at ways of invoking those powers in any lesson.

## Specific powers

Here are three pairs of powers from amongst the many that children bring to lessons.

### Imagining and expressing

Every child can imagine what is not physically present: this is the domain of fairy stories and fantasies, of hopes and fears. Every child can express some of what they imagine, in movement and in speech, in voice tones and in depiction, in words and in other symbols. But this power needs to be called upon and exercised, and expression needs to be developed in various media. If imagination is not called upon, a powerful link to the emotions is neglected, and motivation-interest may suffer; if expression in multiple forms is not encouraged, then students may form the impression that mathematics does not offer opportunities for creativity. If students encounter a very limited range of images, and a very limited range of expressions, they are likely to form the impression that mathematics is a very limited domain of human experience.

### Specialising and generalising

> Given two numbers which sum to 1, which is greater, the smaller added to the square of the greater, or the greater added to the square of the smaller added to the greater?

What is your immediate response? Panic? Aroused interest? 'It's obvious'? Trying an example? Most people immediately try a particular case (specialising). Some try a very special case such as 0 and 1, or ½ and ½, but then need to try something else. A popular choice is ⅓ and ⅔, or ¼ and ¾. Few people try something like ¹¹⁄₃₇ and ²⁶⁄₃₇, or 2.8376 and −1.83786.

Some people are so confident with symbols that they immediately write things down in general (let the numbers be $x$ and $(1 - x)$). In a sense they are specialising too, because specialising means making use of confidently manipulable objects (for most people, numbers, for some, letters) to express the situation and to see what is going on. This is an example of using the power to specialise in the face of a generality in order to see what is going on. The point of the special or particular case is to get a sense of what *always* happens.

Whenever I encounter a generality, I find myself testing it against particular cases. If I am trying to decide *whether* the general assertion is true, or *when* it is true, I consider special, often extreme cases. The purpose of trying out particular cases is not just to seek a counter-example, but to attend to *how* the calculations are done, with an eye to seeing if they generalise. This is exactly what students are expected to do when learning a new technique: do some exercises *in order to see how the technique works* (not just to 'get the answers'). Specialising is an act I can perform in order to make sense of what *always* happens, in order to appreciate and reconstruct generality.

> Having disposed of the particular question, it is natural to ask what role the 'sum to 1' is playing. What happens if they sum to something else? Are there other computation sequences that have a similar effect?

This is an example of enquiring further, of not being content with one result, but trying to put it in a more general context, to generalise.

There are two important perceptions here:

- seeing the *particular in the general* (seeing not just a general assertion but the opportunity to try out specific particular cases and being aware of what constitutes particular instances of the general);
- seeing the *general through the particular* (seeing specific numbers or other aspects as placeholders for other possibilities).

When you find yourself 'doing an example' in front of students, you are probably seeing through the particular numbers, the particular computations, and are aware of generality. But some numbers may be structural rather than particular. What are you doing to draw students' attention to the difference?

> For example, in finding the circumference of a circle of radius 2, there are two 2s in the calculation: $2 \times \pi \times 2$. Are students clear which one is the radius? In finding the area of a trapezium with parallel sides 2 and 4 and height 2, there are potentially three 2s in $\frac{(2+4) \times 2}{2}$, one of which is structural. Even if the numbers are all chosen to be different, are students aware of the different status of the 2 in the denominator and the numbers appearing elsewhere? It may seem obvious, but it is easy to make an inappropriate connection when, as a student, you don't know what is going on.

Working through a particular example provides an opportunity to stand back, without doing any arithmetic, and to see how the calculation works. Then you can 'see the general through the particular' by following a particular number through the calculation as if it were a placeholder, and this can be more easily displayed by giving it a special symbol, such as $x$ or $n$.

> For example, to find the distance between the points $(13, -6)$ and $(-7, 14)$ involves considerable arithmetic. Actually doing the arithmetic may attract attention into that arithmetic. Writing the calculation out without doing the arithmetic makes it possible to track what happens to various numbers, and so supports expressing this as a generality, thereby producing a formula for the general situation.

Tony Gardiner (1993) points out that mentally manipulating small numbers, as now recommended in the National Numeracy Strategy, provides plenty of opportunity to experience the use of brackets to express the way students do computations mentally (e.g. $7 + 8 = 7 + (3 + 5) = (7 + 3) + 5 = 10 + 5 = 15$). The general principles they are using, when expressed verbally, provide a stepping stone to expressing in general the rules of arithmetic.

### Conjecturing and reasoning

Algebra can be seen as a language in which to express generalities. These usually have the status at first of conjectures: they may be correct, but they may need modifying or qualifying. In a conjecturing atmosphere, everything that is said is said because by expressing it, by getting it outside of yourself, you make it possible to stand back from it and to test it and reason about it and with it. If you try to keep all your conjectures in your head, they will end up tumbling around like clothes in a dryer, getting tangled up. In a conjecturing atmosphere, other people invite you to modify your conjecture, or to consider a particular example that might challenge your conjecture. You do not declare someone else to be 'wrong'; you invite them to 'modify their conjecture'. In a conjecturing atmosphere you take opportunities to struggle to express when you are unsure, and you take opportunities to listen to others and to suggest modifications or amplifications or challenging examples, when you are sure.

Algebra seen as a language for expressing conjectured generalities is also ideal for reasoning, because it is succinctly manipulable. In school the study of algebra often degenerates into rehearsing the rules of algebra on algebraic expressions in an attempt to gain facility with manipulating symbols. But algebra is quintessentially a language within which, as well as about which, to reason logically.

## Pedagogic implications

On the face of it, *fill and drill* (exposition and practice) seems a reasonable teaching strategy. But does it call upon students' powers fully? Does it encourage them to try to formulate generality for themselves? Asking students to construct a question of the same type, to construct an easy and a hard question, a challenging question and one that shows that you know how to do questions of this type, stimulates students to move away from mindless rehearsal and to seek structure. Algebra is the language in which to express such structure, and in which to demonstrate that you can do any question of a given type. (See also Chapter 17 on questioning.)

## Roots of algebra in ignorance

For example, asked to find all numbers for which multiplying by 10 and subtracting 5 gives the same as multiplying by 4 and adding 10, you can guess and improve, or you can acknowledge that you do not know, express that ignorance by the symbol x, and then write down what you know, which is how you would check that x is the answer, namely, $10x - 5 = 4x + 10$. Now you can manipulate the symbols to discover x.

Mary Everest Boole (1832–1916) suggested that algebra arose when someone *acknowledged the fact of their ignorance* as to the answer to a problem (Tahta, 1972).

Acknowledgement takes the form of using a letter to represent what I do not as yet know. If I can't solve a problem, can I see how I would check an answer if someone proposed one? If so, denote that answer by a symbol, write down the calculations involved in checking it, and produce one or more equations or inequalities. Then I have at least reduced the problem to manipulating symbols. This mirrors what happened historically: attention suddenly shifted from solving complicated arithmetic problems, to developing techniques for solving the equations produced by using letters to denote the as-yet-unknown in problems.

This was an extremely important and powerful move. On the one hand it seems obvious, but it requires a considerable shift of thinking, an acceptance of denoting the as-yet-unknown and allowing it to participate in computations that previously only involved numbers. In arithmetic you move from the known (numbers) to the unknown (find the answer by doing calculations); in algebra you move from the as-yet-unknown to the known (what you are told, expressed using the unknown). This shift comes as a considerable surprise to students. François Viète, who developed the use of letters to produce equations (and settled on using early letters in the alphabet for constants and later ones for unknowns) was so entranced by the power of this as an approach, that he hoped to solve 'all problems' in this way. The study of algebra became the study of solving equations. Historically, and even currently, many texts fail to support students in making this same shift, and instead begin immediately with the arithmetic of expressions.

## Roots of algebra in structure

In this section I indicate some of the roots of algebra to be found in encountering and expressing mathematical structure. These are only particular cases of a more general principle, which is that a lesson without the opportunity to express a generality is not a mathematics lesson, because generality pervades all of mathematics. Caleb Gattegno (1970) went so far as to suggest that 'something is mathematical only if it is shot through with infinity', by which I believe he meant that somewhere there is a potential infinity, a possibility of generalisation, even if constraints have then been added to make the domain of possibilities finite.

## TUNJA sequences: with and across the grain[1]

Detecting patterns is a possibility in many syllabus topics, and not simply an extra activity as part of mathematical exploration and coursework. Indeed, coursework will not be effective in stimulating exploration if pattern-detecting and expressing has not pervaded every topic. For example, suppose you want to introduce the idea of expanding brackets. Pick a version of the general rule, and exemplify it in a sequence of special cases, such as the following. Offer it line by line (in silence!), pausing obviously after the equality sign and at the end of each line to check the calculation mentally, so that students are induced to do likewise:

$$1 \times (1 + 2) = 1 \times 1 + 1 \times 2$$
$$2 \times (2 + 2) = 2 \times 2 + 2 \times 2$$
$$3 \times (3 + 2) = 3 \times 3 + 3 \times 2$$
$$4 \times (4 + 2) = 4 \times 4 + 4 \times 2$$
$$5$$

Everyone will know how to complete this line. If some are not sure, their attention can be drawn (still silently) to the patterns running down the sequence of lines. Then they can be asked to write out the seventeenth line and, after exposure to several such examples depending on their experience, to generalise.

Attention at first is on the downward pattern (going with the grain). But the really important mathematical awareness lies in making sense of each line in itself, in going across the grain. The expression of a general line *is* a rule both of arithmetic and of manipulating algebra. The Tunja Sequence idea can be extended backwards (with the grain) to encounter products of negative numbers, suggesting how these ought to work so that each line continues to be a correct statement. They can also develop into products of brackets each with two (or more) terms, and the statements can be arranged with the products first or with the expansion first in order to put emphasis on factoring.

## Counting objects in structural patterns

The following sequence of pictures follows a rule for drawing the next pattern from the previous, using matchsticks. Express in words a rule that accounts for all the pictures shown and which can be used to draw further pictures in the sequence.

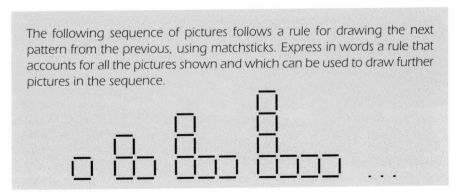

How many squares will be formed, and how many matchsticks will be needed for the next picture? For the tenth picture? For the hundredth? Can we tell someone how to calculate the number of matchsticks required to build a particular picture, even if we don't yet know which one it will be? Can you connect the number of squares and the number of matchsticks?

It is vital that there be an agreed rule which generates the terms of a sequence. So often one sees questions such as 'What is the next term in the sequence 1, 2, 4, 8, … ', as if there were a unique answer. *Only* where the sequence of numbers is generated from some agreed structure or situation, is it possible to decide what the 'next' term might be.

Again it is very useful to draw some further examples for myself, not just for the sake of drawing, but paying attention to *how* I draw them, because I may be able to express the 'how' in terms of the picture-number.

This sort of task also provides opportunities to compare expressions of generality in which the number required for the $n^{th}$ is expressed in terms of the number required for the previous picture (or pictures) as in a Fibonacci sequence, and an expression which expresses how to build the $n^{th}$ from scratch. Recursion-iteration (using previous values) and direct formulae (using only $n$) are quintessential formats for mathematical generalities. While formulae make it easy to manipulate the generality for some further purpose (e.g. using the formula for the solution to a quadratic equation), iteration or recursion relationships are often easier to express and, with computers, are just as easy to calculate.

What is the sum of five terms of the arithmetic progression 1, 4, 7, … ? Consider the following diagram in terms of this problem to find a formula for doing all such questions, using only the area of a rectangle.

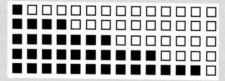

It may be useful to draw another example for yourself, but the invitation is to see the general through the particular, both in terms of adding other numbers of terms of the same progression, and for adding any number of terms of any arithmetic progression. There is also a certain similarity to finding the area of a triangle by completing it to a parallelogram.

## Babylonian area calculations

Omar Khayyham (1027–1123), who developed rules of algebra for solving quadratic equations, followed a long tradition going back to Babylonian scribes (see van der Waerden, 1983; 1985), in which multiplication of two quantities is depicted as a calculation of the area of a rectangle. This notion is exploited somewhat by some teachers of algebra, and extensively by a few teachers with impressive results (Bidwell, 1986; Kieren, 1996; Fairchild, 2001).

Interpret the diagram above as a statement about expanding (a + b)(c + d) as a sum of four terms. Interpret the diagram as a statement about expanding (a − b)(c + d), (a + b)(c − d) and (a − b)(c − d), by choosing different lengths to be represented by a and by c.

Here the diagram provides an image of what expanding brackets entails, in terms of areas. Of course the purpose of the diagram is to provide an image to aid in developing facility, because it is considerably more difficult to use the same idea for multiplying three factors together, and very difficult for more factors! Again the diagrams, although apparently particular, provide an opportunity to see the general through the particular.

## Rules of arithmetic

What is a number?

This turns out to be a very challenging question, but no more so than trying to answer 'What is a chair?' or 'What is beauty?' As Socrates suggests through the writings of Plato, the easiest way to address such a question is to give examples. But examples do not capture generality, merely illustrate or point to particulars. Another approach, suggested by the inspired Greek mathematician Euclid, and exploited profoundly since the nineteenth-century, is to say what you can do *with* them, what their properties are.

(Whole) numbers can be ordered, added, subtracted (sometimes), multiplied, and divided (sometimes) (we could allow ourselves positives and negatives, and fractions).

What are the rules for doing these?

Expressing those rules (order does not matter when adding or multiplying, subtraction is the reverse of addition, division is the reverse of multiplication, multiplication distributes over addition, presence of identities, etc.) using words, then letters, produces the rules not just for arithmetic, but also for algebra! Being invited to stand back from engaging in particular arithmetic calculations, and considering what happens in general, is akin to standing back from social situations and considering what happens: it contributes to your awareness as a citizen. It raises awareness of processes, and provides a much needed overview, which in the case of mathematics, as in other situations, opens up the possibility of making choices which may be obscured when you are caught up in the details.

## Spreadsheets as a support and impetus for expressing generality

Spreadsheets provide an excellent medium in which to express generality, especially when there is some rule which is applied repeatedly. The most powerful features of a spreadsheet are the opportunity to express a calculation in one cell, using the contents of other cells even when you do not yet know what is in those cells, and the fill-down and fill-right features that enable you to apply the same operation repeatedly on a succession of numbers.

Research investigations (Sutherland and Rojano, 1993; Abramovich and Nabors, 1999) have shown that students quickly grasp the use of a letter–number pair as the way to refer to the contents of a cell, which supports the notion of a symbol–letter as denoting an as-yet-unknown value. Attention is attracted to the form or shape of a calculation, the generality, and away from the particularity.

For example:

A constant row of 1s can be entered by inserting a 1 in cell A1, and then using
fill-right from A1 to repeat that as far as desired.

|   | A | B | C | D | E | F | G |
|---|---|---|---|---|---|---|---|
| 1 | 1 | 1 | 1 | 1 | 1 | 1 | 1 |
| 2 |   |   |   |   |   |   |   |
| 3 |   |   |   |   |   |   |   |
| 4 |   |   |   |   |   |   |   |
| 5 |   |   |   |   |   |   |   |
| 6 |   |   |   |   |   |   |   |

|   | A | B | C | D | E | F | G |
|---|---|---|---|---|---|---|---|
| 1 | 1 | 1 | 1 | 1 | 1 | 1 | 1 |
| 2 | 1 | =A2+B1 | =B2+C1 | =C2+D1 | =D2+E1 | =E2+F1 | =F2+G1 |
| 3 |   |   |   |   |   |   |   |
| 4 |   |   |   |   |   |   |   |
| 5 |   |   |   |   |   |   |   |
| 6 |   |   |   |   |   |   |   |

The natural numbers can be produced in consecutive cells by inserting a 1 in cell A2, the formula A2+B1 in cell B2, and then using fill-right from B2 to continue the operation.

Using fill-down in column B from row 2, then fill-right in each row from column B produces triangular numbers and row after row of figurate numbers, as well as the Jia Xian triangle (eleventh century), known in the west as Pascal's triangle.

|   | A | B | C | D | E | F | G |
|---|---|---|---|---|---|---|---|
| 1 | 1 | 1 | 1 | 1 | 1 | 1 | 1 |
| 2 | 1 | 2 | 3 | 4 | 5 | 6 | 7 |
| 3 | 1 | 3 | 6 | 10 | 15 | 21 | 28 |
| 4 | 1 | 4 | 10 | 20 | 35 | 56 | 84 |
| 5 | 1 | 5 | 15 | 35 | 70 | 126 | 210 |

|   | A | B | C | D | E | F | G |
|---|---|---|---|---|---|---|---|
| 1 | 1 | 1 | 1 | 1 | 1 | 1 | 1 |
| 2 | 1 | =A2+B1 | =B2+C1 | =C2+D1 | =D2+E1 | =E2+F1 | =F2+G1 |
| 3 | 1 | =A3+B2 | =B3+C2 | =C3+D2 | =D3+E2 | =E3+F2 | =F3+G2 |
| 4 | 1 | =A4+B3 | =B4+C3 | =C4+D3 | =D4+E3 | =E4+F3 | =F4+G3 |
| 5 | 1 | =A5+B4 | =B5+C4 | =C5+D4 | =D5+E4 | =E5+F4 | =F5+G4 |

The possibility of finding a direct formula for any particular figurate number arises, as does the opportunity to change the initial 1 to something else, to use a non-constant sequence, to explore Fibonacci, and so on. The opportunities are to experience iterative use of generality to produce increasingly complex particulars, and then to address the question of whether the cell entries could be predicted by means of a direct formula.

## Graphics calculators

Graphics calculators already do quite a lot of algebraic manipulation in addition to

> For example, what happens to an equation solver if the lines become very nearly parallel? Alternatively, what conditions on a pair of equations make them unsolvable?

plotting graphs. Having a machine that performs some operations is excellent, because it raises the question of what the machine is doing, and under what conditions one might want that done.

Graphics calculators draw attention to the graphic display of expressions which are functions: straight lines, quadratics in $x$, and so on. They show what it means to solve two equations simultaneously, and even provide approximate solutions graphically as well as arithmetically. They facilitate working on questions such as what is the effect of changing every occurrence of $x$ by $x + 2$, and what is the effect of changing the constant term, or indeed any coefficient in an expression. They raise problems concerned with how one chooses different scales in order to reveal different features of a graph, such as zeros, local maxima and minima, and points of inflection, for it is often difficult to arrange to see all of these clearly at the same time. Students can learn to identify the shapes of different curves ($x^2$, $x^3$, $\sin x$, $\cos x$, $\tan x$, $\sin^{-1} x$, $\tan^{-1} x$, $e^x$, $\log x$, etc.) by being shown scaled and translated versions.

> • Using only the fact that the area of a rectangle is the product of the lengths of two adjacent edges, use the following pairs of diagrams to express formulae for the area of a parallelogram and trapezium. Use a special form of the second pair to depict and then express the area of a triangle. In what ways is a triangle a special case of a trapezium? Does the 'picture' always work (what happens if the parallelogram is so tilted that the top edge does not lie directly above the bottom edge)?

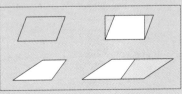

> - What are the maximum and minimum perimeters of figures made up of s squares joined edge to edge?
> - In a school hall there are rectangular tables which seat two people along the short edge and four people along the long edge. How many tables are needed to seat 175 people in the hall if you can only put at most four tables end-to-end across the hall, and five end-to-end down the length?

### Generalising in geometry

Geometry has its own generalities in the form of facts about lines and circles, etc. But geometrical shapes can also be the source of stimuli for algebraic generalisations.

Geometrical configurations are a rich source of opportunity to express generality, and often the geometry turns into number or algebra calculations, particularly when they are to do with perimeters and areas. Note the similarities between area calculations for trapezia and sums of arithmetic progressions.

### Approaching algebra

Algebra is actually present in every mathematics lesson, for if there are no opportunities to encounter and express generality in a lesson, that lesson is not about mathematics. Whatever technique is being developed or rehearsed, whatever concept is being exposed and described, there is always generality present. If you and the text book *always* start with some particular cases (for example 'worked examples'), and then draw out a generality, or if you *always* start with a generality and then illustrate it with particular cases, you are likely to train students to expect the same format in each lesson, and hence their own powers are likely to atrophy through lack of use. If instead you vary your approach, sometimes starting from the general, and getting them to specialise, sometimes starting from some particular cases and getting them to generalise, you are more likely to help students strengthen their own powers, and at the same time, because of the pleasure experienced in exploiting their own powers, actually find mathematics enjoyable, creative and involving.

#### Multiple expressions

Algebra is also about the manipulation of expressions. If you can find contexts in which different people express the same generality but in different ways, then you open up the possibility that it might be possible to manipulate the expressions themselves, without having to return to the original context which spawned them. Furthermore, each expression of generality expresses a way of seeing. Sometimes manipulating an expression can suggest other ways of seeing. For example, in the classic 'paving stones round a pond' there are multiple ways of seeing how to count the number of square slabs needed to surround a square pond of side $s$. We can take a particular case ($s = 3$) and see through it to the general:

The first breakdown suggests a reading of 'four lots of $s$ and four for the corners' or $4s + 4$. The second suggests 'four lots of $s + 1$, or $4(s + 1)$. After considerable experience of multiple expressions for the same thing, the fact that both express the same generality (number of paving tiles) will suggest that it might be possible to get from one expression to the other without recourse to the tiles around the pond. Thus the notion of manipulating symbols as if they were numbers can arise quite naturally, and the rules for these manipulations can be worked out by the students in order to make the calculations 'work in every particular case'. Once rearranging is established, you can use a rearrangement to see if it expresses a direct perception of how to count. For example:

Another rearrangement of the expression is $2(s + 1) + 2s + 2$.
What grouping of the tiles would be expressed in this way?

### The dual nature of algebraic expressions

Arithmetical and algebraic expressions have a dual nature: on the one hand they express something and so constitute an answer in themselves (hence arithmetic to find *the* numerical answer). On the other hand, they indicate a sequence of calculations which could be performed (hence an algorithm, and as such provide access to generality). Many students only have a single view of arithmetical expressions (as things to simplify). When they encounter algebraic expressions like $2x - 7$, they expect that it should be reducible to a single 'thing', and so they try out various erroneous 'rules' for eliminating the $+$ and $-$ signs (Booth, 1984). If they saw $5 \times (37 - 26)$ as a thing, as an answer in an 'exposed' form, they might be more willing to accept $2x - 7$ as a thing also. Algebraic expressions are quintessentially dual in nature, for the expression *is* the answer to a question (an expression of generality), as well as indicating a calculation which could be carried out if one had a specific particular value for $x$. Time spent exposing this dual nature in both arithmetic and algebra is time well spent.

## Exploiting algebra

'Word problems', that is, problems involving numbers in some context, have been present in mathematics teaching since the beginning of recorded time. They have also provided a watershed for a majority of students, and an object of particular dislike for many. The following three problems come from Bonnycastle (1849), but are repeated exactly in Hutton (1833, p. 222) and probably come from much earlier:

- A's age is double of B's, and B's is triple of C's, and the sum of all their ages is 140; what is the age of each?
- A person bought a chaise, horse, and harness, for £60. The horse came to twice the price of the harness, and the chaise to twice the price of the horse and harness; what did he give for each?

- A person has two horses and a saddle worth £50. Now if the saddle be put on the back of the first horse, it will make his value double that of the second; but if it be put on the back of the second, it will make his value triple that of the first; what is the value of each horse?

There is more to these, and to word problems in general, than challenges for the quicker students while the others are practising manipulating symbols. They provide opportunity to extract mathematical calculations from a context. They also offer insight into social conditions of the time (what authors felt were worthy contexts to employ). They do not, usually, provide examples of the use of mathematics in society, for most word problems are fanciful creations designed to challenge the solver.

For problems which are 'real' because they are of importance in society, you can look for questions derived from newspapers and everyday events (Frankenstein, 1997), and for mathematics embedded in the way society is structured (for example, why are wage rises always in percentages; if a restaurant or auctioneer or agent makes a service charge, is it appropriate for them to raise the percentage they charge when there is inflation?).

Much more importantly for students' appreciation of the power of mathematics in general, and of algebra in particular, each word problem can be taken as typical of a class of problems. Students can be invited to make up a different context using the same numbers, and a different context with the same and with different numbers. Furthermore, they can be invited to generalise each problem individually, and they can use a collection of problems to indicate scope for extensive 'complexification': for example, the three problems as inspiration for making even more complex problems involving horses, harnesses, saddles, carriages, etc.. Rather than seeing each problem as a burden, each can be seen as an exemplar of a general class, and as a stimulus to generalise.

## Summary

I have offered a number of conjectures for consideration, from which the remainder of the chapter can be derived.

- Children come to school with the requisite powers to think mathematically, and in particular, to 'think' algebraically.
- Doing someone else's algebra (answering manipulation questions on tests and exams) is greatly facilitated and motivated by generating one's own algebra first, that is, by expressing generalities so that you see where algebraic expressions come from, and by creating your own questions of a given type.
- Algebra appears as symbols, but these are an expression of generality or of an as-yet-unknown quantity, and algebraic thinking is supported and generated by kinaesthetic and imagistic experiences (paying attention to how something is done and imagining doing something without actually doing it physically).

- Algebra is a succinct manipulable language in which to express and reason about generality, and about the as-yet-unmanifested.
- A lesson without a sense of infinity, without an opportunity to experience generality, is not a mathematics lesson.
- Asking 'does it always, sometimes, never work?' leads to encountering the infinity in situations, and to learning to control that infinity.
- Expressions have dual meanings: as answers or expressions of generality, and as rules for doing a sequence of calculations with specific numbers, as in a formula.

There has been an enormous amount of research effort devoted to the teaching of algebra, accounts of which can be found particularly in Wagner and Kieran, 1989; Bednarz *et al.*, 1996; Giménez *et al.,*1996; and Reed, 1999.

## Note

1       This expression was coined and exploited by Anne Watson in Watson, A. (2000) 'Going across the grain: mathematical generalisation in a group of low attainers', *Nordisk Matematikk Didaktikk (Nordic Studies in Mathematics Education)* 8(1) p. 7–22. The title Tunja Sequences arose because teachers in the city of Tunja in Columbia asked me for suggestions concerning teaching algebra to children not confident with negative numbers. See Mason, J. (2000), Tunja Sequences…, *Arithmetic Teacher.*

## References

Abramovich, S. and Nabors, W. 'Spreadsheets as generators of new meanings', in *Middle School Algebra*, www2.potsdam.edu/EDUC/abramovs/Technology_Classroom.htm

Bednarz, N., Kieran, C. and Lee, L. (1996) *Approaches to Algebra: perspectives for research and teaching*, Dordrecht: Mathematics Education Library, Kluwer.

Bidwell, J. K. (1986) 'A Babylonian geometrical algebra', *The College Mathematics Journal*, 17: 22–31.

Bonnycastle, J. (1849) *An Introduction to Algebra: with notes and observations: designed for the use of schools and places of public education*, London: Longman.

Booth, L. (1984) *Algebra: children's strategies and errors*, Windsor: NFER-Nelson.

Fairchild, J. (2001) *Transition from Arithmetic to Algebra using Two-dimensional Representations: a school-based research study*, Occasional paper 2, Oxford: Centre for Mathematics Education Research, University of Oxford.

Frankenstein, M. (1989) *Relearning Mathematics: a different R – radical math(s)*, London: Free Association.

Gardiner, A. (1993) 'Recurring themes in school mathematics', *Mathematics in School*, March: 20–2.

Gattegno, C. (1970) *What We Owe Children: the subordination of teaching to learning*, London: Routledge and Kegan Paul.

Giménez, J., Lins, R. and Gomez, B. (1996) *Arithmetics and Algebra Education: searching for the future*, Tarragona, Spain: Dept. of Engineering, Universitat Rovira I Virguli.

Hutton, C. (1811) 'A course of mathematics: composed for the use of the Royal Military Academy', London: by order of his Lordship the Master General of the Ordnance.

Kieren, T., Simmt, E. and Mgombelo, J. (1997) 'Occasioning understanding: understanding occasioning', in J. Dossey, J. Swafford, M. Parmantie and A.Dossey (eds) *Proceedings of the PME-NA Annual Conference*: 627–34.

Mason, J. (2001) 'Tunja Sequences as examples of employing students' power to generalise', *Mathematics Teacher*, 94(3): 164–9.

Mason, J., Graham, A., Pimm, D. and Gowar, N. (1985) *Routes to, Roots of Algebra*, Milton Keynes: The Open University.

Reed, S. (1999) *Word Problems: research and curricular reform*, Mahwah, NJ: Lawrence Erlbaum Associates.

Sutherland, R. and Rojano, T. (1993) 'A spreadsheet approach to solving algebra problems', *Journal of Mathematical Behavior*, December 12: 353–83.

Tahta, D. (1972) *A Boolean Anthology: selected writings of Mary Boole on mathematics education*, Derby: Association of Teachers of Mathematics.

van der Waerden, B. (1983) *Geometry and Algebra in Ancient Civilizations*, Berlin, Springer-Verlag.

van der Waerden, B. (1985) *A History of Algebra from al-Khwarizmi to Emmy Noether*, Berlin: Springer-Verlag.

Wagner, S. and Kieran, C. (1989) *Research Issues in the Learning & Teaching of Algebra*, Research Agenda for Mathematics Education, vol. 4, Reston: Lawrence Erlbaum & NCTM.

# 8 Issues in the teaching and learning of geometry

Keith Jones

## Preamble

In the Sherlock Holmes story, *The Adventure of the Priory School* (written by the British writer Sir Arthur Conan Doyle and published in 1904), the great detective and his assistant, Dr Watson, are examining some bicycle tracks.[1] The following conversation takes place:

| | |
|---|---|
| *Sherlock Holmes* | This track, as you perceive, was made by a rider who was going from the direction of the school. |
| *Dr Watson* | Or towards it? |
| *Sherlock Holmes* | No, no, my dear Watson. The more deeply sunk impression is, of course, the hind wheel, upon which the weight rests. You perceive several places where it has passed across and obliterated the more shallow mark of the front one. It was undoubtedly heading away from the school. |

Holmes' insight of examining the depth of the tracks made by the bicycle is undoubtedly the most straightforward thing to do. However, by using some knowledge of geometry, Holmes could have found that it is not necessary to have information on the depth of the tracks to discover the direction in which the bicycle had travelled. See if you can work out which way the bicycle went in Task 8.1, below.

---

### Task 8.1

These tracks fit a bicycle moving forward either up the page or down the page (but not both). Which is it?

Hints:

- Think about which of the two paths will fit the rear wheel and which will fit the front wheel.
- Think about how bicycle wheels sit along the tracks at any time.

Which way did the bicycle go?

*An enlargement of the illustration may be helpful.*

---

## Introduction

Geometry is a wonderful area of mathematics to teach. It is full of interesting problems and surprising theorems. It is open to many different approaches. It has a long history, intimately connected with the development of mathematics. It is an integral part of our cultural experience, being a vital component of numerous aspects of life from architecture to design (in all its manifestations). What is more, geometry appeals to our visual, aesthetic and intuitive senses. As a result it can be a topic that captures the interest of learners, often those learners who may find other areas of mathematics, such as number and algebra, a source of bewilderment and failure rather than excitement and creativity. Teaching geometry well can mean enabling more students to find success in mathematics.

These aspects and considerations also tend to make geometry a demanding topic to teach well. Teaching geometry well involves knowing how to recognise interesting geometrical problems and theorems, appreciating the history and cultural context of geometry, and understanding the many and varied uses to which geometry is put. It means appreciating what a full and rich geometry education can offer to learners when the mathematics curriculum is often dominated by other considerations (the demands of numeracy and algebra in particular). It means being able to put over all these things to learners in a way that is stimulating and engaging, and leads to understanding, and success in mathematics assessments.

The aim of this chapter is introduce some of the special features of geometry and its teaching and learning. The chapter examines the nature of geometry, the reasons for its inclusion in the school mathematics curriculum, and how it can best be taught and learnt. The chapter contains a number of tasks that you might like to tackle, either at the point at which they occur in the chapter or at some later, convenient, time. Hopefully, you might be inspired to try some of them out with learners or with professional colleagues. At the end of the chapter there are commentaries and/or hints on many of the tasks.

## What is geometry?

The word 'geometry' comes from two ancient Greek words, one meaning earth and the other meaning to measure. These Greek words, as well as the word 'geometry', may themselves be derived from the Sanskrit word *Jyamiti* (in Sanskrit, *Jy a* means an arc or curve and *Miti* means correct perception or measurement). The origins of geometry are very ancient (it is probably the oldest branch of mathematics) with several ancient cultures (including Indian, Babylonian, Egyptian and Chinese, as well as Greek) developing a form of geometry suited to the relationships between lengths, areas, and volumes of physical objects. In these ancient times, geometry was used in the measure of land (or, as we would say today, surveying) and in the construction of religious and cultural artefacts. Examples include the Hindu Vedas, which are thought to have been composed between 4000 BCE[2] and 3100 BCE, the ancient Egyptian pyramids, Celtic knots (see Task 8.2), and many more examples. Sources of further information on the geometry of some religious and cultural artefacts are given in the commentary to Task 8.2.

## Task 8.2

The Celts were a dominant force in Europe during the fourth and fifth centuries BCE. Intricately designed jewellery and illustrations in texts such as the 'Book of Kells', survive as examples of Celtic knot patterns.

- Work out how to construct these relatively simple Celtic knot patterns.
- Find other examples of the use of geometry in cultural and religious artefacts.

Around 300 BCE much of the accumulated knowledge of geometry was codified in a text that became known as Euclid's *Elements*. In the thirteen books that comprise the *Elements*, and on the basis of ten axioms and postulates, several hundred theorems were proved by deductive logic. The *Elements* came to epitomise the axiomatic-deductive method for many centuries. It is likely that no work, except perhaps the Christian Bible, has been more widely used, edited, or studied, and probably no work has exercised a greater influence on scientific thinking. While some parchments do exist from the ninth century, it is said that over a thousand editions of Euclid's *Elements* have appeared since the first printed edition in 1482, and for more than two millennia this work dominated all aspects of geometry, including its teaching.

In the nineteenth century, geometry, like most academic disciplines, went through a period of growth that was near cataclysmic in proportion. Since then the content of geometry and its internal diversity has increased almost beyond recognition. The geometry of Euclid became no more than a subspecies of the vast family of mathematical theories of space. If you do a search for geometry using the web version of the *Encyclopaedia Britannica* (www.britannica.com), you get the following message: did you mean differential geometry, hyperbolic geometry, Lobachevskian geometry, projective geometry, elliptic geometry, algebraic geometry, Euclidean geometry, analytic geometry, plane geometry, Riemannian geometry or coordinate geometry? It is possible today to classify more than 50 geometries (see Malkevitch, 1991). This illustrates the richness of modern geometry but, at the same time, creates a fundamental problem for curriculum designers: what geometry should be included in the mathematics curriculum?

---

**Task 8.3**

Find out something about the contribution of some (or all) of these mathematicians to the development of geometry:

| | | |
|---|---|---|
| René Descartes | Isaac Newton | Leonhard Euler |
| Max Noether | Jean Victor Poncelet | Bernhard Riemann |
| Lobachevsky and Bolyai | Felix Klein | Sophus Lie |
| Luitzen Brouwer | | |

---

The question of what geometry to include can be applied to the curriculum at any level, from pre-school to (university) graduate school. In order to approach this problem it is worth returning to the question of what is geometry and also to consider the aims of teaching geometry.

A useful contemporary definition of geometry is that attributed to the highly-respected British mathematician, Sir Christopher Zeeman: 'geometry comprises those branches of mathematics that exploit visual intuition (the most dominant of our senses) to remember theorems, understand proof, inspire conjecture, perceive reality, and give global insight' (Royal Society/JMC 2001). These are transferable skills that are needed for (but not taught by) all other branches of mathematics (and science). The Royal Society/Joint Mathematical Council report suggests that the aims of teaching geometry can be summarised as follows:

a  to develop spatial awareness, geometric intuition and the ability to visualise;
b  to provide a breadth of geometrical experiences in two and three dimensions;
c  to develop knowledge and understanding of and the ability to use geometrical properties and theorems;
d  to encourage the development and use of conjecture, deductive reasoning and proof;
e  to develop skills of applying geometry through modelling and problem-solving in real world contexts;
f  to develop useful ICT skills in specifically geometrical contexts;
g  to engender a positive attitude to mathematics; and
h  to develop an awareness of the historical and cultural heritage of geometry in society, and of the contemporary applications of geometry.

Given the above definition of geometry, and a consideration of the aims of teaching geometry, it is possible to say why it should be included in the school mathematics curriculum.

## Why include geometry in the school mathematics curriculum?

The study of geometry contributes to helping students develop the skills of visualisation, critical thinking, intuition, perspective, problem-solving, conjecturing, deductive reasoning, logical argument and proof. Geometric representations can be used to help students make sense of other areas of mathematics: fractions and multiplication in arithmetic, the relationships between the graphs of functions (of both two and three variables) and graphical representations of data in statistics. Spatial reasoning is important in other curriculum areas as well as mathematics: science, geography, art, design and technology. Working with practical equipment can also help develop fine motor skills.

Geometry provides a culturally and historically rich context within which to do mathematics. There are many interesting, sometimes surprising or counter-intuitive results in geometry that can stimulate students to want to know more and to understand why. Presenting geometry in a way that stimulates curiosity and encourages exploration can enhance students' learning and their attitudes towards mathematics. Encouraging students to discuss problems in geometry, articulate their ideas and develop clearly structured arguments to support their intuitions can lead to enhanced communication skills and recognition of the importance of proof. The contribution of mathematics to students' spiritual, moral, social and cultural development can be effectively realised through geometry. As mentioned above, some ideas for using geometry to support spiritual and cultural development can be found in the references included in the commentary to Task 8.2. Useful sources of material for supporting moral and social development can be found in the publications of the Stapleford Centre in Nottingham (for example, the Charis Mathematics resources for Key Stages 3 and 4), the 'Summing up the World' series from Development Education in Dorset, and the Maths and Human Rights Resources Book published by Amnesty International. See the Appendix for more details of other resources supporting the teaching and learning of geometry.

Geometry is a rich source of opportunities for developing notions of proof. While more is said about this in a later section, it is worth emphasising that visual images, particularly those that can be manipulated on the computer screen, invite students to observe and conjecture generalisations. To prove conjectures students need to understand how the observed images are related to one another and are linked to fundamental 'building blocks'. In dynamic geometry software (see Task 8.6 and the Appendix) understanding observed images means working with points, circles and parallel and perpendicular lines. In the programming language Logo, it involves understanding the way in which the 'turtle' moves (see Task 8.7 and the Appendix).

We live on a solid planet in a three-dimensional world and, as much of our experience is through visual stimulus, this means that the ability to interpret visual information is fundamental to human existence. To develop an understanding of how spatial phenomena are related and to apply that understanding with confidence to solve problems and make sense of novel situations has to be part of the educational experience of all students. Geometry offers a rich way of developing visualisation skills. Visualisation allows students a way of exploring mathematical and other problems without the need to produce accurate diagrams or use symbolic representations. Manipulating images in the head can inspire confidence and develop intuitive understanding of spatial situations. Sharing personal visual images can help to develop communication skills as well as enabling students to see that there are often many ways of interpreting an image or a written or spoken description.

Much of our cultural life is visual. Aesthetic appreciation of art, architecture, music and many artefacts involves geometric principles – symmetry, perspective, scale, orientation, and so on. Understanding many scientific principles and technological phenomena also requires geometric awareness, as do navigation, orienteering and map-reading. Recognition of the familiar and the unfamiliar requires an ability to characterise and note key features.

Numerous current applications of mathematics have a strong geometric component. In many cases, the problem includes getting 'geometric' information into a computer in a useful format, solving geometric problems and outputting this solution as a visual or spatial form, as a design to be built, as an action to be executed, or as an image to entertain. Solving these problems requires substantial geometric knowledge. Here, briefly, are a few illustrative examples as suggested by Whitely (1999):

*Computer Aided Design and Geometric Modeling* A basic problem is to describe, design, modify, or manufacture the shapes we want: cars, planes, buildings, manufactured components, etc. using computers. The descriptions need to be accurate enough to control the manufacturing directly and to permit simulation and testing of the objects, usually prior to making any physical models. Indeed, for example, the most recent Boeing aeroplane was entirely designed using computers, without the use of any physical models.

*Robotics* To use a robot, we must input (using cameras, sensors, etc.) a geometric model of the environment. The whole issue of the geometric vocabulary used (e.g. solid modelling, polyhedral approximations, etc.) and how the information is structured, is a major area of research in a field called 'computational geometry'.

*Medical Imaging* Generating non-intrusive measurements (usually some form of picture) requires the construction of an adequate three-dimensional image of parts of the body. This can involve, for example, a series of projections or images from ultra-sound, or magnetic resonance imaging (MRI) from several directions or points. This raises questions about how many measurements are needed to construct the full three-dimensional image and what algorithm can be used to reconstruct the full image from the pieces. Such questions have led to some substantial new results in fields such as geometric tomography.

*Computer Animation and Visual Presentations* How can the computer generate sufficiently rich images to fool our human perceptions of the static form and the moving objects? One of the computer scientists / geometers who worked on the full-length animation video 'A Bug's Life' described it as an 'exercise in handling texture and modeling clothing with new levels of mathematics'. New mathematics with a geometric base, such as fractals, is a part of this work. So is geometric modelling.

Further areas where geometric problems arise are in chemistry (computational chemistry and the shapes of molecules), material physics (modelling various forms of glass and aggregate materials), biology (modelling of proteins, 'docking' of drugs on other molecules), Geographic Information Systems (GIS), and most fields of engineering. Task 8.4 provides an opportunity to explore one of these developments.

---

### Task 8.4

GPS, or global positioning system, is a satellite navigation system operated by the US Department of Defense.

- Find out how GPS works.

- Investigate another modern application of geometry.

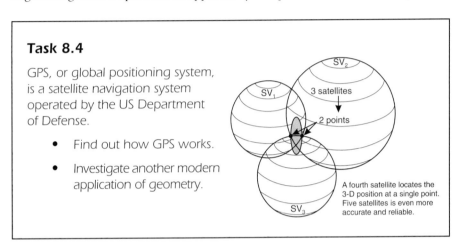

3 satellites

2 points

A fourth satellite locates the 3-D position at a single point. Five satellites is even more accurate and reliable.

---

As shown above, there are a whole host of reasons why geometry should be a major part of the learning experience of mathematics at all levels. There is also a whole range of geometry to consider. The question remains: what geometry should be included in the mathematics curriculum? We examine this question more closely in the next section.

## The geometry curriculum

Mention geometry and school in the same sentence to anyone who was at secondary school before 1970 and it means only one thing: geometry in the Euclidean tradition. In fact, up to around the turn of the twentieth century, for those who were able to attend school, it meant Euclid as written by Euclid, perhaps in an English translation but possibly as translated into Latin (probably dating from the fifteenth or sixteenth century), or even in the original Greek. Given that the books of Euclid were primarily an orderly compilation of what was known about geometry and arithmetic at the time they were written (around 300 BCE), and not a teaching programme as we know it today, the use of Euclid's *Elements* as a school textbook was not without problems. Indeed, the forerunner of the UK Mathematical Association was formed in 1871 as the Association for the Improvement of Geometry Teaching. A major issue of the time was whether or not any required proof *had* to be reproduced by students *exactly* in the form given in Euclid (including in the order the proof occurred in Euclid). For very many pupils their experience of geometry was far from positive.

As Euclidean geometry lost its status as the only geometry, following the work on other geometries, by the middle of the twentieth-century it became of little more than historic interest at university research level. Other geometries became the object of research. Then, in the wake of the launch of the Sputnik by the Soviets in 1957, a major revision of school mathematics (and science) was begun in most western countries. One of the reform ideas was to base much more of school mathematics on the idea of function and to aim more at the mathematics that would lead to calculus and linear algebra. The room for this innovation was made by reformulating all parts of the mathematics curriculum, but the practical effect seemed to be to remove solid geometry and to convert the trigonometry component into part of a course about functions. The impact of these changes was to reduce the amount of geometry while, at the same time, increasing the emphasis on coordinate geometry and introducing some elements of transformation geometry and topology. As a result the amount of geometry taught in the Euclidean fashion steadily declined.

For students completing secondary school in the UK since around 1970, their experience of geometry is likely to have been quite varied. While it is difficult to be precise about the form of geometry teaching practised at that time (due to a lack of good evidence), a review of geometry in the mathematics curriculum published in 1977 (Willson, 1977, p. vi) set out 'to show that the introduction of modern transformation geometry does not rule out the teaching of more traditional Euclidean type proofs, and indicates some of the many fruitful points of contact between the two areas'. Thus it is likely that geometry in the Euclidean fashion persisted in some places, while in others approaches based on transformations dominated. Popular textbooks of the time, including those produced by the School Mathematics Project favoured the transformations approach.

To illustrate that various approaches can be used to prove theorems in plane geometry, you might like to tackle Task 8.5. The aim of the task is to see how many different, but valid, proofs you can find for the theorem that the angle in a semicircle is invariant and that it is equal to 90°. The theorem is often referred to as Thales' theorem, after Thales of Miletus in Greek Ionia who died in about 546 BCE, and who is credited with the first known proof.

---

## Task 8.5

One of the surprising results in plane geometry is that the angle in a semicircle is invariant and that it is equal to 90°.

- See how many proofs you can find for this theorem.

Your proofs could be Euclidean, use transformation geometry, analytic (coordinate) geometry, complex numbers, or vectors.

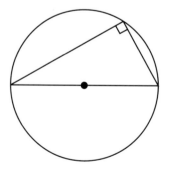

The introduction of the National Curriculum for school mathematics in the UK in 1988 reflected the developing practice in the teaching of geometry. The specification focused primarily on plane geometry, covering aspects of the Euclidean, transformation and coordinate approaches to geometrical objects and problems. There was also a little bit of topology. Reflecting this wide view of geometry, the specification was called 'Shape and Space'.

Since 1988 the curriculum has been revised a number of times. If one wanted to be particularly unkind one could conclude that the 2000 version of the curriculum for shape, space and measure for England is a strange mixture of smatterings of antique geometric construction (using a ruler and protractor is required by law!), nineteenth-century arithmetic, 1950s' grammar school geometry, and 1970s' SMP-style transformation geometry. Coordinate geometry, by contrast, is negligible as is explicit development of spatial awareness and skills in visualisation. A more generous perspective might be to observe that, given the rich diversity that is geometry (as mentioned above, it is possible to categorise more than 50 geometries within mathematics), the 11–16 age-range curriculum attempts to introduce pupils to a variety of important approaches to the study of the Cartesian plane.

For students in the 16–19 age-range, there is even less geometry than in the 11–16 mathematics curriculum. The core curriculum specification for 2000 onwards has a section entitled 'coordinate geometry' but the specification is actually about the algebraic formulae for straight lines and circles. Similarly, while there is a section headed 'vectors', the specification is predominantly algebraic (with 'geometrical interpretation'). Information is less readily available about the amount of geometry taught in higher education. Some university mathematicians have called for more geometry to be taught at university level (and by geometers rather than logicians or historians of mathematics). It is unclear how much success they have had (for example, see Mathematical Association, 1993). It is certainly unhelpful to expect teachers to teach geometry competently given that they are likely to have studied little geometry since the age of 16 (and maybe not much even then).

There is little doubt that the driving force behind curricular decisions in high school mathematics is the goal of preparing students for the study of calculus. A great deal of the manipulative skill in algebra, trigonometry and analytic geometry is clearly prized because of its usefulness in calculus, or at least calculus as it has been traditionally conceived. Geometry, in its many guises, gets neglected, with spatial intuition and visualisation being particularly so. An emphasis on numeracy, through initiatives such as the National Strategy for Key Stage 3, may only serve to reduce the coverage of geometry in schools just at the time when geometrical education has so much to offer the education of students.

Given the curriculum, we now turn to how best to teach it.

## Teaching and learning geometry

There is a considerable amount of research in mathematics education that concerns the teaching and learning of geometry. It is neither sensible nor feasible to attempt to summarise it all (for a comprehensive review, see Clements 2000). Instead a selection of issues is addressed in the following pages, covering theories of geometric thinking, learning, and teaching.

## Theories of learning geometry

Of the range of theoretical work concerned with geometrical ideas, that of Piaget (and colleagues) and of van Hiele are probably the most well known. The Piagetian work has two major themes. The first theme is that our mental representation of space is not a perceptual 'reading off' of what is around us. Rather, we build up from our mental representation of our world through progressively reorganising our prior active manipulation of that environment. Second, the progressive organisation of geometric ideas follows a definite order and this order is more experiential (and possibly more mathematically logical) than it is historical. That is, initially topological relations, such as connectedness, enclosure and continuity, are constructed, followed by projective (rectilinearity) and Euclidean (angularity, parallelism and distance) relations. The first of these Piagetian themes, concerning the process of the formation of spatial representations, remains reasonably well supported by research. The second hypothesis has received, at best, mixed support. The available evidence suggests that all types of geometric ideas appear to develop over time, becoming increasingly integrated and synthesised.

The van Hiele model also suggests that learners advance through levels of thought in geometry. Van Hiele characterised these levels as visual, descriptive, abstract/relational and formal deduction. At the first level, students identify shapes and figures according to their concrete examples. At the second level, students identify shapes according to their properties, and here a student might think of a rhombus as a figure with four equal sides. At the third level, students can identify relationships between classes of figures (for example, that a square is a special form of rectangle) and can discover properties of classes of figures by simple logical deduction. At the fourth level, students can produce a short sequence of statements to justify a conclusion logically and can understand that deduction is the method of establishing geometric truth. According to this model, progress from one of van Hiele's levels to the next is more dependent upon teaching method than on age. Given traditional teaching methods, research suggests that most lower secondary students perform at levels 1 or 2 with almost 40 per cent of students completing secondary school below level 2. The explanation for this, according to the van Hiele model, is that teachers are asked to teach a curriculum that is at a higher level than the students.

According to the van Hiele model it is not possible for learners to bypass a level. They cannot see what the teacher sees in a geometric situation and therefore do not gain from such teaching. While research is generally supportive of the van Hiele levels as useful in describing students' geometric concept development (in the absence of anything better), it remains uncertain how well the theory reflects children's mental representations of geometric concepts. Various problems have been identified with the specification of the levels: for example, that the labelling of the lowest level as 'visual' when visualisation is demanded at all the levels; and the fact that learners appear to show signs of thinking from more than one level in the same or different tasks, in different contexts. An integral component of the van Hiele model is a specified teaching approach involving four phases. There is little research on this aspect of the model and hence little idea whether it is successful.

## Key ideas in teaching and learning geometry

In order to teach geometry most effectively, and give some coherence to classroom tasks, it is helpful if, in your preparation and teaching, you keep in mind, and highlight where appropriate, key ideas in geometry. These include:

*Invariance* In 1872, the mathematician Felix Klein revolutionised geometry by defining it as the study of the properties of a configuration that are invariant under a set of transformations. Examples of invariance propositions are all the plane angle theorems (such as Thales' theorem in Task 8.5), and the theorems involving triangles (such as the sum of the angles of a plane triangle is 180°). Pupils do not always find it straightforward to determine which particular properties are invariant. The use of dynamic geometry software (see Task 8.6) can be very useful in this respect.

*Symmetry* Symmetry, of course, is not only a key idea in geometry but throughout mathematics, yet it is in geometry that it achieves its most immediacy. Technically, symmetry can be thought of as a transformation of a mathematical object which leaves some property invariant. Symmetry is frequently used to make arguments simpler, and usually more powerful. An example from plane geometry is that all of the essential properties of a parallelogram can be derived from the fact that a parallelogram has half-turn symmetry around the point of intersection of the diagonals. Symmetry is also a key organising principle in mathematics. For example, probably the best way of defining quadrilaterals (*except* for the general trapezium, which is not an essential quadrilateral in any case, since there are no interesting theorems involving the trapezium that do not also hold for general quadrilaterals) is via their symmetries.

*Transformation* Transformation permits students to develop broad concepts of congruence and similarity and apply them to all figures. For example, congruent figures are always related by a reflection, rotation, slide or glide reflection. Studying transformations can enable students to realise that photographs are geometric objects, that all parabolas are similar because they can be mapped onto each other, that the graphs of $y = \cos x$ and $y = \sin x$ are congruent, that matrices have powerful geometric applications, and so on. Transformations also play a major role in artwork of many cultures – for example, they appear in pottery patterns, tilings, and friezes.

## The teaching and learning of proof in geometry

While the deductive method is central to mathematics and is intimately involved in the development of geometry, providing a meaningful experience of deductive reasoning for students at school appears to be difficult. Research invariably shows that students fail to see a need for proof and are unable to distinguish between different forms of mathematical reasoning such as explanation, argument, verification and proof. For example, a large-scale survey in the US found that only about 30 per cent of students completing full-year geometry courses that taught proof reached a 75 per cent mastery level in proof writing. Even high-achieving students have been found to get little meaningful mathematics out of the traditional, proof-oriented high school geometry course. Corresponding difficulties with proof have also been found with mathematics graduates. A number of reasons have been put forward for these student difficulties with proof. Amongst these reasons are that learning to prove requires the coordination of a range of competencies each of which is, individually, far from trivial, that teaching approaches tend to concentrate on verification and devalue or omit exploration and explanation, and that learning to prove involves students making the difficult transition from a computational view of mathematics to a view that conceives of mathematics as a field of intricately related structures. Further reasons are that students are asked to prove using concepts to which they have just been introduced and to prove things that appear to be so obvious that they cannot distinguish by intuition the given from what is to be proved.

Nevertheless, despite the sheer complexity of learning to prove and the wealth of evidence suggesting how difficult it can be for students, there are a few studies that show that students can learn to argue mathematically. One promising approach is that being developed by de Villiers (see de Villiers, 1999). De Villiers points out that, in addition to explanation, proof has a range of functions, including communication, discovery, intellectual challenge, verification, systematisation and so on. These various functions, de Villiers argues, have to be communicated to students in an effective way if proof and proving are to be meaningful activities for them. In fact, de Villiers suggests that it is likely to be meaningful to introduce the various functions of proof to students more or less in the sequence shown in Figure 8.1.

Explanation ⟶ Discovery ⟶ Intellectual challenge ⟶ Verification ⟶ Systemisation

**Figure 8.1** *The likely learning sequence of functions of mathematical proof*

Focusing on explanation, de Villiers argues, should counteract students becoming accustomed to seeing geometry as just an accumulation of empirically discovered facts in which explanation plays no role.

## Resources for the teaching and learning of geometry

There can be a tendency to teach geometry by informing students of the properties associated with plane or solid shapes, requiring them to learn the properties and then to complete exercises which show that they have learned the facts. Such an approach can mean that little attempt is made to encourage students to make logical connections and explain their reasoning. Whilst it is important that students have a good knowledge of geometrical facts, if they are to develop their spatial thinking and geometrical intuition, a variety of approaches are beneficial. For example, some facts can be introduced informally, others developed deductively or found through exploration.

To teach geometry effectively to students of any age or ability, it is important to ensure that students understand the concepts they are learning and the steps that are involved in particular processes rather than solely learning rules. More effective teaching approaches encourage students to recognise connections between different ways of representing geometric ideas and between geometry and other areas of mathematics. The evidence suggests that this is likely to help students to retain knowledge and skills and enable them to approach new geometrical problems with some confidence.

When planning approaches to teaching and learning geometry, it is important to ensure that the provision in the early years of secondary school encourages students to develop an enthusiasm for the subject by providing opportunities to investigate spatial ideas and solve real-life problems. There is also a need to ensure that there is a good understanding of the basic concepts and language of geometry in order to provide foundations for future work and to enable students to consider geometric problems and communicate ideas. Students should be encouraged to use descriptions, demonstrations and justifications in order to develop the reasoning skills and confidence needed to underpin the development of an ability to follow and construct geometric proofs.

At Key Stage 4, for many students, the teaching of geometry requires similar teaching approaches to those used in earlier years. A formal, deductive approach to learning geometry needs to be treated with great care if it is to be appropriate for all pupils. With more able students it is possible to encourage a greater understanding of the need for definitions and of the laws of deductive logic. This can include notions of the place of axioms, an appreciation of the importance of proof, understanding of some proofs and the ability to construct simple proofs themselves. For all students, there should be an emphasis on problem-solving involving real-life applications of geometrical skills. See the Appendix for some sources of materials on geometrical problem-solving.

The geometry in the National Curriculum for Key Stages 3 and 4 can be taught making little use of practical resources but this is not necessarily the best way of doing so. It is useful to consider geometry as a practical subject and provide opportunities for students to use a range of resources to explore and investigate properties of shapes and geometrical facts. Particular consideration should be given to ways in which the ICT resources, which are increasingly available in schools, can be used to enhance the teaching and learning of geometry. The use of dynamic geometry enables the teacher or individual students to generate and manipulate geometrical diagrams quickly and explore relationships using a range of examples. Task 8.6 involves using dynamic geometry software to explore the various 'centres' of a triangle. While use of such software can enliven geometry teaching it should be noted that it is not always clear what interpretations students make of geometrical objects encountered in this way (see Jones, 1999). There is also the possibility that the opportunity afforded by the software of testing a myriad of diagrams through use of the 'drag' function, or of confirming conjectures through measurements (that also adjust as the figure is dragged), may *reduce* the perceived need for deductive proof (Hoyles and Jones, 1998).

## Task 8.6

Use dynamic geometry software to construct the circumcircle of a triangle such that the figure is invariant when any object used in its construction is dragged (using the mouse).

- What other 'centres' of the triangle can you find?

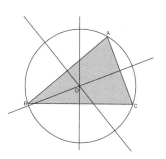

Other software can also be invaluable. Logo can be used to describe journeys and investigate properties of shapes (see Task 8.7). Graph-drawing packages are useful for coordinate and transformation geometry. All of these resources can be used individually by students or for whole-class lessons using an interactive whiteboard.

## Task 8.7

Use Logo to construct designs such as these.

- What geometry are you doing?

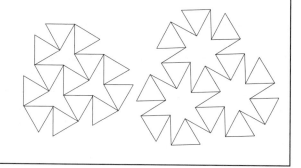

## Concluding comments

Geometry is the part of the mathematics curriculum where it is possible to have the most fun. It is visual, intuitive, creative and demanding. Use your imagination and tap into that of your pupils. Create striking classroom displays, suspend geometrical models from the ceiling of your classroom, involve your pupils in making things and imagining things, get them to decide on definitions and then explore the logical consequences. Too many students vote with their feet and choose to give up studying mathematics. Geometry can help to keep them engaged.

New developments in computing technology mean that the twenty-first century will be one where spatial thinking and visualisation are vital. Geometry is where those all-important skills are nurtured. Engage with geometry yourself and get your pupils thinking geometrically.

## Postscript: a few geometrical jokes

Here are a few jokes with a geometric flavour. They may amuse you and you might find them useful at some point (although there is no guarantee that anyone else will find them funny).

What do you say when you see an empty parrot cage?
*Polygon*

What do you call a crushed angle?
*A rectangle*

What do you call an angle that is adorable?
*Acute angle*

What do you call a man who spent all summer at the beach?
*Tangent*

What do you call people who are in favour of tractors?
*Protractors*

## Commentaries and/or hints on tasks

*Task 8.1: Which way did the bicycle go?*  If you have tried the hints given with this task and are still stuck then you are likely to be aware that this is not that easy a problem. Indeed, the idea is to challenge you and get you interested in such problems. Hopefully you have had the opportunity to discuss the problems with others. A further (big) hint is to think about the geometry of the bicycle frame. Bicycle wheels are, at all times, tangent to the curve they make as a track. The frame of the bike is a direct extension of the tangent vector from the back wheel. So, it is a straight-line segment extending out from the back wheel to the point just above where the front wheel is tangent to the other curve.

Thus, given any position of the rear wheel, and a selected direction of travel, you know where the front wheel is at the same time. (Extend the tangent vector until it crosses the other curve). If you move this rear wheel along one curve you see a series of measurements for the length of the part of the bicycle frame called the 'top tube'. Are the measurements constant? If they are *not* constant, you are looking at an impossible path for the bike.

For more on the mathematics of bicycles see: Whitt *et al.* (1984) *Bicycling Science*, Cambridge, MA: The MIT Press.

*Task 8.2: Celtic knots*  Probably the best thing to do is consult a resource which gives details of how to construct Celtic knot patterns, such as *Celtic Knotwork*, by Iain Bain, Constable and Company, 1986 (although you could start with a grid with an even number of squares in both directions and place dots at alternate vertices, making sure to miss the corners).

*The Book of Kells* is housed in the Library of Trinity College Dublin and is one of the most sumptuously illustrated manuscripts to have survived from the early Middle Ages in Europe. It was completed in 800 CE and contains transcriptions of the four Gospels, lavishly illustrated and ornamented.

Other examples of the use of geometry in cultural and religious artefacts include:

- Moorish and Islamic architecture and design (perhaps the most famous example being the Alhambra Palace in Granada in southern Spain). See, for example, El-Said *et al.* (1987) *Geometrical Concepts in Islamic Art*, Palo Alto, CA: Dale Seymour Publications.
- The tradition of sand drawings in Africa south of the Equator (see, for example, Gerdes, P. (1998) 'On possible uses of traditional Angolan sand drawings in the mathematics classroom', *Educational Studies in Mathematics*, 19: 3–22).
- Weaving patterns from many cultures (for example, Knight, G. (1984) 'The geometry of Maori art: weaving patterns', *New Zealand Mathematics Magazine*, 213): 80–6).

Many more examples can be found in publications such as Lawlor, R. (1992) *Sacred Geometry: philosophy and practice*, London: Thames and Hudson, and in the chapter on native American geometry in Michael Closs (ed.) (1986) *Native American Mathematics*, Austin, TX: University of Texas Press: 387–407. Some fascinating (and difficult) geometrical problems have been found in Japanese Temples written on wooden tablets. The oldest one in existence dates from 1683, see: Fukagawa, H. and Pedoe, D. (1989) *Japanese Temple Geometry Problems*, Winnipeg, Canada: Charles Babbage Research Foundation.

*Task 8.3: the development of geometry* Among the developments you should be able to find out about are:

- the development of analytic geometry, in which algebraic notation and procedures are used for the description of geometric objects;
- the study and classification of conic sections and other families of plane curves and the solution of problems involving them;
- how the problem of perspective (in painting and other areas) became the basis of projective geometry;
- how the field of differential geometry was initiated (by providing analytic expressions for the length of arc and the curvature of plane curves and, subsequently, surfaces) and how these ideas were generalised to spaces of any number of dimensions;
- the development of non-Euclidean geometry;
- the classification of geometries;
- the development of topology.

*Task 8.4: What is GPS (and how does it work)?* The GPS system relies on 24 satellites that orbit the earth twice each day. The distribution of these near circular orbits is even, such that they provide a uniform net around the entire surface of the earth. At any location, at any point in time, up to ten of these satellites may be 'visible' to a receiver of GPS signals. The satellites orbit the earth at a speed of about 4 km s$^{-1}$ at a height of a little over 20 000 km. They are orbiting radio transmitters and the user's GPS instrument is a receiver. The signals from a number of satellites are received and processed by the GPS to provide position, height and time information. The process involves calculating the distance to each of the satellites in range and the intersection of circles produced using those calculated radii (as shown in the diagram accompanying this task). For more information, see GPSCO (1998) *Exploring GPS. A GPS users guide*, The Global Positioning System Consortium.

For information on some other modern application of geometry (and other mathematical topics) try: Savage *et al.* (1999 5th edn) *For All Practical Purposes: mathematical literacy in today's world*, W.H. Freeman and Co.

*Task 8.5: The angle in a semicircle* There are any number of proofs of the theorem that that angle in a semicircle is 90°. These can be of the Euclidean (synthetic geometry) form, use transformation geometry, analytic (coordinate) geometry, complex numbers or vectors. As long as it is a valid proof, no one method is a priori superior to any other. For examples of such proofs see: Willson, 1977, p. 122–3, or Barbeau, E.J. (1988) 'Which method is best?', *Mathematics Teacher*, February 1988: 87–90.

For more than 350 different proofs of Pythagoras' theorem, see Loomis, E.S. (1968) *The Pythagorean Proposition*, National Council of Teachers of Mathematics.

*Task 8.6: A dynamic circumcircle* At its simplest, dynamic geometry software allows the user to create and then manipulate points, lines and circles on a computer screen. Some points and lines may be created so that they are freely movable. These are referred to as the 'basic' objects. Other objects can be created using geometric relationships with these basic objects, such as the midpoint or perpendicular bisector of a line, or the bisector of an angle. Any such relationships created in this way are maintained consistently when any basic object is dragged using the mouse. See the Appendix for some details on different versions of dynamic geometry software.

There are many defined 'centres' of a triangle. For a comprehensive discussion, see the Encyclopedia of Triangle Centers at http://cedar.evansville.edu/~ck6/encyclopedia/

*Task 8.7: Designs on Logo* Logo is the term used to describe a range of programs that in various ways provide the user with the means of controlling the movement of an object on the screen (the 'turtle'). As Seymour Papert (credited as the inventor of Logo) described it: powerful ideas in mind-sized bites. The controls consist of some simple instructions such as fd 40, bk 30, lt 90, rt 60. See the Appendix for some details on different versions of Logo.

## Acknowledgments

I would like to record my appreciation to the following people with whom I've had the pleasure of sharing many ideas on the teaching and learning of geometry:

Members of the Geometry Working Group of the British Society for Research into Learning Mathematics (BSRLM). Reports of the working group are available in the proceedings of the BSRLM, see www.bsrlm.ac.uk.

Colleagues I have had the privilege of working with on the Royal Society / Joint Mathematical Council inquiry into the teaching and learning of geometry.

A group of prospective secondary mathematics teachers I had the pleasure of working with on aspects of the teaching and learning of geometry while on secondment to the mathematics education unit in the Department of Mathematics at the University of Auckland, New Zealand, during the second half of 2000.

## Notes

1   This use of this example of geometry was inspired by a course on 'Geometry and the Imagination', led by some of the greatest mathematicians of our time, John Conway, Peter Doyle, Jane Gilman and Bill Thurston at the Geometry Center in Minneapolis, USA, June 17-28, 1991.

2   BCE is the acronym for 'before the common era'. BCE and CE (common era) are increasingly being used to denote years as used across the world, in place of the solely Christian BC (before Christ) and AD (*anno Domini*, Latin for the year of [the] Lord).

## Appendix

### Some resources for teaching geometry

The information below is designed to support some of the ideas in this chapter. Space does not allow for a comprehensive list. Some further resources are given with the commentaries of some of the tasks in the chapter (see above).

Tarquin Publications (Stradbroke, Diss, Norfolk, IP21 5JP) are a good source of materials for teaching geometry. Examples include:

*Mathematics in Three Dimensions*
*3-D Geoshapes and Polydron*
*Escher, Illusions & Perception*
*Geometrical Pattern Making*
*Tilings & Tessellations*
*Paper Engineering & Pop-ups*
*DIME 3-D Visualising & Thinking*
*Tangrams, Pentacubes & Pentominoes*

Dale Seymour Publications (P.O. Box 10888, Palo Alto, California, USA) publish some useful materials, including:

*Mathematical Investigations, Books 1–3* (problem-solving tasks covering a range of mathematics, including geometry)
*Logic Geometry Problems*
*Blueprint for Geometry* (designing and building a scale model of a house)
*Designing Playgrounds*
*By Nature's Design* (geometry in nature)
*Structures: The Way Things are Built*
*Designing Environments*

*The Mind's Eye: Imagery in Everyday Life*
*Real-Life Math Problem Solving* by Mark Illingworth (Scholastic, 1996) contains a
   number of problems involving geometrical ideas.

Dynamic Geometry Software
   *Cabri* is available from Texas Instruments.
   *SketchPad* is available from Key Curriculum Press.

Logo
   *WinLogo* and *SuperLogo*, a new version for Windows, are available from Longman
      Logotron.
   *LogoWriter* and *MicroWorlds Logo* are produced by Logo Computer Systems Inc.
   *StarLogo* is produced by the Media Lab at MIT, Boston, USA.

Note: all websites mentioned in this chapter were correct at the time of going to
print.

## References

Clements, D. (2000) 'Teaching and learning geometry' in Kilparick, J. (ed.) *Research
   Companion to the NCTM Standards for Mathematics*, Reston, VA: NCTM.
de Villiers, M. (1999) *Rethinking Proof with Geometer's Sketchpad*, CA: Key Curriculum
   Press.
Hoyles, C. and Jones, K. (1998) 'Proof in dynamic geometry contexts' in C. Mammana
   and V. Villani (eds) *Perspectives on the Teaching of Geometry for the 21st Century*,
   Dordrecht: Kluwer.
Jones, K. (1999) 'Students' interpretations of a dynamic geometry environment' in I.
   Schwank (ed.) *European Research in Mathematics Education*, Osnabrück: Forschungs-
   institut für Mathematikdidaktik.
Malkevitch, J. (ed.) (1991) *Geometry's Future*, Arlington, MA: COMAP.
Mathematical Association (1993) *Geometry in the Undergraduate Syllabus: report from
   Group III, mathematical content at university*, Leicester: Mathematical Association.
Royal Society/Joint Mathematical Council (2001) *On Geometry Education Teaching
   and Learning pre-19*, London: Royal Society/Joint Mathematical Council.
Whitely, W. (1999) 'The decline and rise of geometry in 20th century North
   America', *Proceedings of the 1999 Conference of the Mathematics Education Study Group
   of Canada*, St. Catharines, Ontario: Brock University.
Willson, W.W. (1977) *The Mathematics Curriculum: geometry*, Glasgow: Blackie/
   Schools Council.

# 9 Probability and randomness
## Dave Pratt

## Introduction

Pascal, in correspondence with Fermat in 1654, first set out the principles of the *theory of probabilities* in response to a request from Chevalier de Mere for some advice about how to play certain gambling games. Since then probability has been formalised and acknowledged as an important part of the discipline of mathematics. At the same time, the language of chance has more and more pervaded our everyday lives. Today, we hear sports commentators talking about a 50/50 ball; we hear weather forecasters announcing a 60 per cent chance of rain; health and other risks are assessed in terms of probabilities; it seems that no aspect of our daily rituals can escape the vagaries of chance. Thus, the study of probability and randomness has a relevance to children's culture that is all too difficult to find in some other mathematical domains.

Nevertheless, the National Curriculum for 2000 in Mathematics for England and Wales gives little space to probabilistic ideas. In Key Stage 2 (7–11 years), there is precisely one statement concerning probability:

> Pupils should be taught to … explore doubt and certainty and develop an understanding of probability through classroom situations; discuss events using a vocabulary that includes the words 'equally likely', 'fair', 'unfair', 'certain'.
>
> (DfEE, 1999, p. 27)

At Key Stage 3 (11–14 years), the curriculum includes the notion of a probability scale, the use and comparison of probability based on theoretical models and actual data (as in relative frequencies), and the notion that the probabilities of mutually exclusive events sum to 1. Two further statements indicate what the study of probability at this age is expected to cover:

> Pupils should be taught to … understand that if they repeat an experiment, they may – and usually will – get different outcomes, and that increasing sample size generally leads to better estimates of probability and population characteristics.
>
> (op.cit., p. 55)

Thus the curriculum suggests that around at the age of 12 years, children begin to consider informally the Law of Large Numbers.

Pupils should be taught to compare distributions and make inferences, using the shapes of distributions and measures of average and range.

(op. cit., p. 55)

Although this statement may be intended to focus on the distribution of data, I see it as related to the notion of a theoretical probability distribution. For the majority of pupils, there are no new probabilistic ideas introduced in Key Stage 4 (14–16 years). Although the minority who follow Key Stage 4 higher will study (i) adding and multiplying of probabilities, and (ii) dependent and independent events, these ideas lies outside the curriculum for the majority. Below the age of 16, no pupils are required to study conditional probability, the notion of discrete and continuous distributions, or many other aspects of probability.

Why then is the curriculum in England and Wales restricted to such a small number of ideas relating to probability when it is clear that this is an area of mathematics that impinges directly on the lives of everybody? In fact, experienced teachers will stress how difficult probability is to teach. When the curriculum relating to probability was broader, it was not unusual to see teachers resorting to formal methods, using definitions for probabilities based on sets and attempting to drill pupils into using *heuristics*, rough rules of thumb, for when to apply addition and when to apply multiplication to given probabilities. Inevitably, without a firmer basis for their understanding, many pupils applied the rule incorrectly or simply applied the wrong rule. Lack of success has led to the abandonment of probability for the majority except for a small number of fundamental ideas. Indeed, we will see that even the most basic ideas about probability and randomness are problematical.

In the next section, I will provide evidence that such ideas are not well understood amongst the population at large. The remainder of the chapter will then focus on some ideas and principles, based on insights gained from my own research, to guide the teaching of those fundamental ideas that remain in the national curriculum for the majority.

## Making sense of random experiments

Here is a short anecdote that will be recognisable to practising teachers.

A child was repeatedly tossing a coin, while each time her friend wrote down the result, a head or a tail. The teacher had asked them to count the number of heads and tails. To pass the time, the children were playing a game in which they tried to guess the next outcome before each toss. The last four results had all been tails. The teacher saw them playing the game and asked one child what the result would be after the next toss. The child said, 'Heads haven't come up now for ages. I think it will be a head this time.'

Over two decades, Kahneman and Tversky, (1982) researched how adults (mostly university students) made judgements of chance. They found that many adults made similar judgements to the child in the above anecdote and they argued that their subjects expected the results from such experiments to resemble the set of possible outcomes. According to their research the child in the anecdote may have believed that heads were under-represented in recent results and so a head was the likely outcome of the next toss 'to correct this imbalance'[1].

Kahneman and Tversky collected and categorised many heuristics that people apparently use to make judgements of chance. The following anecdote illustrates a second of their heuristics.

> Two children were about to play Ludo, a board game in which the player moves counters around a board, but the counters are not allowed to begin moving until a six is thrown. One child said, rather disconsolately, 'I don't like this game. I'm hopeless at throwing sixes.'

The child in the above anecdote was perhaps recalling playing Ludo, or games like Ludo, and remembering how often she had failed to throw a six. Her judgement of the relative frequency of such failures may have been biased by the feeling of hurt that accompanied those failures. According to Kahneman and Tversky, judgements of chance are often based on the recollection of similar events. Such judgements are subject to bias since the significance of some events makes them more easily evoked.

Now consider this anecdote from the classroom:

> A teacher had set up a circus of activities. In one corner of the classroom there was a bag containing two orange-flavoured sweets and one lemon-flavoured sweet. When Adam and Mary sat down to do this activity, the sweets were on the table. Mary placed the sweets in the bag while Adam watched. Mary shook the bag and asked Adam to pick out a sweet without looking. Before picking out the sweet, the two children discussed what flavoured sweet Adam was most likely to choose. Adam said, 'It's just a matter of luck. They are equally likely.'

LeCoutre (1992) has reported that 15- to 17-year-olds tend to assume that outcomes in a wide variety of situations are equally likely. In fact, LeCoutre found that this tendency to assume *equiprobability* was related to the chance element of the experiment; when the chance element was removed, her subjects were more likely to obtain the correct answer. LeCoutre concluded that correct cognitive models are often available but not spontaneously associated with the situations at hand.

Similarly, 10-year-old children have been found to say that, when two dice are thrown, no total is easier or harder to obtain than any other (Pratt, 2000). In the same research, when the children's attention was drawn to the combinations that made up the different totals, the children were usually able to recognise that some totals were obtainable in more ways than others. Nevertheless, it is entirely feasible that the children might still believe that all totals are equally likely.

Young children seem to recognise random experiments as involving (Pratt, 1998):

- *Unpredictability* If the next outcome is not predictable, a child might regard the experiment as random.
- *Irregularity* If there is evidently no patterned sequence in prior results, a child might refer to the experiment as random.
- *Unsteerability* If the child is unable to exert physical control over the outcome of the phenomenon, the experiment might be seen as random.

- *Fairness* If there seems to be a rough symmetry in the experiment, a child may think of the experiment as random.

At first glance, these characteristics of randomness seem largely uncontroversial and probably fit reasonably well your own intuitions. Further reflection, though, reveals three problems from the mathematical perspective.

1   In the standard mathematical view, random variables simply have associated with each value a corresponding probability. Thus, mathematically speaking, variables that are biased towards certain values are in fact random. We would not want to associate fairness with randomness too strongly as such a view is far too restrictive; a mathematical view of randomness needs to extend beyond fairness. (Note that an intuition of fairness can be seen either as an obstacle that stands in the way of a proper appreciation of distribution or as an impoverished view of distribution with the potential for enrichment.)

2   The four aspects of randomness focus entirely on immediately observable aspects of the experiment. Mathematically, the exciting property of random experiments is not so much their unpredictability in the short term but how random experiments become MORE predictable over a large number of trials, in the sense that the relative frequency of an outcome tends towards that outcome's probability. (Note that the long-term predictability of random experiments can be seen as counter-intuitive because of the unpredictability of experiments in the short-term, but I prefer to think of the attention placed on unpredictability as a means for refocusing attention on those aspects of random experiments that turn out to be predictable after all.)

3   The four characteristics of randomness can be self-contradictory. A child will regard experiments with a uniform spinner as fair and so random. The same child may regard a non-uniform spinner (i.e. one in which the sectors are not all equal in size) as unfair and so non-random. Both these spinners are largely unpredictable and unsteerable and will generate irregular results, and so in these respects the experiment with the non-uniform spinner might have been regarded as random too. Such inconsistencies do not seem apparent to many young children, who typically adopt whichever stance is cued by the most obvious characteristics of the situation in question. What stands out about the second spinner is its unfairness and so the experiment is seen as non-random.

Many researchers of randomness and probability have been struck by the inconsistency of responses by children and adults (see, for example, Konold *et al.*, 1993). It seems that children (and adults) simultaneously hold many intuitions for making sense of random experiments. In any instance, the particular intuition used to make sense of the experiment will be cued by the characteristics of that situation. The pedagogic question is: 'How do we tune children's thinking so that appropriate intuitions are used across a wide range of circumstances?' Many people think of these intuitions, with their obvious fallibilities and biases, as misconceptions – to be wiped out. In my view, these heuristics often possess grains of truth on which richer understandings can be built. I prefer to think of these intuitions as resources – to be used, built upon or finely tuned. (For a deeper analysis of this reconceptualisation of misconceptions, see Smith *et al.*, 1993). Such a view is consistent with the research, which shows how children and adults have many ways of making judgements of chance, often used inconsistently and inappropriately, but that these intuitions include the potential for normative thinking.

In the remainder of the chapter I wish to consider some principles and guidelines for building on these intuitions to encourage the development of intuitions for distribution and the Law of Large Numbers, two of the fundamental ideas remaining in the curriculum for the majority.

## Pedagogic objectives and approaches

Consider these two scenarios:

1   Two children have been asked by their teacher to roll a dice 100 times, record the results and discuss their conclusions.
2   Two children have made a game that needs a spinner containing the numbers 1, 2, 3, 4, 5 and 6. They have not yet made the spinner. The children know that their spinner should be equally likely to land on 2, 3, 4, 5 or 6. However, they need 1 to be twice as likely. Their immediate task is to design and make the spinner and then to decide whether their spinner is 'working properly'.

I wish to compare these two scenarios to illustrate some important research-based pedagogic considerations (Pratt, 1998; 2000).

## Purpose and utility

A challenge for the teacher when addressing any topic is to find an approach that is likely to generate in the child a sense of purpose that will drive and guide the child's investigation. When children find a task meaningful, they will become fully engaged and take ownership of it. Without this sense of ownership, children may complete a task as required but they will not feel any need to extend their work. In contrast, when children take ownership, they will be motivated to continue, extend or even deepen their studies. They will begin to pose their own questions simply because they want to know the answer, rather than because the teacher has asked them to do it.

All too often it seems classroom statistical activities are reduced to the monotonous collection of data, following the teacher's instructions. In the first scenario above, the children may easily complete the task without any reflection on why the experiment involved 100 throws, rather than, say, just 10. They are even less likely to question whether 100 throws is enough, or what would happen if they used a spinner – perhaps even a non-uniform spinner – instead of a dice. A lack of purpose will probably mean that scenario 1 will fail to involve the children in the extended work needed to generate intuitions for distribution or the Law of Large Numbers.

In contrast, scenario 2 is likely to generate a sense of purpose and allow the children to take ownership of the task. If the children have made their own game or have become involved in the idea of the game, they will want to make a spinner that works properly. As a result they will wish to explore data that might suggest their spinner is not working properly.

In trying to make the activity purposeful, there is a converse danger that the task is inappropriately directed. For example, there are many fun games that involve the use of probabilistic thinking implicitly to play the game well. I used an anecdote earlier in which children were playing Ludo. Most of us have played such games in the past. Playing Ludo focuses our attention on the game itself, the need to do well, to beat our opponent. We become interested in what happens here and now. Will we get the six that we need to get our counter started? The game is not in itself well directed as an instrument for reflecting on distribution and the Law of Large Numbers. The design of the task must somehow focus attention on the important mathematical ideas, without impinging on the child's sense of purpose and ownership of the task. In the case of scenario 2, the child is directed by the task towards the consideration of distribution (how the spinner is made) and how this affects the results of the spinner. If they are going to be sure that their spinner works properly, the child will also need to consider the effect of small versus large numbers of trials. In scenario 2, the child is likely to gain a *utility* for distribution and the Law of Large Numbers, a sense of how these ideas can be used in the context of making spinners.

## Testing personal conjectures

Consider this research-based anecdote (Pratt, 1998):

> Anne and Rebecca were playing with a uniform spinner, testing it by throwing the spinner about 50 times and examining the pie chart of the results. The pie chart was not uniform.

Mathematically, this outcome is not in the least surprising, since 50 trials are hardly sufficient to expect any sense of uniformity in the relative frequencies. Anne and Rebecca, however, responded to what they saw as an unfair pie chart by searching for the causes of this unfairness. In so doing, the girls proposed a series of personal conjectures that might explain the lack of fairness in the results. They needed to test out these ideas to explore their power to explain the strangeness of the pie chart.

They wondered whether the lack of fairness might be the consequence of:

- how the spinner was thrown;
- where the numbers were positioned on the spinner;
- whether some numbers (like 1) were special, and just occurred more often.

Anne and Rebecca tested each of these conjectures by setting up mini-experiments, and it was some time before they concluded that none of these factors seemed consistently to explain the lack of fairness in their results.

Typically, when children feel ownership of the task, they will want to carry out relatively prolonged investigations to find an explanation for the behaviour of their spinner. The process can be made less laborious by using technology. Anne and Rebecca used a computer to generate their graphs though a similar effect could have been obtained using a graphing calculator. Pie charts give an excellent visual check on the relative proportions and bar charts provide a means of seeing the frequencies in absolute terms (Figure 9.1).

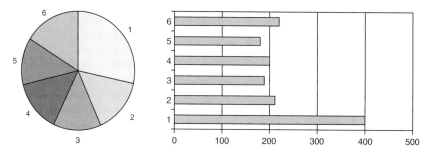

**Figure 9.1** *These two graphs were generated for data from 1400 trials of the spinner in task 2. In both the pie chart and the bar chart, it is clear that the spinner has thrown up many more 1s. However, in the pie chart, the other numbers appear to be roughly equal, whereas the bar chart tends to emphasise the differences between the frequencies of 2, 3, 4, 5 and 6. By displaying the relative frequencies, the pie chart supports an intuition of 'evening out', whereas the bar chart supports an intuition of variation.*

## Large scale experiments

In the anecdote above, Anne and Rebecca had rejected several conjectures about why the pie chart was non-uniform. What happened next? In fact, Anne and Rebecca spontaneously wondered whether they needed to throw the spinner more often. This was probably because they had seen a similar effect when tossing a coin. If it had been necessary, an intervention by the teacher would have been justified, since it was vital that they considered the effect of carrying out many trials.

It is instructive to use technology to generate pie charts at regular intervals so that the children are likely to see the pie chart tending towards the same proportions as the sample space, as more and more trials are used (Figure 9.2).

The right-hand pie chart looks remarkably like the spinner itself in scenario 2. There is the possibility here for confusion between the pie chart and the random generator. I see this connection as positive since there is a real sense in which the appearance of the spinner is a representation of the probability distribution. This linkage of the pie chart and the spinner is a specific illustration of how the distribution of relative frequencies tends towards the probability distribution as the number of trials becomes large. Thus, although there may be some initial over-simplification in children's thinking, the connection between the spinner and the pie chart has potential to become a deeper understanding of the Law of Large Numbers.

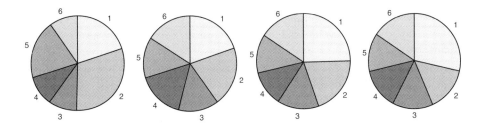

**Figure 9.2** The left-hand pie chart is generated from just 10 spins of the spinner in task 2. Gradually the number of trials is increased to 50, 100 and 1400. The proportions tend towards those in the sample space.

## Varying the context

Intuitions about distribution and the Law of Large Numbers derived from scenario 2 are likely to be highly context-dependent. For example, if the effect of a large number of trials on the pie chart is understood in terms of the equivalence of the pie chart and the spinner, what is the child meant to make of using large numbers of trials with a dice? When Anne and Rebecca followed up their work with the spinner by investigating a dice, they began by making the same sorts of personal conjectures as before and appeared to ignore the conclusions that they had made, based on their work with the spinner.

In one sense this is not surprising. Many researchers have written about the contextualised nature of mathematical knowledge (for example Lave, 1988). Indeed, if we accept that children hold many meanings for randomness simultaneously, we might suppose that longer-held intuitions would be more significant than recently-constructed ones. Intuitive ideas about the Law of Large Numbers will only be used reliably when experience has shown that the ideas work across a range of situations. (This model of intuitive knowledge in which many pieces of knowledge are held simultaneously with varying degrees of significance has been formulated by Professor Andy diSessa, see diSessa, 1988).

For example, as Anne and Rebecca continued their work with further random devices, they were increasingly willing to reject personal conjectures and they began to adopt large numbers of trials for every device (Pratt, 2000). The pedagogic implication is that children need at least two or three mathematically equivalent experiences in different contexts if recently acquired 'mathematical' intuitions are to be regarded as more important than longer-standing, less normative intuitions for random experiments.

## The role of the computer

I have found the computer to be an indispensable aid in the teaching and learning of randomness and probability. Let us examine why by reviewing the above pedagogic objectives.

Spreadsheets can handle data and carry out computations very quickly. Virtually all schools have access to spreadsheets so one might expect teachers to exploit such facilities to enable children to generate and analyse large sets of random data. In practice, the counting and grouping facilities in a spreadsheet tend to be rather clumsy and difficult to use. Nevertheless, there are interesting examples of how spreadsheets might be used to carry out probability simulations (see, for example, Bridges, 1999).

Scenario 2 above requires children to make their own spinner and to test out whether it is working properly. With 'real' spinners, it is not easy to redesign the spinner itself, but computers have the potential to enable the user to draft and redraft ideas. I have used software that offers the possibility of quickly changing what the spinner looks like and generating a new set of results.[2] By using this software, the children took ownership of the task because it was relatively easy for them to test out their personal conjectures about the behaviour of the various spinners (and other devices) that they built on the computer.

The speed of the computer makes it ideal for generating large sets of data very quickly. The child can examine what happens when many trials are carried out in a matter of minutes. Indeed the graphic facilities of a computer mean that the child does not need to divert attention towards the task of producing a graph by hand. One piece of software, Probability Simulator,[3] is particularly good for allowing the child to change the sample space and generate many results, although the software does not encourage the exploration of different contexts.

Children might reasonably argue that the computer must generate random numbers from a predefined sequence of numbers, and, since it 'knows' the next number, the experiment is not random. The children are, of course, entirely right and for that reason most people refer to random numbers generated on a computer as *pseudo-random*. I have found that when children were encouraged to play with the computerised random numbers, they failed to predict the next outcome or to discover patterns in recent results with any prolonged success, and so they began to trust that the numbers were 'random'.

I believe that, once this level of trust has been negotiated, children will treat the computer situation much as they do any conventional situation. This is not to say that they will immediately apply new intuitions constructed during the computer experience to conventional contexts. On the contrary, I would expect them to be just as unlikely to apply such newly acquired knowledge as Anne and Rebecca were when moving from one random device to another. The computer-based intuitions possess potential that will be released if the children are given the opportunity to recognise that those same intuitions explain a whole range of situations, both on and off the computer, better than many longer-held (less mathematically precise) intuitions.

## Notes

1   This is an example of 'negative recency' where the repeated occurrence of one outcome leads the subject to assign a higher likelihood for the alternative outcome. Alternatively, there is also the possibility of 'positive recency' where the subject considers the current trend to be more likely to continue.

2   Chance-Maker can be downloaded free of charge from: http://fcis1.wie.warwick.ac.uk/~dave_pratt/   You will first need Boxer, a programming language in the style of Logo. At present it is only available for the Macintosh computer but will soon be available for

the PC. You can find out more about Boxer, including free download, from: www.soe.
berkeley.edu/~boxer/

3    You can order or find out more about Probability Simulator (for the Macintosh
computer only) from www.umass.edu/srri/serg/probsim.html

## References

Bridges, R. (1999) 'Probability simulation with a spreadsheet', *Mathematics in School*, 28(4).

DfEE (1999) *National Curriculum for 2000 in Mathematics*, London: HMSO.

diSessa, A.A. (1988) 'Knowledge in pieces', in G. Forman and P. Pufall (eds) *Constructivism in the Computer Age*, Hillsdale, NJ: Lawrence Erlbaum Associates, Inc.: 49–70.

Kahneman, D., Slovic, P. and Tversky, A. (1982) *Judgement Under Uncertainty: heuristics and biases*, Cambridge: Cambridge University Press.

Konold, C., Pollatsek, A., Well, A., Lohmeier, J. and Lipson, A. (1993) 'Inconsistencies in students' reasoning about probability', *Journal for Research in Mathematics Education* 24: 392–414.

Lave, J. (1988) *Cognition in Practice*, Cambridge: Cambridge University Press.

Lecoutre, M.P. (1992) 'Cognitive models and problem spaces in "purely random" situations', *Educational Studies in Mathematics*, 23(6): 557–68.

Pratt, D. (1998) 'The coordination of meanings for randomness', *For the learning of mathematics*, 18(3): 2–11.

Pratt, D. (2000) 'Making Sense of the Total of Two Dice', *Journal for Research in Mathematics Education*.

Smith, J.P., diSessa, A.A. and Rochelle, J. (1993) 'Misconceptions reconceived – a constructivist analysis of knowledge in transition', *Journal of Learning Sciences*, 3(2): 115–63.

# 3 Pedagogical issues

# 10 Teaching for understanding
## Anne Watson

*'Understanding' has several different meanings: knowing how to perform and use mathematics (instrumental and procedural); knowing about usefulness in context (contextual); relating mathematical concepts (relational); knowing about underlying structures (transformable, generalised and abstract); having overcome inherent obstacles.*[1]

## Levels of understanding arising from a tables exercise

To illustrate these meanings I shall describe an exercise given to a Year 9 class of very low achievers to help them practise the seven times table. It may come as a shock that pupils of 13 and 14 needed such practice, but I shall focus on the structure and aim of the exercise.

Pupils were given a sheet on which they could fill in answers to four columns of calculations. Here is an excerpt, which could be used as a teaching tool in a variety of ways:

| | | | |
|---|---|---|---|
| $5 \times 7 =$ | $7 \times 5 =$ | $35 ? 7 =$ | $35 ? 5 =$ |
| $6 \times 7 =$ | $7 \times 6 =$ | $42 ? 7 =$ | $42 ? 6 =$ |
| $7 \times 7 =$ | $7 \times 7 =$ | $49 ? 7 =$ | |
| $8 \times 7 =$ | $7 \times 8 =$ | $56 ? 7 =$ | $56 ? 8 =$ |

Pupils filled the first two columns vertically, usually by adding seven each time. Few knew answers without this adding process. No pupil connected the columns and worked horizontally.

In what sense was this exercise enabling them to practise? If the aims of practice are fluency and recall, how does repeated addition help? It is likely that the pupils were focusing on adding seven with the aim of getting the worksheets completed, rather than thinking about the number facts they had generated. Appropriate teacher intervention, restructuring the task to focus on aspects other than filling in the answers, can make a crucial difference to learning outcomes.

Here are some ways in which this task can be used to encourage a range of understandings.

### To encourage instrumental and procedural understanding

To recall and use multiplication facts one has to be able to know them individually, rather than only have inefficient routes to find them. This worksheet is physically structured to encourage recursion. To focus on individual facts a different physical layout would be essential, one in which '6 × 7' cannot easily be related to '5 × 7' except in the pupil's head. Some pupils might have a visual memory which enables them to imagine the worksheet layout to get the right answer; some might rapidly reconstruct the answer from a small bank of memorised facts; others may use rhythms of words to aid recall (as in 'seven elevens are seventy-seven'); others might reorganise facts into groups which make sense to them in some other way. Pupils have personal ways of remembering and the teacher has to intervene to get their attention off the page and into their imaginations. The task, therefore, is not finished when the gaps are filled, but after the completed tables have been used to aid memory and recall. To do this, there needs to be focused questioning and further tasks, such as a game in which quick answers are required, repeated over several lessons so that pupils can be aware of their progress.

Can the task be developed to help pupils develop a deeper understanding of multiplication procedures? A teacher might draw pupils' attention to the commutativity of multiplication, which always suggests an alternative procedure, and ask when it might be useful.

### To encourage contextual understanding

This exercise is purely about number relationships which could be applied in contexts. In primary schools pupils are often asked to tell a story that illustrates a number fact. If teachers choose contexts they need to ensure relevance for the pupils; it might be better to get pupils to provide their own contexts. It is highly likely that some contextual knowledge of number facts might come first with answers being treated as abstract number facts. For example, a pupil might know that 3 × 7 is 21 from playing darts, or that 7 × 5 is 35 from handling money. These may seem trivial examples but it is always worth asking pupils what they already know.

### To encourage relational understanding

The exercise provides opportunity to relate each number fact to three other expressions of the same relationship. The pupils' concentration on vertical relationships may lead them to ignore both commutativity and the relationship between multiplication and division. Intervention by the teacher could redirect the focus towards the horizontal patterns (Watson, 2000) by separating one line from the others and asking 'What do you see?' or 'Where do the same numbers appear?', then offering '7 × 23' as the start of a line and expecting pupils to complete it. Pupils are almost forced to look at the relationship as a structure. Looking for non-obvious patterns makes structures more important than answers and gives pattern-spotting a powerful role in learning mathematics.

The omission of an entry in the '7 × 7' line can be discussed to bring out the relationship between this exercise and square numbers. The positioning of the numbers in the last two columns can be discussed and pupils asked to explain the relationship between divisor and quotient.

## To encourage transformable, generalised and abstract understanding

Although this is such a simple piece of mathematics, it is worth noticing that it can be generalised. The four forms for each multiplication fact can be expressed algebraically, and pupils asked to transform between them. For example, pupils can pose questions of the form '112 × 34 = 3808, so what is 3808 divided by 34?' or 'If $pq = m$, what does $q$ equal?'

At a higher level of abstraction, pupils could be asked to find another operation which is commutative and set up a row of its different representations, and one which is not. This is a further shift, beyond generalisation, towards the abstract notion of binary relationships.

The reader may like to imagine further whether the task could be used to overcome inherent obstacles in multiplication. The appropriateness of the task for 13- and 14-year-olds clearly depends on how the teacher interacts with pupils about possible ways to reflect on their work.

## Task choice, lesson structure and interaction

Each of the approaches described above requires more from the teacher than merely selecting the exercise and helping pupils finish it correctly. In fact, given unmediated without teacher intervention, and without some reflective discussion afterwards, the task does not promote even the simplest levels of memory or understanding. But this is not to suggest that pupils gain nothing from it. Understanding is achieved by a process of personal 'sense-making' by the learner, and a pupil who is mentally engaged with even a mundane task may develop some level of understanding. Conversely, it is possible for some of the above ideas to be treated on a superficial level by the learner, and little growth of understanding to be the outcome. The teacher cannot guarantee understanding, but *can* plan for pupils to have experiences that are likely to lead to higher levels of understanding (or to memorising and fluency, if those are the aims) by structuring tasks and discussion to focus sharply on the desired features. To understand requires mental effort (Newton, 2000) and the teacher has to channel this towards goals of understanding.

Consideration of the simple repetitive exercise above shows that teachers need to be clear about the kind of understanding they wish pupils to achieve, and use strategies that are likely to create appropriate learning experiences. This cannot be done by simply choosing 'good' tasks. The task above was fairly mundane but could be used to create purposeless or purposeful activity according to the way it was used in the classroom.

The National Strategy recommends a three-part lesson consisting of a mental and oral starter, a main part and a plenary at the end. It is possible to interpret a fairly traditional UK mathematics lesson as fitting with this pattern. Exposition could be described as an oral starter because it contains some questions and answers, but the questions would often be procedural and the answers perfunctory; the main part would be working through a textbook exercise; in the plenary answers can be read out and further explanation might be given. Superficially, a three-part lesson structure has been followed, but only instrumental or procedural understanding has been programmed into it.

Using the tables task, a better three-part lesson might start by sharing ideas about how to fill in the answers, the main part could consist of filling in the answers and looking for patterns within and between columns and seeing if similar patterns occur with other tables, and the plenary could be a substantial whole-class discussion of the relationship between multiplication and division, or a game highlighting rapid recall of multiplication facts which might be repeated at the start of the next lesson. A particular lesson structure, like a particular task, does not guarantee understanding.

## Strategies which promote understanding

The following sections describe strategies which are likely to foster understanding. You will probably notice that, although each part starts with different intentions, there is convergence towards practices that overlap all sections.

### Teaching for instrumental and procedural understanding

Learning new procedures often entails using previously-learnt procedures fluently in complex situations. The teacher has to help pupils sort out what ought to become fluent and what can be reconstructed from a deeper understanding. Here are two examples: it is a good idea to know fluently what 'cosine' means and not have to look it up when it appears in a mathematical context; it is a good idea to know fluently that 48 is the product of several pairs of numbers so that when it appears as the constant term in a quadratic one has a possible starting point for factorisation.

Learning theoretically, combined with frequent opportunities to use what has been learnt so that it becomes fluent in context, seems to be the way we all learn how to use new mental and technological tools. Unfortunately a fragmented mathematics curriculum makes this hard to organise, but learning by heart with the expectation of later recall, and without regular rehearsal through contextual use, does not foster fluency for most pupils.

When the aim is for pupils to know what to do and how to do it, demonstration and procedure-following is useful. But if they have been shown a worked example, pupils will often slot different numbers into the structure they have been shown, like filling in some blanks of a sentence. At the end of an exercise of similar calculations they may have a set of correct answers but not recall how to repeat the calculation on another occasion. Rather than slotting in numbers, the teacher probably hopes that pupils achieve a sense of the procedure and absorb it through using it several times. What actually happens is like drivers being given step-by-step directions by a passenger: they may get to the destination, but may be unable to repeat the route alone on another occasion. Doing something by depending on step-by-step instructions may lead to successful 'doing' but not to learning.

In order to focus on the procedure as the thing to be remembered, something else has to happen; pupils have to generalise about what they are doing. One way to achieve this is to ask them to give instructions for the procedure in their own words.

This can be done orally to each other, in writing, as a letter to a mythical younger pupil, as a 'make your own textbook' exercise, or to make up an example and work it through themselves. In subsequent lessons pupils can demonstrate worked examples for each other and share the 'inner speech' they use as they do them. Not all students can readily describe what they do in words as they may have other ways to 'see' procedures (this can apply even to gifted mathematicians), so I am not suggesting that this kind of activity is essential for everyone, but it does provide reflective action which can aid recall of the procedure. Hiebert and Wearne (1996) found that pupils who were encouraged to develop their own procedures and explain them to each other improved in their ability to learn later procedures, and to recall, and to develop procedures where none had been taught.

Consider teaching the conventions of order of operations in algebraic representation. To some extent this is a set of rules that have to be followed and pupils can be told, 'This is the agreed way of indicating the order in which operations are to be done'. This can lead to a lesson in which it is explicitly learnt and practised as an essential tool.

Another approach would be to explore ambiguities which are resolved by having a conventional order, such as BODMAS[1]. Such explorations and resolutions are important for pupils who are going to use calculators and spreadsheets extensively. They can find out that choosing which operation is done first affects the answer, so there is clearly a need for agreement. They can devise their own rules by indicating button sequences on a calculator. In the end it is important not to leave pupils with the view that their own notations are as valuable as the international convention … they need to conform. However, BODMAS is not the only way to establish the conventional order of operations.

An established teacher, seeing pupils develop through several years of mathematics, can develop language forms to be used when brackets appear. Reading arithmetical and algebraic expressions out loud is a powerful way of relating symbol to meaning. The expression:

$$2(x+3)$$

is often read as 'two into $x$ plus three'. The word 'into' is usually associated with division so is rather inappropriate. A literal reading 'two, bracket, $x$ plus three, close brackets' says nothing about meaning. More meaningful readings could be devised: 'two lots of (pause) $x$-plus-three' or 'all of $x$ plus three … times 2'.

Reading out loud can establish useful articulations of symbols, and can also reveal helpful and unhelpful ways of reading mathematics which pupils have already developed. In this example, the distributive law (a fundamental structural feature of arithmetic and algebra) can be embedded in the way the symbols are read. There may be no need to recall BODMAS.

## Teaching for contextual understanding

For many, the reason for teaching mathematics in school is so that pupils become numerate out of school. Being able to choose and apply appropriate methods in situations outside school is, in itself, a skill that needs to be learnt and practised. Modern curricula take this into account requiring that uses of mathematics be discussed in school, that pupils have experience of problem-solving and multi-answer situations, and that contextual questions are worked on regularly. What often results is the use of artificial contexts in mathematics lessons, in which mathematics has to be used in ways in which it would not really be used outside the class. For example, pupils might be asked to answer questions about filling petrol tanks and calculating prices, when in reality most people might fill up to a fixed value, or let the machine do the calculations. Pupils who can imagine themselves into the situation might be confused by its unreality, and those who cannot are impeded by the contextual details. Contexts that are relevant for pupils and use mathematics with integrity are hard to find. Perhaps one of the teacher's tasks is to extend the pupils' awareness of possible ways in which mathematics might be relevant, starting with their obvious current interests, but indicating other possibilities outside their experience so far.[2]

In Holland, the 'realistic mathematics' movement uses tasks that attract the interest of adolescents and allow them to work as problem-solvers, so that different pupils might use different mathematical approaches (van den Heuvel-Panhuizen, 1994). Cooper and Dunne (1999) have shown that pupils of lower social classes can respond less well than others to contextual questions used for assessment, even in contexts with which they are familiar.[3] A further issue is whether context should be introduced after techniques have been taught, so that the role of context is to provide a forum for practising techniques, or whether context should be the forum for introducing the technique. The first approach requires abstract learning about simple situations to be applied in real, hence complex, situations (general to particular); the second implies that learning can take place by simplifying and abstracting aspects of real, hence complex, situations (particular to general).

Boaler (2001) reports on a school in which pupils were routinely given complex mathematical questions to explore, and thus became used to having to choose and develop methods for themselves. Examination questions held few terrors for them, because they were seen as just more problems to solve. For example, many were able to choose between multiplication and division on the merits of the question, rather than by looking for cues or guessing. Pupils reported recognising how their approach to mathematics in the classroom was similar to their approach to mathematical issues that arose elsewhere. The pupils did not expect every mathematical situation to have an obvious algorithm and were experienced in having to try things out and evaluate the outcome.

Older pupils who have to choose between integration methods, when some questions can be resolved several ways, and some by neither, will be disadvantaged if they have not experienced trying, adapting, using past knowledge, making judgements and hence developing a 'feel' for choice of method. If working with mathematics includes analysing complex situations, deciding what is important, choosing appropriate methods and adapting them if necessary then application of mathematical techniques in context, and in examinations, will be less problematic.

## Teaching for relational understanding within mathematics

Returning briefly to BODMAS, suppose that we try to avoid a rule-based approach and look for opportunities to make links with other areas of mathematics. If pupils had already accepted the distributivity of multiplication over addition (and their inverses) because it had been developed as a feature of their arithmetical work, brackets will have arisen as a way to express this. For a new teacher, teaching 'order of operations' and knowing nothing of the pupils' past experience, it would be impossible to start from scratch, but it would be possible to find out something about what they already knew by starting a class with some discussion, or activity, which is designed to reveal the range of understanding and experience they have already, and then to vary what happens next to take account of this prior knowledge.

In a study of methods of teaching mathematics, Askew et al., (1997) found that teachers who were explicit about connections between different aspects of arithmetic were more successful than those who taught topics separately. Mathematics provides links between procedures, symbols, contexts, purposes, and concrete experiences, so there are many connections to be made. Since most theories of learning agree that we learn by relating new experiences to what we already know, teaching approaches which exploit this by making it easier to build *helpful* relationships might be more successful than those which leave pupils to form their own, perhaps idiosyncratic, relationships. For example, a pupil who thought that solving linear equations was like simplifying equivalent fractions because 'do the same to both sides' was like 'do the same to top and bottom' may have formed an unhelpful relationship. Without guidance, pupils can assume chance or superficial features of mathematical examples are important, and miss the essential features (Anthony, 1994).

Nevertheless, teaching for relational understanding takes time. Skemp (1976) gives four possible reasons for rejecting a relational approach to teaching mathematics: (i) relational understanding may take longer to achieve; (ii) a relational approach may be too hard since relationships can be more abstract than the aspects being related; (iii) pupils may need to learn to perform the skill or technique, say in science or technology lessons, before they can work on the deeper meanings of it; (iv) a teacher might work in an environment where instrumental approaches are the norm and attempts to work relationally are unsupported. If anything, these pressures are more likely now than in 1976 because of the pace of coverage required by the NC for mathematics and the demands of the assessment system. However, where instrumental mathematics might be easier to follow, give immediate rewards and produce right answers, relational learning promotes adaptability, easier recall and an atmosphere of growth of understanding and can help pupils become intrigued by the subject in its own right, not merely as a service tool or a set of test hurdles.

To teach for relational understanding requires awareness of what pupils already know, and how it is known. For instance, knowledge of common misunderstandings is useful because some, if not all, pupils will have similar problems and activities can be planned to address them explicitly. In these cases, the relationship being sought is with what is already known, and restructuring of understanding is the desired learning outcome.

Being told by the teacher that a current topic has links with previous work is not enough to ensure that pupils make useful links for themselves. Newton (2000) suggests that pupils can be asked to create concept maps and flow diagrams to show how they connect different topics for themselves, and to establish the expectation that topics will interconnect. Connections might be through language ('square' being the name of a shape and numbers raised to the second power); through imagery (points on a plane being seen as coordinate pairs, or complex numbers, which can also be related to vectors); through underlying commonality (rotations of order four having similar structure to addition in modulo 4); through the growing complexity of mathematics (equivalence of fractions relating to simplifying rational algebraic expressions); or through making distinctions (irrational numbers are those which cannot be expressed as ratios). Pupils can be asked, when meeting a new piece of mathematics, if it reminds them of anything else; what existing knowledge they have to use to help them understand or do the new mathematics; what is totally new to them and what is already familiar. The teacher has to be adaptable enough to incorporate pupils' responses into the lesson.

## Teaching for transformational understanding, generalisation and abstraction

Much secondary mathematics depends on recognising when to use a technique and being able to use it appropriately. Recognition of mathematical situations occurs when the pupil sees a familiar structure lurking within a problem or question. For this reason, pupils need experience of different ways to express mathematics, and of being flexible with what they know.

Pattern-spotting can help here, because patterns give the raw material for generalisation which, in turn, enables us to describe facts, properties and techniques in general terms. For example, if pupils look at a collection of quadratics and their factorisations, they might begin to spot patterns in the coefficients and factors. Talking about these, conjecturing and testing their ideas, can lead to a description of a method of factorising. In the same way, looking at the ratio of certain sides in similar right-angled triangles might lead to conjectures about such ratios, which can be tested and then articulated as rules for finding sine, cosine and tangent. In each of these the teacher has directed pupils to look for similarities in structure by comparing examples, reflecting on their work in a way which goes 'across the grain' of the work done (Watson, 2000).

To transform between representations is an important tool in mathematical thinking. Working explicitly with parallel representations establishes this as a normal feature of mathematics. Sometimes this is traditional, such as when demonstrating a geometrical proof with a diagram, writing a Euclidean argument beside it and speaking an everyday language version at the same time. Teachers can exploit the power of this by using different representations in conjunction so that they are more likely to be linked by pupils. This example is used by many teachers: every time a relationship with structure $a = bc$ is given, the two other expressions of it are also given: $b = a/c$ and $c = a/b$. Pupils with whom this is an established practice have little difficulty with, say, transforming trigonometric formulae.

An important feature of mathematics is that structures which first appear as generalisations eventually become examples of more general concepts. Some examples of this process of abstraction can be seen in secondary mathematics: counting numbers become examples of rational numbers, which are examples of points on the number line; isolated coordinate pairs become examples of the continuous set of points on lines, and the lines themselves become manipulable as linear equations, which could be members of a system of equations. It would be tempting to say that pupils should not be asked to work at a higher level of abstraction until they understand the previous level, yet it is also true that some features of an object become clear when one attempts to use it alongside others to fulfil some higher purpose. In mathematics, it can be illuminating to use a concept in a more complex mathematical context, and trying to make sense of complexity can teach us more about simple ideas. There is no obviously 'right' way to treat this issue. In a healthy classroom there would be frequent flow between simplicity and complexity, generality and specificity (Mason and Watson, 1999).

## Teaching to overcome obstacles

For formative and diagnostic purposes pupils can be asked to explain how they did some mathematics, thus showing what sort of reasoning led to incorrect, or even correct, answers. This method requires close one-to-one attention and is hence difficult to manage. However, a teacher can use similar methods with a whole class in order to be better informed about a range of misunderstandings which they might have.

There are some common errors or misunderstandings in mathematics that occur so frequently, however the topic has been taught, that they can be seen as inherent difficulties in mathematics. Some of them occur because mathematical terms may have a looser meaning in everyday use. For instance, the word 'regular' applied to shape in mathematics means 'having equal sides and equal angles' but in everyday use it may mean simply that the shape is ordinary or symmetrical in some way. Knowing this potential confusion, teachers can use it as a focus for a lesson, rather than just giving the technical word and hoping that pupils will use it with precision in mathematics. Unless shapes loosely called regular are specifically discussed during the lesson, it is unlikely that pupils will make the required distinction. A related common error is for pupils to believe that the diagonal of a rectangle is an axis of symmetry. Again, it is easy to see why, and even good pupils of mathematics may get this wrong because they see that two halves of the rectangle are congruent, so it feels as if *something* should be said about the diagonal! If the focus for a lesson on reflective symmetry is the rectangle, rather than something less problematic such as a square, it is more likely that this obstacle can be overcome.

The examples just given relate to precise use of language, but there are other sources of common obstacles. The belief that multiplication is repeated addition is very strong because, for much of the pupils' lives so far, that is exactly what it means. To shift to understanding it as scaling requires an undoing of images of repeated addition. In fact, if pupils still have an adding rather than a scaling metaphor, great confusion can occur in ratio problems (Hart, 1981).

To teach for an understanding in which pupils have overcome such obstacles it is not enough just to teach the new meaning and hope that some will 'pick it up'. Bruner's model (1960) of learning concepts is helpful here. He said that learning takes place through manipulating and acting with the concept, then forming an iconic representation of it, such as a mental image, and finally being able to express it in symbolic form. If the objects chosen by the teacher are such that common obstacles will be brought to the fore (such as working with the rectangle when considering symmetry, or working with scaling factors less than unity when constructing two-dimensional enlargements) the iconic understandings have to be adjusted to fit the new enacted experience, and cognitive obstacles are more likely to be overcome.

## Key practices which promote understanding

I have shown that significant thought has to be given to how a task is structured and how the teacher interacts with pupils about it. Several strategies have been given which are designed to focus pupils on procedures, applications, relationships and the underlying structures of the mathematics. These strategies all assume a classroom in which there is exploration and discussion, the teacher giving questions and prompts which guide pupils' thinking in useful directions, while recognising the supremacy of individual 'sense-making'. There would be explicit recognition of pupils' current knowledge, and their difficulties would be worked on as a legitimate part of coming to understand mathematics. Pupils would be asked to write about, create examples of and use the technical language of mathematics. They would be offered mathematical situations to explore, some of which would be chosen to create shifts in their understanding. There would be different representations given, and pupils would sometimes be asked to shift from one to the other, or transform their knowledge some other way. Pupils would be encouraged to see links between different mathematical topics, helped to see what is worth remembering, and helped to remember.

## Notes

1   BODMAS is a common acronym for: brackets, 'of', division, multiplication, addition and subtraction.
2   John Mason (in Chapter 17 of this volume) has named this 'the zone of proximal relevance'.
3   See also chapter 13 by Barry Cooper in the companion volume *Teaching Mathematics in Secondary Schools: a reader*, 2001.

## References

Askew, M., Brown, M., Rhodes, V., Wiliam, D. and Johnson, D. (1997) *Effective Teachers of Numeracy: report of a study carried out for the Teacher Training Agency*, Kings College, University of London.

Anthony, G. (1994) 'The role of the worked example in learning mathematics', in A. Jones *et al.* (eds) *SAME papers*, Hamilton, New Zealand: University of Waikato: 129–43.

Boaler, J. (2001) 'Open and closed mathematics approaches: student experiences and understandings', in L. Haggarty (ed.) *Teaching Mathematics in Secondary Schools: a reader*, London: RoutledgeFalmer.

Bruner, J.S. (1960) *The Process of Education*, Cambridge, MA: Harvard University Press.

Cooper, B. (2001) 'Culture, class and "realistic" mathematics tests', in L. Haggarty (ed.) *Teaching Mathematics in Secondary Schools: a reader*, London: RoutledgeFalmer.

Cooper, B. and Dunne, M. (1999) *Assessing Children's Mathematical Knowledge: social class, sex, and problem-solving*, Buckingham: Open University Press.

Hart, K. M. (ed.) (1981) *Children's Understanding of Mathematics: 11–16*, London: John Murray.

Hiebert, J. and Wearne, D. (1996) 'Instruction, understanding and skill in multi-digit addition and subtraction', *Cognition and Instruction*, 14: 251–83.

Mason, J. and Watson, A. (1999) 'Immersion in multiplicity: complex stories for complex people', *Mathematics Teaching*, 166: 5–8.

Newton, D.P. (2000) *Teaching for Understanding: what it is and how to do it*, London: RoutledgeFalmer.

Skemp, R. (1976) 'Relational and instrumental understanding', *Mathematics Teaching*, 77: 20–6.

Van den Heuvel-Panhuizen, M. (1994) 'Improvement of didactical assessment by improvement of problems: an attempt with respect to percentage', *Educational Studies in Mathematics*, 27(3): 41–72.

Watson, A. (2000) 'Going across the grain: mathematical generalisations in a group of low attainers', *Nordic Studies in Mathematics Education*, 8(1): 7–20.

Watson, A. (2001) 'What does it mean to understand something and how do we know when it has happened?', in L. Haggarty (ed.) *Teaching Mathematics in Secondary Schools: a reader*, London: RoutledgeFalmer.

# 11 Progression in mathematics
## Pat Perks

## Introduction

Teaching is concerned with enhancing pupils' development, in fact according to the National Curriculum, their spiritual, moral, social and cultural development. But what is development? As a teacher I should be able to account to other professionals and to parents for statements such as 'Mary is making good progress'. But what does this mean? Does this mean that Mary was at point x in the curriculum and is now at point y, or that she knew x but now knows x better, or a combination of the two or indeed that she is settling well into the class and is prepared to join in discussion? I suppose the Holy Grail for teachers would be that magic sequence for presenting mathematical ideas that would ensure maximum progression in pupils' learning. Questions remain about whether this is a possibility.

> ... my view of teaching is that of teachers as inquirers attempting to solve peda-
> gogical problems. The pedagogical problems are not of the type ... such as the
> use of audio-visual aids, or how to write on the chalkboard, or how to use one's
> voice; rather they are concerned with more fundamental questions such as the
> conceptual structure of the subject under study or the most appropriate ap-
> proach to teaching for meaningful learning.
>
> (Stones, 1992, p. 14)

Teaching is not just a body of craft knowledge, it is difficult to explain and analyse. Why does the material you use with one class seem to result in learning, but with another just causes confusion? Why does a session appear really exciting and useful to some and yet boring and uninformative to others? In trying to identify how best to help pupils learn, to make progress, the teacher cannot just turn to a formula and apply it. You have to identify the problem, find the parameters, work towards the best solution available at the time, then evaluate the solution in terms of the learning of the pupils and refine the solution. Whilst ideas, materials and methods about lessons can be shared, they cannot always be relied on to provide the expected outcome. A brain surgeon deals with one brain at a time, a teacher deals with 30 brains in a class, along with all those raging hormones if you work in a secondary school.

This chapter is concerned with exploring issues related to progression in mathe-matics – a concept that lies at the very heart of becoming and being a teacher. There are those in public life that think that answers to progression questions ought to be easy, who think that progression is equivalent to acceleration through the defined curriculum. Not so, this chapter is not about acceleration (Gardiner, 2000) but about working with pupils learning mathematics in a deep and meaningful way with all the consequent complexity.

## Defining progression

'Progression' is one of the key words in many of the documents and policies for teachers. Teachers are expected to plan for progression, to account for it and to ensure that it happens. A first task is to define the 'it'. What is progression? Does it only happen in the long term? Or can it be accounted for in the short and medium terms? There are two main ways to describe progression, the first relates to teaching sequences and the second to pupil development. As a teacher you need an understanding of these two types of progression – which are often confused in policy documents:

- progression through the curriculum in order to develop teaching sequences; you need an understanding of your subject knowledge, the content and the processes, the connections and interrelations, you need an understanding beyond getting the right answer;
- progression of the learner as they experience the curriculum in order to assess their development against the teaching sequence; you need an understanding about learners, their different needs, the fact that they learn differently, engage with mathematics differently.

And once you have an understanding of these two definitions you then have to ask what the relationship between teaching and learning is. For the teacher the honest answer is that teaching does not imply learning. There may be clear hierarchies such as the historical classification of number, there may be clear paths of development which sees the questions getting harder. You may feel that you can map the stages to the final goal, but teaching to these stages may not result in the learner coming to know them in the expected order.

Vygotsky (1986) trialled some investigations to consider the relationship between instruction and 'the development of the corresponding psychological function.' (p. 184). The conclusions that he gives, from plotting the curves of these two, shows that far from coinciding, the curves reveal an exceedingly complex relation. 'Development and instruction have different rhythms ... but by and large instruction precedes development.' (p. 185):

> ... for example, the different steps in learning arithmetic may be of unequal value for mental development. It often happens that three or four steps in instruction add little to the child's understanding of arithmetic, and then, with the fifth step, something clicks; the child has grasped a general principle, and his development curve rises markedly. For this particular child the fifth operation was decisive, but this cannot be a general rule. The turning points at which

a general principle becomes clear to the child cannot be set in advance by the curriculum.

(Vygotsky, 1986, p. 185)

About the time of the first writing of the National Curriculum, a research project was devised to investigate how attainment targets (for the National Curriculum) might be formulated and whether assessment techniques could be devised for diagnosis and for monitoring of pupils (Denvir *et al.*, 1987). One of the topics was division and the project looked closely at defining subordinate skills in understanding division. A variety of data was gathered about the children's understanding of division word problems. Data from investigations and practical problems were also used. After trialling, 14 pupils were interviewed for about 20–30 minutes. From this range of data a hierarchy of mathematics, for division, was hypothesised by observing the many variations in strategies used and, from these, a small number were selected as they were judged to be important in the development of the concept of division. Figure 11.1 shows a possible hierarchy, with arrows showing links that appear to be prerequisite, i.e. counting, addition and subtraction appear to be necessary to the skill for selecting division. Other skills appear to be related, such as modelling and number bonds. The diagram lays out a progression through the learning of division.

An investigation was given to four children and their results were matched against the hierarchy. The conclusions were that the hierarchy was a crude indicator rather than a provider of accurate information and that it was not always possible to assess whether some of the possible strategies had been used, as it was not easy for children to reflect on how they solved a problem. (For example, the researchers found that certain children were intimidated by a class assessment and were not able to articulate their workings.)

> The 'strategies' used by children vary in their complexity. The picture of children's acquisition of skills which emerged from the observation was extremely complex and it was necessary to make a crude simplification in order to produce a hypothesised framework of strategies which describes the development of children's understanding of division. Because the hierarchy was obtained from results with different children at a single point in time, there can be no assurance that children do progress through it. It is important to emphasise that these hypothesised orders of development do not represent a natural order but the order for a small sample of pupils each of whom has followed similar school curricula.
>
> (Denvir, 1987, p. 106)

Brown (1993), quoting earlier research conducted with Denvir (Denvir and Brown, 1986), showed, like Vygotsky, that the rhythms of learning and teaching are different and individual. Diagnostic tests were used to establish what understanding individual pupils had attained; a teaching programme was implemented to teach skills that were considered to be the next skills in the hierarchy and post-tests were given. The results showed that such an approach was useful for describing each pupil's knowledge but it was less useful as a predictor for next learning. Some

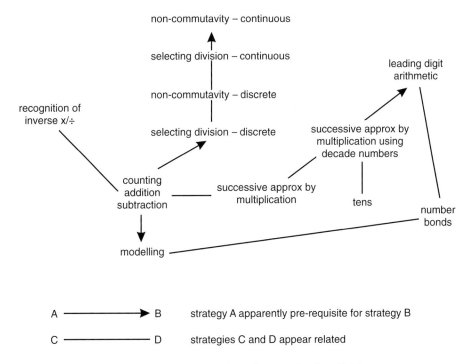

**Figure 11.1** *Denvir's possible hierarchy of strategies for division*

attained the new skills being taught, others did not but made progress in different parts of the hierarchy. Teaching will affect what is learnt but cannot determine it, 'pupils can learn that which is not taught, while failing to learn what is taught' (Brown, 1993, p. 16).

So, because of these complications, if we are going to identify progression, we must have an understanding of the mathematics, along with an awareness that, although we may have an understanding of some learners, we can only have a best shot at progression to help understanding of a particular pupil. Knowing that all pupils will be learning as individuals, we need to provide as much background opportunity for learning as possible. We first have to come to know the mathematics for teaching and then we have to come to know the pupils.

## Progression in a single area of mathematics: developing connections

Advice on what to teach for the 5–16 curriculum comes from the four key-staged Programmes of Study in the National Curriculum (NC). The order of the mathematics is very generalised and leaves the teacher free to create his or her own teaching sequences. The Attainment Targets in the NC do impose an order of the expected learning for a 'generalised' pupil. The language of levels implies progression upward, with the content of level 4 being easier than level 5, or that moving from level 4 to level 5 is making progress. However, even these level descriptions are end points for pupils at the end of a Key Stage, requiring best-fit judgements from teachers. So there is some indication of order but little help for creating teaching sequences. But the NC does offer a starting point for analysing a single area of mathematics.

## Example 1  Percentages

Let us take numbers and the number system, and the subset in the Key Stage 3 Programme of Study called percentages (p. 30 Ma2 in the mathematics NC). This excludes the section on page 31 concerned with calculating with percentages.

> Understand that 'percentage' means 'number of parts per 100' and use this to compare proportions; interpret percentage as the operator 'so many hundredths of'.
> (DfEE, 1999, p. 30)

The Key Stage 4 (foundation) reads:

> Understand that 'percentage' means 'number of parts per 100' and use this to compare proportions; interpret percentage as the operator 'so many hundredths of'; use percentages in real-life situations.
> (op. cit. p. 44)

The Key Stage 4 (higher) reads:

> Understand that 'percentage' means 'number of parts per 100' and use this to compare proportions; interpret percentage as the operator 'so many hundredths of', (for example, 10% means 10 parts per 100, and 15% of $Y$ means $\frac{15}{100} \times Y$.
> (op.cit. p. 58)

Well, that hasn't helped much (and in fact there is a lot of repetition from Key Stage 3 to Key Stage 4) and I find the explanation of the mathematics in the brackets unappealing (this is printed grey in the book, which is non-statutory; and because of the repetition, only extracts from Key Stage 4 higher have been given here). The Attainment Target for Ma2 (pp. 88–9) however does gives some sense of movement.

> Level 4: they recognise approximate proportions of a whole and use simple fractions and percentages to describe these.

> Level 5: … they calculate fractional or percentage parts of quantities and measurements using a calculator where appropriate.

> Level 6: pupils are aware of which number to consider as 100 per cent, or a whole, in problems involving comparisons and use this to evaluate one number as a fraction or percentage of another; they understand the equivalences between fractions, decimals and percentages, they add and subtract fractions.

Immediately the pathway is muddied as the level 6 statement of being 'aware of which number to consider as 100 per cent' seems very necessary to the level 4 statement about proportions of a whole. I need to remember that these are *attainment* descriptions for the end of a Key Stage. For teaching, if I know that I want the pupils to know about equivalences at level 6 and I know my mathematics, I will draw connections early on in the teaching of labelling parts of a whole in various ways (level 4). But a picture is beginning to emerge of possibilities in the mathematics.

Next I would draw on my own knowledge about percentages and then I would look at other sources to see what examples and types of questions they offer in order to extend my thinking. I may look in a textbook (maybe the departmental textbook) or at worksheets.

I would also look in the framework of the National Strategy (2001), which offers questions that pupils should be able to do and suggested methods of calculation. They are split between mental, pencil and paper and calculator methods. See Table 11.1.

**Table 11.1** Extracts from the National Strategy for Key Stage 3

---

**Calculate percentages of numbers and measures**

---

**Use mental methods. For example, find:**

| | |
|---|---|
| 10% of 37g | by dividing by 10; |
| 5% of £5 | by finding 10%, and then halving; |
| 15% of 40 | by finding 10% the 5% and adding the results together. |
| | (Section 4/p. 72) |

---

**Use informal written methods. For example, find:**

| | |
|---|---|
| 11% of £2800 | by calculating 10% and 1% as jottings, and adding the results together; |
| 70% of 130g | by calculating 10% and multiplying this by 7 as jottings; or by calculating 50% and 20% as jottings and adding the results. |
| | (Section 4/p. 72) |

---

For calculator use, two methods are offered for finding 12% of 45

Converting a percentage calculation to an equivalent decimal $0.12 \times 45 =$

Converting a percentage calculation to an equivalent fraction $12 \div 100 \times 45 =$

We are told that the second method should be reocognised as being less efficient than the first.

---

These examples offer an idea of the type of mathematics pupils must learn to do. Within the single area the hierarchy of difficulty may be easy to create, but the teach-

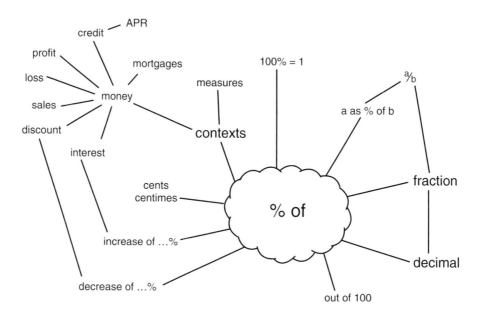

**Figure 11.2** 'Splurge' diagram for 'percentages of ... '

ing strategies and interconnections may be harder to identify. By working through the sources listed above, I begin to connect my thinking on 'percentages of'. In order to capture this thinking I use a 'splurge' diagram. Figure 11.2 shows some first connections. Questions in textbooks offer contexts, the other ideas can be seen in the NS, extract from which are in Table 11.1.

Figure 11.2 can be added to, but I find it useful to begin to capture the first links within the topic. If we take another topic, the work above has to be done, but you can consider the implications of ICT on the links within a topic.

## Example 2  Equations

Certain things are traditionally seen to be hard and history has greater influence on our teaching order than the introduction of technology. For example, negative numbers are not considered with pupils in the early learning stages, yet young children with a calculator, using the constant key, will often discover the negative numbers and deal with them in terms of a usage of 'the other side of 0'. Equations with a variable on both sides trap pupils who can cope with equations when the variable is on one side. We usually teach equations with the variable on one side, practising this type of question exhaustively, before moving on to equations with the variable on both sides. We then find that pupils find these more difficult. This particular teaching order is reinforced by the *idea* that the pupils find this type of equation harder. A better solution might be to work on such equations very early on so they do not appear harder. Using a spreadsheet or a graphical package can set up images that give meaning to the mathematics beyond the algorithmic solutions. Here are some thoughts about the impact of technology upon the teaching of solving equations.

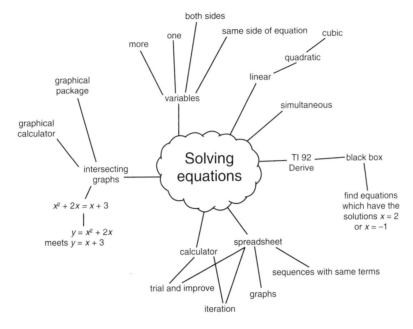

**Figure 11.3** *'Splurge' diagram for solving equations*

Equations with the variable on both sides can be worked on by pupils using graphical packages before formalising any particular method for solving them. Formalising the method is then set at a different level of progression. Access to ICT for teaching and learning challenges some of the traditional orders in the curriculum and means that we need to consider very carefully how we link and how we define progression through a topic.

## Progression in a single area of mathematics: developing pupils' understanding

There is a sense in which progression can be thought of simply as 'gaining more' skills within a single area. There are in mathematics more facts that can be learned and more skills that can be developed. For skills it is difficult to know whether the refining of skills is merely an old skill made better, or a new skill. However, consider the calculation:

$$8 \times \text{something} = 6$$

Imagine offering this question to a group of pupils (in whatever context you choose). One set of responses might be:

- There is no solution since I know that multiplication always makes numbers bigger.
- Not sure, but I'm prepared to have a go at finding the answer, using trial and error.
- I can find the answer, using division.

These three responses demonstrate a range of mathematical development from particular (imaginary) pupils to a particular problem, from those whose knowledge of multiplication is limited to a particular set of numbers, to those who know that division and multiplication are inverse operations. In fact it is possible to imagine one pupil offering these responses over a period of time. There are many dimensions to progression. Finding solutions to problems, even to the apparently straightforward one above, involves a complex interplay of many factors: familiarity with the context, personal qualities such as confidence and perseverance (is trial and error an acceptable method and will it help me to find a solution?), available problem solving and investigational strategies and command of mathematical concepts and techniques. Is it possible to define progression in each of these areas?

Consider another calculation.

Calculate $6^3$.

If asked for $6^3$, my answer may come from:

- instant recall;
- recall plus the use of an operation $6^3 = 6^2 \times 6$
  I know $6^2 = 36$, $36 \times 6 = 180 + 36 = 216$;
- the recall of the definition of powers from its first stages $6^3 = 6 \times 6 \times 6$;
- my knowledge of factors, using it to change the calculation to rely on different recall: $6^3 = 2^3 \times 3^3 = 8 \times 27$.

My answers could be achieved with a calculator, but for many purposes it is more efficient to remember and use recall. The stages involved, as described above, offer a way of considering progression in the learners' understanding of the mathematical facts.

- Recall of the answer requires no understanding but has to be memorised – no checking or linking mechanism is involved. Teaching for recall involves no ways of making connections and may lead to overload and inefficient learning.
- Recall plus operation: $6^2 = 36$ is easier to remember, it belongs to the set of mathematical multiplication facts and is thus connected to other knowledge; $6^3 = 6^2 \times 6$ demonstrates a strong understanding of the connection between powers – it offers opportunities for checking and for noting facts such as the last digit is 6.
- Working from first principles (and using recall as well) i.e. $6 \times 6 \times 6 = 36 \times 6$ – but prompted by a structure, the method used may or may not indicate a deeper understanding of powers.

The mathematician has to have recourse to many strategies in order to organise and use memory efficiently; effective progression in learning may necessitate working on these different strategies more explicitly.

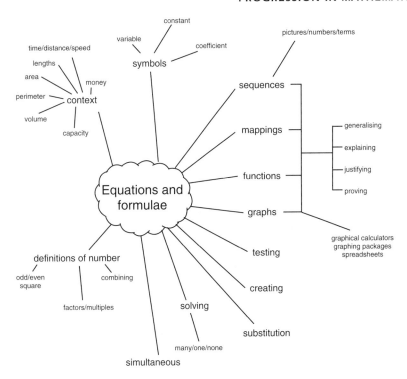

**Figure 11.4** 'Splurge' diagram for equations and formulae

## Progression around an area: developing an integrated understanding for teaching and for learning

For a beginning teacher, many first lessons are based on the immediate concerns of teaching this topic now. With experience a wider frame can be used, which again can help to define 'coming to know the mathematics better'. If you plan with a syllabus, this can help you to find other links.

It is useful to start with a single area and then build out and around the area connecting across the Attainment Targets, Programmes of Study, textbook and the NS. In the NS, the 'Example planning chart and possible units for Year 7' (p. 1/48) has equations and formulae appearing in all three terms: in a 5-hour block in the autumn term; in a 4-hour block in the spring term; and in an 8-hour block, along with sequences, functions and graphs, in the summer term. The related examples in Section 4 help to see what pupils have to come to do by the end of the year. However, this still leaves the teacher with the decision about exactly what to teach and when within the year. Looking at the framework for Years 5 and 6, the properties of number and reasoning about numbers appear to be the closest link for what has come before. This suggests number sequences, general statements (from words to formulae), multiples, squares, primes, factors and explaining methods, patterns and relationships. All of this information offers connections to identify the many strands in equations and formulae. The 'splurge' diagram in Figure 11.4 shows some of these connections.

The routes a learner may take through the understanding of the material are likely to be idiosyncratic, but if as a teacher you have identified the possible linkages, you can offer alternative. How can you do this? You have to know the mathematics. You have to try to identify the connections. All of this takes practice and experience, to build up your knowledge of the connections. 'Splurge' diagrams are a tool to practise making links. A diagram such as Figure 11.4, suggests possible teaching routes. You could begin with graphs, or sequences or a context such as perimeter, or link these.

Table 11.2 shows some possible starting points. The teaching sequence can then take alternative routes and the learners' progression will be different as a result.

**Table 11.2** Starting points for equations

| Graphs | Sequences | Context |
| --- | --- | --- |
| Using a graphical calculator find the value of x when $y = x$ meets $y = 5 - x$ | Extend the arithmetic sequence 3, 5, 7, … Find the pth term, the nth term. Which term is 25? Which term is 123? | Draw some rectangles, on centimetre squared paper, where the length is one centimetre more than the width. What is the width of the rectangle if the perimeter is 26 cm, 58 cm, 126 cm? |

If such links are made, identifying an individual's progress can be assessed in response to the various tasks devised to exploit these links. Task 11.1 provides a context for working on sequences and mappings.

**Task 11.1**

Using centimetre squared paper, draw some rectangles with sides of whole centimetre lengths where the lengths are three centimetres longer than the widths. Find the perimeter of each rectangle. Predict the perimeter for a rectangle that is 15 cm wide, 90 cm wide, 1000 cm wide, a cm wide, g cm wide. Draw a graph to show the relationship between width and perimeter.

Can you draw such a rectangle with a perimeter of 30 cm, 44 cm, 33 cm?

The generality can be sought from pupils and an explanation requested. The formula can be connected to the general formula for the perimeter of rectangles. The graph is initially just points, because of the constraints on integer lengths, but it can be extended. Pupils' understanding can be assessed by such tasks as they come to know how to deal with equations better.

## Progression based upon prerequisite knowledge, understanding and skills

This aspect is a daily concern for the teacher. Your lesson is unlikely to go well if your pupils do not have the necessary knowledge to work on the tasks you offer. Denvir *et al.*, (1987) offered an analysis of division (see above) but this only provides a general framework for thinking about links within the topic, not one that offers a strategy for teaching so that all learners learn. The 'splurge' diagram can help you with this. By considering the many connections, you will become more aware of the interconnected concepts and skills that feed the topic so that, even if your plans are upset by unexpected questions or misconceptions, you may have alternative teaching sequences to fall back on. More complex knowledge may depend on the acquisition of other knowledge, but this may not always have to be taught beforehand. Some simpler skills may be obtained when working on a more complex skill. Certainly they may be better practised in such a context.

Do you need to make sure that the pupils know all of level 3 before teaching level 4? Can you teach some of level 7 if the pupils are working at level 5? Well, as you might have guessed, it all depends. The way that you choose to present the mathematics will change the demands upon previous knowledge needed. What becomes important is that you know about mathematics rather than you know about progression. Consider, for example, working on solutions to $y = 2x + 4$ and $y = 7 - x$. At one level pupils could input them into a graphics package and read the coordinates of the intersection. I could ask the class to change the value of the constants and make predictions about what happens to the images of the lines as well as the value of the intersecting coordinate. I could imagine constructing a very interesting lesson around this. What is the prerequisite knowledge needed in this instance? Alternatively, I might want to develop an algebraic solution to solve these simultaneous equations that would require a facility with algebra not needed in the first instance. Or, I might want the class to practise substitution into linear expressions, and so with three pupils at the front of the class, one with a card $2x + 4$, one with a card $x$ and the third with a card $7 - x$, I might ask $x$ to declare values for the other two to use for substitution. With the help of the whole class, the three at the front could converge to a 'same' solution.

## Making choices: planning for teaching

In planning for teaching there are a number of cycles to go through. These will be repeated throughout your teaching career and so the information will become more and more automatic.

Firstly, you need to define what the learners in your charge are expected to know. This means referring to the National Curriculum, the syllabuses for the external examinations and past papers, the scheme of work for your school, textbooks, worksheets, other teachers and the departmental plans and then professional journals and research. The syllabus offers structure; teachers and textbooks offer methods, activities and ideas; journals such as *Mathematics in Schools* and *Mathematics Teaching* offer experiences from others as well as useful activities; research offers insight into children's errors and ideas useful to the beginning teacher. All of these contribute to knowledge about mathematics and about learners.

Figure 11.2 showed a diagram for thinking about percentages. Having thought about the connections, you can use these to work on the teaching of percentages. Textbooks will offer their own versions of order, worked examples and exercises to practise. Each source will choose its own methods and orderings for development within the topic – as a teacher you have to choose which methods you want your learners to come to know and in which order you will present them. You also need to make sure that you know how you do any of the questions on percentages. Are these the methods you use or are there others? Do the methods offered confuse you? If so, why? This is the beginning of thinking about progression, about making choices available to you for planning for teaching and for the pupils' learning.

The link of 'divide by 100' immediately prompts the connection to place value (a huge topic deserving a 'splurge' of its own) but this is probably the strongest link in the chain. This is *why* 'per cent' – we use a decimal system, and it is this idea which needs to underpin our teaching. Expressing 74 per cent as 0.74 becomes an obvious way of connecting, and leads to a calculator method linked to place value. '10 per cent of … ' shifts everything one place and can become a strong image, with links to one-tenth, $0.1x$; and divide by 10. All of these fraction, decimal, percentage connections must never be separated from ratio and proportion but, more importantly, the work must be underpinned by the place value system. By using percentages, pupils are coming to know the place value system better, but only if this aspect of the mathematics is made explicit.

Having ensured that you know how to do the mathematics, you need to discover what you will do as a teacher. There are many ways of working on developing tasks – textbooks offer a source of ideas, other teachers can help you to develop these ideas and journals can give you examples of what other teachers may have done. Your ability to choose will develop and the approaches may change as you revisit the topic.

Once you have worked on understanding the material that is available, you are ready to plan lessons. What methods do I want to teach? How will I approach mental methods? Will I use one per cent or ten per cent as my starting point? Do I feel my students are ready for two different ways of using a calculator, will I stick to one method? Which? What errors do pupils make? Are these more likely with some methods than others? You may, for example, choose to work on certain images. Language may act as an important reminder, per cent, cents and dollars. One per cent is one penny in the pound. Is there a link to 1 cm in 1 m? The 100 square or a circle divided into 100 sectors might offer ways of linking to fractions, or the use of overlays might show equivalence.

Evaluating your teaching will help you to assess the effectiveness of the sequence of activities you have offered. You will also need to consider pupils' learning:

- Why do pupils not remember?
- Why did I choose some methods?
- How do I link this mathematics to other content?
- How do I help pupils to learn this?
- What is this topic connected to?

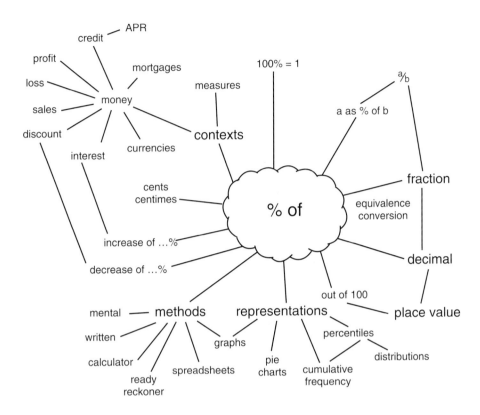

**Figure 11.5** More 'splurge' on percentages

The last question returns us to the starting point, the need to try to capture connections.

All of this analysis, awareness of the type of questions pupils have to answer, evaluation of teaching sequences and strategies will help to identify the many levels within a topic and give you the sense of the 'coming to know better' that can be developed in the pupils' learning.

## Conclusion

Progression in learning mathematics can only be assessed over long periods of time. Teachers can plan teaching sequences, choosing the order and pace at which to offer the content, but the learner may not work to that plan. Teaching sequences need to be constantly re-evaluated to look for better matches to the needs of the learner.

Progression can be considered in three ways, more knowledge and skills (e.g. moving Year 7 onto the Year 8 syllabus), better knowledge and skills (e.g. being able to use your algebra to solve problems, setting up the equations to solve) and better-connected knowledge and skills (e.g. knowing how graphs, sequences and equations relate to each other). Our assessment system seems to focus only on obtaining more: higher levels in the Standard Assessment Tasks, greater numbers of primary pupils taking GCSE examinations. There is a tension between performance (as measured by tests) and progression. True progression leads to the development of future mathematicians, people who want to study the subject at higher levels, who want to enjoy it. This type of progression depends on our pupils getting to know the mathematics better, with greater depth in wider contexts and with a strong sense of the inter-connectedness of the subject.

## References

Brown, M. (1993) 'Clashing epistemologies: the battle for control of the National Curriculum and its assessment', inaugural lecture, Kings College, University of London, 20 October 1993.

Denvir, B. and Brown, M. (1986) 'Understanding number concepts in low-attaining 7–9 year olds: I and II', *Educational Studies in Mathematics*, 17: 15–36 and 143–64.

Denvir, B., Brown, M. and Eve, P. (1987) *Attainment Targets and Assessment in the Primary Phase: report of the mathematics feasibility study*, Kings College, University of London.

DfEE (1999) *Mathematics: the National Curriculum for England and Wales*, London: HMSO.

DfEE (2001) *Key Stage 3 National Strategy: framework for teaching mathematics Years 7, 8 and 9*, London: DfEE Publications.

Gardiner, A. (2000) *Acceleration or Enrichment*, UK Mathematics Foundation, University of Birmingham.

Stones, E. (1992) *Quality Teaching*, London: Routledge.

Vygotsky, L. (1986) *Thought and Language*, Cambridge, MA: The MIT Press.

# 12 Language issues in mathematics
## Tim Rowland

## Preamble

Judith is a newly-qualified mathematics teacher in an 11–16 secondary school. She is working with a class of Year 9 pupils, who have various rectangular arrays of points on 'dotty' paper, and have to connect them by drawing line segments between pairs of points. What is the least number of segments necessary so that they form a continuous line connecting all of the points? The brief episode that follows will be used in this chapter to raise and illustrate a number of issues about language in the mathematics classroom. As you read it, you might make a note of some of the issues that it raises for you.

One pupil, Allan, starts with a 3 × 3 array of dots, and counts eight line segments. Judith enquires:

| | |
|---|---|
| *Judith* | All right then, so what are you going to do now? |
| *Allan* | I'll try a, um, four by four grid. |
| *Judith* | Right. Can you make any predictions before you start? |
| | *After some hesitation, Allan eventually replies.* |
| *Allan* | The maximum will probably be, er, the least'll probably be about fifteen. |
| *Judith* | So why did you predict fifteen? |
| *Allan* | Uh … because I thought there might be a pattern between … if there was um, a certain amount of, um … if it's three by three say … |
| *Judith* | Uh-hum. |
| *Allan* | If you ti…, three times three is actually nine. |
| *Judith* | Uh-hum. |
| *Allan* | But as, if you went round all the dots, it would only come to about, if you did it once it would come to one, uh, less than nine, you got, uh, because, because there's o…, there's only … 'cause you only have, y … you can miss out a line exactly, 'cause you, you can miss out a gap, 'cause you, um, y'd 'ave to go all the way round the whole dots. |
| *Judith* | OK … So why did that make you say fifteen? |
| *Allan* | Because uh, f…for the same reason, 'cause if you w… tried to go round the whole all the dots you'd get sixteen but if you just did it once all the way round the dots but missing out gaps you'd still come to uh, you just minus one basically and just … |
| *Judith* | So what would happen in some other squares? |

*Allan*     Probably if you minus one from the …, if you square the number you'd
           probably find that if it was actually, if you minus one from that you'd prob-
           ably find that that would be the answer …

Allan would hardly win a prize for clarity or conciseness, nor for the elegance of his
mathematical articulation. You probably found that you had to expend some effort to
make sense of what he is trying to tell Judith. We might infer that Judith is working
hard towards the same end. You will come upon a good many 'Allans', struggling
hard to summon up words to communicate the mathematical ideas in their heads.
Actually, you will be fortunate if the pupils you teach are as willing as Allan to speak
the mathematics, and as persistent in the struggle to do so. His willingness probably
says something about the relationship that Judith has built with this class.

    Notice that Judith's contributions are limited to requests for Allan to explain his
reasoning, and to assurances that she is listening to his answers ('uh-hum'). She does
not attempt to correct or improve Allan's expression of his thinking. Do you think
that she should? What would be an elegant way to express the generalisation in the
last of Allan's utterances above?

## Vocabulary

The *Standards* for Qualified Teacher Status in England (DfEE, 1998) insist that
mathematics teachers should enable pupils to learn to speak and write mathematics
'correctly'.[1]

> Trainees must be taught that pupils' progress in mathematics depends upon
> them teaching their pupils the correct use of mathematical language, including
> the importance of using mathematical definitions and vocabulary precisely –
> especially where a word, e.g. *similar*, has an everyday meaning and a mathemati-
> cal meaning which is more subject-specific.
>
> (DfEE, 1998, Annexe G, A2ai)

> Trainees must be taught to recognise the factors which may contribute to low
> levels of numeracy including … insecure grasp of the vocabulary of number,
> e.g. *square root, prime*.
>
> (DfEE, 1998, Annexe G, A4vii)

    Learning to speak and write mathematics as a mathematician is part and parcel of
learning to become a mathematician. This is not simply a case of learning to use
jargon. Rather, one is endeavouring to achieve fluency in a particular linguistic 'register' (rather as teachers, fire-fighters, clinical health professionals, lawyers and computer scientists each have their own register) for the sake of conceptual clarity and
elegance of communication. The most straightforward aspect of this register for
young mathematicians to identify and to acquire is perhaps the vocabulary.
However, when pupils encounter mathematical language at school, they must learn
to cope with the ambiguities and misunderstandings that arise from the fact that
many words from 'ordinary' English have been adopted and given specialised meanings in mathematics. As the poet and scientist Goethe famously remarked:

Mathematicians are a kind of Frenchmen. When one talks to them, they translate the talk into their own language, and soon it is something entirely different.
(Goethe 1829, *Maxims and Reflections*)

Well-known examples of such 'translation' include *difference, product, similar, face, volume* and *table*. An extensive list is given in Durkin and Shire (1991, p. 74). Before reading on, think about the mathematical meaning (or meanings) of each of these six words, then suggest why pupils might fail to realise this particular mathematical meaning.

I shall elaborate on just two of these words, one from arithmetic, the other geometrical.

*Difference* There is no shortage of anecdotes of naive interpretation of this word. Pimm (1987, p. 8) cites two responses by nine-year-olds to the question 'What is the difference between 24 and 9?' The first replied, 'One's even and the other's odd'. The other said 'One has two numbers in it and the other has one'. The word 'difference', with all its attendant ambiguities, has traditionally had a high profile in school texts compared with *sum, product* and *quotient* – the names of the outcomes of addition, multiplication and division. This anomaly has been redressed in ambitious guidance on vocabulary in the National Numeracy Strategy (DfEE, 1999) which gives *sum* and *difference* in the checklist for the Reception year, with *product* and *quotient* in Years 3 and 4 respectively. The checklist is also extended to Year 7, 8 and 9 (DfEE, 2001), where *divisor* and *commutative* are amongst the new words for pupils to incorporate into their vocabulary in Year 7.

You might like to pause for a moment to construct two sentences, demonstrating 'correct' usage of the words *quotient* and *divisor*. What would you anticipate if you offer the same challenge to a maths set in Year 9, say?

The problem with three of the four operation–outcome words is that familiar words with very broad application in ordinary English have been borrowed and assigned, by convention, very narrow and specific mathematical meanings. Even *sum* is commonly taken to mean any kind of calculation. At least *quotient* is unlikely to be mistaken for anything else: its meaning is almost exclusive to the mathematical register.

In a seminal school-based enquiry, Otterburn and Nicholson (1976) studied 15- to 16-year-old pupils' comprehension of the mathematical language used in their public examination course. Whereas nearly all could give a satisfactory account of the meaning of *multiply*, only one-fifth gave evidence of confident understanding of *product*. A follow-up of the Otterburn and Nicholson study (Hardcastle and Orton, 1993), with 12- to 13-year-olds in Leeds, included the word 'difference', for which rather more than a half of the pupils gave a correct (mathematical) meaning.

*Similar* Only one-fifth of the 15- to 16-year-old students in the Otterburn and Nicholson study gave evidence of understanding the technical meaning of this word, referring to a relationship between shapes, one of which is an enlarged version of the other. In fact, pupils often resort to 'the same' to make reference to a wide range of relationships between shapes (e.g. same number of sides, same shape and size but different position or orientation) including that of similarity.

It is a challenging but worthwhile teaching task to try to tease out what sort of sameness the pupil is (intuitively) aware of, to encourage him or her to articulate it.

Dylan Jones (1993) highlights the ambiguity of *similar* in an analysis of 224 GCSE scripts, half being English-medium papers and half Welsh-medium versions of the same paper. The mean marks of the two halves were virtually identical. However there was a significant difference in the responses to a four-part geometry question. The Welsh-medium candidates did on average twice as well as the English-medium on the final part, which began:

Three triangles, similar to the triangles, *ABC*, *JKL* and *PQR* above, will fit together …

Now the Welsh word for similar is cyflun, a word with no meaning in ordinary Welsh, and is used only in the mathematical sense, rather like the noun *cosine* in English. Jones surmises that the Welsh-speaking candidates were alerted to a specific mathematical property of the triangles in the last part of the question, whereas many English-medium candidates understood a vague 'sameness' relation which lacked the precision necessary for successful completion of the question. The examining board, understandably, had made no distinction between the two versions of what, on the face of it, seemed to be the same mathematics.

Hardcastle and Orton suggest that 'ways certainly do need to be found to *compel* pupils to use specialist vocabulary.' (1993, p. 12). Well, compulsion is unlikely to be productive, and in any case we should expect pupils to derive some intrinsic satisfaction from developing the capacity to 'speak mathematically'. One way of enabling this is first to point out and emphasise, on a regular basis, that mathematical words are not always what they appear. Then to take just a few minutes in most lessons to ask individuals or pairs of pupils to offer the class a sentence to illustrate or exemplify the meaning of a particular word. Give them enough notice of the question to think about it without feeling 'in the spotlight'. Ask, for example, 'Can you make up a sentence containing the word *multiple*?' Specify in advance that definitions are not accepted, nor are sentences such as 'I could never understand the meaning of the word *multiple*!'

When pupils more spontaneously offer mathematical insights in the day-to-day interaction of the classroom, we need to be more flexible and accepting of their modes of expression, in order to demonstrate appreciation of their contributions. It is counter-productive to impose a kind of lexical fascism on the mathematics classroom, but it is positively helpful for the teacher to model the mathematics register in their own speech. Later in the transcript with which I began this chapter, Allan generalises his 'rule' from squares to rectangles as follows:

*Allan*   Well I did it on the same basis as the square … if you um, times both sides, the amount of dots, you um minus by one it might be the same amount.

An appropriate response might be 'Good, well done. So you multiply the two sides and then subtract one. Is that right, Allan?' On other occasions, a degree of negotiation may be judged to be necessary for the sake of effective communication. Indeed, teachers may readily accept natural (or naive) language for the sake of communication and sustained confidence. I illustrate this by reference to a snapshot from a conversation with an able, nine-year-old pupil.

*Tim*      What are you like at multiplication?
*Susie*    What's that?
*Tim*      Um, times?
*Susie*    You mean so-and-so lots of so-and-so? That sort?
*Tim*      Yes, that's called multiplication. I'll say 'lots of'.
*Susie*    I'm trying to get divide and times together, 'cos I keep getting muddled up about what to do.
*Tim*      We'll try one. Suppose we have five lots of … um …
*Susie*    Fives is easy.

Having begun by talking about multiplication, I made a spontaneous but conscious decision to go along with 'lots of'. Was the decision well-judged?

## Communication

Not all pupils will be as direct as Susie about potential sources of confusion. In any case, a person must be aware of inner confusion before they can declare it. When I ask groups of teachers and student teachers what 'language' is for, responses typically centre around the idea of communication – spoken, written, gestural, body language, and so on. But it is simplistic to suppose that words and symbols act as pure vehicles of shared meaning. Ernst von Glasersfeld (1983, p. 66) cautions that 'Knowledge is not a transferable commodity, and communication is not a conveyance'. Glasersfeld's point is that, ultimately, each person constructs his or her own version of the world, and his or her own version of knowledge about the world. We cannot expect to pass on to another person a simple copy of our own version of what we know, because we cannot be sure that our communicative intentions have been realised when another person makes sense of our words for themselves. Glasersfeld (1995) asserts that it is naive to suppose that words refer to independent objects, or that a universal meaning is shared by independent speakers. He argues that the function of words is to evoke or generate 're-presentations' of experience (actual or imaginary). Conversely, experiences may call up, for an individual, the words associated with those experiences. The essence of successful reference is not sameness, but compatibility. Each language user coordinates a word–experience pair; linguistic communication then consists of coordinations that are compatible rather than identical. This dilemma, if that is what it is, is at the heart of radical constructivism as 'a way of thinking about knowledge and the act of knowing' (Glasersfeld, 1995, p. 15). But the way out of the dilemma is by communication! Barbara Jaworski has written:

> In order to help pupils make sense of mathematics [ … ] there must be communication between teacher and pupils [ … ] The teacher has somehow to get into the minds of her pupils [ … ] Linguistic communication becomes supremely important – teachers encouraging children to talk, and listening to them;

providing opportunities for pupils to talk and listen to each other; encouraging open negotiation of meanings without fear of being thought foolish or wrong.

(Jaworski, 1988, p. 295)

Diagnostic mathematics talk is useful insofar as it explores and reveals the extent of the compatibility of the teacher's coordinations and the pupil's, within the domain under discussion. Talk about rectangles, for example, or about multiples, may expose incompatibilities that necessitate renegotiation – or correction – of word–concept coordinations, depending on the circumstances. If a pupil insists that a square is not a rectangle, which of the following would you be inclined to do?

- Point to a mathematical dictionary to show that the pupil is wrong?
- Say that mathematical definitions are arbitrary, and his misconception is understandable?
- Explain that mathematical definitions, like this one, tend to include rather than exclude; that a square is also a trapezium?
- Sketch a 'diamond' and ask whether it is a square?

## Explanation and logical language

In addition to mathematical vocabulary, the *Standards* also attach substantial importance to the language of logic that underpins mathematical argument.

Trainees must be taught that pupils' progress in mathematics depends upon them teaching their pupils the correct use of mathematical language, including the importance of using: ...

ii   mathematical sentences and connectives like 'therefore' and 'because' to indicate the logical connections between consecutive sentences;
iii  qualifiers and quantifiers correctly, e.g. $\Rightarrow$, 'and', 'or', 'not', 'if', 'then', 'for all', 'there exists'.

(DfEE, 1998, Annexe G, A2a)

The issue behind (ii) above is the need for teachers to urge and encourage pupils to engage in explanation and justification. Mathematics is, above all, a rational discipline: mathematical truths are (and should be) justified by argument, not by the authority of the teacher. Both *therefore* and *because* serve to express the logical notion of entailment, but there are no hard and fast rules about how they do so. They also have a number of informal but perfectly acceptable equivalents, such as *so* and *since*. The language of explanation ought to be apparent in the language of the teacher, and is primarily invoked in pupils when teachers ask 'why' questions.

Recall Allan and Judith earlier:

*Judith*  OK ... So why did that make you say fifteen?
*Allan*  Because uh, f ... for the same reason, 'cause if you, um, w ... tried to go round the whole all the dots you'd get sixteen but if you just did it once all the way round the dots but missing out gaps you'd still come to uh, you just minus one basically and just ...

The answers to 'why' questions will include explanatory words such as *because* and *so*, occasionally *since* and very rarely *therefore*. 'What' and 'how', by contrast, invite answers of a factual or a procedural kind. A more detailed account of the language of explanation is given in Donaldson (1986). Notice, incidentally, how Allan makes recourse to *you* in his explanation as an informal way of expressing a generality, something that is true for everyone. This use of pronouns in pupils' explanations is explored further in Rowland (1999).

The concerns raised in (iii) are associated with the appropriate use of the special-ised logical language that is deeply embedded into mathematical language. This logical register appears superficially to be natural language, yet the words are subtly redefined for logical purposes. Consequently, the range of permissible propositions becomes bizarre by conventional norms. For example, the sentence:

John is a boy or Mary is a girl.

seems nonsensical. The everyday *or* is typically exclusive ('If he feels hot, give him a couple of aspirin or paracetamol'), whereas its use in formal logic (known as logical disjunction) is inclusive, corresponding to the union of two sets, and including their intersection. Similarly, common sense offers no guide to the truth of the statement:

If daffodils are red then grass is green.

in that we are inclined to say that since daffodils are not red, the statement is silly, or even that it is false. On the other hand, formal logic judges it to be true, given only our usual experiences of grass. 'If P then Q' is false only when P is true and Q is false. This is a hard lesson to learn, although it is for this reason that every set has the empty set as one of its subsets.

Before leaving such matters, suppose a pupil were asked to 'show that the sum of any two odd numbers is even'. How would you assess the response '5 and 9 are two odd numbers, $5 + 9 = 14$, and 14 is even'? The fact is that the quantifier *any*, despite widespread use in mathematics at all levels, is irredeemably ambiguous, and may in turn be intended, as in this case, to mean 'every' (this is the universal quantifier *for all*) or – as interpreted in the response given above – 'some' (the existential quantifier *there exists*). So the question:

Is any rectangle a rhombus?

can legitimately be answered both 'Yes, a square is', and 'No, unless it happens to be a square'.

Finally, experience leads me to suggest that the symbolic ⇒, if it is no more than a shorthand for 'and so', 'it follows that' or 'therefore', is best avoided since the explan-atory intention of the prose is clearer. Indeed, the symbol can degenerate to, at best, a kind of 'carriage return' in students' mathematical arguments.

To summarise: the process of decoding mathematical 'text' (written or spoken) necessitates recognising and separating several different kinds of language subtly rolled together. Consider, for example, the sentence:

A tetrahedron has four faces, any two of which meet at an edge.

This innocent statement contains one or more examples of each of the following language categories:

- explicit logical language – 'any' is an informal equivalent of the universal quantifier 'every';
- implicit logical language – here, the indefinite article 'A' has the force of 'every'; the mid-sentence comma needs to be read as if it were the connective 'and';
- words peculiar to the vocabulary of mathematics, such as 'tetrahedron' and, to a lesser extent, 'two';
- words like 'has' and 'meet', borrowed from natural language, which subtly personify the tetrahedron and its faces;
- words such as 'face' borrowed from natural language and redefined for mathematical purposes.

Awareness of these distinctions is one aspect of the teacher's professional knowledge, so that pupils' misunderstandings arising from these complexities and lexical ambiguities may be anticipated and understood.

## Language and thought

The role of language in the teaching and learning of mathematics is a special component of a wider problem: the general relationship between language and thought. It is tempting to suppose that the two are intimately interrelated. We encapsulate and communicate our thoughts with language, and language, in turn, conjures up particular ideas in our minds. Vygotsky (1962) proposes, however, that thought and language (speech, to be precise) are best considered as two intersecting circles. The intersection of the circles is verbal thought, but there exist other forms of thought and other forms of speech. Vygotsky cites the thinking manifested in the use of tools as evidence of thought with no direct relation to speech. This is especially true of automated tool use, car-driving being a sophisticated example of the kind. The disabling necessity for the learner driver to think, under instruction, in words about things like 'clutch' and 'third gear' is, in time, replaced by an automatic bodily response to road conditions by limbs and fingers.

Conversely, says Vygotsky, a person may recite a poem learned by heart in the absence of 'intellectual activity in the proper sense of the term' (p. 48). The phenomenon of speech divorced from thought has multiple manifestations in, and significant implications for, mathematics education. Before entering school, a child may be able to rehearse the counting numbers to ten, without any awareness of their cardinal or ordinal significance. Later, the child may be able to say the 'seven times table', but without the sense of any model of multiplication. Some time ago, the Open University produced video material for a course *Developing Mathematical Thinking*. In a memorable clip, a 13-year-old boy, Charlie, is asked to subtract 70 from 109. He writes the 'sum' in the usual vertical format, with the digits of 70 below 09, and intones:

*Charlie*  Nought from nine you can't do that, so you put nought down. Then it's seven take nought, you can't do it, so you put nought down again. Then there's nothing to take from one, so you put one down.

Charlie writes 100 as his 'answer'. Whilst we cannot claim that no thought has accompanied his speech, it is apparent that he has chanted a kind of 'magic spell' to accompany the performance of a syntactic task (a faulty algorithm) with little attention to the meaning of the individual components of the task. This is by no means as stupid as it might at first appear. The whole point of an algorithm is that the user is freed from semantic considerations for the sake of efficiency and fluency. This is a theme which David Pimm explores at length (Pimm, 1995). Over a century earlier, Thomas Hill wrote:

> The most striking characteristic of the written language of algebra … is the sharpness of definition, by which we are enabled to reason upon the symbols by the mere laws of verbal logic, discharging our minds entirely of the meaning of the symbols, until we have reached a stage in the process where we desire to interpret our results.

> (Hill, 1875, p. 505)

Suppose, for example, I were asked to find the roots of the equation $2x^2 - x - 5 = 0$. Having established that the quadratic expression does not factorise, I am likely to apply the algorithm – 'the formula' – without thought for its derivation. The point about 'understanding' in mathematics education is not so much that one should always mentally refer to the meaning of signs and actions, but that recourse to such meanings is possible when it is prompted by necessity or curiosity. Thus, having solved my quadratic expression, I might start to build up a mental image of the graph of the quadratic function, and so give some meaning to the two solutions in terms of the relationship of the parabola to the coordinate axes.

## The language of uncertainty

Annexe G of the *Standards* promotes, perhaps inadvertently, the commonly-held view of mathematics as a discipline characterised by precision and exactness, with a sharp boundary between truth and error. The questions which teachers ask pupils are usually not genuine requests for information, but 'testing questions', to which – contrary to normal social convention – they already know the answer. For pupils, there are intrinsic and extrinsic penalties associated with 'wrong' or even hesitant responses to questioning. The official documentation of the National Numeracy Strategy makes much of 'well-paced lessons', characterised in training materials by quick-fire questions and confident answers. Yet uncertainty is a valid response to a mathematical challenge, and such a cognitive state is to be expected when, like Allan, pupils are asked to make predictions and generalisations in enquiry-based, problem solving activity. A conjecture needs to be articulated before a prediction can be verified or a generalisation justified. Describing the qualities of what he calls a conjecturing atmosphere, John Mason advises '… let it be the group task to encourage those who are *unsure* to be the ones to speak first … ' so that '… every utterance is treated as a *modifiable conjecture*!' (Mason, 1988, p. 9). In such circumstances, uncertainty must be recognised, and handled with care and sensitivity. Knowledge of language is the key to such sensitivity, but a rather more subtle appreciation of language than that set out in the *Standards*. Vygotsky warns against belief that intellect and affect are somehow separable, since 'every idea contains a transmuted affective attitude towards that bit of reality to which it refers.' (1962, p. 8).

In Rowland (1995), I describe and analyse a number of transcripts of interviews based on an investigative activity that I call 'Make 10'. This begins with consideration of the number of ways that 10 can be made as a sum of two numbers, and proceeds to making other positive integers as such sums. The intention, as the task develops, is to provoke pupils into making predictions about untried numbers, and conjectures about what might happen with 'any' number; in some cases to testing the generality of such conjectures, and trying to see why they might be true.

One striking feature of the transcripts is the use of words such as: *about, around, maybe, think, normally, suppose, (not) sure, (not) exactly*. Such words are called 'hedges'. They convey a sense of uncertainty – a state which, as I have already noted, one would expect to prevail in a conjecturing moment. The following examples are drawn from a discussion with two girls, Frances and Ishka. At this point, having considered 10, 20, 13 and 30, they are invited to predict the number of ways of making 100 as a sum of two numbers.

*Frances*  Fifty?
*Ishka*  About fifty, yeah.
*Tim*  About fifty [ … ] do you really think it is fifty?
*Ishka*  Well, maybe not exactly, but it's around fifty basically? [ … ]
*Frances*  Maybe around fifty.

The linguist George Lakoff coined the term 'a hedge' for a word or phrase that makes a proposition 'fuzzy' or vague in some way. The short extract above is chosen for the dense concentration of 'hedges' which it contains, arguably including the rising intonation on Frances' 'Fifty?', indicating her lack of full commitment to her prediction. The same tentativeness is evident in Allan's speech in his interaction with Judith (the portion above, and elsewhere) when he is invited to generalise, to make the leap from certain knowledge to a plausible conjecture.

*Judith*  So what would happen in some other squares?
*Allan*  Probably if you minus one from the s …, if you square the number you'd probably find that if it was actually, if you minus one from that you'd probably find that that would be the answer.

*Maybe, probably* and *possibly* are examples of so-called 'plausibility shields', which point to a less than complete commitment to a proposition. These 'hedges' are called shields because their function is to protect the speaker from accusation of being committed to a false proposition. Incidentally, teachers more often use 'attribution shields' such as 'so-and-so says that … ', distancing themselves from a proposition by attributing it to someone else. This is a pedagogical strategy which avoids 'closing' on a problem, in order to sustain discussion and invite a variety of proposals. For example:

*Teacher*  John says you can't divide 739 by 9. What do other people think?

A second category of 'hedge', 'approximators', such as *about, around, approximately*, as well as *sort of, kind of, basically*, can, like shields, also have the effect of withholding commitment to a proposition. They achieve this by inserting vagueness into the substantive proposition itself. (Shields, by contrast, stand outside the proposition.) Sadock (1977, p. 437) observes that:

> the role of an approximator [ … ] is to trivialise the semantics of a sentence, to make it almost unfalsifiable.

The short extract with Frances and Ishka provides a rich source of approximators *about, around* and *not exactly*. The two pupils' lack of certainty is conveyed in the 'hedged' predictions ('Fifty?'; 'About fifty'), but I press them to nail their colours to the mast ('Do you really think it is fifty?'). Ishka responds with a consummate display of multiple 'hedging', implicating in no uncertain terms that she is not yet ready to make the commitment that I seem to be wanting. The linguistic pointers are there for teachers whose ears have been sensitised.

## Summary

Language is essential if teachers and students are to communicate and share mathematical ideas and beliefs. In our culture, an elaborate edifice of 'proper' mathematical language has evolved, which has an elegance and beauty of its own for individuals who learn to speak and write it with confidence. Pupils should be encouraged and assisted to speak and write mathematically. Yet, in the teaching and learning of mathematics, the language of communication is a language of struggle, of compromise and negotiation. Students can fail to understand the meanings intended by teachers, because of the different language types to be found in mathematical speech and writing – Ordinary and Mathematical English, logical language, meta-language – which are rarely superficially evident. If we are at least aware of the ambiguities and misunderstandings inherent in classroom mathematical language, we are in a stronger position to diagnose learning difficulties whose cause may be linguistic.

The language used by pupils as they respond to mathematical tasks is capable of conveying feelings, anxieties and degrees of commitment in subtle ways, including the use of 'hedges' as protection against accusation of being wrong. These 'hedges' may be recognised by sensitised teachers as subtle pointers to vulnerability in conjecturing activity.

## Note

1    In their call for 'correctness', the authors of Circular 4/98 inadvertently invite us to consider whether correctness is absolute or conventional. Their formulation 'pupils' progress in mathematics depends *upon them teaching* their pupils ...' brings to mind H. W. Fowler's comment that 'It is perhaps beyond hope for a generation that regards *upon you giving* as normal English to recover its hold upon the truth that grammar matters.'

## References

DfEE (1998) *Teaching: high status, high standards: Circular 4/98*, London: HMSO.

DfEE (1999) *The National Numeracy Strategy: mathematical vocabulary*, Sudbury: DfEE Publications.

DfEE (2001) *Key Stage 3 National Strategy: framework for teaching mathematics Years 7, 8 and 9*, London: DfEE Publications.

Donaldson, M. (1986) *Children's Explanations*, Cambridge: Cambridge University Press.

Durkin, K. and Shire, B. (eds) (1991) *Language in Mathematical Education*, Milton Keynes: Open University Press.

Hardcastle, L. and Orton, T. (1993) 'Do they know what we are talking about?', *Mathematics in School*, 22(3): 12–14.

Hill, T. (1875) 'The uses of "mathesis"', *Bibliotheca Sacra and Theological Eclectic*, 32.

Jaworski, B. (1988). '"Is" versus "seeing as": constructivism and the mathematics classroom', in D. Pimm (ed.) *Mathematics, Teachers and Children*, London: Hodder and Stoughton.

Jones, D. (1993) 'Words with a similar meaning', *Mathematics Teaching*, 145: 14–15.

Lakoff, G. (1973) 'Hedges: a study in meaning criteria and the logic of fuzzy concepts, *Journal of Philosophical Logic*, 2: 458–508.

Mason, J. (1988) *Learning and Doing Mathematics*, London: Macmillan.

Otterburn, M.K. and Nicholson, A.R. (1976) 'The language of CSE mathematics', *Mathematics in School*, 5(5): 18–20.

Pimm, D. (1987) *Speaking Mathematically: communication in mathematics classrooms*, London: Routledge and Kegan Paul.

Pimm, D. (1995) *Symbols and Meanings in School Mathematics*, London: Routledge.

Rowland, T. (1995) 'Hedges in mathematics talk: linguistic pointers to uncertainty', *Educational Studies in Mathematics*, 29(4): 327–53.

Rowland, T. (1999) *The Pragmatics of Mathematics Education: vagueness and mathematical discourse*, London: Falmer.

Sadock, J. M. (1977) 'Truth and approximations', *Berkeley Linguistic Society Papers*, 3: 430–9.

von Glasersfeld, E. (1983) 'Learning as a constructive activity', in J.C. Bergeron and N. Herscovicz (eds) *Proceedings of the Fifth Meeting of PME-NA*, University of Montreal.

von Glasersfeld, E. (1995) *Radical Constructivism: a way of knowing and learning*, London: The Falmer Press.

Vygotsky, L.S. (1962) *Thought and Language*, Cambridge, MA: MIT Press.

# 13 Differentiation
## Linda Haggarty

What kinds of strategies are available to help mathematics teachers in mainstream secondary schools meet the educational needs of all their pupils? Responding to pupil differences is called differentiation.

This chapter is divided into three sections. The first is about why differentiation is an important issue, the second looks at general strategies for differentiation and the third looks in detail at mastery learning.

## Why is differentiation important?

Think back to your own schooldays and try to remember how it felt when you finished your work before everyone else. There were, no doubt, feelings of pleasure at having completed the work set – but then what? Were you set even more of the same to do? Were you left to your own devices? Did you actually waste a lot of time in your mathematics lesson or were you able to set yourself new challenges while you waited for everyone else to catch up?

Perhaps you were rarely in the situation described above. Maybe you felt rushed in your particular class; perhaps you often felt that the teacher moved the class on before you quite mastered something. Were there times when it seemed that everyone else could do something so you didn't like to draw attention to yourself by asking for help?

Mathematics is a difficult subject to learn and the mathematics teacher has the task of trying to meet the needs of all the individuals in his or her care. How can this be done when learners are all so different from each other? A common response is to say that by grouping learners into achievement groups – sets – it is possible to meet those needs. Whilst it is possible – and probably easier to do this in a setted situation – it is by no means certain that differentiation needs will be met. There are still difficult decisions to be made. Take, for example, the common scene in the mathematics classroom of teacher explanation followed by pupil practice. Where should the teacher begin the explanation – where the lesson ended yesterday or at some point before then? Perhaps begin with questions to pupils, but which pupils and which questions? Perhaps with an example in context, but what sort of example, and who is the context likely to appeal to? Then we move onto the practice phase. Questions from the textbook or another source? Which questions? How many? For how long? How do you avoid the situation described above about two extremes of learners? There are many choices to be made, but by not attending to differentiation, there is a danger that the teacher actually ends up using the lesson opening to 'manage' whoever the dominant minority in the classroom happens to be. For all sorts of complex and understandable reasons, unless differentiation is firmly on the agenda of any teacher, teaching in a setted situation ends up suiting only a notional 'middle' group of learners and leaving all the rest to make the best of what is on offer.

It is useful to begin by looking at some of the differences between learners.

## Educational Differences

Educational differences can be described as differences in what pupils already know, understand and can do in relation to the issue which is the subject of a planned educational experience (Postlethwaite, 1993). It is worth thinking about this more carefully.

Imagine you are teaching a topic on ratio and, in particular, you want pupils to learn how to divide a quantity in a given ratio. What do you assume pupils already know? What do pupils already know? Are these the same thing? It is tempting to say they are, because you taught it to them yesterday / last week / in the last chapter … or because the last teacher said so. But they are likely to know different things – have different constructions from each other – and are also likely to have a different construction from the one in your head. Of course, they might never have 'known' it in the first place, at least to the extent you anticipate for this lesson. They might also have forgotten much of it – and no doubt different pupils have forgotten different bits. So even within a setted class, it is perfectly reasonable to expect different pupils to know different things before you even start a topic. For this reason, many teachers give a quick reminder or recap before beginning a new topic. Of course, whilst this is much better than nothing, it does little to help those who failed to learn first time round or those who, for a variety of reasons, were missing the first time round. Nevertheless, there is a clear need for the teacher to try to address the educational differences pupils bring with them to each lesson in order to give all pupils a fair chance of being successful in new learning.

## Psychological differences

Psychological differences include both general and specific cognitive characteristics as well as preferred learning styles, feelings about school, the subject, and themselves. A general cognitive characteristic, in common-sense terms, describes how some people seem genuinely more intelligent than others across a wide range of activities. Although there is a link between IQ scores and performance in school, so that it may be tempting to argue that, within a particular set in mathematics, IQ scores are likely to be similar, there is a danger in thinking that IQ scores are fixed and therefore determine success in school. In fact, Feuerstein (1980) has demonstrated that IQ is not fixed and can be altered through a programme such as Instrumental Enrichment. So pupils in the same set might have different IQ scores, and it is by no means certain that the higher the score, the more likely they are to be successful in mathematics. The converse is also dangerous: mathematics classes are set according to notions of generalised ability, measured through something like an IQ test so that some are excluded who might otherwise have been successful.

More specific psychological differences in mathematics include those of cognitive style – about the ways people think. For example, some people are better at visualising than other people and may therefore have little need for a diagram in mathematics –

certainly not one imposed by the teacher. Some people are field-dependent while others are field-independent. A field-dependent learner has difficulty extracting the general from the particular: of recognising a 'type' of situation because of the complexity surrounding it. Thus in mathematics, while a field dependent learner can be confused when a right-angled triangle is shown in an unfamiliar orientation, a field independent learner is much less likely to have the difficulty. (See Cronbach and Snow, 1977 for a discussion of the significance of this.)

Another difference is that between people who adopt a serialist approach in their work and those who adopt a holist approach. The former are likely to proceed methodically through a mathematical problem whilst the latter see the problem (and are therefore more likely to recognise a problem type) as a whole. (See Backhouse et al., 1992, for further discussion.) What is important here is that Pask (1975) has shown that people learn more effectively when they are taught in a style that matches their preferred learning style.

Thus in terms of cognitive characteristics and preferred learning styles, learners differ from each other and some learners' performance is likely to be significantly affected if the teacher only adopts a narrow range of teaching strategies and learning opportunities. Indeed, a teacher who adopts a 'rule of thumb' that dismisses an approach because they would not have liked it as learners themselves, is in very great danger of ensuring that only learners who learn just like them are likely to be successful in their classes.

Whilst it goes beyond the scope of this chapter to examine other psychological differences in detail, such as differences in attitude to school, to mathematics, to ways of working in mathematics, to ways in which pupils perceive the teacher as helping their learning, diversity in motivation, variation in self-esteem and academic self-image and so on are also important differences between pupils.

Again, we have to draw the inevitable conclusion: even within a setted group, pupils have significant differences. In turn, since teachers can't suit all learners all of the time, it seems that teachers can have an effect if they choose from a range of approaches which at least (realistically) suit all of the pupils some of the time. In addition, as pupils experience increasing amounts of success, other psychological differences are also attended to, relating to self, to mathematics and to mathematics learning (e.g. Bloom 1976; Postlethwaite and Haggarty, 1998).

## Other differences

As well as educational and psychological differences, McIntyre and Postlethwaite (1989) argue there are also physical differences (which may be temporary or long-term and are the consequences of illness, prolonged physical or sensory handicap, or chronic medical difficulties), social differences (i.e. the different ways pupils behave in the social situation of the classroom – so that a pupil not answering may not understand, may be introverted, may feel they have experienced failure too often in the past to take a risk, may have a poor self-image, may have a negative attitude towards mathematics … ) and socio-economic and cultural differences (relating to race, gender, socio-economic background, etc. and the ways in which the experiences they have affect the explanations and experiences they construct for themselves.

So moving beyond the simplistic notion that a setted class is already sufficiently differentiated is important and necessary for teachers. Learners are individuals in terms of the wide variety of differences already outlined, and trying to meet their learning needs is the responsibility of their teacher. However, having argued that, pupils know, understand and can do different things (even after the same learning experience in the classroom), they have particular preferred ways of learning, they are individuals with their own affective characteristics, they have their own physical and social characteristics, and so on, it is important for the teacher not to conclude that with so many differences, it becomes impossible to meet any of them very sensibly. Indeed, the oft-quoted remark from Ausubel (1968) springs to mind:

> If I had to reduce all of educational psychology to just one principle, I would say this: the most important single factor influencing learning is what the learner already knows. Ascertain this and teach him accordingly.

Well yes, and no! The task starts to sound like that of the plate spinner, attempting to keep plates spinning at the tops of an ever-increasing number of sticks! There are strategies, and we look at some of these now.

## Strategies for differentiation

HMI (1992) report that differentiation, where it exists, is usually done in classrooms in four ways:

- *by outcome*, giving a common task to elicit different levels of response;
- by rate of progress, allowing a pupil to proceed through a course at his or her own speed;
- *by enrichment*, giving a pupil supplementary tasks intended to broaden or deepen skills or understanding;
- *by setting different tasks* requiring greater sophistication within a common theme or topic.

They further report that where there was sufficient planning with explicit pathways to higher order cognitive and intellectual development, it was almost always associated with good practice. Thus, although investigations or investigative activities are often seen to offer *differentiation by outcome* by their very nature, and although it is possible to elicit different levels of response from pupils from the same starting point, HMI suggest that this in itself may not be enough to ensure all pupils are sufficiently challenged. Rather, teachers need to be sure that a range of cognitive responses is possible from an activity, that they are aware of the possible routes through the activity leading to different levels of cognitive response and that different pupils are encouraged to move down routes that are appropriate to their own learning needs. An investigation can become as impoverished and unchallenging to a learner as a routine exercise from a textbook unless the pupil can tackle it at an appropriately demanding level.

*Differentiation by rate of progress* through a course is often referred to as acceleration in relation to high attainers. The equivalent for low attainers is rarely practised in this country, although in France, for example, the practice of *redoublement* – repeating a year – is relatively common. Of course, it could be argued that setting in England allows for differentiation by rate of progress, but the arguments presented in the previous section should alert the reader to the shortcomings of this reaction.

Acceleration is usually understood to refer to 'grade-skipping', although it can also mean individualised provision of any sort that takes the pupils on faster. (Note that this use of the term 'acceleration' is different from that referred to as 'cognitive acceleration' referred to in the next chapter by Maria Goulding). In relation to mathematics teaching in this country, there are many examples reported in the media of pupils who have gained mathematics qualifications well beyond that expected of pupils their age. However, it is also possible for pupils to work on individualised programmes in their own classroom, or to 'sit in' on A level classes, or to engage in study with a local Higher Education institution.

Acceleration is essentially a reactive measure in that it is a tactic based on a learner's already recognised advancement. Thus one problem with this strategy is that it only addresses issues of differentiation for those already attaining highly within the learning experiences offered. It does not address the learning needs of those who may be equally capable if different learning experiences had been offered.

There are arguments for and against acceleration, and the research remains inconclusive about its effectiveness. While it may seem to proponents of acceleration that it allows the learner to reach their potential when they are ready rather than being restricted by age expectations, opponents may see it as resulting in a narrowing of mathematical experience as well as being likely to have a negative effect on emotional development.

*Enrichment* is understood to be a deliberate attempt by the teacher to broaden or deepen skills and understanding. Clearly it is desirable for all pupils to be offered enriching experiences but it is particularly important for high-attaining pupils in any particular topic since it allows them to go well beyond the core objectives of a particular sequence of lessons to meet new and more challenging objectives. It is assumed that engaging in enrichment activities keeps learners on the same broad topics as their classmates, but that they broaden or deepen their knowledge of that topic within the teaching time allowed for it. Enrichment can be considered to be proactive in that it can promote hidden potential. Thus, all learners have opportunities throughout the year to engage in enrichment activities when they are offered (whereas few have such opportunities through acceleration).

Maria Goulding examines (in the next chapter) a strategy developed by the Cognitive Acceleration in Mathematics Education (CAME) Project (Adhami *et al.*, 1998), in which higher-order thinking is developed through particular types of lessons. A more general strategy (which can be used in all mathematics lessons) is offered by Bloom (1956) in his taxonomy of educational objectives. He identifies the following in an increasingly demanding hierarchy: knowledge, comprehension, application, analysis, synthesis, evaluation. It is useful to think about each of these and the kinds of associated questions that might be asked in a mathematics classroom. Because his list is not mathematics specific, it is not clear whether this hierarchy applies strictly in the subject, nor whether these interpretations are those intended. Nevertheless, it provides us with a useful start for general thinking about the types of problems that might lead to higher-order thinking.

1   Knowledge, with questions relating to remembering. For example:
   - describe a regular pentagon …
   - state Pythagoras' theorem …
   - write down the coefficient of $x$ in the expressions listed …

2   Comprehension, assuming a low level of understanding and without necessarily making links with other ideas. For example:
    • answering the next 10 questions (which are virtually the same as the worked example)
    • answering questions from a worksheet which practise skills in isolation from each other

3   Application, using generalised methods. For example:
    • answering questions that are not like the worked example
    • answering questions requiring a choice of method

4   Analysis, understanding parts of the whole. For example:
    • how are those questions similar and how are they different … ?
    • what was the main idea behind that activity … ?
    • recognising connections between ideas in mathematics
    • which of the ideas can be deduced from the others?

5   Synthesis, putting ideas together to generate new ideas. For example:
    • making conjectures and generalisations
    • asking how else you could convince someone …
    • asking how new work links with what was learnt in science …
    • developing a plan to tackle a complex and unfamiliar problem

6   Evaluation, judging the extent to which an argument is acceptable. For example:
    • consider the different strategies you have learned about and decide when each is most useful and in what circumstances …
    • develop an alternative argument from the point of view of another interest group within the context of the problem
    • find fallacies in mathematical arguments
    • read through the proofs and consider the effectiveness of each of the arguments …

It is useful at this point to consider the extent to which questions from textbooks require pupils to engage in some of these higher order activities. Usually, they rarely go beyond application (level 3). However, activities that genuinely extend those in the enrichment group without moving them on to new content learning can be developed using question types found in levels 4 to 6. (For more ideas on making the most of your textbook, see Chapter 16 by Laurinda Brown.)

Thus, tasks such as 'draw the graphs of the following equations: $y = 2$, $x = 3$, $y = 2 + 3x$, $y = 7 - 2x$, $y = x/5$, $2y - 5x = 10$ …' can generate enrichment questions such as:

• Design a set of cards to play 'pairs' where two pupils turn over pairs of cards. Player 1 turns over two cards and if he or she has two that match, they keep them and have another turn – otherwise Player 2 has a turn. The winner is the one with more pairs at the end. In each pair of cards, one will have the equation and the other its graph. You will need to decide how many pairs to design in order to make a worthwhile game.

• You have drawn some straight line graphs in science of … . Explain how they relate to what you have learnt about $y = ax + b$.

- Look at the questions set in the textbook exercise and (without drawing them) try to group them in terms of their similarities and/or differences. Explain the classification you have used.

However, there are very many ways of generating such activities and many more examples. A useful starting point is to have the list above available until you become familiar with the headings and types of examples. These can then help to generate comparable ones requiring a similar order of thinking.

*Differentiation by setting different tasks*, requiring greater sophistication within a common theme or topic, is essentially a strategy in which some pupils move straight into enrichment activities, bypassing whatever is taught to the rest of the class. Rather than restrict this opportunity to those identified as 'able' in mathematics it is possible to offer this route to any pupils following diagnostic assessment at the beginning of a topic. In other words, because of the educational differences between pupils it is possible that any pupil might meet the learning objectives of any topic before it is even taught. Ascertaining what everyone knows at the beginning in order to plan teaching is therefore a useful strategy as long as the possibility is available for some pupils to move forward to appropriate enrichment activities.

Indeed, one teacher we worked with in a research project tried out a strategy using diagnostic assessment at the beginning of a unit on scale reading (Haggarty *et al.*, 1995). She found in a mixed Year 7 class – and before any teaching had taken place in the school – that three of her pupils could successfully read some scales on instruments as long as the scales were annotated with whole numbers. On the other hand, eight could successfully carry out interpolations to two or three decimal places and to a higher degree of accuracy than the annotated numbers. The others in the class were somewhere between these two extremes. This provided her with enough information to develop learning materials at three levels of input as well as an enrichment activity for those meeting all her identified learning objectives. It has to be said, though, that this was a challenging and time-consuming job!

## Mastery learning as a strategy for differentiation

Although there are a number of possible strategies for differentiation, one which seems particularly appealing to teachers, as well as leading to successful outcomes, is Mastery Learning (Bloom, 1976). (See, for example, Postlethwaite and Haggarty, 1998.)

It is probably sensible, before providing more details of the strategy, to tackle its critics. Not only does it *sound* mechanistic but it has also been criticised as limiting education to the pursuit of behavioural objectives (e.g. Cohen, 1981), and for encouraging an atomistic approach to teaching and learning. Indeed, many may have dismissed the strategy as unhelpful and outdated along with behaviourism! However, my argument would be that despite its name, it sits comfortably within newer paradigms of learning! Indeed, with a broad view of objectives, and within newer understandings about learning, it is possible to take the view that Mastery Learning simply requires teachers to decide on the outcomes that all pupils are intended to achieve for each unit of work, and on deeper objectives which can be truly enriching for those who meet the objectives ahead of the rest of the class. As in

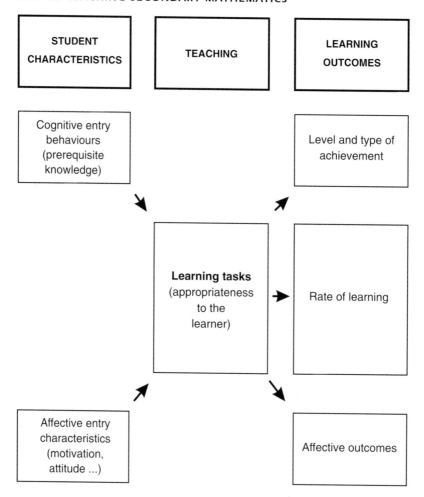

**Figure 13.1** *Variables in the learning process, all of which can be controlled by the teacher. (Based on Bloom, 1976)*

almost all Government publications, teachers are urged to tell their pupils what the lesson is intended to achieve (see also, for example, Brophy, 1986), this can be seen as helpful rather than limiting.

Bloom's assertion is that if pupils have the necessary prior knowledge and positive attitudes to learning the subject, and if the learning tasks and teaching are well designed, almost all pupils can be successful in their learning (see Figure 13.1). He claims that under the appropriate conditions, and given 20 per cent of additional time on a topic, approximately 80 per cent of pupils can master work that, under conventional teaching, only 20 per cent would be able to comprehend. Where Mastery Learning has been used, evaluations of its impact on learning have often been positive (see Postlethwaite and Haggarty, 1998).

The 'appropriate conditions' which Bloom mentions require the teacher to take account of each of the variables in the diagram (Figure 13.2) and these are elaborated next.

The key elements of mastery learning are that:

1   It requires teachers to break down their course into relatively short units of work. This is not unusual for mathematics teachers since Programmes of Study, schemes of work and textbooks follow this pattern anyway. However, Bloom's assumption is that the unit is about two weeks long – so the concepts taught in *some* textbook chapters would have to be put together (a good idea for opportunities to explore connectivity and coherence).

2   It calls for the setting of (and making explicit) specific objectives for each unit. This is entirely in line with Government recommendations, not only in relation to setting learning objectives but also in making them known to pupils (see, for example, DfEE, 1998, Circular 4/98 – the sections on Standards and in Annex G for secondary mathematics).

3   It expects teachers to plan their initial treatment of each unit to take account of pupils' pre-existing knowledge and understanding. Thus it is important that the teacher has a secure understanding of the likely progression within each topic. (See Chapter 11 for more suggestions about this.) Given the educational differences between pupils explored above, this seems a reasonable requirement. Bloom himself did not make specific mention of the possibility of pupil misconceptions in pre-existing knowledge but it is clearly relevant at this point in that the teacher can use these as a stimulus to discussion.

4   It recognises that pupils' attitudes will be relevant to their performance on the unit and may be altered by their work on that unit. This is in line with some of the psychological differences identified above. According to Bloom, many pupils have experiences that fall well short of mastery in conventional teaching. However, his argument is that under Mastery Learning conditions, many such pupils will begin to experience success and therefore their affective characteristics will become increasingly positive.

5   After initial teaching of the unit, using a wide range of activities and approaches, it calls for diagnostic assessment of each pupil's learning. The wide range of approaches is important and takes account of the diversity of preferred learning styles of pupils. It is also assumed that the teacher uses as rich a variety of learning opportunities as possible. Diagnostic assessment requires the teacher to target assessment at the achievement of the particular learning objectives set.

6   Pupils who have not 'mastered' – or successfully achieved – the objectives of the unit are, on the basis of the diagnosis, directed towards remediation work on a small group or individual basis; pupils who have 'mastered' the objectives are provided with enrichment work which addresses new objectives suitable for more successful learners in the topic, but not objectives that are to be tackled by the whole class in a later unit of the course. There are a number of important issues raised here.

    •   The end of unit test (which achieves little for anyone beyond providing numbers for a mark book) is replaced by diagnostic assessment made a lesson or so before the end of the unit so that meaningful remediation can take place (rather than the often hurried 'going over' of the test). In other words, the teacher is genuinely asking which pupils have achieved

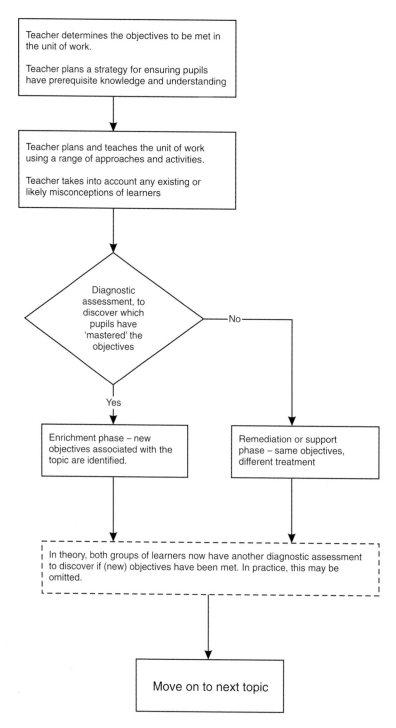

**Figure 13.2** Flowchart for a Mastery Learning unit of work

which objectives and which pupils have what kinds of difficulties achieving each of those objectives. Then, rather than simply telling pupils where they are wrong – or pressing on with the next topic – the teacher finds alternative strategies for helping those who have difficulty.

- 'Mastery' of objectives needs some thinking about. What counts as 'mastery'? What would you expect to see from a pupil who had 'understood'? (See Chapter 10 by Anne Watson for further discussion of this idea.)
- Remediation is assumed to mean something rather different from 'going over' or 're-teaching' using the same explanations, activities and examples as in the initial teaching. Pupils who did not find it a helpful way to learn first time round are unlikely to do so the second time round. Instead, remediation tries to help the learner meet the objectives, using alternative strategies and approaches.
- Enrichment allows pupils who have met the objectives to engage in more demanding activities associated with the same range of objectives. This goes well beyond 'more of the same', but allows them to engage in higher order thinking. Notice also that this keeps all pupils together – i.e. working on the same topic rather than allowing some pupils to race ahead.

Mastery Learning seems to be acceptable to teachers because units of work can be developed over time: a whole course does not have to be developed before pupils can learn through such an approach. In addition, very much of what teachers already do can still be done: it does not require a whole new way of working in the classroom, nor does it threaten the existing expertise of mathematics teachers. Further, this is a strategy that student teachers can use successfully within departments locked into particular schemes of work: for much of the time the student can fit into existing ways of doing things. In addition, the strategy lends itself to student and mentor developing approaches collaboratively since the development of alternative remediation materials and enrichment materials may well require additional time to devise or discover new materials.

I have chosen to write most extensively about Mastery Learning because it has been so well received by teachers and learners I have worked with on a number of research projects. I therefore end the chapter with two anecdotes.

The first concerns a doctoral student from Cameroon who wanted to improve the teaching and learning of mathematics in his country. One strategy he trialled was that of Mastery Learning – and it is salutary to think that he trialled this with class sizes of 80 plus and with few, if any, teaching resources. One outcome, which none of us had anticipated, was that many of the pupils asked (and turned up) for extra lessons at weekends because they said they realised, with the 'new' way of teaching, that 'at last, someone is trying to help us to learn'. They were referring to the remediation phase of each unit where those who had difficulty first time round were being helped by their teacher's extra efforts.

The second concerns some pupils in a secondary school in Britain. Teachers were again using Mastery Learning and one pupil commented afterwards that '… it was great fun, especially the enrichment work because you can let your mind run riot'.

Attending to differentiation helps all pupils to learn more effectively and allows minds to run riot!

## References

Adhami, M., Johnson, D. and Shayer, M. (1998) *Thinking Maths. Accelerated learning in mathematics*, Oxford: Heinemann.

Ausubel, D.P. (1968) *Educational Psychology: a cognitive view*, New York: Holt, Rinehart and Winston.

Backhouse, J., Haggarty, L., Pirie, S. and Stratton, J. (1992) *Improving the Learning of Mathematics*, London: Cassell.

Bloom, B.S. (ed.) (1956) *Taxonomy of Educational Objectives. Book 1: cognitive domain*, New York: Longman.

Bloom, B.S. (1976) *Human Characteristics and School Learning*, New York: McGraw-Hill.

Brophy, J. (1986) 'Motivating students to learn mathematics'. *Journal for Research in Mathematics Education*, 17: 341–6.

Cohen, A.S. (1981) 'In defense of mastery learning', *Principal*, 60: 35–7.

Cronbach, L.J. and Snow, R.E. (1977) *Aptitudes and Instructional Methods: a handbook of research on interactions*, New York: Irvington.

DfEE (1998) *Circular number 4/98: Requirements for courses of Initial Teacher Training*, London: DfEE.

Feuerstein, R., *et al.* (1980) *Instrumental Enrichment: an intervention programme for cognitive modifiability*, Baltimore: University Park Press.

Haggarty, L., Postlethwaite, K. and Burgess, J. (1995) 'Scale reading', *Mathematics in School*, November 1995.

HMI (1992) *Education Observed: the education of very able children in maintained schools. A review by HMI*, London: HMSO.

McIntyre, D. and Postlethwaite, K. (1989) 'Attending to individual differences: a conceptual analysis' in N. Jones (ed.) *Special Educational Needs Review*, vol. 2, Lewes, Falmer Press.

Pask, G. (1975) *The Cybernetics of Human Learning and Performance*, Hutchinson, London.

Postlethwaite, K. (1993) *Differentiated Science Teaching. Responding to individual differences and to special educational needs*, Buckingham: Open University Press.

Postlethwaite, K. and Haggarty, L. (1998) 'Towards effective and transferable learning in secondary school: the development of an approach based on mastery learning', *British Educational Research Journal*, 24(3): 333–53.

# 14 Developing thinking in mathematics

Maria Goulding

## Introduction

All the writing in this book is concerned with aspects of mathematical thinking and the ways in which it can be developed by teaching. In this chapter, I have chosen to describe a particular intervention project that sets out to accelerate pupils' mathematical thinking. My interest was aroused by teachers and students working in participating schools, which led me to research their perspectives and experiences, but I do not represent the project in any other way.

## Different levels of thinking

The Cognitive Acceleration in Mathematics Education (CAME) programme comes with a ready-made inducement: pupils who followed the earlier sister project in science (CASE) achieved significantly better GCSE results than students in a control group. This is understandably very attractive to schools who are trying to improve their examination statistics.

Both projects are based on the social constructivist theory of learning. The idea of children passing through stages in their thinking comes from Piaget, but the idea that teachers have a crucial part to play in this process originates in the work of the Soviet psychologist, Vygotsky. In CAME terms this means that teachers can intervene to move children's thinking onto higher levels so that they can develop the reasoning patterns enabling more of them (particularly those between the seventieth and twenty-fifth percentile) to achieve a grade C or better at GCSE mathematics. More detail of this theoretical base for the project is given later, after some background and exemplification.

## The Thinking Maths Programme

The 'Thinking Maths' (TM) materials that have grown out of the CAME project are intended for pupils in Years 7 and 8. They offer opportunities to develop higher order reasoning patterns in mathematical contexts related to content areas of the National Curriculum. The programme runs over two years, with four or five lessons per term. Over the two years, teachers are expected to meet in order to plan, to discuss lessons, to observe each other and to reflect on progress in an ongoing way.

The programme is meant to be an enrichment to existing teaching, and followed separately from it.

For each of the 30 TM activities, underlying mathematical 'thinking strands' and 'curriculum links' are specified, together with appropriate technical mathematical terms which can be introduced, and guidance on how to use the tasks in a lesson. Specimen lessons are included in the first fifteen tasks. Although these are not intended as templates, they give a very detailed description of what a CAME lesson could be like, with examples of the teachers' questions and the pupils' responses.

The learning style advocated is highly interactive and collaborative. The teacher, and peers with slightly better understanding, act as mediators in moving a child from one state of thinking to another.[1] This mediation should unlock learning potential, as these reasoning patterns are constructed by the children themselves in interaction[2] with adult or peer mediators. In this way, the child's thinking is moved on more rapidly than it would be on its own, hence the term 'cognitive acceleration'. This is not to be confused with the use of acceleration to mean moving pupils beyond their age group as discussed in the previous chapter by Linda Haggarty.

Pupils are actively encouraged to use their present understandings in accessible tasks, the development of which requires 'higher order' thinking. Working as a whole class and in small groups, they discuss and explain their findings, share conjectures and explanations, and review the key learning that has taken place. The teacher manages the learning by making sure there is a common understanding of the tasks, organising the groups and moving through the lesson briskly. Above all the teacher manages pupils' talk, challenging and developing children's thinking by appropriate prompts, introducing the use of technical mathematical language and stimulating the review discussion.

Pupils sit where they can talk to each other in small groups, but face the teacher for the teacher–whole-class interactions. The advice is not to put pupils at the extremes of attainment in separate groups or to put pupils at the opposite extremes together in groups. Pupils are expected to use the pupil sheets but there is no pressure to work neatly as the sheets are only to record findings and aid the pupils as they 'struggle on the way' to a better understanding of the underlying concepts.

The next section gives a detailed description of a CAME lesson taught by a student teacher with some help from her mentor.

## Exploring the rectangle

The student teacher (Fiona), with the help of her mentor (Elaine), is teaching a middle attaining Year 7 class set of about 22 pupils. The school is in an area of economic deprivation, with GCSE results below national averages.

Note that the transcript has been prepared from a video and so not all of the interactions are audible and attributable to named pupils. The interspersed commentary offers interpretation and evaluation.

Phase 1

Fiona asks the class for examples of rectangles in the room and writes them on the board.

*Fiona*      Now who can describe to me what it is that makes it a rectangle – what's a rectangle?

*Pupil*      It's got four sides and the four sides aren't the same size.

Fiona draws a shape on the board.

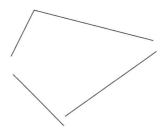

*Michelle*   Two sides the same and two sides different.

*Boy*       Two straight lines going down the sides are the same and two … .[*inaudible*] along the top are a bit bigger.

*Fiona*      Isn't that what Michelle said?

*Michael*   Two smaller lines going down the sides straight … [*inaudible*] a line along the top …

Fiona draws:

and then changes it for this.

*Fiona*      You did say straight.
         (*laughter from some of the class*)

*Stacey*    Miss, two parallel lines going down the side and two parallel lines along the top.

*Fiona*      Isn't that what we've got – those are parallel.

*Kimberley* Two straight lines going down, a line at the top going straight across and a line at the bottom going across straight.

*Lee*       Two vertical lines and two horizontal lines.

Fiona draws a square.

*Fiona*     I did what Lee told me – I did two vertical lines and two horizontal lines.
*Brian*     Miss, the two top and bottom lines a bit wider.

She draws an 'oblong' rectangle next to the square:

*Fiona*     So hang on a bit ... this one isn't a rectangle (*several voices from the class say,*
            *'it's a square'*). Everyone says this is a square and this is a rectangle ... One
            more thing ... what can you tell me about the corners?
*Michelle*  They're ninety degrees.
*Fiona*     Does anyone disagree and think this is a rectangle (*pointing to the square*)?
*Michael*   They're both the same.
*Fiona*     So this is a rectangle and this is a rectangle?
*Michael*   No.
*Fiona*     No? This is a ...?
*Michael*   (*and others*) A square.
*Fiona*     Is everybody sure that this isn't a rectangle? ... 'Cos I think it is.
*Boy:*      If you half it in the middle it will be.
*Fiona*     Yes if I draw a line here ...

            ... it'll be two rectangles but it's also one rectangle because a square is a
            type of rectangle ... so if a square is a type of rectangle what's the only thing
            we can describe to draw a rectangle ...?
*Boy*       Miss, the square's ninety degrees as well.
*Fiona*     Yes ... what's the only thing we can describe?
*Girl*      All sides the same.
*Fiona*     No because this is a rectangle as well, and these two are, and this is ...
            what's the only thing you can describe?
*Girl*      It's got four sides.
*Boy*       Four corners.

*Fiona*    What about these corners ... Gemma?
*Gemma*  They're all ninety degrees.

In this lesson the introduction does not link directly with the later activities concerning area and perimeter. Fiona starts by using examples from the pupils' own experience (concrete preparation)[3], and then draws out the pupils' own implicit definition of a rectangle. She forces them to clarify their ideas by drawing examples that conform to what they say but are not what the pupils mean. Fiona spends a long time encouraging the class to develop their ideas (construction)[4] and then shows her cards, 'Is everybody sure that this isn't a rectangle ... 'cos I think it is'. This challenge to the pupils' preconceived ideas gives them an opportunity to restructure their theories (cognitive conflict).[5] It looks as if Michael's thinking starts to wobble just before Fiona's statement when he says 'They're both the same', but then he goes back to safety by agreeing with the others that the square is a square. An unnamed boy comes in with, 'The square's got ninety degrees as well' but an unnamed girl goes too far the other way and now suggests that the rectangle has to have equal sides.

This episode comes to a close very soon after and we are left with the question of which pupils, if any, have restructured their ideas to accept that a square can be a square and a rectangle at the same time. We may also question why Fiona's definition of a rectangle assumes superiority. Perhaps she could have stressed that this a matter of definition or encouraged pupils to think up similar examples from their own everyday experience e.g. that a rose is both a rose and a flower at the same time.

### Phase 2

In the second phase of the lesson, pupils are presented with a worksheet on which three differently shaped rectangles, similar to those below, are drawn.

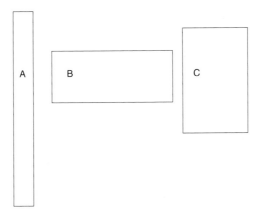

The pupils spend time in pairs constructing theories;[4] first they have to put the rectangles in order of area and give reasons.

> 'I thought B was biggest because it's got the longest length', 'It hasn't got a large width if you fold it up ...' are examples where some reason is given. In contrast to, 'It looks bigger', which is one boy's untheorised response.

There are several examples of the teachers deliberately encouraging the pupils to reflect on their thinking (metacognition):[6]

'What were you talking about to me?', 'What did you write down, Paul?', 'You put the width and the length were bigger', and later ... 'But you did have a conversation where you thought they were the same'.

The pupils now measure the dimensions of the rectangles and calculate the areas. Teachers circulate, giving help with the calculation.

At this point pupils may have experienced conflict between their intuitive judgements and the results from measuring and calculating the areas. Their attention was not drawn to the differences between their estimates and calculations and there is no evidence on the video of pupils making the comparison themselves.

Finally Fiona discusses the method of working out the area and moves on to an algebraic formula. Only one method, that of multiplying length by width, was taken without asking for alternatives. If several methods had been shared, including the counting of squares and repeated addition, it would have been particularly interesting to see if this produced some conflict when it came to the symbolism. How would they generalise counting squares or repeatedly adding the number of squares in each row? Would they see the relationship between $A = l \times w$ and these methods?

## Phase 3

| Fiona | Right some people described the per ... What did you say the perimeter was? |
|---|---|
| Pupil | The sides ... add the sides. |
| Fiona | What is the perimeter? |
| Pupil | Length around the shape. |
| Fiona | So the perimeter is the length around the shape and the area is ... [several pupils join in] ... inside the shape ... So think of a football field, the perimeter is the white lines and the grass in the middle is the area ... Or in this room the skirting board is the perimeter and the carpet is the area. Now what I want you to do is questions 1 and 2 on notesheet 2 – work out the perimeter for each one for the rectangles A, B and C ... Discuss in your pairs how you worked out the perimeter. |

The class starts working and teachers circulate. Audible comments include:

'Do you need to measure that again ... measure that one and that one ... yes – just check – did you measure round the whole shape ... ?... Check it again ... that's what we're going to do next ...'

One interchange between Fiona and two pupils takes place close to the video.

| Fiona | What did you do? (*Reading out what the boy has written*) 'I measured round the whole shape' ... You measured every single side ... and so what did you do (*speaking to the other pupil*) ... ? |

| | |
|---|---|
| *Girl* | Miss, you measured the lines and timesed it by the numbers … On that one we measured that and that came to three and that came to eight and then you did eight times three … |
| *Fiona* | Hang on …are you sure that's what we did? That's what we did to find the …If you multiply them together what do you find out … ? The … ? |
| *Girl* | Oh, is that the area? The perimeter you've got to get all the measures and add it all up … |
| *Fiona* | See if you can find a different way … you've found one way. |

Both teachers start discussing different pupils' work amongst themselves.

| | |
|---|---|
| *Fiona* | (*Writing up calculated perimeters to the nearest centimetre on the board*) What we want to talk about is how you did it. |
| *Michelle* | I added the top and the side and I doubled it. |

Fiona starts to write this on the board in words.

| | |
|---|---|
| *Elaine* | That's what she came up with for the quicker method but she did something else before. |
| *Fiona* | What was your first method? |
| *Michelle* | Added them all up. |
| *Fiona* | (*Writing Michelle's words on the board*) Anyone else have a different method … ? Kimberley, what did you do? |
| *Kimberley* | Length times two and width times two. |

Fiona writes this on the board in words and then writes 'plus' at the end.

| | |
|---|---|
| *Pupil* | Added the length and the width and then doubled it. |
| *Fiona* | Isn't that the same as Michelle's? |
| *Elaine* | No, she said the top and the sides. |
| *Fiona* | Anyone do anything different? |
| *Darren* | *l* two plus *w* two equals *P*. |
| *Fiona* | Hang on, say it again Darren. What does that mean? Where did you get that from? |
| *Darren* | Length times two plus width times two equals the perimeter. |
| *Fiona* | Does everyone see where he got that from …? He did the length times two add the width times two to get the perimeter … Remember earlier we changed things around a bit … we tidied things up a bit … how could we change that … ? It's good but we could write it better. |
| *Boy* | *P* equals *l* two plus *w* two. |
| *Fiona* | Anyone else think of something that would make it even better than that? |
| *Stacey* | *P* equals *lw* times two. |
| *Fiona* | Nearly …you're getting a different thing there … I think. |
| *Boy* | *l* two *w* two. |
| *Fiona* | Not quite – if we take out the add then we're timesing … remember when we put the numbers first … (writes) … $P = 2l + 2w$ … If we look at this one we've got two times the length and two times the width … which one does that describe …[links this on the board with the corresponding statement written in words] … That's a formula for that one, can anyone see a formula for the middle one? |

| | |
|---|---|
| *Girl* | P equals *l* plus *l* plus *w* plus *w*. |
| *Fiona* | Can everyone see that she's added length and length and width and width … Excellent so if we circle that one … now this is a difficult one … add the top and side together … think of that first and then double them. |
| *Kayley* | *lw* two. |
| *Fiona* | What does that mean? |
| *Girl* | Length times width times two. |
| *Fiona* | So that's not going to work but it's nearly right. |
| *Stacey* | *l* plus *w* and two here. |
| *Fiona* | That would mean *l* add *w* timesed by two but it's only the *w* timesed by two. |
| | *(Long silence)* |
| *Elaine* | I don't think they're going to get this. |
| *Fiona* | We want to times the whole thing by two so we can put it together with brackets round it … you know when you're writing in English and you don't want it to be exactly in the sentence and you put brackets round it … and then what do you think you're going to put in front of the brackets? |
| *Michelle* | Times two. |
| *Fiona* | You can just put two in front – we don't need to put a times by. |

She writes $P = 2(l + w)$ on the board and the lesson draws to a close.

It is interesting to compare the final phase of the lesson with the lesson summary notes given in the support materials. The first part goes according to plan with pupils finding the three different methods expected for calculating the perimeters, in some cases starting with one method and then finding a better one. Fiona then decides to go straight on to the algebra, skipping the suggested discussion of the conjecture – 'a longer perimeter gives a longer area' – as in the materials. The support materials advise the teacher to:

> Finalise the discussion by getting pupils to appreciate that algebraic notation, e.g. *W + L + W + L, 2W + 2L*, and *2(W + L)* are shorter versions of their ordinary language phrases, where the letters stand for any numbers.

This 'getting pupils to appreciate' sounds so straightforward but the reality turns out to be much more complex. The initial attempts at generalising are in words but Fiona does not have to introduce algebraic notation herself. It is Darren who makes the transition from words to symbols with his '*l* two plus *w* two equals *P*' interjection from the back of the room. The order here is interesting. Darren takes the length and *then* multiplies it by two, does the same to the width and then adds to find the perimeter. In his formula the addition has been placed in between the two products and the perimeter is at the end of the chain. He is comfortable with the compression of $l \times 2$ into '*l* two', but sees no need to bring the two 'to the front' since this does not mirror his method. In fact Darren's formulation is perfectly appropriate and could have been left as it is, or expanded to the fuller version $l \times 2 + w \times 2 = P$ for the benefit of the others in the class.

In Fiona's desire to 'write it better' some of the students lose the thread. Some of them have picked up the trick of removing the multiplication sign and unfortunately decide to remove the addition sign as well. They are moving away from the sensible methods they were using with particular rectangles and are now manipulating symbols in a meaningless way. Instead of glossing over these formulations, Fiona could have seen if they would work in particular cases thus setting up a conflict situation that may have encouraged the pupils to revise their formulations.

It is not surprising that 'add length and width' and 'multiply by two' came out as $l + w \times 2$ and that pupils needed to be introduced to brackets here. For them the order here is not ambiguous because the addition is completed before the multiplication by two. Again, it is debatable whether bringing the two to the front and dropping the $\times$ is helpful. The important learning point that there are three different but equivalent algebraic expressions; representing different general strategies for calculating perimeters is more important than the conventions for the order in which symbols are written. There is no discussion of this is in the materials.

Clearly all this is difficult for even an experienced teacher to judge, especially in a lesson where the students' own methods and thinking are being invited, and the teacher needs to respond to pupils' ideas quickly. The teacher may be able to look ahead to some extent but there will always be an element of unpredictability. This is where the importance of reflection and discussion of common experiences with other teachers may be very valuable, particularly when focused on specific incidents.

Analysing this CAME lesson gives some idea of the principles underlying the design of the materials and the way they are intended to be used, but it also indicates how much is left to the judgement of the teacher even within this tight structure. For me, the most interesting aspect is the insight into children's thinking.

## The theoretical background to CAME

> … some time between the ages of about 12 and 18 many people's thinking goes through a qualitative change, something like shifting up a gear …
>
> (Adhami *et al.*, 1998, p. viii)

What exactly is this qualitative leap in thinking? Piaget's description of a movement from the concrete to the formal operational stage has been criticised and misinterpreted but is influential nonetheless. The concrete operational stage does not necessarily mean a stage in which children's mathematics consists of moving bricks around. It is better to think of this as a stage in which pupils' thought processes are used to describe their own perceptions, for example, of a practical activity, a conversation, a diagram in a book. At the formal stage, pupils develop reasoning patterns that allow them to construct and interpret abstract models drawn from particular situations. These reasoning patterns are characteristics of 'higher order thinking'. The balance of opinion (e.g. Donaldson, 1978; Desforges and Brown, 1979) seems to be that thinking of children moving through separate stages is not helpful. Others (e.g. Orton, 1992) point out how the construct of formal operations still seems to be as good a way as any of characterising the process of abstraction common to much of secondary school mathematics.

In the lesson described, for instance, the pupils derived different formulae for the perimeter of a rectangle. We could say that their formulae, expressed first in words and then in symbols, were *abstracted* from the methods they used for particular rectangles and that the formulae could then be generally applied.[7]

An alternative to the idea of 'higher order thinking' is the identification of the mathematics that secondary pupils find particularly difficult. There is a considerable body of evidence (e.g. Hart, 1981; Hart, 1984; Kerslake, 1986) which points to difficulties with ratio and proportion, and with algebra. In problems involving ratio and proportion, reasoning patterns that require muliplicative strategies seem to present enormous difficulties (see Orton, 1992, p. 14). Such understanding is required, however, in so many aspects of the curriculum at Key Stages 3, 4 and beyond, for example, for fractions, decimals and percentages, similarity in geometry, gradients and rates of change. In algebra, many pupils find the manipulation of symbols meaningless because their thinking requires memorising countless rules for different situations, rather than reasoning based on an understanding of the underlying ideas of unknowns, variables and functions. This may be a product of teaching, but it may also be that these big algebraic ideas are conceptually difficult. Again, this is very problematic since algebra, as generalised arithmetic, becomes increasingly important in the Key Stage 3 and 4 curriculum.

Ratio and proportion, and algebra, or more accurately *the reasoning patterns associated with them,* are clearly present in the list of characteristics of formal operations given in the introduction to the CAME materials:

- control of variables, exclusion of irrelevant variables
- ratio and proportionality
- probability and correlation
- the use of abstract models to explain and predict

Probability and correlation may seem out of place here and it is true that we have less empirical evidence of children's difficulties here than we have of other topics. In probability, however, difficulties do stem from problems with fractions and with the reasoning patterns needed to explain situations, not uncommon in probability, where intuition is confounded (Garfield and Ahlgren, 1988). In correlation, the mechanical aspects of learning how to draw a scatter diagram and plot a line of best fit may not present many difficulties, but understanding the nature of the relationship between two variables is a more demanding activity altogether, with echoes of direct and inverse proportion. This CAME list, representing formal operations or higher order thinking, has parallels with the areas of secondary mathematics which we know to be challenging for many pupils.

In Piagetian terms their thinking needs to move up a level, but rather than wait until they are 'ready' or give up on them altogether, social constructivists believe that this move is possible with the right sort of teaching. This involves eliciting the ways in which pupils are currently thinking by providing the sort of activities that encourage them to explain and justify their ideas and strategies in discussion with peers and the teacher. This idea of starting where the children are is not confined to the CAME project. We know that eliciting misconceptions through carefully designed diagnostic tasks followed by cognitive conflict through group discussion and resolution is successful in promoting long-term retention from the Diagnostic Teaching project (Bell, 1993). Here we also have the idea of cognitive conflict being deliberately engineered:

> Drawing attention to a misconception before giving the examples was less effective than letting the pupils fall into the 'trap' and then having the discussion.
>
> (Askew and Wiliam, 1995, p.13)

Other aspects of the Vygotskyan perspective, particularly the idea of scaffolding as pupils construct knowledge, and the idea of reflection or 'thinking about' thinking have similarly been advocated by writers advocating a social constructivist approach (Jaworski, 1992; Wood, 1988). What CAME appears to have done is to package this approach within a programme of professional development, and within an evaluation framework directly related to examination performance.

This attention to professional development, as much as the psychological rationale, may in part explain the successful effects of the programme. It may also have found its own particular window of opportunity by aiming at the only two years in the secondary school when the pupils are not preparing for public examinations.

At the school level, there is an expectation that the process of working together on the programme could build up a new culture within the department and contribute to the teachers' professional development. This may result in teachers finding ways to use the strategies from CAME in their other mathematics lessons (*bridging*).[8] My own interviews with a sample of 21 teachers reveal a very complex picture here. There are some teachers who have clearly experienced the benefits of collaboration, but there are others who remain unconvinced or resistant to what they see as an imposition.

For the learners, the emphasis on enquiry and collaboration may introduce pupils to an alternative way of being and thinking in the mathematics classroom. They too may learn to link ideas[9] from CAME with those in other lessons. This may, however, only apply to particular groups of pupils. A common perception amongst the teachers in my sample was that the CAME lessons were preferred by pupils, usually boys, who liked the opportunity to dominate the talk and the lack of emphasis on written recording. It has also been suggested (Leo and Galloway, 1995) that CAME may suit those pupils who are mastery-oriented, i.e. those who are not put off by difficulty or failure and are prepared to 'have a go' at tackling problems. On the other hand, those who tend to give up or those who fear loss of face through failure may be disadvantaged. Much would seem to depend on the ability of the teacher to support students with different motivational styles.

## Conclusions

It should be clear that the principles underlying CAME are not exclusive to the project and its associated materials, although the structure and support is attractive to many teachers. Are there any general ideas here, which the reader could use to promote higher order thinking?

Clearly the activity itself is crucial. This should embody some of the big underlying ideas that the teacher wants the pupils to encounter. So, for instance, if one of the big underlying ideas is 'ratio and proportion', the teacher could use activities based on metric sizes of paper (see Gibb, 1990). Probability theory can all be taught through games and experiments. Collecting real data and fitting curves to it, or exploring families of curves with graphic calculators can engage pupils with the big ideas of functionality. Professional journals such as *Mathematics Teaching* and *Mathematics in Schools*[10] are a rich source of potential activities.

The activity needs to be accessible and have some element of surprise. Asking pupils to make predictions or forcing them to clarify definitions, as Fiona did, are two possible strategies. It should also give the pupils something to talk about in small groups and with the whole class. Finding lots of different ways of coming to the same result is a strategy which can be used in numerous situations, for example, comparing all the different ways you could calculate the area of kites starting from A3, A4, A5 … paper, comparing all the different algebraic ways that the function $2y = x - 3$ can be represented, and checking with graphs.

Also crucial is the way in which the pupils work and the teacher responds. The teacher needs to create situations for the pupils to talk in an exploratory way and to explain their reasoning. The teacher can then help to refine and develop the pupils' thinking, using similar prompts to those from the earlier lesson extract. Only if the teacher circulates and really listens to the pupils as they work in groups can that material be used to stimulate a review in which pupils can reflect on their own and others' strategies, and evaluate alternatives.

The CAME activities were developed and tried out in schools and teachers in the project are advised to meet and share experiences. Again this is not exclusive to CAME but there is no substitute for this form of professional development. If the meetings focus upon real examples of pupils' thinking and talk, the stumbling and difficult-to-fathom responses, as well as the flashes of genius, then teachers may:

- begin to think more deeply about mathematics;
- become more aware of the difficulties presented by the subject;
- become more aware of how children are thinking;

and they may be better able to help pupils:

- attach some meaning to mathematics;
- struggle towards concepts with the support of teachers and peers;
- find their voices.

## Notes

1   Zone of proximal development – the gap between what the learner can achieve on his own, and what the learner can achieve with help from a more knowledgeable adult or peer.

2    Scaffolding (or contingent teaching) – the process by which a more knowledgeable adult or peer can help a child move from their actual performance level to their potential level.

3    Concrete preparation – the teacher introduces the pupils to a problem embedded in their own experience, draws out links with previous ideas and clarifies the expectations for the next phase.

4    Construction – the pupils work together in small groups to develop ideas to solve the problem.

5    Cognitive conflict – the pupils start to develop theories and may be driven to restructure them in the light of contradictions.

6    Metacognition – this is a period when the pupils have stopped working on the tasks and are reflecting on their actions and their thinking.

7    People also use abstract in a derogatory sense to denote symbol manipulation for the sake of it. This sort of activity is characterised by phrases such 'multiply out the brackets', 'simplify' and 'factorise'.

8    Bridging – linking the underlying concepts to situations in other subjects, in other mathematics lessons or in later CAME lessons.

9    In 'Exploring the rectangle' the thinking strands are described as:
     • comparing multiplicative and additive relations;
     • representing rules in natural language and algebra;
     and the curriculum links are:
     • measuring and symbolising.

## References

Adhami, M., Johnson, D. and Shayer, M. (1998) *Thinking Maths: accelerated learning in mathematics*, Oxford: Heinemann.

Askew, M. and Wiliam, D. (1995) *Recent Research in Mathematics Education 5–16*, London: Ofsted Reviews of Education HMSO.

Bell, A.W. (1993) 'Some experiments in diagnostic teaching', *Educational Studies in Mathematics*, 24(1): 115–137.

Desforges, C. and Brown, G. (1979) 'The educational utility of Piaget: a reply to Shayer', *British Journal of Educationnal Psychology*, 49(3): 277–81.

Donaldson, M. (1978) *Children's Minds*, London: Fontana.

Garfield, J. and Ahlgren, A. (1988) 'Difficulties in learning basic concepts in probability and statistics: implications for research', *Journal for Research in Mathematics Education*, 19(1): 44–63.

Gibb, W. (1990) 'Paper patterns with metric paper', *Mathematics in School*, 19(2): 24.

Hart, K.M. (ed.) (1981) *Children's Understanding of Mathematics 11–16*, London: John Murray.

Hart, K.M. (1984) *Ratio: children's strategies and errors*, Windsor: NFER-Nelson.

Jaworski, B. (1992) 'Mathematics teaching: what is it?', *For the Learning of Mathematics*, 12(1): 8–14.

Kerslake, D. (1986) *Fractions: children's strategies and errors*, Windsor: NFER-Nelson.

Leo, E. and Galloway, D. (1995) 'Conceptual Links between acceleration through science education and motivational style: a critque of Adey and Shayer', *International Journal of Science Education*, 18(1): 35–49.

Orton, A. (1992) *Learning Mathematics*, London: Cassell.

Wood, D. (1988) *How Children Think and Learn*, Oxford: Blackwell.

# 15 Mental mathematics
## Chris Bills

## What is mental mathematics?

Try to do the following without drawing or writing anything, think for several minutes about the problem then reflect on what was going on in your mind when you were thinking about it. You may find it helpful to close your eyes after you have read it:

---

**Task 15.1**

Imagine a quadrilateral. Now imagine a circle that has each of the vertices of the quadrilateral on its circumference.
   What can you say about the position of the centre of the circle?

---

Unless your mind was totally inactive, or full of thoughts unrelated to the problem, then what you have been engaged in is mental mathematics and metacognition (thinking about your own thinking). It could be that you were able to visualise a quadrilateral mentally and circumscribe a circle and to 'see' them in your head sufficiently vividly to be able to answer the initial question. Many people do not have clear 'pictures in the head'; you may have been bringing to mind memories of diagrams you had drawn or had seen. You may instead (or as well as) have been trying to recall any circle theorems that might help or trying to remember if you had ever done anything like this before. Mixed up with these images and thoughts may well have been feelings of frustration and despondency if you were unsuccessful or a sense of euphoria if you enjoyed working on the problem.

Even if you were unable to say anything about the position of the circumcentre of the quadrilateral you may well have been engaged in mathematical activity – specialising, conjecturing, generalising, predicting, verifying, refuting, proving – as you turned the problem over in your mind. Alternatively, you may have stopped after you had done as asked and simply imagined the situation for a particular quadrilateral. This problem, and your reactions to it, are illustrative of what is involved in mental mathematics and the problems associated with doing mathematics without any aids to memory. You may wish at this stage to try the problem on paper or using dynamic geometry software. If you do not feel the need to do so, simply think about how much less (or more) mental mathematics is involved when physical diagrams are allowed. It is likely that before you draw you imagine what you are going to draw. As you draw the second edge of the quadrilateral, for instance, you will probably start to imagine the rest of the quadrilateral to decide in advance whether it will be possible to put a circle through the vertices. You might have decided that it would be much simpler to draw the circle first then imagine various quadrilaterals in relation to the centre before drawing a few illustrative examples. Looking at your drawings may have generated more mental mathematical activity.

We necessarily engage in private mathematical thinking when we are working with more public 'signs' (diagrams, words, symbols) so that 'mental mathematics' is interspersed with sign production in order to generate and communicate our mathematical activity. For the purposes of this chapter, however, I shall use the term 'mental mathematics' for the mathematical thinking that we can engage in without physical aids.

## What is a mental image?

Try a non-geometric problem in your head.

---

### Task 15.2

x squared subtract x is equal to x multiplied by three. What is the value of x?

---

If you have found a solution (or two) you have used an image. It is possible that again you had a vivid mental visualisation, a picture in your mind of the equation written out in your own writing or like a teacher's board work, printed in a book or on a computer screen. It is just possible that as you worked on the equation you 'saw' the subsequent lines of symbols appearing as you thought through each step in the procedure for solving equations. You may have supplemented this with (or used instead) instructions to yourself such as 'collect the unknowns', 'add the same to both sides', 'take the $x$ outside the bracket', etc. These words are just as much images as are the visualisations because they 're-present' previous experiences to your mind. You may for instance 'know' that equations of the form $x^2 - ax = 0$ give the solutions 0, and because this is an image formed from the numerous examples you have done of this type, not because you learned this as a general rule. Even if you do not need to verbalise it, it is part of your thought process and is an image that you use subconsciously.

The word 'image' is used most commonly for quasi-sensory experiences. Try thinking of some food or drink you really like, or hate, to test if you have images. Long years of chocolate consumption may have left you with vivid sight, taste and smell images as well as emotional images such as comfort or guilt. Just *one* acquaintance with chilli may have left you with equally vivid images. Where images are concerned it is quality not just quantity of previous experiences that matter. Not everyone, however, has quasi-sensory images. If you did not visualise the quadrilateral, equation, or chocolate (and could not now even if you concentrated very hard on trying to 'see' it) then you are not alone. Even people with strong imagery, however, would find it easier to form a variety of mental images for familiar everyday objects than for mathematical objects.

In order to communicate what was in my head I have to describe or draw something visual, or say or write words or symbols. To this extent the visual and verbal are the most easily communicable images. We need to be aware, however, that in transforming our thoughts into communicable form we might well transform the thought. I might say or draw something that I think is more acceptable to my audience than that which was actually in my head. Or what is in my head may not be expressible in any common language so what I express is my attempt at a translation into visual, verbal or written form. Thus, mental images may not be in the format that we use to describe them but those pictorial or verbal communications are an approximation to what was in our minds.

Try this in your head.

---

### Task 15.3

*Calculate negative three subtract negative eight.*

---

I gave that problem, orally, in a seminar and was told by one of the group that she had pictured the numbers on a number line but had panicked when she couldn't remember what to do. Her mind had gone blank – the visualisation on its own was no use without images of the procedure.

Your own thinking may have involved imagining the question written in mathematical symbols with or without a number line, you may have experienced head or body movements as you re-enacted turning and walking backwards, you may have seen sandcastles and holes, thermometers, staircases or any other pictures that had been used by teachers to illustrate this type of problem to you. You may have found yourself muttering 'an enemy of an enemy is a friend' or 'two minuses make a plus'. It is likely that you have had a variety of experiences of integers that have left you with images. In reading my list of possibilities some more may have come to your mind but when you first did the calculation it was probably your preferred image that was used. If you just 'knew' the answer and were not aware of any thinking it may be because the imagistic thinking has been condensed into a subconscious procedure that, though based on some physical representation or verbally expressed rule, happens automatically.

I shall use 'mental image' to imply that what comes to mind for the purposes of thinking has been influenced by previous physical or mental activity – what we have seen or done or talked about or thought about before. Images are re-presentations of previous experiences.

## What is a verbal image?

Whilst many people do not claim to have mental visual images the language they use to describe their thinking shows the influence of their previous experiences. I have asked children between the ages of 7 and 9 years to perform mental calculations and have then asked, 'What was in your head when you were thinking of that?'. Their responses revealed the influence of previous activities. Some used language associated with counting objects, for instance:

17 + 8    I *added* ten *onto* seventeen and I *took away* two and that *gave me* twenty-five.

48 + 23   Forty *with* twenty is sixty, forty-eight *add* twenty *comes to* sixty-eight and then you *add* three *on*.

Others used words associated with manipulation of materials and numbers:

97 + 10   I *move the seven* and then I knew which one, I know I got to add a ten on, I can't add a ten so I *put the one in front* of it and then a *nought in the middle*.

30 + ? = 80   I know that three add five is eight so just *turn it into* tens.

Others used the language of the written algorithms:

48 + 23   Eight and the three made eleven, so I *carried a figure* and *put it under there* then four and the two.

65 – 29   Five take away nine, but you can't do so you *cross out* the six, *make that* five, and *make that* fifteen.

All these pupils had the same variety of classroom experiences yet they each had different ways of expressing their process of calculation. It is this use of language associated with previous activities that I shall refer to as a 'verbal image'. The variety of images suggests that they are the pupils' own constructions, influenced by one or many of the physical representations used by the teacher, and not just learned rules. Many of the words are common in the classroom but different pupils show preference for different images. These responses were recorded before the teaching of specified mental calculation strategies was commonplace in primary schools.

## What are mental calculation strategies?

*The National Numeracy Strategy: Framework for teaching Mathematics* implemented in all English primary schools from 1999 with the extension for Years 7–9 piloted in 2000, stresses that an ability to calculate mentally lies at the heart of numeracy, that mental methods should be emphasised and that written algorithms should develop out of mental methods. In the guidance for teachers, 'Teaching mental calculation strategies' (QCA, 1999), it is made clear that:

...children should learn number facts 'by heart' and be taught to develop a range of mental strategies for quickly finding from known facts a range of related facts that they cannot recall rapidly.

And furthermore:

For much work at Key Stages 1 and 2, a mental approach to calculation is often the most efficient and needs to be taught explicitly.

(p. 3)

It lists the facts that children should be able to recall, the mental strategies they should be able to use and the mental calculations they should be able to perform in each year. For instance, by Year 3 children should recall addition and subtraction facts for all numbers to 20, they should use the strategy of adding or subtracting a 'near multiple of ten' to or from a two-digit number (e.g. $36 + 42 = 36 + 40 + 2$), 'bridge through a multiple of ten then adjust' (e.g. $36 + 42 = 36 + 4 + 38$) or 'use knowledge of number facts and place value to add or subtract pairs of numbers' (e.g. $36 + 42 = 30 + 40 + 6 + 2$) so that they should be able to decide the most efficient method to calculate mentally. As outcomes of teaching, Year 7 pupils should, for example: add or subtract 0.1 and 0.01 to or from any number, multiply and divide a number by 1, 10, 100, 1000, 0.1, 0.01, derive quickly decimal complements in 1 to one or two decimal places (e.g. $1 = 0.8 + 0.2$, $1 = 0.41 + 0.59$).

The key to the pupil's development of this range of strategies is thought to be classroom discussion of different strategies. Teachers use questions such as, 'How did you work that out?', 'Who did it another way?', 'Which is the easier/easiest way?' to stress that efficiency, the speed and ease with which strategies lead to a correct answer, is important. In addition QCA (1999) recommends informal recording and the use of tools such as number lines and hundred squares to develop understanding of number. It explicitly states that mental calculation is not the same as mentally picturing a written algorithm. Paper and pencil can, it suggests, be used to support mental calculation particularly through the use of diagrams that encourage the development of mental imagery. An empty number line, for instance, can provide a visual representation to demonstrate to others the way in which the calculation is being performed.

The emphasis on, and frequent practice of, mental calculation in primary schools is likely to result in some pupils forming images that were not previously common. Sharing ideas through class discussion and through pupils communicating different strategies to one another may well lead to mental visual and verbal images that go beyond images related to counting or to written algorithms.

## Is a mental visual image seen?

---

### Task 15.4

*Imagine a number line. Look at the number thirty-six. Now add twenty.*

---

Much of the research on mental visual imagery has demonstrated that it has many of the characteristics of visual perception – the same area of the brain is in use when people are thinking about an image as when they are looking at something, the time taken to scan or rotate mental visual images is consistent with the time taken with pictures and physical objects. It seems reasonable then to talk of 'seeing' a picture in the mind but it is clearly not like a photograph. When we have an image of something we have previously seen it is our own construction and is thus dependent on what we noticed about the object when we were looking at it and how much we can remember. It is also dependent on our ability to recreate it in our mind. If I choose to imagine a number line I might have a hazy idea of a straight horizontal line with some vertical markers on it and a zero. As I think more about it I can imagine bolder markings for the tens and longer lines for the fives because I have seen number lines like that and noticed those features. As I 'scan' along the line from 36 to 56 I may imagine the numbers along the way because I know what they are.

This dependence on 'having seen', and noticed what has been seen, is an important aspect of visual imagery. If a child is asked to get a picture of a four-sided shape in their head, they most often visualise a square or a rectangle and it is always in the stereotypical orientation, with sides vertical and horizontal, that has been used as illustration by teachers. The pernicious effect of 'fixed' images that we bring to mind when asked to imagine objects is illustrated by the following example:

---

## Task 15.5

*Imagine a wooden cube. Imagine suspending it by a piece of string attached at one vertex. Lower it onto a bed of damp sand so that a vertex just touches the surface and then push the cube down so that the vertex makes a hole in the sand. Remove the cube and look at the hole. What shape is it?*

---

About half of the people who visualise this situation say that the hole is a square based pyramid. The most likely reason for this is that the only polyhedron they have ever seen in this orientation (i.e. vertex uppermost) is a regular octahedron. If you reasoned that the hole had to be a triangular based pyramid and made no attempt at visualising you were still reliant on having previous experience of cubes and to this extent you were relying on your image of a cube.

All this seems to imply that we can only imagine what we have already seen yet surely the power of imagination is that it is creative? This is true, but I can only imagine a two-headed elephant because I have seen a normal elephant and with this as a base my imagination can transform it into something I have never seen. I can imagine the vertical calculation for 346 subtract 172 not because I have seen it before but because I have seen calculations *like it* before. To this extent an image is 'seen' if there is a memory of having seen something like it. We need not feel that we cannot mentally visualise something simply because we do not have a vivid, video-screen type picture in the mind. I shall refer to a mental visual image as simply an awareness of spatial relationships in whatever way they are manifested in the mind.

## Is a mental visual image useful?

I have given the number line problem in Task 15.4 to 9-year-old children. The majority have said they could 'see' the number line and the 36 but did not use their image for the addition. This is not surprising since, for most of us, a considerable mental effort is required to keep a picture in mind and we have difficulty doing the calculation and creating the image at the same time. Only if the calculation is performed without conscious effort might we be convinced we have seen it happen on the number line. For many people the image seems epiphenomenal – it is created to go with the calculation but does not guide thoughts, it is an optional extra.

Seen simply as an aid to mental calculation, a mental image would seem likely to be more of a hindrance than a help if we are using up mental processing capacity in creating it. It is not unusual for young children to visualise objects to count when given a mental addition question, and for other mental calculations to be performed by visualising the written algorithm, or at least performing procedures as if the written calculation were being performed. These forms of image might even inhibit the development of more efficient strategies for mental calculation.

The value of visual imagery, on paper or in the head, thus lies in its potential to facilitate and generate mathematical thought. Visualisation is an important aspect of mathematical activity and if visual thinking can occur without recourse to paper or electronic means of production then it seems likely to be beneficial. So as teachers we need to consider how we might encourage pupils to develop the ability to use mental visual images. The National Curriculum suggests that at Key Stage 1:

> pupils should be taught to: describe properties of shapes that they can see or visualise

and

> pupils should be taught to: observe, visualise and describe positions.

At Key Stage 2:

> pupils should be taught to: visualise and describe 2-D and 3-D shapes ... , visualise 3-D shapes from 2-D drawings ... , visualise and describe movements, visualise and predict the position of a shape following a rotation, reflection or translation.

The clue to how this might be achieved lies in the suggestion in the 'Breadth of study' for Key Stage 3 which recommends:

> practical work with geometrical objects to develop their ability to visualise these objects and work with them mentally.

There appears to be no suggestion that all pupils should be trained to form mental visual images so we can only teach pupils how to create physical visualisations, on paper or computer screen, and encourage them to visualise mentally as a result.

## Can mental imagery be 'taught'?

It is clear that the National Curriculum, both for pupils and trainee teachers, and the Mathematics Framework are written on the assumption that children can be encouraged to use mental visual imagery as a result of experiences with physical visual images. There is also the assumption that a facility with mental calculation will develop as a result of frequent practice and that an understanding of different strategies will result from classroom discussion. It is tempting to think that visual representations such as the number line and verbal imagery developed from it (e.g. 'bridging through multiples of ten' and 'jumping forward and backward to landmarks') will be as useful to pupils as they are for teachers. There is a well-known paradox, however, that a representation may only be understood if one already possesses the concept that it is supposed to represent. Simply encouraging pupils to visualise a number line is of no practical use unless the concepts it can illustrate are understood.

The 'constructivist' view of learning is that each individual constructs their own picture of reality from their own experiences and 'social' constructivists emphasise the role of the community of the classroom in providing these experiences. Whilst learners do not construct a copy of a pre-existing mathematical reality, or work on an 'internal representation' of a 'physical representation' of number, their images are based on their classroom experiences and particularly their experience with the representations used by their teachers. The images that are used in subsequent thinking are re-presentations of those experiences. The teacher needs to be aware, however, that not all pupils will form images at the same pace and that some may not form images at all. It is also likely that many pupils will not use the same image as the teacher.

In order to promote the construction of mental images that can be used in future thinking, classroom activities need to provide the experiences, and encouragement for reflection on them, that might lead to formation of those images. Geometry provides obvious examples for mental visual images but also illustrates how physical visualisations can lead to mental visualisations that restrict rather than generate mathematical thinking. Try this.

---

### Task 15.6

*Imagine a triangle and a straight line drawn near it. Now reflect the triangle in the line.*

---

That task could be meaningless if you have not had the usual classroom experiences. If you have had some experience of drawing reflections of plane shapes you may have been able to form a picture in your mind or at least have a vague recall of what it looked like when you did draw it. The 'usual classroom experiences' however often lead to errors since reflection is invariably in a vertical or horizontal line. The mental image that is formed as a result often leads to the common error, when working without aids, of drawing the reflection as if the line of reflection were vertical or horizontal, even when the line is at an angle to the vertical. To combat this the learner's attention needs to be focused on the process of reflection, they need to work with many orientations of shape and line, and they need to notice the features of the relationships between a shape and its reflection. They need to use this awareness to construct the 'mathematical object', reflection, not simply as a stereotypical visualisation but as an understanding of its characteristics. The teacher's role is thus to educate this awareness and this is done through discussing examples and counter-examples and encouraging pupils to communicate their own thinking about what a reflection is.

## Can mental mathematics be taught?

There is a concern that the attempt to teach mental calculation strategies will be as unsuccessful for some pupils as previous attempts to teach written algorithms. If rules of manipulation of numbers on paper, or of manipulation of quantities in the mind, appear arbitrary to pupils then they are likely to be misapplied. It is too easy to make the assumption that if those who are unsuccessful at mathematics are shown what it is that successful mathematicians do then they, too, can become successful. The mental calculation strategies that are now being actively taught are the efficient strategies that people have previously developed for themselves. They were developed as a result of an understanding of quantity and the way in which combinations and decompositions of quantities relate to the numerals that are used to express them. Those pupils who have not made sense of the connection between the signified (quantity) and the signifiers (number words and numerals) are unlikely to make sense of any of the ways of manipulating the symbols, even if they can do the manipulations. Similarly, mental images of algebraic manipulation, for instance, can only be formed if the learner has noticed what is happening when the process is performed physically, when it is described or when the result is seen.

There is another aspect of pupils' individual cognitive abilities. The mental image may manifest itself as visual or verbal or both and the extent to which thinking involves either or both of these modalities may be due to individual differences in thinking styles as well as differences in experiences. Presmeg (1986) showed that few able high school students are 'visual thinkers', i.e. prefer to use methods involving diagrams (physical or mental images) rather than 'analytic' methods (words and symbols). She noted that there was often little encouragement from teachers for visual methods and so they were not valued by students. She also discovered that visual thinkers seemed to be most successful in the classes of teachers who used both visual and non-visual methods rather than in the classes of teachers who were either strongly visual or strongly non-visual. Preference for visual methods was also found to be independent of the student's mathematical attainment (Presmeg, 1995).

## What are the implications for teaching and learning?

---

### Task 15.7

*Think of a number between one hundred thousand and one million. Now round it to the nearest ten thousand.*

---

Did you 'see' it or say it to yourself or have some other way of thinking about it? Does it matter whether it was a visual or verbal image or both or neither? If the number in your head was just a collection of words would it help to visualise before writing it or rounding it? If you can visualise it do you need to verbalise before writing or rounding? Could you even do this in your head? Most people are on the limit of their ability to hold a number in mind when it is has six digits so you may have found yourself writing it with your finger on the table. If you could be trained to keep larger numbers in mind would it be worth the effort?

When teachers ask pupils to work out in their heads the mean of a small set of data, imagine the graph of $y = (x - 2)(x + 3)$ and say where it intersects the $x$-axis, mentally rotate and reflect a triangle to decide if two drawn triangles are congruent, or any other task without physical aids available, the teacher and the pupils will be using a variety of images. If the teacher and pupils are only interested in the answer then it does not matter what was in their heads when they were doing it. If they are interested in the way they think and whether they might think in different ways then that variety does matter and is worth exploring. If mental mathematics is to be any more than learning efficient mental calculation strategies or training for mental visualisation then there needs to be more discussion about mental imagery in all modalities and how it relates to the learning of mathematics. Being more aware of the way we think is a first step toward taking more control of our thinking.

On a more mundane level, an awareness of the variety of images that others use may help with communication. If the teacher assumes that all pupils have the same thing in mind then communication will not be possible. Consider for example $12 \div 3$. How did you read it and what images come to mind when you think about it? You may have said '12 shared by three', '12 divided by three', '12 shared into three (parts or lots)', '12 divided into three (parts or lots)', '12 shared into threes', '12 divided into threes', 'How many threes in 12?', 'Threes into 12 go ... ', etc. You may or may not have visualised something and if you did it may or may not have been a picture appropriate to the way you said it. Now imagine a class of children working on $12.8 \div 3.2$. Many will have a preferred, fixed verbal image for division, 'shared by' perhaps, the teacher may be talking about 'how many of these in this'. It is likely that there will be, at least initially, some confusion. Try this.

---

### Task 15.8

*Four point six multiplied by seven.*

---

Many people can perform that calculation entirely as words in their heads, the partition is transparent in the language and there is not too much to hold in the mind. Other people need to visualise it. Is either group behaving in a more desirable way? It has been argued that children who rely on physical materials and particularly on counting strategies for calculation are disadvantaged in not developing more efficient mental skills. It is also suggested that a reliance on visual thinking can delay the beginnings of abstract thinking. Teachers concerned with pupils' cognitive development need to be aware of these possibilities and encourage flexible thinking through discussion and through a change in emphasis away from the answer toward the processes for getting answers. Imagery in all its guises needs to be recognised and included in that discussion.

## References

Presmeg, N. (1986) 'Visualisation in high school mathematics', *For the Learning of Mathematics*, 6(3): 42–6.

Presmeg, N.C. (1995) 'Preference for visual methods: an international study', in L. Meira and D. Carraher (eds) *18th International Conference for the Psychology of Mathematics Education*, vol. 3, Recife, Brazil: Programme Committee: 58–65.

QCA (1999) *The National Numeracy Strategy. Teaching mental calculation strategies.* QCA, London.

# 16 Making the most of your textbook

Laurinda Brown

## Where are you coming from?

---

**Task 16.1**

Look back on your own learning of mathematics, from as early as you can remember in the primary school, through secondary school, to university or college and maybe as part of a job. Focus on the use of textbooks. Did you have one at the various stages? How did you use one when you had one? Did this change over time? Write down a few stories and reflect, as someone learning to teach mathematics, on some positive and negative aspects of using textbooks in different ways. Keep a record of these positive and negative aspects and refer back to your two lists as you work through this chapter.

---

Here's a story, from the early years of secondary schooling, of using a set of textbooks. It is told by Richard Barwell, currently studying for a doctorate in mathematics education, who previously did a mathematics degree and taught mathematics both in the UK and abroad. As you read the story notice what aspects of using textbooks this way you agree and disagree with.

The secondary school I attended was involved in a pilot of the School Mathematics Project (SMP) 11–16 individualised learning scheme: booklets and worksheets and not much teacher input. As we were the first year to do it, everything was new. New booklets, new equipment. Some things weren't available as they hadn't been produced. We stayed in mixed ability form groups throughout the two years of the booklet scheme. The tables were hexagonal. When we started on the booklets, I thought they were stupid. I think the first booklet I did was Reflection 1. I spent a week with a number of other boys who were also doing Reflection 1, making each other laugh by using the little mirrors to make strange or obscene reflections from the pictures in the booklet. Amongst us students, performance was measured by how many booklets had been completed. We weren't all very competitive. The weeks passed as slowly as the booklets. Gradually the class spread out. I remember Carl and Julian were both miles ahead of anyone else. They're on block G! What really? Yeah. I suppose I liked the autonomy.

Do a booklet, take as long as you like. Mark it. Look up the answer if you're not sure. Do the 'Suppex' (Supplementary Exercise) and get it marked by the teacher. Do a block test and then a level test every once in a while. I didn't have much to do with the teacher, apart from the marking. I was rarely stuck, not so stuck that I couldn't work it out from the answer. At some point during the two years, I started working faster. I can't remember why. Perhaps the teacher rearranged the tables so I was sat with someone more diligent. From halfway through the first year I started putting time in. I would take home four booklets at a time and do them all in one evening. Some of them were only eight pages long. In the second year we had a couple of different teachers. It didn't make much difference. Some time in the summer term of my second year I finished the last book of the last block. I felt satisfied with myself. I was one of the first of only a handful who managed to do every single booklet.

---

## Task 16.2

How would you describe this use of texts? The sets of booklets are usually called an individualised learning scheme. Have you experience of using individualised schemes as a learner of mathematics? Make a list of issues raised for you by the writing. Some people find it useful to do this in the form of questions. Try also to think what Richard is portraying positively, negatively or neutrally about his experiences.

For each of the points you saw Richard as viewing positively, such as 'autonomy', try to see the issue from a range of different perspectives, some positive, some negative, some neutral, e.g. for a non-competitive person who is self-motivated and careful there can be a pleasure in doing the books at their own speed … and yet another child might be prone to day-dreaming and never get to the end of the book, let alone the whole scheme!

Similarly for your negative list, try to find some perspectives from which the same effect could be viewed positively.

Richard presents some issues neutrally, e.g. having different teachers. The school may have chosen to do the individualised learning scheme because of a high turnover of teachers. The head of mathematics may feel negative about the high turnover of teachers but positive about the scheme for having supported a way of working with that problem. We do not know. Whatever you yourself preferred as a learner there will be other learners who find it does not work for them and other contexts in which it might not work at all. One mathematics teacher I was talking to, who had moved in September 2000 from a school with a scheme of work based on a textbook to a school that sometimes uses textbooks, said that the scheme of work based on a textbook boosted the confidence of the new teacher that they had covered the same work as the other teachers in the department. This is a use of the textbook to define the curriculum in some way. What other uses of textbooks have you thought of? Here are some suggestions:

- children are each issued with a textbook which acts as a resource to support their learning as the teacher works with them;
- sets of exercises for the students to practise which saves the teacher time making up their own. Sometimes the students do not get issued with their own textbook;
- teaching materials, explanations and worked examples actually in the textbook which can support the non-specialist mathematics teacher as they can ask students to read the explanation;
- mainly for the students to use but supported by a teacher's guide with suggestions for introductions to lessons, extension and assessment materials;
- the book of the examination course with questions closely linked to those that will be asked in the related examination (happens often at A level).

Whatever the range of textbooks in your mathematics department, they will be used by teachers who will stress and ignore different things depending on how they view mathematics and the teaching of mathematics. How will you learn what is important? Talking to other teachers in the department and finding out what they do is a good start. Another is to read through a range of textbooks and teacher's guides to see what they have to say and compare their approaches.

Here's a list of problems that SMP (Little *et al.*, 1994, p. 34) identified in relation to learning mathematics solely from the written word:

- the language may be too difficult;
- you cannot have discussion with a book;
- you cannot interpret easily what is in a book;
- you cannot hear how the words sound;
- reading can be very passive;
- working on real understanding can be difficult without articulating your interpretation of the written word;
- tasks are often easier to explain orally;
- tasks initiated by books often lack challenge.

---

**Task 16.3**

*Which of these problems are illustrated in Richard's writing? Are there any more you can identify if you reflect on what the experience may have been like for a different child or the teacher in his mixed ability classroom?*

---

The reality of the situation is that you will be entering a department where there will be a scheme of work in place that will be supported in some way, either by resources which the department provides, or by a textbook or booklets. You, as a new teacher in the department, will be concerned to make the best use of what is available to you – for all the learners in your classes. Given the problems highlighted above, developing strategies for supporting discussion in your classroom seems an important focus to support your students' learning using a textbook. Unlike Richard, when he was taking home four booklets a night, most students need support when engaging with texts. SMP individualised learning schemes were at one extreme of the use of the written word in learning mathematics and they are not so commonly in use today because there were perceived problems with the scheme when the National Curriculum and GCSE coursework were implemented in the schools. The following were missing (Little, 1994, pp. 64–5):

- technology (the pace of change in this area means that curriculum materials will always lag behind the potential of software and hardware);
- the mathematics itself (the mathematical agenda remains largely hidden from the pupils);
- you the teacher.

There was very little material in the SMP booklets linked to technology, only perhaps some work with calculators. In some schools the scheme was being used independently of the teacher. Importantly, what eventually led to the rewriting of the booklets was their focus on skills without the investigations, problem-solving and discussion between teacher and pupils and between pupils themselves, recommended as supporting a mathematical agenda in the Cockcroft report (para. 243, DES, 1982).

SMP have recently published a new set of textbooks called 'Interact'. This scheme addresses the 'missings' above, but the pace of change is fast. Given the current move of the National Numeracy Strategy (NNS) into Key Stage 3, numeracy could be added to your list of what to look out for as needing to be covered in addition to what is in your textbook. SMP are currently rewriting their Year 7 'Interact' books to take account of NNS. Which version of the National Curriculum is the textbook your department uses written for? You will need to make decisions, often with colleagues in the department, how to implement what does not exist in the textbook.

SMP's (Little *et al.*, 1994) discussion of effective teaching focused on four 'maxims' which still seem powerful for 'better mathematics teaching' using any textbook:

*Maxim 1*   Don't let the scheme run you. You are supposed to be running the scheme!

*Maxim 2*   Individualised learning alone is not sufficient to learn mathematics effectively.

*Maxim 3*   Good mathematics teaching involves conscious choices about how you want to teach!

*Maxim 4*   No teaching material is complete without the teacher.

The focus of this chapter is on you making the most of your textbook. For the rest of this chapter, we are going to be thinking in general principles, even when we consider particular examples from particular texts. The following discussion supports your planning from a textbook, focused and organised through each of the four maxims above.

We will be thinking about the teaching of algebra. You're faced with the two pages below from the Key Maths scheme (Chapter 8, Book $9^3$, pp. 152–3) as you start thinking about teaching that chapter to your Year 9 top set. The book is targeted at levels 6–8 according to the Teacher File and on the back of the book it says 'Providing full coverage for the 1995 order'.

## 1   Brackets

... *continued* on page 159 ...

◀◀ REPLAY ▶

| Collecting terms | $a + a + a + a + a = 5a$<br>This is called **collecting terms**. *Remember*: $5a = 5 \times a$ |
|---|---|
| Power | $a \times a \times a = a^3$<br>The **power** '3' tells you how many *a*s are multiplied together. |

**Exercise 8:1**

Write each of these expressions in a shorter form by collecting terms or using a power.

**1**  $b + b + b + b + b + b$          **6**  $k + k$

**2**  $m \times m$          **7**  $r \times r \times r \times r$

**3**  $g + g + g + g$          **8**  $j \times j \times j \times j \times j \times j$

**4**  $y \times y \times y \times y \times y$          **9**  $p + p + p + p + p$

**5**  $t + t + t$          **10**  $h \times h \times h$

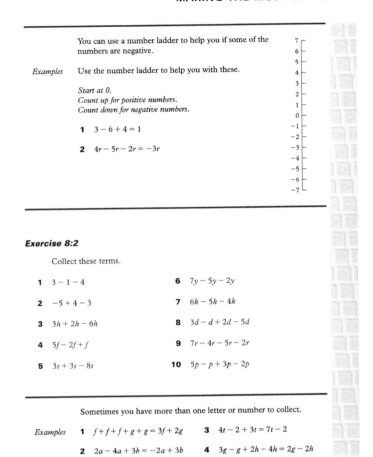

You can use a number ladder to help you if some of the numbers are negative.

*Examples*    Use the number ladder to help you with these.

*Start at 0.*
*Count up for positive numbers.*
*Count down for negative numbers.*

**1**  $3 - 6 + 4 = 1$

**2**  $4r - 5r - 2r = -3r$

**Exercise 8:2**

Collect these terms.

**1**  $3 - 1 - 4$              **6**  $7y - 5y - 2y$

**2**  $-5 + 4 - 3$            **7**  $6k - 5k - 4k$

**3**  $3h + 2h - 6h$        **8**  $3d - d + 2d - 5d$

**4**  $5f - 2f + f$            **9**  $7r - 4r - 5r - 2r$

**5**  $3s + 3s - 8s$         **10**  $5p - p + 3p - 2p$

Sometimes you have more than one letter or number to collect.

*Examples*    **1**  $f + f + f + g + g = 3f + 2g$      **3**  $4t - 2 + 3t = 7t - 2$

**2**  $2a - 4a + 3b = -2a + 3b$      **4**  $3g - g + 2h - 4h = 2g - 2h$

---

## Task 16.4

Take some time now to think what you can imagine yourself doing before you teach this chapter.

---

In order to give you some things to try out and react to I have tried to illustrate planning and practice through a particular context, a research project that is looking at the 'developing algebraic activity'[1] of Year 7 pupils in four classrooms in three schools. The teachers continue to use their own department's scheme of work and textbooks, but they also worked on a classroom culture developed through sharing with their pupils that the year was about them 'becoming mathematicians'. They worked with the pupils explicitly on what that meant, as well as on the mathematics. It's important that whilst you teach you are developing your practice through strategies that you experience as effective *for you* in achieving a purposeful learning environment. Your task is to identify strategies to try out in your own classroom (you are a teacher who can make conscious choices!) as you learn through experience what classroom culture you want to develop, and can develop, supported by all the resources at your disposal.

There will be four strands for each maxim:

1 Overview: general suggestions of what accepting the maxim might make you do ... ;
2 ... illustrated through writing about practice; a story or stories;
3 What happens in the research project?
4 Using the previous discussion to work with the pages from Key Maths.

## Where are you going to?

In the previous section there were stories, actions and discussions. Here, throughout the text, you will be identifying strategies that you will consciously apply in your planning, teaching and reflection on teaching. I will be reminding you of the task occasionally throughout the text by perhaps discussing a particular strategy, but don't forget to be actively engaged in committing yourself to future action and reflection on action to produce further actions. This cycle is the beginnings of a process which is sometimes called action research. You're finding out about your teaching by seeing what works for you.

---

### Task 16.5

To focus your first reading, identify strategies you could use to support discussion in your classroom. This will help you to minimise some of problems with using text, identified above.

---

Remember, throughout the rest of the chapter we will be addressing what to do in teaching from the two pages (Figure 1) from Key Maths, Year 9, top set, starting a chapter on algebra.

### Maxim 1    Don't let the scheme run you. You are supposed to be running the scheme!

Overview

- Be critical – what's not in the text? How can you build in technology, numeracy, a range of teaching styles, a sense of sharing with the children what it is to be mathematical?
- Look backwards and forwards in the scheme. What's in the Year 7 and 8 textbooks related to what you're planning? Where is this chapter leading?

Work at distilling out some crucial points. What is algebra?! Make a topic web. The textbook does not save you having to think things through.

- Using others – look at the teacher guides if they exist, talk to other teachers in the department, look at the development in other textbook schemes, read through what John Mason has to say about algebra in Chapter 7 in this book! Look on the internet.

Stories: looking backwards, what's in Year 7?

A student teacher planned a lesson on algebra for his university tutor who was coming to visit. He read around the subject, talked to other members of staff and decided to do a lesson on Codes (below). After viewing the lesson the tutor simply said, 'What have codes got to do with algebra?' (Bernard Murphy, Somervale School, in a personal communication).

I was interviewing some Year 7 pupils for a teacher. The first statement to explore was: f + f + f + f + f. I found myself surprised when the response came back 30. When I asked 'Why?' the pupil said 'f equals six'. I was reminded of Bernard Murphy's story and checked in the textbook. The school uses Key Maths and there is a section on codes in the Year 7 textbook that was used.

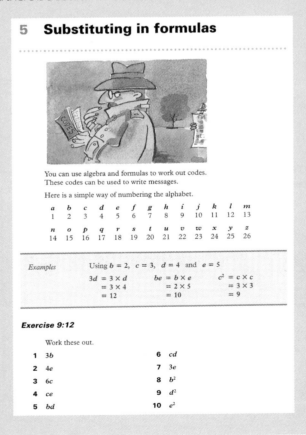

### 5  Substituting in formulas

You can use algebra and formulas to work out codes.
These codes can be used to write messages.

Here is a simple way of numbering the alphabet.

| a | b | c | d | e | f | g | h | i | j | k | l | m |
|---|---|---|---|---|---|---|---|---|---|---|---|---|
| 1 | 2 | 3 | 4 | 5 | 6 | 7 | 8 | 9 | 10 | 11 | 12 | 13 |

| n | o | p | q | r | s | t | u | v | w | x | y | z |
|---|---|---|---|---|---|---|---|---|---|---|---|---|
| 14 | 15 | 16 | 17 | 18 | 19 | 20 | 21 | 22 | 23 | 24 | 25 | 26 |

*Examples*  Using $b = 2$, $c = 3$, $d = 4$ and $e = 5$

$$3d = 3 \times d \qquad be = b \times e \qquad c^2 = c \times c$$
$$= 3 \times 4 \qquad\quad = 2 \times 5 \qquad\quad = 3 \times 3$$
$$= 12 \qquad\qquad\; = 10 \qquad\qquad = 9$$

**Exercise 9:12**

Work these out.

1  $3b$       6  $cd$

2  $4e$       7  $3e$

3  $6c$       8  $b^2$

4  $ce$       9  $d^2$

5  $bd$       10  $e^2$

There is no right or wrong answer here. What's crucial is that an experienced teacher using that textbook would talk to the children about the mathematics and point to the differences between being able to do codes and 'collecting terms'. Even then some children will still respond to the interview statement with their valid view of the world that f is six. Experience allows you to notice what are often called the students' misconceptions. You may hear stories about where such an idea is coming from. In the same way, Bernard Murphy's story supported my 'noticing' when I was interviewing the Year 7 students.

---

## Task 16.6

What would you do or what would you offer as teacher to the child who uses codes when collecting terms?

---

### Research project: using others

The four teachers on the project (A, B, C and D) met for a day meeting six times during the year, mainly to support each other in planning lessons and sharing resources. We also talked to each other on e-mail. The idea of 'Loop Cards'[2], which I first came across through Adrian Pinel at University College Chichester, appeared

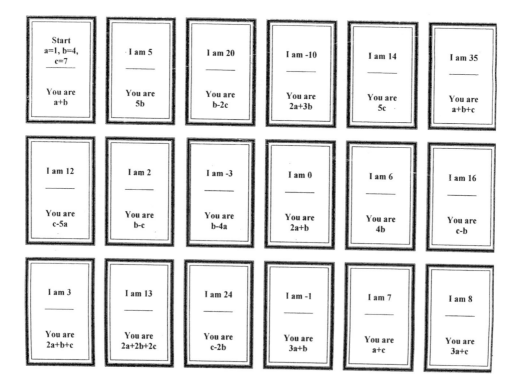

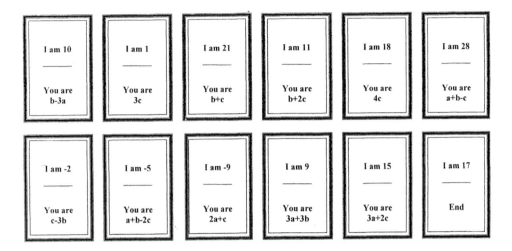

from one member of the group. Soon everyone was using 'Loop Cards' in some form. The basic idea (in the figure below) is that the set of cards is shuffled and dealt out to the class. Some children may end up with more than one card. The person with 'Start' begins and reads out that card. The loop continues to its end. You can make up sets or get them from the internet for almost any topic. One of the teachers from the project described successfully adapting this idea with a Year 8 top set, where they had to design their own set of algebraic loop cards in groups. Not an easy task. There was a realisation that an extension question for students who finish quickly, when using any textbook exercise, would be to write their own questions for each other. The ones they come up with themselves are usually more difficult than any they are asked to do!

Key Maths: exploring the Year 7 textbook

Looking backwards: Reading p. 152 in the Year 9 textbook (see page 232) there is a sense of 'replay' and the word 'remember'. There's definitely a history of how these ideas have been introduced before. Let's go back and have a look at where 'collecting terms' (which some textbooks call 'collecting like-terms') was introduced. (Key Maths have now revised their textbooks to comply with the 2000 National Curriculum but it really is worth making sure you know which curriculum your textbook was written to cover and what the differences are. Remember: You may have Revised Year 7 textbooks and old Year 9 textbooks!)

On a page of the Revised Year 7 textbook, Figure 16.1 (overleaf), is some indication that the pupils have been encouraged to remember and learn the 'rules of algebra'.

## 3  How to make everyone understand

$$[証明] \quad かりに \ a+b\sqrt{2} \ が無理数でないとすると,$$

$$a+b\sqrt{2}=p$$

は有理数である. $b \neq 0$ であるから, この式を変形して,

$$\sqrt{2}=\frac{p-a}{b}$$

となるが, $a, b, p$ は有理数であるから, 右辺は有理数とな

る. 左辺が無理数であるから, これは不合理である.

したがって, $a+b\sqrt{2}$ は無理数である.

There are some simple rules that everyone uses.
Algebra is the same in all languages.
You can see the algebra in this Japanese maths book.

Try to learn these rules and use them from now on.

---

### Rules of algebra

We miss out multiplication signs because they look too much like the letter x.

We write the formula $t = 4 \times C + 3$  as  $t = 4C + 3$

$5y$ means multiply 5 by $y$.
The number is always written first.
We never write $y5$.

Always put the letter you are finding on the left hand side.
Write $t = 4y + z$  not  $4y + z = t$

Miss out any units.
You do not put cm in any formulas involving lengths.

Write divide like a fraction.

Write $5 \div y$  as  $\frac{5}{y}$

---

**Figure 16.1** At the beginning of this chapter, the first on algebra in this Year 7 textbook, 'writing simple formulas' is discussed: the **t**otal length will be **4** m plus the length of the **c**aravan (Key Maths $7^2$, p. 195). So, t = 4 + c. This is a valid entry point but there can be problems with it as well as advantages. The problems come when the idea of variable is lost. Given a = apple and b = banana, a + a + a + b + b = 3a + 2b. Fine. But an experienced teacher will be aware of the children who continue to think like this and, consequently, have problems later in their lesson when, in Linear Programming say, W needs to stand for 'number of washing machines'. In the Teacher File Year $7^1$, which I looked at in my preparation, there were some supportive assessment materials and the student can tick if they can 'collect terms' (see Figure 16.2).

9. Introduction to Algebra

Name                                        Class

_____

☐     I can write simple formulas.

☐     I can use simple formulas.

☐     I can work out two-stage formulas.

☐     I can write two-stage formulas using algebra.

☐     I know the rules of algebra.

☐     I can use the rules of algebra to write formulas.

☐     I can collect terms when all the letters are the same.

☐     I can collect terms when there is more than one letter.

☐     I can substitute numbers into formulas.

☐     I can use algebra to solve problems.

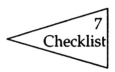

**Figure 16.2** Assessment sheet from Key Maths Teacher File Year 7 Chapter 9 Algebra

It really is possible to appear to go backwards in mathematics whilst in fact understanding more as you ask or are challenged with deeper questions. I must not assume that these Year 9 pupils 'can do' collecting terms because they have got ticks on their assessment sheets in earlier years. There are many interpretations of the task that could lead to them being successful. In my planning I need to try to find out what they know now, and whether there are any problems, bearing in mind codes and variables as possible misconceptions.

## Maxim 2  Individualised learning alone is not sufficient to learn mathematics effectively

### Overview

- Develop strategies in your classroom for running discussions to allow the language of mathematics to be used.
- The teacher's task can be thought of as stressing and ignoring (Love and Mason, 1992, p. 6) from their greater experience of mathematics. For example, you can stress the variable as you work with the students or ignore it to give experience of the technique. Ask other teachers what they see as essential in this chapter and what they stress and ignore in it.

### Strategies for discussion

David Wheeler (1970) wrote an article in *Mathematics Teaching* (MT50) called 'The role of the teacher' from which the following points have been paraphrased. If you like these strategies, find the article and read more.

- A teacher never collects answers from the whole group to check that they all have the correct one, nor does the teacher collect all the different answers without working on the differences.
- A teacher does not praise or blame particular responses or particular children, but may exhort or reassure by expressing faith in the children's capabilities.
- A teacher obtains as much feedback from the children as possible, by observing, asking questions, and asking for particular actions.
- A teacher works with this feedback immediately.
- Except on rare occasions a teacher does not indicate whether a response is right or not, though often asks the children which it is.
- A teacher accepts errors as important feedback which indicates more than correct responses. By directing the children's attention back to the problem the teacher urges them to use what they know to correct errors themselves.

### Research project: stressing variable

The students had been working on a problem. They were drawing squares on square dotted paper and working with the areas of the squares. The whole class were working together to present their work in an organised way. A notation was being used where an $n \times m$ square would be drawn with one side sloping so that it was $n$ squares along and $m$ squares up.

| n x 0 | 1 x 0 | 2 x 0 | 3 x 0 | 4 x 0 | . . . . |
| n x 1 | 1 x 1 | 2 x 1 | 3 x 1 | 4 x 1 | . . . . |
| n x 2 | 1 x 1 | 2 x 1 | 3 x 1 | 4 x 1 | . . . . |
| . | | . | | | |
| n x m | | | | | |

*Pupil 1*   I've noticed a pattern in the *n* by 0 squares, um, the dots inside is the same as the area of the one before.

*Teacher*   Could someone else say that, someone else say what they heard?

*Pupil 5*   The dot in the middle is the area of the one before.

*Teacher*   The number of dots in the middle is the area of the one before.

I want to draw attention to two things from this transcript.

1   The teacher is using a strategy to get the children to articulate what they heard so that they explore what they are thinking in different ways. You could actually try that form of words.

2   This teacher is clear that they are stressing 'the number of dots'. Becoming more aware of misconceptions is important for you to develop what you stress and what you will ignore. You can only stress what you notice and you will only notice what you care about.

*Key maths: finding a start which provokes discussion*

Looking ahead: Let's leave Year 7 and go back to the Year 9 text (pp. 232–3) to carry on planning. Below in the illustration, BODMAS is introduced and this feels like a place where I might want to start my planning. I am aware of problems that can arise for students from using this rule; common misconceptions will lead to there being a variety of answers that will lead to a discussion, as the students work at sorting out their differences. For years I used the rule pretty much as is given below.

### Multiplying out brackets

You can use BODMAS to remind you what to do first.

| You do | Brackets first |
|--------|----------------|
| then powers | Of |
| Next you do | Division |
| and | Multiplication |
| Then you do | Addition |
| and | Subtraction |

*Example*  Work these out using the rules of **BODMAS**.

a  $3 \times (5 + 9)$  b  $2 \times 4 + 3 \times 5$

a  $3 \times (5 + 9) = 3 \times 14$
$= 42$

b  $2 \times 4 + 3 \times 5 = 8 + 15$
$= 23$

### Exercise 8:6

1  Work out part (1) and part (2) of **a** to **d** using the rules of BODMAS.
   a  (1) $2 \times (3 + 7)$    (2) $2 \times 3 + 2 \times 7$
   b  (1) $5 \times (9 - 4)$    (2) $5 \times 9 - 5 \times 4$
   c  (1) $10 \times (7 + 8)$    (2) $10 \times 7 + 10 \times 8$
   d  (1) $7 \times (6 - 5)$    (2) $7 \times 6 - 7 \times 5$

2  Write down what you notice about the answers in question **1**.

## Task 16.7

Use BODMAS to see what you get for $2 + 25 \times 6 - 3 + 5$

You know what the rules are. No problem! If I present a number sentence to a class they usually come up with more than one answer, even when applying BODMAS. We can then explore how they got their answers. This gives me a chance to stress the wording of the explanation to make it possible for them to apply the rule more accurately. Where do you think a problem might be?

See if you can make 154 and 144. Are you having problems seeing how to get 144? I'm assuming you can see that you have to do multiplication before subtraction and addition. This leaves you with 2 + 150 – 3 + 5. If BODMAS gets understood as 'do them in order', then some students do addition first! 2 + 150 – 8 = 144!!! Offering a problem like this, and listening to the discussion which ensues as they discuss their range of answers, helps me to know what to stress to allow them to apply BODMAS effectively. If there are no problems, fine, I don't need to worry about explaining in a way that might suddenly confuse!

All the examples in this section of the Key Maths text can be answered without experiencing this potential problem. If the problem exists, unless it is tackled now it will emerge at some time in the future! There is nothing to stop you extending the work of the chapter. Why not make up some extra exercises?

## Maxim 3  Good mathematics teaching involves conscious choices about how you want to teach!

### Overview

- It's worth doing some work now on what you think being a mathematician or thinking mathematically means. Then you can work consciously on strategies to employ, to develop and stress these behaviours in your students.
- Start to try out strategies and evaluate their use in developing the mathematical classroom culture that you want. Sometimes this is called action research; it involves you making conscious choices against a question you have and then adapting from there.

### Story: action research

A story of a newly qualified teacher making a conscious choice to support the development of her teaching styles:

> 'Pupil-led teaching or teacher-led teaching?' seemed to be the question I was asking here.
>
> The school I was about to start at had a very prescribed scheme of work in place (Key Maths) and expected the chapters of the textbook to be worked through in a certain order, with a prescribed time limit on each chapter. I had been given two Year 7 classes, so it seemed an ideal opportunity to try to make a comparison. Class 7K would be taught 'pupil-led', barely using the textbook, but covering the relevant topics in other ways (after checking with my Head of Department). Class 7G would be taught, 'teacher-led', as the school prescribed. As well as an interesting experiment, this would be a good challenge for me, to see if I could teach in any prescribed style, and whether I could switch straight from one to the other (the classes frequently followed each other).
>
> (Becky Silvester, unpublished MEd assignment, 2000).

The story of how Becky adapted from this starting point is told in the rest of her assignment which is not included here. Keep a research diary of notes giving evidence for and against, and exploring the questions you are working on as you teach.

*Research project: 'becoming a mathematician'*

Here's a brainstorm of what 'being a mathematician' meant to a group of teachers:

- looking for connections
- logical
- wanting to know 'why'
- explaining and writing
- talking and discussing
- open to new ideas – listening
- persevering, struggling, satisfaction
- enthusiasm, interest, enjoyment
- power, efficiency, elegance, beauty
- sorting it out for yourself
- getting organised, looking for simpler cases

(Notes from Steering Group Minutes, TTA Teacher Research Grant[3] 20/1/99)

The teachers in the project then used their awareness of what being a mathematician meant to them in their thinking, planning and organising of lessons. For example, one common practice was stressing the question 'Why?' and some students started to ask, 'Why does this work?' for themselves.

**Task 16.8**

Sit down now and make some statements about what being a mathematician is for you. What will this mean you would notice in your classroom? Are you committing yourself to action?

*Key Maths: conscious choices*

In developing my conscious choices about how I teach I am currently aware of using beginnings of lessons where students are invited to compare and contrast two diagrams or two situations. This helps me to plan for using discussion in my classroom. I'm sure that's what made me think of the idea for introducing the rule of BODMAS to my lessons.

This kind of focus takes the same time as an explanation at the beginning of a lesson, but the students are involved in the discussion and have a chance to clear up misconceptions, followed by practice from the textbook. You might want to use a longer introduction such as Loop Cards to practise, actively as a class, the ideas of solving equations, or changing the subject of a formula. The textbook will not introduce the ideas you want, nor establish a mathematical culture in your classroom by itself. For instance, inverse is mentioned in this chapter and I would want to stress the concept as being a common mathematical idea which will keep cropping up in other contexts, and invite the students to watch out for it.

### Maxim 4   No teaching material is complete without the teacher

Overview

- The textbook writers bring a lot of implicit assumptions to their work, to which you do not have access. Question your own assumptions and listen to the problems the children have and learn from them, asking yourself: 'What have I got to offer to a child with that partial understanding?'
- Where's the motivation and engagement? That's part of the teacher's role. Can the pupils see algebra do something for them that they couldn't do without it? What about any part of the syllabus? Then the work from the textbook might become more accessible and be the practice that the pupils want rather than simply words without an interpretation.

Story: motivation and engagement

Some of the best introductions to lessons come from a teacher having realised the potential of one of the questions in the textbook. One of the research project teachers suggested the following.

'Can you draw a shape with …

1   one line of symmetry and rotational symmetry of order three;
2   no lines of symmetry and rotational symmetry of order two;
3   two lines of symmetry, but no rotational symmetry?

This is lifted straight from a textbook (Vickers level 5). It generates all sorts of discussion on the structure of shapes.'

(Teacher B, e-mail communication)

Research project: what have I got to offer?

The teaching material described above is not complete without the teacher and the culture of the classroom in which that teacher operates. Teacher B's pupils are used to discussion and so will avoid some of the problems associated with language. But children do not just discuss if asked to do so. Your task is to develop teaching strategies to support the learning of your students.

Teaching strategies include anything that you DO that supports (or hinders!) your aims (explicit and implicit) in the classroom. Examples are:

- getting students to discuss, in pairs, what they found in their homework;
- always saying '$a$ times $b$' when you write '$a.b$';
- getting a student to go through an example on the board;

- getting a student to say what they understood another student to mean;
- modelling a mathematician (e.g. by asking, 'Why?');
- getting students to use a common board to collect their results.

(Alf Coles, ESRC project, minutes of a meeting)

## Key Maths

There isn't the need for me to commit to what I would do. It's not my class although I hope that you have a sense of what I would be looking for and how I would behave as a teacher given my experiences on the research project this year. You are a different person although I hope that here there are many strategies that you can pick up and try, especially to do with supporting discussion. Use the book for practice but also encourage the asking of questions. Often as pupils talk through their problem it goes away. In the Teacher Files to Key Maths there are lots of extension ideas to do with use of technology and graphic calculators, points for discussion, concept maps, extra worksheets, answers. The most important way in which you can make the most of your textbook is to engage with it and find out all the things the scheme has to offer, as well as what's missing.

---

### Task 16.9

Make a list of all the strategies you could use to encourage discussion in your classroom from all resources available to you, including observation of other teachers. Keep adding to it, both in terms of other strategies and comments about what worked for you in what circumstances.

---

## Conclusion

When you start teaching you'll have your own particular circumstances to cope with: your school not allowing textbooks to be taken home, not liking the explanations, feeling constrained by time to get through chapters – but there are many things you can do in terms of distilling and expanding. If you can create an atmosphere in your classroom where children feel supported in learning mathematics they will start to question when they are unsure, discussing with the teacher and each other, knowing that they will be listened to even if there isn't always an easy answer! This is a journey for you, too, where there isn't an easy answer to how to teach. Enjoy learning about the children in your classes and how to support them in their learning.

## Notes

1   'Developing algebraic activity in a "community of inquirers"' Economic and Social Research Council (ESRC) project reference R000223044, Laurinda Brown, Rosamund Sutherland, Jan Winter, Alf Coles. Contact: Laurinda.Brown@bris.ac.uk or University of Bristol, Graduate School of Education, 35 Berkeley Square, Bristol BS8 1JA, UK.

2   For 'Loop Cards' go to the Sandwell Numeracy Web Site, www.emu.org.uk/numeracy.

3    For more information about the evidence-based practice teacher research grants go to www.teach-tta.gov.uk/research/grant/index.htm

## References

Department of Education and Science (DES) (1982) *Mathematics Counts (The Cockcroft Report)*, London: HMSO.

Gattegno, C. (1981) *Animated Geometry*, New York: Educational Solutions Inc.

Little, C. (ed.) (1994) *Effective teaching with SMP 11–16: A newcomer's guide*, Southampton: School Mathematics Project.

Love, E. and Mason, J. (1992) *Teaching Mathematics: action and awareness, EM236 Monograph T*, Southampton: The Open University.

SMP (1978) *Supplementary Booklet 5*, Cambridge: Cambridge University Press.

SMP (2000) *Interact Cambridge*, Cambridge: Cambridge University Press.

Key Maths *Book $7^2$*, Stanley Thornes.

Key Maths *Book $7^2$* Revised, Stanley Thornes.

Key Maths *Book $9^3$*, Stanley Thornes.

Vickers, K.M. and Tipler, M.J. (1991) *National Curriculum Mathematics: Level 5*, Chiddingstone Causeway, Canterbury Educational.

Wheeler, D. (1970) *Mathematics Teaching*, 50: 23–9.

# 17 Minding your Qs and Rs
## Effective questioning and responding in the mathematics classroom
John Mason

## Introduction

Asking learners (especially children) questions is so strongly embedded in our culture that most adults do it when in the company of children, and most children do it when playing 'school'. Furthermore, in these types of interactions the adult usually knows the answer and most children quickly work out that this is the case. Questions are seen as some sort of testing process, through which learners supposedly learn. An extreme form is the *cloze* technique of pausing and expecting students to fill in the missing word. Adults are more likely to ask each other questions that are actually seeking information, genuinely enquiring. Where do questions come from? How can we use them effectively in classrooms? How can we stimulate learners to ask their own questions? These issues are addressed through a number of conjectures which cannot be proved, merely tested out in your own experience.

## Where do questions come from?

Not all utterances with a question mark are questions, and some assertions are actually questions. For example, 'We don't do that in here, do we?' is an assertion not a question, and 'Tell me what you are thinking', or 'Tell me what you have been doing' are commands that expect a response. Here I consider any utterance that expects a response as a form of question. So where do questions come from? How do they arise?

> *Conjecture*: an adult asks a learner a question when the adult, in the company of the learner, experiences a shift in the focus of their own attention. The question is intended to reproduce that shift of focus in the learner.

> In particular, enquiry-questions are asked when people become aware that they are uncertain, confused, stuck, struck by something they cannot account for or realise that some expectation is contradicted.

This conjecture has to be tested in your own experience, through trying to catch yourself suddenly asking children or other learners some question. Then you ask yourself, where did that question come from? What was the impulse that prompted the question? For example, here are some situations in which I have caught myself:

- I am with a child, I notice something, and I want the pupil to see it as well; I find myself asking a pointed or focusing question.
- A technical term comes to mind that the learner is supposed to know so I ask …
- I become aware of a logical consequence of something I was thinking about so I ask …
- I become aware that some situation is a particular case of a more general phenomenon, theme, technique, etc., so I ask a pointed question …

These experiences suggest that questions often arise when I experience a contrast or a change in my focus, and without even being aware of it, I use the format of a question to try to direct learners' attention. Furthermore, I often find that it is only when I hear the learner's response that I am aware that it conflicts with what is in my head, and so I become aware that I have asked a question with a specific answer in mind. Before that, I am immersed in the flow of my own attention.

Questions such as 'How did we do this last week?', 'What is this diagram saying?', 'Why did you … ', and so on, all try to focus attention on something that I believe is being overlooked or needs stressing. Even when I am using an enquiry-question because there is something I don't know, the question itself arises because of a sense that there is a gap or uncertainty in my own mind. The question format comes naturally, if tentatively (I have been enculturated not to display my ignorance) to focus others' attention on my problem.

Thus it seems that questions have the effect of focusing or directing other people's attention. They arise from the flow of attention of the asker, and they are likely to be a disturbance to the flow of other people's attention. Unfortunately, that disturbance may not always be welcome.

## Controlling questions

Because it is an accepted cultural norm that questions are supposed to be answered, questioning is one way to exert social control, to assert authority or power (Ainley, 1987; Love and Mason, 1992). For example, 'What do we do when we come into the classroom … ?', 'We don't do that, now do we?', 'Where do we put the equals sign?' This applies especially in a class where, by picking on certain individuals to respond and by stopping one line of discussion through introducing a new one, the teacher retains control. It follows, however, that *not* answering can be used by some learners as a form of reaction or even revolt. This is most likely when learners feel buffeted by questions, and they detect that questions are being used for control purposes.

Similarly, we retain control over learner attention by asking focusing questions such as, 'What is in front of the $x$?', 'What is next to the three?', 'What do we do with the variable?', 'What does the diagram tell us?' and, more generally, 'What did we/you do last time?', 'Can you give me an example?', 'Have you seen something like this before?', 'What does it say in the question?', 'What do you know and what do you want?' In many cases, if the learner knew the answer to the question, they would probably not be stuck so the question would not have to be asked in the first place! Yet somehow we naturally ask the question.

## Cloze technique

Pausing in a flow of statements and expecting students to fill in the missing word is a common format for testing-questions in classrooms. For example, 'This shape is called a ____.', and 'The next thing we do is to carry down the ___.' Note that the missing word is usually at the end of a sentence. The idea is that students have to pay attention and are rehearsing patterns of inner speech that will help them carry out the technique. But there is effective use and ineffective use of this technique, and the two are rather hard to tell apart. If you listen to a lesson in which there is a lot of this going on, you will soon see that children can chorus out an expected word without knowing anything of what is going on because the reasoning is being done by the teacher, and the missing word becomes clear even if you do not know what is going on. Far from rehearsing the useful inner incantations of a technique, students are only called upon to fill in a technical term. If you catch yourself pausing and expecting children to complete your statements, make sure that you are getting them to fill in the reasoning, not the technical terms.

## Genuine enquiry

Not all questions exert control explicitly, though they do direct attention. For example, it is possible to enquire genuinely about what someone is thinking: 'How did you get that?', 'Why did you add these two numbers?', 'Can you tell me how to do this type of question in the future?' But it is important to recognise that no matter how genuine a question is, the fact that it is being asked by a teacher is likely to lead the learner into believing that the teacher knows the answer and expects the learner to know it too, and/or that what the learner has been doing is not correct or not appropriate. Thus the fact of a question being asked is likely to generate a defensive stance. Unless, that is, a different working atmosphere has been developed in the classroom. (See 'Creating a conjecturing atmosphere' later in this chapter).

## Meta-questions

Meta-questions are questions about the process that draw learner attention out of the particularities of the current task with a view to making them aware of a process. For example: 'What would you have to do next time to answer a similar question?', 'What led you to choose this approach?', 'What question am I going to ask you?'

This last question is typical of a range of increasingly indirect prompts used to encourage learners to internalise questions that they could usefully ask themselves. When a particular type of question is proving fruitful such as 'Can you give me an example?', or 'What do you *know* in this problem, and what do you *want* to find?', the teacher can explicitly refer to the use of these questions, perhaps by asking themselves out loud and replying in front of the learners while working on a problem, then using them with learners. After a period of time it is important to become less and less direct, and more and more indirect so that learners begin to internalise the question. Eventually you can ask questions such as, 'What question do you think I am going to ask you?' Of course the first time you ask this they will probably not know what you are asking, but you can tell them, then use the same prompt again later.

Teachers sometimes put up a poster for a time, with a few pertinent questions listed. But if the poster remains up all term or all year, then learners are likely to become dependent on it. If the teacher has to keep asking the same questions, the learners are not being educated. By the teacher's obscuring the poster after a while and referring to it indirectly, then later removing it, and by using more and more indirect prompts (such as meta-questions), learners can be induced to incorporate those questions into their way of thinking. That frees you to make use of a further collection of additional questions.

The process of moving from *directed questions*, through increasingly *indirect prompts* towards *spontaneous use* by learners is also known as scaffolding (the direct questions) and fading (increasingly indirect prompts). The term *scaffolding* was introduced by Wood *et al.* (1976) with Bruner (1986) bringing ideas of the Russian psychologist Lev Vygotsky to the West. The effectiveness of scaffolding lies not in the actual scaffolding but in the fading, the increasingly indirect prompts so that learners internalise the support (Brown *et al.*, 1989).

## Using questions effectively

### Interrogating your own experience

The first thing necessary is to try to catch yourself using questions, to try to check the conjectures out for yourself. If you find some agreement with the conjectures, then you may want to work at changing the way you use questions. The rest of this section makes suggestions to this end. If you do not agree with the conjectures, then the rest of this section may provide further food for thought and experimentation.

### Reducing the use of questions for controlling

The conjectures put forward imply that all questions asked by a teacher are to some extent controlling, and are certainly intended to disturb the learner's flow (or 'stuck') thoughts. But it is possible to reduce the use of questions for social control and for exerting authority, so as to allow questions to be used for teaching mathematics.

The rhetorical form of questioning which masks an instruction or a criticism is used more often than most of us care to admit. For example, 'What do we do when we come in the room?' is typical of an attempt to exert control and to remind learners of social norms. To locate a question asked for the purposes of social control, ask yourself how you would feel if the learners asked the same question of you! What sorts of questions from a learner would be acceptable and what kinds would be seen as impertinent? The impertinent ones are probably the ones used for controlling and *norming*. The use of 'we' is also characteristic, and can be used to catch yourself asking this form of question:

when you find yourself using 'we', stop and ask yourself who the 'we' is. Notice also that when a teacher reports that in a lesson 'we discussed ... ' there is no evidence to distinguish between a *norming* and controlling sequence of questions and a genuine discussion or enquiry. As a form of interaction, controlling and *norming* questions are perfectly common, but they may get in the way of developing a conjecturing, enquiring atmosphere in the classroom. There are other equally effective ways of socialising and controlling learners, such as by making a direct instruction or statement.

Questions that reverse the power structure of the classroom are probably being used to maintain that structure. Where maintaining the power structure is necessary, try using assertions rather than questions. Learners quickly recognise that questions are being used for control purposes, and it merely muddies the water for creating a questioning, conjecturing atmosphere in the classroom, one which supports rather than obstructs mathematical thinking.

## Enculturating learners into using specific questions themselves

### Task 17.1

Make a list of the types of questions you would like learners to internalise, such as the following:

| | |
|---|---|
| What do I know? | What do I want? |
| What do the words mean? | Can I state the question in my own words? |
| Can I depict the situation on a diagram? | Am I convinced? |
| Will it always work or happen? | Can I find an example? |
| Can I simplify the problem first? | What helped me get unstuck? |
| How is it similar to or different from what I've done before? | |

Select a few and work on using those consistently over a period of time, then begin to use more and more indirect references to them. Establish a pattern of work in which learners ask each other for help when they are stuck, before asking you.

### Funnelling

Asking a learner a question is one thing, but what happens if they do not respond? Perhaps the question is too difficult? Perhaps a more pointed, more focused, more precise question will make it clear? So begins a process of funnelling (Bauersfeld, 1995; Wood, 1998), of playing the game 'Guess what is in my mind'. The teacher keeps asking one or more learners more and more precise and detailed questions in an attempt to find something that they can answer. John Holt (1964, p. 24–5) gave an example of funnelling:

I remember the day not long ago when Ruth opened my eyes. We had been doing math, and I was pleased with myself because, instead of telling her answers and showing her how to do problems, I was 'making her think' by asking her questions. It was slow work. Question after question met only silence. She said nothing, did nothing, just sat and looked at me through those glasses, and waited. Each time, I had to think of a question easier and more pointed than the last, until I finally found one so easy that she would feel safe in answering it. So we inched our way along until suddenly, looking at her as I waited for an answer to a question, I saw with a start that she was not at all puzzled by what I had asked her. In fact she was not even thinking about it. She was coolly appraising me, weighing my patience, waiting for the next, sure-to-be-easier question. I thought, 'I've been had! The girl had learned how to make me do the work for her, just as she had learned to make all her previous teachers do the same thing. If I wouldn't tell her the answers, very well, she would just let me question her right up to them.'

How can you break out of a funnelling sequence? As soon as you become aware that you are playing some form of 'Guess what's in my mind' you have the option of admitting to yourself, or even to them, that you do indeed have something in mind. You can go to one extreme, perhaps, and play a quick game of 'Hangman' as you indicate the length of the word you are looking for; at the other extreme you can simply tell them the answer, and then perhaps genuinely enquire why they had not thought of that themselves, and how they might learn to think of it in a similar situation in the future.

## Creating a conjecturing atmosphere

A mathematical or conjecturing atmosphere is one in which whatever is said is said tentatively as a conjecture in the hope of receiving feedback and suggestions for modification. Those who are confident they 'know the answer' tend to keep quiet, or perhaps ask pointed questions in order to support and assist others, while those who are uncertain take every opportunity to say what they can say, and then get help in extending or completing it. Struggle is valued, even praised. No one says 'No that's wrong', they say, 'I invite you to modify your conjecture'.

How might a conjecturing atmosphere be developed? The first essential is to adopt a conjecturing stance yourself, treating everything said by you or by others as a conjecture which may require modification, not as an assertion that has to be right or wrong. Secondly, take opportunities to praise learners for changing their mind, for modifying what they previously said or did. Thirdly, take opportunities to praise learners for making a conjecture (without implying judgement about the quality or aptness of the conjecture). This enables you to attend to the process and ethos of the topic development rather than to the correctness or otherwise of what is said. Try to put the onus on learners to test out what others conjecture. Finally, especially at the beginning, label conjectures as such. (Someone asserts something forcefully, and you say, 'Conjecture'; someone says, 'No' or, 'That's not right' to someone else, and you invite them to change what they say to 'I disagree with your conjecture' or 'I invite you to modify your conjecture'.)

Earlier I suggested that questions cause a disturbance to learners, and that disturbance may not always be welcome. In a conjecturing atmosphere learners are confident to contribute because they know they are learning. In an atmosphere of questions that constantly test whether learners know facts, learners may display signs of anxiety (Anderson and Boylan, 2000): if questions are perceived as too simple, there may be anxiety about not getting them correct; if questions of different levels of difficulty are offered to learners in accordance with what the teacher thinks they can do, there may be embarrassment; and a learner who answers a hard question may be disliked by peers for whom it is too difficult. To gauge atmosphere in a lesson, pay attention to the gestures and postures of learners *after* they have answered a question, as well as to the enthusiasm with which they volunteer.

'Guess what is in my mind' is not always initiated by the teacher. If a learner does not have a response to a question, then they are likely to revert to trying to work out what answer was expected. Tell-tale signs are a sequence of increasingly unthinking responses with a taste of 'guesswork'.

## Being genuinely interested

The secret of effective questioning is to be genuinely interested in what the learners are thinking, in how they are thinking, in what connections they are making and not making. Genuine interest in the learners produces a positive effect on them, for in addition to their feeling that they are receiving genuine attention, you can escape the use of questions to control and disturb negatively. Instead of asking for answers, which in most cases you probably already know, you can genuinely enquire into their methods, their images, their ways of thinking. In the process, you demonstrate to learners what genuine enquiry is like, placing them in an atmosphere of enquiry which is, after all, one view of what schooling is really intended to be about.

If you are genuinely interested, you will wait for an answer when you have asked a question. Learners pick up quickly from the habit of asking and then answering your own question, or from a barrage of questions with little pause between them, that the questioner is not actually interested in an answer. Try holding yourself very still when you ask a question, and think about it yourself while waiting for an answer. If no response is forthcoming, get them to talk to each other about the question for a few seconds, and then ask for contributions. Make it clear that every contribution is valued (e.g. record on a board everything that is said). Sometimes smiling (with an eyebrow raised, *not* staring or glowering) while looking at a learner will encourage them to respond.

## Using attention

If there is something to the conjecture that questions disturb the flow of attention of learners, then effective use of questions would be built around gaining insight into what learners are attending to, and being aware oneself of how learner attention could most usefully be focused. To do this you must be aware of how your own attention is structured.

### What is the learner attending to?

A teacher is demonstrating how to work through a particular problem. The teacher is aware that this problem is a particular case of a general class of problems, and sees it that way (seeing the particular in the general). The numbers are merely representative of any (relevant) numbers that could appear, while the structural constants are seen as common to all such problems. But the learners may only be aware of the particular problem being solved. They may be trying to work out what the rules are, what the steps are in solving it, without being aware of generality. They may not be ready to attend to and distinguish what is generic and what is particular in the resolution of the problem.

An important factor therefore is what learners are attending to: what features are they stressing, and what are they consequently ignoring? Unfortunately, asking such questions directly is rarely informative: learners usually don't know how to answer. However, there are some less direct ways of revealing something of what they are stressing.

One way is to get learners to read a problem or statement out loud, as they may reveal from voice tones and stress what is meaningful and what not. Another is to get them to 'say what they see' as they look at an expression, a diagram, a picture, a poster, a computer screen, etc.. No fancy technical terms are needed, just let them describe some aspect or feature. What they choose to describe is most informative, as long as you remember that absence of evidence is not evidence of absence: just because something is not mentioned does not mean that it is not seen, only that no one has chosen to refer to it. Probably the most effective way to enquire into what learners are attending to is to get them to construct examples: examples of similar questions, examples of mathematical objects satisfying certain properties or conditions, and so on (Watson and Mason, 1998), which is taken up in the section on 'Stimulating learners to question'.

### What do I want the learner to attend to?

In order to use questioning effectively for focusing attention, it is necessary to do more than simply ask a question whenever an idea pops into your head. As a first step, it is necessary to become aware of what features you are stressing, and to make sure that your actions, both overt and covert, serve to stress or highlight those same features. By pausing after saying something significant, by pointing physically and verbally, by getting learners to try to say to each other something you have just said, you can assist them to focus on what you think is central and essential. You can also try out various forms of questions in an attempt to bring those features to the fore in learners' minds, however subtly or explicitly. This is the role of meta-questions mentioned earlier.

## Open and closed questioning

There is a penchant for classifying questions as being open or closed, or more specifically, open-ended or open-fronted, and closed-ended or closed-fronted. For example:

- 'What is a triangle with three equal sides called?' and '⅓ − ¼ = ?' are clearly closed at both ends, because what has to be done is specified, and there is a single correct answer.
- 'Explore the relationship between a polygon being equiangular and equilateral' and 'What fractions can be the difference of two unit fractions?' are open-fronted, because the learners have to decide what they are actually going to work on, and perhaps open-ended because there is no specific well-known answer to be found.
- 'For which polygons does equilateral imply equiangular and vice versa?' and 'In how many ways can a given unit fraction be the difference of two unit fractions?' are fairly open-fronted because the learners have to decide what polygons or fractions to work on, but are closed-ended because there are definite and known answers.
- 'What can you tell me about this shape?' or 'What do you notice?' is open-ended but closed-fronted because the shape or object is specified but the features the learner chooses to stress and express are not, though it is also likely to be received as a 'Guess what is in my mind'.

However, questions are just words with a question mark: the notion of 'openness' and 'closedness' is more to do with how the question is interpreted than with the question itself. Thus 'What is a triangle with three equal sides called?' could be taken as a stimulus to explore the use of the term *equilateral* for other polygons, while 'For which polygons does equilateral imply equiangular and vice versa?' could be taken as an instruction to locate and prove a theorem concerning triangles.

## Stimulating learners to question

How can learners be encouraged to take initiative, to be active learners rather than passive receivers?

The action of getting learners to generate their own questions transforms the learners' relationship with authority and with tests (John Holt, 1968, p. 147) while, at the same time, giving them opportunity to exercise their creativity (even silliness) and still developing their mathematical thinking and their skilful use of techniques. Learners who have regularly and consistently made up their own questions, similar to standard questions, are more likely to be independent of their teacher and in the position of recognising not only the type of question being asked (and hence having access to a method of approach), but also of having developed their confidence in being able to tackle *all questions of a given type*, not just those they have done for revision.

Good starting points for the teacher to stimulate this include:

- Construct a question with the same numbers but different context that makes some sense.
- Construct a question with different numbers in the same context and with the same structure.
- Construct a question with different numbers and different context but the same structure.

- Construct a question with more features in addition to those in this problem but with the same basic structure.

## Responding to learners' questions

Suppose a learner asks you how to do something, perhaps using a fact or some technique they are supposed to know already. You have a choice: you can decide that it is more important that they make progress on the main topic (and so tell them directly), or you can decide that they need to refresh their skill and reconstruct it for themselves (and so make some suggestion or ask a pertinent question). Answering a question with a question may be attractive, but it can be excruciatingly irritating to a learner seeking information, as many teachers find when their own children get the 'teacher treatment' when seeking help with their homework: 'Don't ask me a question, just tell me!' In such cases it is valuable to establish an overt contract with the learners, by finding out what sort of response they are seeking and then providing it, but making an agreement to work on the issue later.

However, what learners need is not for a teacher to resolve all their uncertainties, answer all their questions, tell them what they do not remember. Rather, what they need is to become familiar with *how* to deal with getting stuck: for example, looking for confidence – inspiring examples to try out to see what is going on, looking up technical terms to check meaning and replace them with something more confidence inspiring, and clarifying what they actually know and what they need to know in order to solve the problem.

If a learner does not understand, they are most likely to ask for a repetition ('Could you say that again please?', 'Could you go through that again please?'). If, as teacher, you always accede to this request, you train learners in dependency and you preserve your role of authority. You can choose instead, sometimes, to get someone else to 'say what they think you said', and you can choose to get the learner to say or do as much as they can, in order to reveal where it is that they are actually getting stuck. If you can establish a practice in which learners are willing to struggle out loud because they know that others will help them (not mock them), then you and they will find that learning becomes more efficient as well as more satisfying.

## Summary

Although a very common activity, asking questions is at best problematic and at worst an intrusion into other people's thinking. By catching yourself expecting a particular response you can avoid being caught in a funnelling sequence of 'Guess what is in my mind'. By being explicit at first, then increasingly indirect in your prompts, you can assist learners to internalise useful questions that they can use for themselves to help them engage in effective and productive mathematical thinking. Above all, the types of questions you ask will quickly inform your learners of what you expect of them and, covertly, of your enacted philosophy of teaching.

The key to effective questioning lies in using *norming* and controlling questions rarely, focusing questions sparingly and reflectively and genuine enquiry-questions as much as possible. This means being genuinely interested in the answers you receive as insight into learners' thinking, and it means choosing the form and format of questions in order to assist learners to internalise them for their own use (using meta-questions reflectively). The kinds of questions you ask learners indicates the scope and breadth of your concern for and interest in them, as well as the scope, aims and purposes of mathematics and the types of questions that mathematics addresses.

## References

Ainley, J. (1987) 'Telling questions', *Mathematics Teaching*, 118: 24–6.

Anderson, J. and Boylan, M. (2000) 'The National Numeracy Strategy: teacher questions and pupil anxiety', in B. Jaworski (ed.) *Proceedings of BSRLM*, 20(1 & 2): 49–54.

Baird, J. and Northfield, F. (1992) *Learning from the Peel Experience*, Melbourne: Monash University.

Bauersfeld, H. (1995) '"Language games" in the mathematics classroom: their function and their effects', in P. Cobb and H. Bauersfeld (eds) *The Emergence of Mathematical Meaning: interaction in classroom cultures*, Hillsdale, NJ: Lawrence Erlbaum Associates: 271–91.

Brown, S., Collins A. and Duguid, P. (1989) 'Situated cognition and the culture of learning', *Educational Researcher*, 18(1): 32–41.

Bruner, J. (1986) *Actual Minds, Possible Worlds*, Cambridge, MA: Harvard University Press.

Holt, J. (1964) *How Children Fail*, London: Pitman.

Holt, J. (1968) *How Children Learn*, London: Pitman.

Love, E. and Mason, J. (1992) *Teaching Mathematics: action and awareness*, Milton Keynes: Open University.

Watson, A. and Mason, J. (1998) *Questions and Prompts for Mathematical Thinking*, Derby: ATM.

Wood, T. (1998) 'Funnelling or focusing? Alternative patterns of communication in mathematics class', in H. Steinbring, M.G. Bartolini-Bussi and A. Sierpinska (eds) *Language and Communication in the Mathematics Classroom*, Reston, VA: National Council of Teachers of Mathematics: 167–78.

Wood, D., Bruner, J. and Ross, G. (1976) 'The role of tutoring in problem solving', *Journal of Child Psychology and Psychiatry*, 17: 89–100.

# 18 Coursework and its assessment
## Candia Morgan

## Introduction

Students develop and follow alternative approaches. They reflect on their own lines of enquiry when exploring mathematical tasks; in doing so they introduce and use a range of mathematical techniques. Students convey mathematical or statistical meaning through precise and consistent use of symbols that is sustained throughout the work. They examine generalisations or solutions reached in an activity, commenting constructively on the reasoning and logic or the process employed, or the results obtained, and make further progress in the activity as a result.

(Ma1, Level 8)

Students specify hypotheses and test them by designing and using appropriate methods that take account of variability and bias. They ... [select] the statistic most appropriate to their line of enquiry.

(Ma4, Level 7)

---

**Task 18.1**

- What sort of tasks must students engage in so that they can achieve these standards?
- How can such levels of mathematical behaviour be assessed?
- And what can teachers do to help their students to attain them?

---

Traditional forms of timed examination questions are not suited to trying out alternative approaches, designing investigations, following individual lines of enquiry, reflecting or commenting. Those who are successful in mathematics examinations generally consider that a quick recognition of the standard methods expected by the examiner and single-minded following of the required procedures are much more effective ways of achieving high marks. Yet exploration, posing problems, reflection, communication and critical comment are important parts of creative mathematical thinking. They are essential problem-solving tools for those who use mathematics in their work and empower all of us in an increasingly 'mathematised' everyday environment. Indeed, they are included in the National Curriculum for England (DfEE, 1999) at all levels and must be assessed at each Key Stage. At Key Stage 4 one of the main ways in which they are assessed is through the coursework component of the GCSE (General Certificate of Secondary Education).

At various times, the word *coursework* has been used in at least three ways, referring to:

- any work that is done during a course;
- a selection from all the work done during a course, chosen for assessment purposes;
- specific tasks done for assessment purposes, completed during a course.

Since the introduction of the GCSE for students in England and Wales in 1988, all subjects have had to include coursework components as well as terminal examinations in the assessment process for students aged 16-plus.[1] In mathematics, the need to make this assessment process manageable has meant that examination boards and schools have increasingly made use of specific tasks, often set by the examination board. It is thus the third meaning of *coursework* that has come to dominate – and it is this meaning that I shall be using in this chapter (unless otherwise specified).

Many post-16 courses, including General National Vocational Qualifications and some A level syllabuses, also involve coursework. While there are some differences in the ways in which assessed coursework at post-16 relates to the work students do during the course, many of the issues are very similar to those at earlier stages. In this chapter, however, I shall focus primarily on Key Stages 3 and 4.

Some beginning mathematics teachers did coursework as part of their own schooling, although for many of them it may only have been a small part of their experience. Others have not experienced assessment by coursework at all. This chapter will therefore start by identifying what coursework in mathematics is – what its objectives are and what forms it takes. We shall then look at some of the issues involved in its assessment, including the difficulties that teachers encounter in their two roles as teachers and as assessors, and the extent to which assessment methods support achievement of the original objectives of the introduction of coursework.

While the use of coursework as part of an external examination system at GCSE is obviously important, it needs to be related to the experiences that students have throughout their mathematics education. The relationship of coursework to the broader mathematics curriculum at Key Stages 3 and 4 will be considered. An important challenge for teachers is to prepare their students for this 'high stakes' assessment by developing the mathematical skills needed to undertake coursework tasks successfully and an understanding of how to communicate their mathematical skills and understanding effectively.

## What is coursework?

Since its inception, the regulations governing GCSE coursework and the interpretation of these regulations by the examination boards have changed several times and will, no doubt, change again. Syllabuses are developed to comply with the current version of the National Curriculum and, while there are minor differences between the examination boards, they have much in common, including (at the time of writing) the following characteristics:

- All syllabuses include a coursework component.
- Marks from coursework constitute 20 per cent of the GCSE, while timed examinations form the other 80 per cent.
- Candidates have to submit two coursework tasks, one of which will be assessed according to the criteria for Ma1 (Using and Applying Mathematics), while the other will be assessed using the criteria for Ma4 (Handling Data).[2]
- The assessment criteria are nationally agreed, though individual examination boards may issue additional guidance (performance indicators) related to specific tasks. The criteria are related to the strands of the National Curriculum: Making and monitoring decisions to solve problems, Communicating mathematically, Developing skills of mathematical reasoning (for Ma1); Specify the problem and plan, Collect, process and represent data, Interpret and discuss results (for Ma4).
- The tasks may be chosen from tasks suggested by the examination board or may be devised by the school or college.
- Each school or college may decide either to assess their own students' coursework tasks (which will then be moderated by the examination board) or to submit them to be assessed by external examiners.

The introduction of coursework at GCSE aimed to enable assessment of important aspects of the curriculum that could not be assessed by traditional timed examinations (DES, 1985), in particular the problem solving processes involved in working on extended- and open-ended tasks. Both Using and Applying Mathematics and Handling Data involve students in defining their own problems (usually from a starting point suggested by a set task) and determining their own approaches to their task. This means that coursework tasks must be open. In other words, different students are likely to choose different approaches and may achieve different (but equally valid) results. There may not be a single right answer – or even a finite number of right answers! This means that coursework tasks are much more difficult to assess than short, closed questions.

## Task 18.2

A class of students were given this task as a starter for their coursework:

Drop a ball onto a flat horizontal surface. How high does it bounce?

All the students started in the same way, dropping a tennis ball from a height of 1 m onto the classroom floor and recording the results. They then continued in different ways:

continued on next page

Student A varied the height from which the ball was dropped and looked for a relationship between this and the height of the bounce.

Student B considered the consistency of the bounce.

Student C checked whether all the balls in a box of six bounced the same.

Student D compared the bounces of different kinds of balls.

- Consider the different mathematics that each of these students might use and the different results they might get. You may find it useful to do the task yourself following one or more approach.
- How could you evaluate these different outcomes?

## Assessing coursework: some issues

Exploring, reflecting, decision-making, interpreting, commenting are among the processes that students are expected to demonstrate in their coursework. These all imply that individual students will respond to their tasks in original ways – and hence that there may be very many different kinds of responses that are equally valid, demonstrating achievement in a variety of ways. This possibility raises real difficulties when it comes to assessing the various responses. In this section I shall assume that the coursework is being assessed by the students' own teachers, though most of the issues are still relevant when coursework is externally assessed.

## Same starting point: different paths, different solutions

The defining characteristic of investigation and problem-solving is openness. Even when students start with the same initial task, they are expected to introduce their own supplementary questions and to make their own decisions about the mathematics they will use. This raises two important sources of difficulty.

First, by going down different paths, two students may end up working on different problems that provide them with unequal opportunities to achieve the assessment criteria. For example, among the GCSE criteria for Ma1 tasks are some demanding the formulation and justification of generalisations and the use of symbols. Dylan Wiliam discusses possible responses to the task 'Investigate integer-sided triangles'. He points out that, if a student chooses to investigate the number of triangles with a fixed longest side, it is very easy to formulate a quite simple algebraic generalisation for the number of possible triangles, whereas investigating the number of triangles with a fixed perimeter would lead to a very complicated generalisation for which the formulation and justification would probably be beyond the capability of any but the best GCSE candidates (Wiliam, 1994). Whereas in some other cases it may be possible for an experienced teacher to anticipate and provide guidance about whether the path proposed by a student is likely to prove fruitful, in this case it is unlikely to be obvious at an early stage. Unequal opportunities to demonstrate achievement (that is, to formulate and justify a correct generalisation in an algebraic form) mean that the assessment task itself is unfair.

The second problem with the possible proliferation of interpretations of tasks and decisions about methods of approach is the difficulty for the teachers who are going to assess the students' work. Teachers must read, make sense of and evaluate several pages of original work for each student in their class, comparing each against the same set of criteria. This problem becomes even more acute when it is borne in mind that students in schools all over the country, with a wide range of different backgrounds and experiences of mathematics in the classroom, working on a number of different tasks, are all to be assessed by the same standards. Teachers of subjects such as English or history sometimes complain that teachers of mathematics have it easy because they only have to mark right and wrong answers rather than making qualitative judgements about original writing. This is certainly not true when it comes to assessing coursework! Indeed, reading mathematics is probably more difficult and more time-consuming than reading in many other subjects because it is not possible to get the sense of a text or to evaluate its reasoning without paying close attention to each statement and to the relationships between them. 'Skimming' is not an option if all students are to be given a fair assessment.

Attempts to resolve these difficulties have tended to result in restricting the possibilities for students to 'investigate' in any genuine sense. Specifying tasks more tightly in order to ensure that students at least start out on fruitful paths restricts opportunities for them to pose their own problems and may also lessen the excitement and fulfilment that they can get from creating and exploring an original piece of mathematics. Providing 'performance indicators' to guide the assessment of particular tasks may also lead teachers to guide their students towards solution paths that will match the indicators and thus be easy to assess (Wiliam, 1994).

## Pattern spotting

A further danger is that, in attempting to ensure that students have a better chance of reaching higher grades, they are guided towards a narrow range of types of tasks and ways of working. It has been recognised since the early years of GCSE that achieving a generalisation in an algebraic form is a good way of getting a grade C for investigative tasks. This led to the proliferation of tasks that engaged students in generating numerical data from multiple examples, looking for a pattern in their data and finally forming an inductive generalisation from the pattern; usually only a minority of students were able to go on to prove that their generalised formula was valid. Two important criticisms have been made of this type of task. First, this is clearly not the only possible kind of mathematical investigation and its overuse restricts the mathematical experience of students. In his article 'Train Spotters' Paradise', Dave Hewitt describes several lessons in which students were working in this way (Hewitt, 1992). He argues strongly against the tendency to focus only on the number patterns found in the data, pointing out that students lose sight of the structure and context of the problem, working only with the numbers. Hewitt suggests many rich mathematical possibilities that might arise from alternative approaches to the same starting points. A second criticism has come from mathematician David Wells, who has argued that what he calls the

Data-Pattern-Generalisation approach is a method of investigation appropriate to the natural sciences rather than to mathematics (Wells, 1993). While induction from data may help mathematicians to generate hypotheses, this is not the primary aim of mathematical activity. Deductive reasoning about the structure of the situation is necessary, both to construct proofs and to generate further understanding of the situation itself.

---

## Task 18.3

Consider this trapezium drawn on isometric paper.

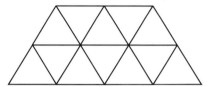

Here are some problems that might be posed related to such trapezia:

a   What relationship is there between the lengths of the sides and the number of small triangles a trapezium contains?

b   The lengths of the sides can be given as an ordered set {4, 2, 2, 2}. What other sets of four numbers would also make a trapezium?

c   How many trapezia can you find in a trapezium?

d   What other polygons can be drawn using isometric paper?

- Pose some further possible problems from this starting point.
- Which problems are likely to lead to a 'pattern-spotting' approach?
- Which are likely to avoid 'pattern-spotting'?
- What range of mathematical ideas and processes might students engage with while working on each of the problems?

---

### How do you know someone has 'worked systematically'?

Many of the criteria for coursework in both Ma1 and Ma4 involve assessing the processes that students go through while working on their tasks. The main source of evidence available to assessors is the written work that is presented at the end of the task, but this written product often does not show clearly all the processes that students have gone through and certainly cannot be thought of as a transparent representation of these processes. For example, when students tackle the problem of finding the relationship between the lengths of the sides of a trapezium and the number of 'unit' triangles in it (as in the task above), they often include a table in their written work – but how can the assessor interpret it? A particular arrangement of data in a one-dimensional table (see the table opposite) may be a record of the way in which the data was actually collected, showing systematic change in one variable at a time. On the other hand it may have been constructed at a later point in the investigation, organising data that was originally collected in a haphazard way.

| Top length | Bottom length | Slant length | Unit triangles |
|---|---|---|---|
| 1 | 3 | 2 | 8 |
| 2 | 4 | 2 | 12 |
| 3 | 5 | 2 | 16 |
| 1 | 4 | 3 | 15 |
| 2 | 5 | 3 | 21 |
| 3 | 6 | 3 | 27 |
| 1 | 5 | 4 | 20 |
| 2 | 6 | 4 | 32 |
| 3 | 7 | 4 | 40 |
| 1 | 6 | 5 | 30 |
| 2 | 7 | 5 | 45 |
| 3 | 8 | 5 | 55 |

**Figure 18.1** A one-dimensional table – does it show systematic data collection?

And what about the student who chooses to use a two-way table to show other aspects of relationships in the data below?

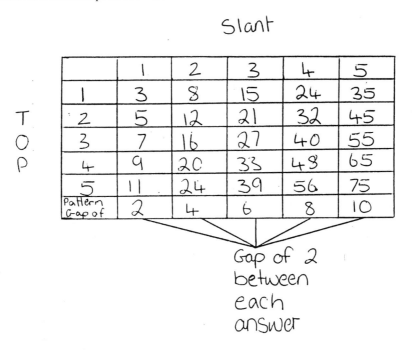

Slant

| | 1 | 2 | 3 | 4 | 5 |
|---|---|---|---|---|---|
| 1 | 3 | 8 | 15 | 24 | 35 |
| 2 | 5 | 12 | 21 | 32 | 45 |
| 3 | 7 | 16 | 27 | 40 | 55 |
| 4 | 9 | 20 | 33 | 48 | 65 |
| 5 | 11 | 24 | 39 | 56 | 75 |
| Pattern Gap of | 2 | 4 | 6 | 8 | 10 |

(T O P)

Gap of 2 between each answer

**Figure 18.2** A two-way table – has this student been systematic?

My research investigating teachers assessing such coursework showed that, while some assessors reacted positively to work containing such a table, at least one complained that there was no evidence that the student had 'worked systematically' (Morgan, 1998). Again there is a danger that stereotypical ideas about coursework and about its writing may lead to unfair assessment.

Particular issues arise when attempting to assess the thinking that goes on during the planning stages of students' work.

- Candidates try different approaches and find ways of overcoming difficulties that arise when they are solving problems. (Ma1 task criteria for Making and monitoring decisions to solve problems, Level 1.)
- Candidates consider the practical problems of carrying out the survey or experiment. (Ma4 task criteria for Specify the problem and plan, Level 6.)

Apart from the fact that many students find writing very difficult, some can be reluctant to write about the problems they encountered during their work, thinking that it is only getting the right answer that counts in mathematics. Helping students to write more effectively will be discussed below; it is not, however, the only approach to resolving this difficulty. Unlike in traditional timed examinations, the written product presented at the end is not the only evidence that can be used. When teachers assess their own students' work it is inevitable that they draw on their personal knowledge of the student and, in particular, their observations of the students' work on the coursework task in class. Moreover, if a teacher is uncertain about any aspect of the written coursework it is possible to talk with the student to seek clarification. This sort of additional evidence needs to be recorded if it is to be used to justify awarding marks for criteria that are not evident in the student's written report.

## What constitutes 'help'?

Although coursework is used for formal assessment purposes, it is expected to be undertaken in normal classroom conditions. This means that students will discuss the task among themselves, both in and out of the classroom, with their teacher and, in some cases, with parents or other family members. Some may get information from reference sources in the library or from the internet; some may even buy ready-made solutions from internet entrepreneurs. One of the arguments against coursework has been that students from middle-class families with educated parents are at an unfair advantage because they have so much help available to them at home. This is clearly a true criticism, though it also applies to more traditional forms of examination in which students from such backgrounds also perform better. In my opinion, however, we should welcome the use of such research methods and support students from less-advantaged homes by providing them with the resources they lack at home. Mathematicians do not work in total isolation but make use of all the resources available to them, including perhaps the most valuable resource of all, discussion with other mathematicians. The crucial question from the point of view of the teacher making a formal assessment of a student's work is not 'Did this student do this work all by himself or herself?' but 'Does the student understand everything that he or she has written?' If some or all of the work has been copied

COURSEWORK AND ITS ASSESSMENT 267

blindly it is usually easy to detect by observing the work done in the classroom and by discussing the final report with the student. Questions such as, 'Why did you decide to do that?', 'What difficulties did you encounter?' and 'How might the result be different if … ?' are useful for probing whether a student has really made this work his or her own.

The classroom setting for doing coursework raises another concern felt by many teachers: how much help can or should they give to students while they are working on their coursework tasks? A useful guideline is the advice given by one of the examination boards in answer to this question:

> Good practice should prevail. It is not good practice to allow candidates to flounder, nor is it good practice to show them solutions to problems.
>
> (Edexcel, 1999, p. 9)

Unfortunately it is not always entirely clear how far you have to go before 'preventing floundering' becomes 'showing the solution'. This has to be a matter of professional judgement. The Edexcel advice goes on to suggest that, where a student is trying to form a generalisation but has data that contains errors, it is acceptable to guide them by making comments such as 'Have another look at your results' or 'Are you sure about this one?' But if you go as far as saying 'This result is wrong and should be … ', this would constitute help that must be recorded and taken into account when deciding the grade for the work as a whole. How much adjustment to make to grades is again a matter of professional judgement. If the student has succeeded in demonstrating unaided achievement of the same criterion in another part of their work, they probably should not be penalised.

## Preparing students

So far I have focused primarily on issues related to the assessment of coursework. It is important to remember, however, that the skills required for using and applying mathematical facts and procedures need teaching and practising, just as the facts and procedures themselves need to be taught and practised. Students should not just be expected to use the necessary skills and ways of thinking in the context of extended tasks and formal assessment but should have opportunities to develop them in situations where they are fully supported by their teacher. Many mathematical thinking and problem-solving skills can be addressed on a regular basis in the context of lessons that are focused on other 'content' areas of the curriculum. The Cockcroft Report, which was very influential in prompting the inclusion of investigation and problem-solving in the curriculum and in examinations, envisaged a mathematics classroom in which these ways of working would be integrated into everyday lessons, stating:

> Investigations need be neither lengthy nor difficult. At the most fundamental level, and perhaps most frequently, they should start in response to pupils' questions, perhaps during exposition by the teacher or as a result of a piece of work that is in progress or has just been completed. The essential condition of work of this kind is that the teacher must be willing to pursue the matter when a

pupil asks 'could we have done the same thing with three other numbers?' or 'what would happen if … ?'

(Cockcroft, 1982, para. 250)

This open attitude on the part of the teacher is crucial, but just being willing to pursue such questions is not enough. How do students come to ask them in the first place? Of course, a safe, supportive and responsive classroom atmosphere is important, but students also need to know what sorts of questions are mathematically interesting and productive. One way for teachers to help students develop these sorts of enquiry skills is to model them by using them themselves in their teaching. However, as Anne Watson and John Mason argue, this is not the end. Such support has to 'fade away' so that students can become independent questioners and mathematical thinkers themselves (Watson and Mason, 1998; and also Chapter 17 by John Mason, in this volume).

Working with pupils on asking questions is a good starting point, but other parts of the investigative and problem-solving processes also need to be addressed. Having asked a question, how do you formulate it mathematically? How do you devise a strategy to attack it? How do you check that your reasoning is valid and your conclusions are reasonable? Again, these aspects can and should be addressed as part of the everyday mathematics classroom procedure. The Association of Teachers of Mathematics makes a number of practical suggestions for doing this with students of all ages in their booklet 'Using and Applying Mathematics' (ATM, 1993). Many of these suggestions involve oral questioning and discussion that gives students responsibility for deciding how to approach problems and for justifying their decisions. For example, teachers might ask students to describe their solution methods and compare different approaches to the same problem, make a habit of asking 'How do you know that is right?' – and help students to begin asking that question themselves, provide opportunities for students to critique other people's solutions and reasoning.

---

**Task 18.4**

Reflect on a lesson you have taught or observed recently.
What opportunities and support were provided for students to:

- pose problems?
- decide what approach to use?
- consider different ways of approaching a problem?
- explain their reasoning?
- critique someone else's reasoning?
- consider whether their answers were reasonable?

How might the lesson be adapted to provide more opportunities and support for students to develop these processes?

---

I have suggested that many of the skills required for being successful at coursework can and should be developed through everyday work on other types of task – through coursework in its first sense of 'any work that is done during a course'. When it comes to GCSE, however, students are generally faced with substantial tasks that may take an extended period of time to work on. This will be daunting if their general experience in mathematics lessons consists only of short tasks, several of which are generally completed within a single lesson. A long-term approach needs to be taken to preparing students for GCSE coursework. Just as schemes of work in secondary schools plan for students to develop from their basic knowledge of arithmetic to high-level algebraic understanding and skills, development in investigational and problem-solving skills must be planned. Here are some possible paths of progression in the types of tasks that students might engage in and in the organisation of these tasks:

- *from* short tasks *to* tasks that take a whole lesson *to* tasks extended over several lessons;
- *from* using small amounts of data *to* dealing with large data sets;
- *from* informal arguments and justifications *to* formal chains of reasoning and proofs;
- *from* oral reporting *to* formal writing;
- *from* whole-class work *to* group work *to* individual work;
- *from* teacher-led *to* teacher-guided *to* independent;
- *from* structured tasks *to* tasks that demand that students decide their own strategies;
- *from* work done as part of everyday lessons *to* formal assessment tasks.

I am not suggesting that these paths are the only possible ones – or even that they are necessarily the right paths for all teachers and all students – but that the development of the ability to cope independently with extended coursework tasks cannot be left to chance.

## Communication skills – mathematical writing needs teaching too

A particular issue in preparing students for assessment by coursework is the development of their mathematical communication skills. Teachers frequently observe that some students who are good at mathematics do not succeed in writing effectively about the mathematics they have done and hence have difficulty in demonstrating their achievement fully. This can be because their general language skills are not as good as their mathematical ones. For example, students for whom English is an additional language sometimes do relatively well in non-verbal aspects of mathematics compared with their performance in other subjects. However, it is also quite possible for students who are good at writing in other subjects to have difficulties with the kind of writing needed for mathematics coursework.

One difficulty is knowing what to write about in the first place. In an article in *Mathematics in School*, Ann MacNamara and Tom Roper describe several examples of mathematical ideas and findings 'overheard' by their tape recorder in a classroom but not recorded in writing by the students or noticed by their teacher (MacNamara and Roper, 1992). They suggest that one useful way of helping students to record their mathematical thinking is to expect them to keep a 'diary' as they work on their coursework task. Many teachers have found this a useful way of helping students to record their processes. However, MacNamara and Roper also point out that that this may not solve every problem: students may deliberately choose not to record part of their work because they do not realise it is significant. In one incident a group of students working on an investigation made a discovery, but then overheard another group who had noticed the same thing so decided not to write about it: 'Someone else knows it as well now ... you don't need to write it down' (p. 13). Teachers cannot be aware of everything students do, so they need to help students realise how much needs to be recorded.

On the other hand, recording *all* the details may not be appropriate either. On reading a piece of coursework that contained the following passage:

> Once Suzanne and I had completed tasks 1 and 2, we set out to discover if there was any connection between the triangular area and the lengths of the sides. First we lettered the sides. In a very short time we had discovered a relationship between the lengths of the sides and the area (triangular). We were able to put this into a formula.

One teacher commented, 'That's one of my pet hates. It's sort of, you know, "Miss put this task on the board and we copied it down", but not quite that bad.' This is not just a language issue, but a mathematical one. Deciding what is significant enough to record is a matter of mathematical judgement and needs to be addressed in mathematics lessons.

---

**Task 18.5**

- How does the passage above need to be changed so that it contains only mathematically significant information? (Some of the information may be missing – try to specify what it is.)
- How could you help the girl who wrote this passage to understand why it is inappropriate and to improve it?

---

Teachers need to help their students develop awareness of good ways of writing about mathematical activity. This must involve being explicit about what these ways are – we cannot expect all pupils just to 'pick up' what is expected. One approach is to start with collaborative writing guided by the teacher. If a class has all been working on the same problem a plenary session might work on constructing a joint report, the teacher taking ideas from members of the class and shaping them into appropriate forms of written language on the board. Another approach, used to help develop children's writing in a number of different areas of the curriculum, is the idea of 'writing frames' (Lee, 1997; Lewis and Wray, undated). Here, useful phrases (for example, 'I noticed that ... ', 'I decided to ... because/so that ... ', 'This will always be true because ... ') are provided for the students to prompt them to remember what needs to be recorded and to give them appropriate words and grammatical forms. Again, as when developing mathematical problem-solving processes, this support needs to 'fade away' so that students develop independent mathematical communication skills.

## Conclusion: professional judgement and professional community

During the discussion of issues in the assessment of coursework, it should have become clear that there are no straightforward, easy answers to the difficulties and dilemmas that teachers are likely to encounter. The very nature of coursework makes this uncertainty inevitable. Tasks that are open enough for students to demonstrate their abilities to pose problems and design solution methods must create opportunities for differences between students and, indeed, for creativity – surely a desirable outcome, however hard it is to assess. Providing supportive environments for students to work in encourages fruitful mathematical discussions, collaboration and research skills at the same time as raising questions about 'help' and students' ownership of their work. If we are to get all the possible benefits from coursework, teachers must accept and work with its problems, having the confidence to use their professional judgement when faced with difficult decisions.

Having said this, we must also be concerned about the reliability of assessment of coursework at GCSE – is it fair to all students? After all, GCSE results are of critical importance to young people in their future educational and occupational opportunities. We must ask whether the processes of assessment carried out by teachers and by the examination boards are good enough to ensure that each student receives the grade they deserve, regardless of which individual teacher or examiner has responsibility for assigning the grade. Experience since the inception of coursework has suggested that, when teachers work together to establish common understanding of standards, they can be successful in achieving a good level of agreement in their judgements of students' work. Moderation meetings within schools and participation in continuing professional development, bringing teachers from different schools together, are essential to maintaining a professional community that is capable of establishing common standards and applying them reliably. Teachers' commitment to developing students' mathematical problem-solving skills and to the work that is required to establish such a professional community is the key to success in achieving the original aims of coursework.

## Notes

1   In mathematics, unlike most other subjects, coursework did not become a compulsory component of GCSE until 1991.
2   In some cases, one of these components may be made up of two or more shorter tasks.

## References

ATM (1993) *Using and Applying Mathematics: strategies for teachers*, Derby: Association of Teachers of Mathematics.

Cockcroft, W.H. (1982) *Mathematics Counts*, London: HMSO.

DES (1985) *GCSE: The National Criteria – Mathematics*, London: HMSO.

DfEE (1999) *Mathematics: The National Curriculum for England*, London: Department for Education and Employment.

Edexcel (1999) *Mathematics 1385 and 1386: The assessment of Ma1*, London: Edexcel Foundation.

Hewitt, D. (1992) 'Train spotters' paradise', *Mathematics Teaching*, 140: 6–8.

Lee, C. (1997) 'The use of teaching strategies to improve students' writing of mathematics', unpublished report to the Teacher Training Agency.

Lewis, M. and Wray, D. (undated) *Writing Frames: Scaffolding children's non-fiction writing in a range of genres*, Exeter: The Exeter Extending Literacy Project.

MacNamara, A. and Roper, T. (1992) 'Unrecorded, unobserved and suppressed attainment: can our pupils do more than we know?', *Mathematics in School,* 21(5): 12–13.

Morgan, C. (1998) *Writing Mathematically: the discourse of investigation*, London: Falmer.

Watson, A. and Mason, J. (1998) *Questions and Prompts for Mathematical Thinking*, Derby: Association of Teachers of Mathematics.

Wells, D. (1993 3rd enlarged edn) *Problem Solving and Investigations*, Bristol: Rain Press.

Wiliam, D. (1994) 'Assessing authentic tasks: alternatives to mark-schemes', *Nordic Studies in Mathematics Education*, 2(1): 48–68.

# 19 Formative assessment in mathematics

Dylan Wiliam

## Introduction

Successive governments have bemoaned the 'long tail of underachievement' in British schools but, in fact, the distribution of achievement in British schools is almost completely symmetrical. The real problem is that the range of achievement in Britain is wider than in almost any other developed country. Our highest-performing students compare well to the best in any other country, but we have many students who leave school or college without adequate capability in mathematics.

This is not because the lack of an adequately skilled workforce harms our industrial competitiveness (there is, in fact, no discernible association between levels of academic achievement and industrial productivity). Rather we should be concerned about the mathematical achievement of young people because too many of them leave school without the mathematical capabilities they need in order to exercise an effective control over their own lives.

A recent review of research studies on formative assessment (Black and Wiliam, 1998) showed that increasing the use of formative assessment in school classrooms would raise the average achievement of students by as much as two grades at GCSE for each subject.

But much more importantly, formative assessment has the power to change the *distribution* of attainment. Good formative assessment appears to be disproportionately beneficial for lower attainers so that, typically, an average improvement of two GCSE grades would actually represent an improvement of three grades for the weakest students, versus an improvement of one grade for the strongest. Formative assessment therefore seems to be the most promising way to reduce the unacceptably wide variation in attainment that currently exists in mathematics classrooms in Britain.

This chapter will discuss formative assessment under three broad headings – rich questioning, feedback, and involving students in their own learning.

## Questioning

Two items used in the Third International Mathematics and Science Study (TIMSS) are shown in Figure 19.1. Although apparently quite similar, the success rates on the two items were very different. For example, in Israel, 88 per cent of the students answered the first items correctly, while only 46 per cent answered the second correctly, with 39 per cent choosing response (b). The reason for this is that many students, in learning about fractions, develop the naive conception that the largest fraction is the one with the smallest denominator, and the smallest fraction is the one with the largest denominator. This approach leads to the correct answer for the first item, but leads to an incorrect response to the second. In this sense, the first item is much weaker than the second, because many students can get it right for the wrong reasons.

---

**Item 1 (success rate 88%)**

---

Which fraction is the smallest?

(a) $\dfrac{1}{6}$ (b) $\dfrac{2}{3}$ (c) $\dfrac{1}{3}$ (d) $\dfrac{1}{2}$

---

**Item 2 (success rate 46%)**

---

Which fraction is the largest?

(a) $\dfrac{4}{5}$ (b) $\dfrac{3}{4}$ (c) $\dfrac{5}{8}$ (d) $\dfrac{7}{10}$

---

**Figure 19.1** *Two items from the Third International Mathematics and Science Study*

This illustrates a very general principle in teachers' classroom questioning. By asking questions of students, teachers try to establish whether they have understood what they are meant to be learning, and if students answer the questions correctly, it is tempting to assume that the students' conceptions *match* those of the teacher. However, all that has really been established is that the students' conceptions *fit* within the limitations of the questions. Unless the questions used are very rich, there will be a number of students who manage to give all the right responses, while having very different conceptions from those intended.

A particularly stark example of this is the following pair of simultaneous equations:

$$3a = 24$$

$$a + b = 16$$

Many students find this difficult, often saying that it can't be done. The teacher might conclude that they need some more help with equations of this sort, but the most likely reason for the difficulties with this item is not to do with mathematical skills but with their *beliefs*. If the students are encouraged to talk about their difficulty, they often say things like, 'I keep on getting *b* is 8, but it can't be because *a* is'. The reason that many students have developed such a belief is, of course, that before they were introduced to solving equations, they were almost certainly practising substitution of numbers into algebraic formulas, where each letter stood for a different number. Although the students will not have been taught that each letter must stand for a different number, they have generalised implicit rules from their previous experience (just as because we always show them triangles where the lowest side is horizontal, they talk of 'upside-down triangles').

The important point here is that we would not have known about these unintended conceptions if the second equation had been $a + b = 17$ instead of $a + b = 16$. Items that reveal unintended conceptions – in other words that provide a 'window into thinking' – are difficult to generate, but they are crucially important if we are to improve the quality of students' mathematical learning.

Now some people have argued that these unintended conceptions are the result of poor teaching. If only the teacher had phrased their explanation more carefully, had ensured that no unintended features were learnt alongside the intended features, then these misconceptions would not arise.

But this argument fails to acknowledge two important points. The first is that this kind of over-generalisation is a fundamental feature of human thinking. When young children say things like 'I go-ed to the shop yesterday', they are demonstrating a remarkable feat of generalisation. From the huge messiness of the language that they hear around them, they have learnt that to create the past tense of a verb, one adds 'ed'. In the same way, if one asks young children what causes the wind, the most common answer is 'trees'. They have not been taught this, but have observed that trees are swaying when the wind is blowing and (like many politicians) have inferred a causation from a correlation.

The second point is that even if we wanted to, we are unable to control the student's environment to the extent necessary for unintended conceptions not to arise. For example, it is well known that many students believe that the result of multiplying 2.3 by 10 is 2.30. It is highly unlikely that they have been taught this. Rather this belief arises as a result of observing regularities in what they see around them. The result of multiplying whole numbers by 10 is just to add a zero, so why shouldn't that work for all numbers? The only way to prevent students from acquiring this 'misconception' would be to introduce decimals before one introduces multiplying single-digit numbers by 10, which is clearly absurd. The important point is that we must acknowledge that what students learn is not necessarily what the teacher intended, and it is essential that teachers explore students' thinking before assuming that students have 'understood' something.

Questions that give us this 'window into thinking' are hard to find, but within any school there will be a good selection of rich questions in use – the trouble is that each teacher will have a stock of good questions, but these questions don't get shared within the school, and are certainly not seen as central to good teaching.

In Britain, the majority of teachers spend most of their lesson preparation time in marking books, invariably doing so alone. In some other countries, the majority of lesson preparation time is spent planning how new topics can be introduced, which contexts and examples will be used, and so on. This is sometimes done individually or with groups of teachers working together. In Japan, however, teachers spend a substantial proportion of their lesson preparation time working together to devise questions to use in order to find out whether their teaching has been successful.

When thinking up questions, it is important not to allow the traditional concerns of reliability and validity to determine what makes a good question. For example, many teachers think that the following question, taken from the Chelsea Diagnostic Test for Algebra (Hart *et al.*, 1985), is 'unfair':

Simplify (if possible): $2a + 3b$

This item is felt to be unfair because students 'know' that in answering questions, you have to do some work, so it must be possible to simplify this expression, otherwise the teacher wouldn't have asked the question. And I would agree that to use this item in a test or an examination where the goal is to determine a student's achievement would probably not be a good idea. But to find out whether students understand algebra, it is a very good item indeed. If in the context of classroom work, rather than a formal test or exam, a student can be tempted to 'simplify' $2a + 3b$ then I want to know that, because it means that I haven't managed to develop in the student a real sense of what algebra is about.

Similar issues are raised by asking students which of the following two fractions is the larger:

$$\frac{3}{7} \qquad \frac{3}{11}$$

Now in some senses this is a 'trick question'. There is no doubt that this is a very hard item, with typically only around one 14-year-old in six able to give the correct answer (compared with around three-quarters of 14-year-olds being able to select correctly the larger of two 'ordinary' fractions). It may not, therefore, be a very good item to use in a test of students' achievement. But as a teacher, I think it is very important for me to know if my students think that $\frac{3}{11}$ is larger than $\frac{3}{7}$ The fact that this item is seen as a 'trick question' shows how deeply ingrained into our practice the summative function of assessment is.

A third example, that caused considerable disquiet amongst teachers when it was used in a national test is based on the following item, again taken from one of the Chelsea Diagnostic Tests:

Which of the following statements is true:

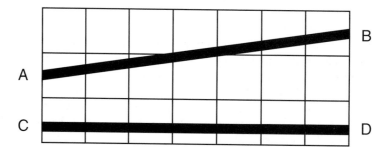

1    AB is longer than CD.
2    AB is shorter than CD.
3    AB and CD are the same length.

Again, viewed in terms of formal tests and examinations, this may be an unfair item, but in terms of a teacher's need to establish secure foundations for future learning, I would argue that this is entirely appropriate.

Rich questioning, of the kind described above, provides teachers not just with evidence about what their students can do, but also what the teacher needs to do next, in order to broaden or deepen understanding.

There is also a substantial body of evidence about the most effective ways to use classroom questions. In many schools in this country, teachers tend to use questions as a way of directing the attention of the class, and keeping students 'on task', by scattering questions all around the classroom. This probably does keep the majority of students 'on their toes' but makes only a limited contribution to supporting learning. What is far less frequent in this country is to see a teacher, in a whole-class lesson, have an extended exchange with a single student, involving a second, third, fourth or even fifth follow-up question to the student's initial answer, but with such questions, the level of classroom dialogue can be built up to quite a sophisticated level, with consequent positive effects on learning. Of course, changing one's questioning style is very difficult where students are used to a particular set of practices (and may even regard asking supplementary questions as 'unfair'). And it may even be that other students see extended exchanges between the teacher and another student as a chance to relax and go 'off task', but as soon as students understand that the teacher may well be asking them what they have learned from a particular exchange between another student and the teacher, their concentration is likely to be quite high!

How much time a teacher allows a student to respond before evaluating the response is also important. It is well known that teachers do not allow students much time to answer questions, and, if they don't receive a response quickly, they will 'help' the student by providing a clue or weakening the question in some way, or even moving on to another student. However, what is not widely appreciated is that the amount of time between the student providing an answer and the teacher's evaluation of that answer is much more important. Of course, where the question is a simple matter of factual recall, then allowing a student time to reflect and expand upon the answer is unlikely to help much. But where the question requires thought, then increasing the time between the end of the student's answer and the teacher's evaluation from the average 'wait-time' of less than a second to three seconds, produces measurable increases in learning (although increases beyond three seconds have little effect, and may cause lessons to lose pace).

In fact, questions need not always come from the teacher. There is substantial evidence that students' learning is enhanced by getting them to generate their own questions. If instead of writing an end-of-topic test, the teacher asks the students to write a test that tests the work the class has been doing, the teacher can gather useful evidence about what the students think they have been learning, which is often very different from what the teacher thinks the class has been learning. This can be a particularly effective strategy with disaffected older students, who often feel threatened by tests. Asking them to write a test for the topic they have completed, and making clear that the teacher is going to mark the questions rather than the answers, can be a hugely liberating experience for many students.

Some researchers have gone even further, and shown that questions can limit classroom discourse, since they tend to demand a simple answer. There is a substantial body of evidence that classroom learning is enhanced considerably by shifting from asking questions to making statements. For example, instead of asking, 'Are all squares rectangles?' which seems to require a 'simple' yes/no answer, the level of classroom discourse (and student learning) is improved considerably by framing the same question as a statement – 'All squares are rectangles', and asking students to discuss this in small groups before presenting a reasoned conclusion to the class.

## Feedback

Ruth Butler (1988) investigated the effectiveness of different kinds of feedback on 132 Year 7 students in 12 classes in four Israeli schools. For the first lesson, the students in each class were given a booklet containing a range of divergent thinking tasks. At the end of the lesson, their work was collected in. This work was then marked by independent markers. At the beginning of the next lesson, two days later, the students were given feedback on the work they had done in the first lesson. In four of the classes students were given marks (which were scaled so as to range from 40 to 99) while in another four of the classes, students were given comments, such as 'You thought of quite a few interesting ideas; maybe you could think of more ideas'. In the other four classes, the students were given both marks and comments.

Then, the students were asked to attempt some similar tasks, and told that they would get the same sort of feedback as they had received for the first lesson's work. Again, the work was collected in and marked.

Those given only marks made no gain from the first lesson to the second. Those who had received high marks in the tests were interested in the work, but those who had received low marks were not. The students given only comments scored, on average, 30 per cent more on the work done in the second lesson than on the first, and the interest of all the students in the work was high. However, those given both marks and comments made *no gain* from the first lesson to the second, and those who had received high marks showed high interest while those who received low marks did not.

In other words, far from producing the best effects of both kinds of feedback, giving marks alongside the comments completely washed out the beneficial effects of the comments. The use of both marks and comments is probably the most widespread form of feedback used in the United Kingdom, and yet this study (and others like it – see below) show that it is no more effective than giving marks alone. In other words, if you are going to grade or mark a piece of work, you are wasting your time writing careful diagnostic comments.

A clear indication of the role that ego plays in learning is given by another study by Ruth Butler (1987). In this study, 200 Year 6 and Year 7 students spent a lesson working on a variety of divergent thinking tasks. Again, the work was collected in and the students were given one of four kinds of feedback on this work at the beginning of the second lesson (again two days later):

- a quarter of the students were given comments;
- a quarter were given grades;
- a quarter were given praise; and
- a quarter were given no feedback at all.

**Table 19.1** Ego- and task-related attributions

| Attribution of | Ego | Task |
|---|---|---|
| **Effort** | To do better than others<br>To avoid doing worse<br>than others | Interest<br>To improve performance |
| **Success** | Ability<br>Performance of others | Interest<br>Effort<br>Experience of previous<br>learning |

The quality of the work done in the second lesson was compared to that done in the first. The quality of work of those given comments had improved substantially compared to the first lesson, but those given grades and praise had made no more progress than those given absolutely no feedback throughout their learning of this topic.

At the end of the second lesson, the students were given a questionnaire about what factors influenced their work. In particular the questionnaire sought to establish whether the students attributed successes and failures to themselves (called ego-involvement) or to the work they were doing (task-involvement). Examples of ego- and task-involving attributions are shown in Table 19.1.

Those students given comments during their work on the topic had high levels of task-involvement, but their levels of ego-involvement were the same as those given no feedback. However, those given praise and those given grades had comparable levels of task-involvement to the control group, but their levels of ego-involvement were substantially higher. The only effect of the grades and the praise, therefore, was to increase the sense of ego-involvement without increasing achievement.

This should not surprise us. In pastoral work, we have known for many years that one should criticise the behaviour, not the child, thus focusing on task-involving rather than ego-involving feedback. These findings are also consistent with the research on praise carried out in the 1970s which showed clearly that praise was not necessarily 'a good thing' – in fact the best teachers appear to praise slightly less than average (Good and Grouws, 1975). It is the quality, rather than the quantity of praise that is important and in particular, teacher praise is far more effective if it is infrequent, credible, contingent, specific and genuine (Brophy, 1981). It is also essential that praise is related to factors within an individual's control, so that praising a gifted student just for being gifted is likely to lead to negative consequences in the long term.

The timing of feedback is also crucial. If it is given too early, before students have had a chance to work on a problem, then they will learn less. In a study, undertaken by Simmonds and Cope (1993) pairs of students aged from 9 to 11 worked on angle and rotation problems. Some of these worked on the problems using Logo and some worked on the problems using pencil and paper. The students working in Logo were able to use a 'trial and improvement' strategy which enabled them to get a solution with little mental effort. However, for those working with pencil and paper, working out the effect of a single rotation was much more time-consuming, and thus the students had an incentive to think carefully, and this greater 'mindfulness' led to more learning.

The effects of feedback highlighted above might suggest that the more feedback, the better, but this is not necessarily the case. Day and Cordon (1993) looked at the learning of a group of 64 Year 4 students on reasoning tasks. Half of the students were given a 'scaffold' response when they got stuck – in other words they were given only as much help as they needed to make progress, while the other half were given a complete solution as soon as they got stuck, and then given a new problem to work on. Those given the 'scaffold' response learnt more, and retained their learning longer than those given full solutions.

In a sense, this is hardly surprising, since those given the complete solutions had the opportunity for learning taken away from them. As well as saving time, therefore, developing skills of 'minimal intervention' promotes better learning.

Feedback is not the same as formative assessment. Feedback is a necessary first step, but feedback is formative *only if the information fed back to the learner is used by the learner in improving performance*. If the information fed back to the learner is intended to be helpful, but cannot be used by the learner in improving performance, it is not formative. It is rather like telling an unsuccessful comedian to 'be funnier'.

As noted above, the quality of feedback is a powerful influence on the way that learners attribute their successes and failures. Recent research has suggested that, in terms of motivation, an even more important factor is whether students see ability as fixed or incremental. Students who believe that ability is fixed will see any piece of work that they are given as a chance either to re-affirm their ability, or to be 'shown-up'. If they are confident in their ability to achieve what is asked of them, then they will attempt the task. However, if their confidence in their ability to carry out their task is low then they will avoid the challenge, and this can be seen in mathematics classrooms up and down the country every day. Taking all things into account, a large number of students decide that they would rather be thought lazy than stupid and refuse to engage with the task, and this is a direct consequence of the belief that ability is fixed. In contrast, those who see ability as incremental see all challenges as chances to learn – to get cleverer – and therefore, in the face of failure, will try harder. What is perhaps most important here is that these views of ability are generally not global – the same students often believe that ability in schoolwork is fixed, while at the same time believe that ability in athletics is incremental, in that the more one trains, the more one's ability increases. What we therefore need to do is to ensure that the feedback we give students supports a view of ability as incremental rather than fixed.

In summary, and perhaps surprisingly for educational research, the research on feedback paints a remarkably coherent picture. Feedback to learners should focus on what they need to do to improve, rather than on how well they have done, and should avoid comparison with others. Students who are used to having every piece of work graded will resist this, wanting to know whether a particular piece of work is good or not, and in some cases, depending on the situation, the teacher may need to go along with this. In the long term, however, we should aim to reduce the amount of ego-involving feedback we give to learners (and with new entrants to the school, perhaps not begin the process at all!) and focus on the student's learning needs.

Furthermore, feedback should not just tell students to work harder or be 'more systematic' – the feedback should contain a recipe for future action, otherwise it is not formative. Finally, feedback should be designed to lead all students to believe that ability – even in mathematics – is incremental. In other words the more we 'train' at mathematics, the cleverer we get.

## Involving learners

An extensive study by Frederiksen and White (1997) showed that all students improved their scores when they thought about what it was that would count as good work. However, much more significantly, the improvement was much greater for students with weak basic skills. This suggests that, at least in part, low achievement in schools is exacerbated by students not understanding what it is they are meant to be doing – an interpretation borne out by the work of Gray and Tall (1994), who have shown that 'low-attainers' often struggle because what they are trying to do is actually much harder than what the 'high-attainers' are doing. This study, and others like it, show how important it is to ensure that students understand the criteria against which their work will be assessed. Otherwise we are in danger of producing students who do not understand what is important and what is not.

Now although it is clear that students need to understand the standards against which their work will be assessed, the study by Frederiksen and White showed that the criteria themselves were only the starting point. At the beginning of a project or piece of work, the criteria do not have the meaning for the student that they have for the teacher. Just giving 'quality criteria' or 'success criteria' to students will not work, unless students have a chance to see what this might mean in the context of their own work.

Because we understand the meanings of the criteria that we work with, it is tempting to think of them as *definitions* of quality, but in truth, they are more like labels we use to talk about ideas in our heads. For example, 'being systematic' in an investigation is not something we can define explicitly, but we can help students develop what Guy Claxton calls a 'nose for quality'.

A possible strategy (used by Frederiksen and White, 1997) is that marking schemes are shared with students, but they are given time to think through, in discussion with others, what this might mean in practice, applied to their own work. We shouldn't assume that the students will understand these right away, but the criteria will provide a focus for negotiating with students about what counts as quality in the mathematics classroom.

Another way of helping students understand the criteria for success is, before asking the students to embark on (say) an investigation, to get them to look at the work of other (anonymous) students on similar (although not, of course the same) investigations. In small groups, they can then be asked to decide which of pieces of students' work are good investigations, and why. It is not necessary, or even desirable, for the students to come to firm conclusions and a definition of quality – what is crucial is that they have an opportunity to explore notions of 'quality' for themselves. Spending time looking at other students' work, rather than producing their own work, may seem like 'time off-task', but the evidence is that it is a considerable benefit, particularly for 'low attainers'.

Whether students can then assess their own performance objectively is a matter of heated debate, but very often the debate takes place at cross-purposes. Opponents of self-assessment say that students cannot possibly assess their own performance objectively, but this is an argument about *summative* self-assessment, and no one is seriously suggesting that students ought to be able to write their own GCSE certificates! Advocates of self-assessment point out that accuracy is a secondary concern – what really matters is whether self-assessment can enhance learning.

However this is just one of the strategies. In fact, there are a huge range of studies, in different countries, and looking at students of different ages, that have found that involving students in assessing their own learning improves that learning. (A striking example is from the work of Fontana and Fernandez, 1994.)

## Putting formative assessment into practice

In a project with mathematics and science teachers, we are currently looking at ways of incorporating these ideas into classroom practice. Teachers are using strategies that include improving their questioning, using comment-only marking and the use of students' work to exemplify quality. Teachers are also trying out a number of strategies related to student self-assessment. For example, half the teachers are using 'traffic-lights' or 'smiley faces' to develop students' self-assessment skills (see Table 19.2). The teacher identifies a number of objectives for the lesson, which are made as clear as possible to the students at the beginning of the lesson. At the end of the lesson, students are asked to indicate their understanding of each objective by a coloured blob or a face. This provides useful feedback to the teacher at two levels. It is possible to see if there are any parts of the lesson that would be worth re-doing with the whole class, but also it provides feedback about which students would particularly benefit from individual support. However, the real benefit of such a system is that it forces the student to reflect on what she or he has been learning.

This feature of 'mindfulness' is one of the crucial features of effective formative assessment – effective learning involves having most of the students thinking most of the time. Effective questioning is that which engages all students in thinking, rather than remembering, and doesn't allow students to relax simply because they've just answered a question, which means that it can't be their turn again until everyone else has been asked a question.

This notion of 'mindfulness' also gives some clues about what sort of marking is most helpful. Many teachers say that formative feedback is less useful in mathematics, because an answer is either wrong or right. But even where answers are wrong or right, we can still encourage students to think. For example, rather than marking answers right and wrong and telling the students to do corrections, teachers could, instead, feed back saying simply, 'Three of these ten questions are wrong. Find out which ones and correct them'. After all, we are often telling our students to check their work, but rarely help them develop the skills to do so.

Other teachers are experimenting with 'end-of-lesson' reviews. The idea here is that at the beginning of the lesson, one student is appointed as a *rapporteur* for the lesson. The teacher then teaches a whole-class lesson on some topic, and finishes the lesson ten or fifteen minutes early. The student *rapporteur* then gives a summary of the main points of the lesson, and tries to answer any remaining questions that stu-

**Table 19.2** Developing students' self-assessment skills

| Level of understanding | Traffic light | Smiley face |
| --- | --- | --- |
| Good understanding | green | ☺ |
| Not sure | yellow (amber) | 😐 |
| Don't understand at all | red | ☹ |

dents in the class may have. If he or she can't answer the questions, then the *rapporteur* asks members of the class to help out. What is surprising is that teachers who have tried this out have found that students are queuing up to play the role of *rapporteur*, provided this is started at the beginning of the school year, or even better, when students are new to the school (Years 1, 3 or 7).

## Summary

In some ways, the ideas presented in this chapter give an old-fashioned message – very similar to the 'good practice' guidelines that were published by HMI in the 1970s and 1980s. What is new is that we now have hard empirical evidence that quality learning does lead to higher achievement. Teachers do not have to choose between teaching well on the one hand and getting good results on the other. Even if all a school cares about is improving its national test scores and exam results, the evidence is that working on formative assessment is the best way to do it. The bonus is that it also leads to better quality learning.

## References

Black, P.J. and Wiliam, D. (1998) 'Assessment and classroom learning', *Assessment in Education: principles policy and practice*, 5(1): 7–73.

Brophy, J. (1981) 'Teacher praise: a functional analysis', *Review of Educational Research*, 51(1): 5–32.

Butler, R. (1987) 'Task-involving and ego-involving properties of evaluation: effects of different feedback conditions on motivational perceptions, interest and performance', *Journal of Educational Psychology*, 79(4): 474–82.

Butler, R. (1988). 'Enhancing and undermining intrinsic motivation; the effects of task-involving and ego-involving evaluation on interest and performance', *British Journal of Educational Psychology*, 58: 1–14.

Claxton, G. (1999) *Wise up: the challenge to lifelong learning*, London: Bloomsbury.

Day, J. D. and Cordon, L.A. (1993) 'Static and dynamic measures of ability: an experimental comparison', *Journal of Educational Psychology*, 85(1): 76–82.

Fontana, D. and Fernandes, M. (1994) 'Improvements in mathematics performance as a consequence of self-assessment in Portugese primary school pupils', *British Journal of Educational Psychology*, 64: 407–17.

Frederiksen, J.R. and White, B.Y. (1997) 'Reflective assessment of students' research within an inquiry-based middle school science curriculum', paper presented at the *Annual Meeting of the American Educational Research Association*, Chicago, IL.

Good, T.L. and Grouws, D.A. (1975) 'Process-product relationships in fourth grade mathematics classrooms', report for National Institute of Education, Columbia, MO: University of Missouri (report no. NE-G–00–0–0123).

Gray, E.M. and Tall, D.O. (1994) 'Duality, ambiguity and flexibility: a "proceptual" view of simple arithmetic', *Journal for Research in Mathematics Education*, 25(2): 116–40.

Hart, K.M., Brown, M.L., Kerslake,D., Küchemann, D. and Ruddock, G. (1985) *Chelsea Diagnostic Mathematics Tests*, Windsor: NFER-Nelson.

Simmon, M. and Cope. P. (1993) 'Angle of rotation: effects of differing types of feedback on the quality of response', *Educational Studies in Mathematics,* 24(2): 163–76.

# Index

A levels 34, 36–7, 48–9; formulae for 43–4; problem of proof in 41; teaching styles 38
ability 10, see also differentiation
Abramovich, S. 114
abstract understanding 155, 160–1
acceleration: cognitive see cognitive acceleration; differentiation 194–5
acquisition: learning as 4, 6, 10
Adhami, M. 195, 211
Advanced Extension Papers 48
Advanced Subsidiary Certificate (AS level) 36–7, 48; formulae for 43–4; problem of proof in 41
Ahlgren, A. 212
Ainley, J. 249
Alexander, P.A. 4
algebra 105–19, 276; approaches to 116–17; arithmetic and 113–14; exploitation of 117–18; generalisation and 105, 106, 107–9; geometry and 115–16; roots in children's powers 107–10; roots in ignorance 110; roots in structure 110–16; use of textbooks 232–9
Anderson, J. 254
Andrews, P. 92
Anghileri, J. 98
Angolan sand drawings 136
animation 126
Anthony, G. 159
apprenticeship scheme 52
area calculations 112–13
Aristotle 93
arithmetic 91–101; algebra and 113–14; basic need to quantify 94–5; calculation 97–8, 112–13; connections 95–7, 159; fundamental theorem of arithmetic 21; investigations 100; mental 12–13, 98–9, 218–21, 225, 226–7; numeracy and 91–2; use of calculators 99–100; value of 92–4
Askew, M. 5, 6, 10, 11, 12, 39, 97, 159, 213

assessment: attainment targets 23–5, 166; coursework 262–6; diagnostic 197; formative 273–83; free standing mathematics units (FSMUs) 65–6; Key Skills Qualification 65–6; post-16 mathematics 38–48; standard assessment tests (SATs) 24; vocational education 65–6
assistance with coursework 266–7
Association for the Improvement of Geometry Teaching 127
Association of Teachers of Mathematics (ATM) 33–4, 268
assumptions 79–81
attainment targets 3, 19–20, 23–8, 166; assessment 23–5, 166
attention 254–5
Augustine, Saint 92
Ausubel, D.P. 194
axioms and assumptions 79–81

Babylonian area calculations 112–13
Backhouse, J. 193
Bain, Iain 135
Baroody, A.J. 4
Barwell, Richard 228
base ten blocks 11, 12, 13–14
Bauersfeld, H. 252
Beaton, A.E. 10
Bednarz, N. 119
behaviourism 197
Beishuizen, M. 12
Bell, A.W. 213
Berry, J. 47
Bibby, N. 44
bicycle tracks 121, 135
Bidwell, J.K. 113
Black, P.J. 273
Bloom, B.S. 193, 195, 197
Boaler, J. 158
Bonnycastle, J. 117

books 228–46
Boole, Mary Everest 110
Booth, L. 117
Bostock, L. 81
Boylan, M. 254
brackets 232–3, 242
Bridges, R. 148
Brophy, J. 44, 198
Brown, G. 211
Brown, J.S. 4
Brown, M. 19, 166
Bruner, J.S. 161, 251
BTEC 52
Butler, Ruth 278

calculation 97–8, 112–13; mental 12–13, 98–9, 218–21, 225, 226–7
calculators 44–5, 46–7, 58, 99–100, 115, 170
Carpenter, T.P. 4, 14
Celtic knots 123, 135–6
Chelsea Diagnostic Test 276
chemistry: mathematics and 63–4
Claxton, Guy 281
Clements, D. 129
closed questioning 255–6
cloze technique 248, 250
Cockroft Report 38, 74, 91, 94, 231, 267–8
codes 235–6
cognitive acceleration 195, 203–4; exploring the rectangle example 204–11; theoretical background 211–13
Cohen, A.S. 197
Coles, Alf 246
commercial mathematics schemes 3
communication 26; coursework and 269–71; language and 183–4
computers 44, 58; animation 126; computer aided design (CAD) 126; equations and 170–1; geometry and 133–4, 137; probability and 147–8; spreadsheets 45, 114–15, 147–8
connections: arithmetic 95–7, 159; connectionist teaching orientation 6, 7–15, 96–7, 159; progression and 167–71
constructivist view of learning 224
contextual understanding 154, 157–8
contradiction: proof by 82
controlling questions 249–50, 251–2
Cooper, B. 5, 158
Cope, P. 279
Cordon, L.A. 280
counter-example 73, 74, 76
counting 94–5
counting strategies 5–6, 12
coursework 259–71; assessment 262–6; communication skills 269–71; definition

260–1; help with 266–7; preparing students 267–71
Cronbach, L.J. 193

Davis, B. 92, 93
Day, J.D. 280
De Villiers, M. 83, 132
Dearing Report 33, 36, 54
Denvir, B. 166, 175
Desforges, C. 211
design: computer aided design (CAD) 126
diagnostic assessment 197
Diagnostic Teaching 213
differentiation 9, 191–201; by enrichment 194, 195–7; by outcome 194; by rate of progress 194–5; by setting different tasks 194, 197; educational differences 192; importance of 191–4; Mastery Learning and 197–201; psychological differences 192–3; strategies for 194–201
discovery teaching orientation 6, 7, 97
DiSessa, Andy 147
Dixon, L. 96
Donaldson, M. 185, 211
Dowling, Paul 53
Doyle, Arthur Conan 121
Drape, S. 34
Du Shiran 78
Dunne, M. 158
Durkin, K. 181

Education Reform Act (1988) 19
educational differences 192
egalitarianism 3
El-Said 136
emotional involvement: proof and 73–7
English A levels 34, 35
enrichment: differentiation by 194, 195–7
equations 170–1
Euclid 79, 113, 123
Euclidean geometry 82–3, 127
examples: role of 106
explanations 77–8; logical language and 184–6
expression 107

Fairchild, J. 113
falsification 73
feedback: formative assessment 278–81
Fernandes, M. 282
Feuerstein, R. 192
field dependency 192–3
Fitch, Joshua 93
Fontana, D. 282
formative assessment 273–83; feedback 278–81; involvement of learners 281–2; practice of 282–3; questioning 273–8

formulae for AS and A level mathematics 43–4
Frankenstein, M. 118
Frederiksen, J.R. 281
free standing mathematics units (FSMUs) 36, 37–8, 54, 56–8, 59; assessment 65–6
French, D. 42, 43
fundamental theorem of arithmetic 21
funnelling 252–3

Galloway, D. 213
Gardiner, A. 165
Gardiner, Tony 109
Garfield, J. 212
Gattegno, Caleb 110
General Certificate of Education (GCE) A levels see A levels
General Certificate of Education (GCE) O levels 34
General Certificate of Secondary Education (GCSE) 34, 37, 38, 49, 260, 271
General National Vocational Qualifications (GNVQs) 37–8, 52, 54, 62, 63–5, 260
generalisation: algebra and 105, 106, 107–9; generalised understanding 155, 160–1
geometry 78, 79, 80, 82–6, 121–37, 240–1; algebra and 115–16; curriculum 127–9; definition 122–4; history of 122–3; jokes in 135; mental images 217, 224; proof in 125, 131–2; reasons for studying 125–7; resources for 132–4, 138–9; teaching and learning 129–34
Gerdes, P. 136
Gibb, W. 214
Giménez, J. 119
Ginsburg, H.P. 4
Glaserfield, Ernst von 183
global positioning system (GPS) 127, 136–7
Goethe, Johann Wolfgang von 180–1
Good, T.L. 279
Gravemeijer, K. 12
Gray, E.M. 11, 281
Grouws, D.A. 279

Haggarty, L. 193, 197, 198
Hanrahan, V. 33
Hardcastle, L. 181, 182
Hardy, G.H. 92
Hart, K.M. 161, 212, 276
Hart, S. 10
hedges 188–9
help with coursework 266–7
Hewitt, Dave 263
Hiebert, J. 157
higher education: preparing for 48–9
Hill, Thomas 187

history of mathematics 92–3; geometry 122–3
Holt, John 252–3, 256
home environment 10
Howson, A.G. 94
Hoyles, C. 133
Huckstep, P. 92, 93
Hutton, C. 117
Hyland, T. 62

imagination 107
information and communications technology (ICT) 22, 44–7, 58; calculators 44–5, 46–7, 58, 99–100, 115, 170, see also computers
instrumental understanding 154, 156–7
investigations 73–4, 100, 267–8
IQ scores 192
irrational numbers 81–2
Islamic art 136

Jaworski, Barbara 183–4, 213
Johnson, S. 62
Jones, Dylan 182
Jones, K. 133
justifications 77–8

Kahneman, D. 141, 142
Kerslake, D. 212
Key Skills Qualification 54–6, 59, 62; assessment 65–6
Key Stages 19
al-Khwarizmi, Muhammad ibn Musa 106
Kieran, C. 4, 119
Kieren, T. 113
Klein, Felix 131
Knight, G. 136
Konold, C. 143

Lakatos, Imre 73
Lakoff, George 188
language 95, 179–89; communication and 183–4; explanation and logical language 184–6; thought and 186–7; uncertainty and 187–9; vocabulary 180–3
Lave, J. 4, 53, 147
learning: as acquisition 4, 6, 10; development of thought 203–14; differences in 192–3; geometry 129–34; Mastery Learning 197–201; as participation 4–6, 10; progress see progression; questions and responses 248–58; theories of 4–6, 10, 130, 161–2, 224, see also understanding
LeCoutre, M.P. 142
Lee, C. 270

lemma 78, 90
Leo, E. 213
Lewis, M. 270
Li Yan 78
Little, C. 230, 231
logical language 184–6
Loomis, E.S. 137
Loop Cards 236–7
Love, E. 249

McIntosh, A. 96
McIntyre, D. 193
MacNamara, Ann 269–70
Malkevitch, J. 123
Maori art 136
Mason, J. 106, 161, 187–8, 249, 255, 268
Mastery Learning 197–201
Mathematical Association (MA) 33, 42, 48, 127
Mathematics in Education and Industry (MEI) 33, 48–9
mechanics 47
medical imaging 126
mental mathematics 217–27; arithmetic 12–13, 98–9, 218–21, 225, 226–7; definition 217–18; mental images 217, 218–19, 221–5; teaching 224–7; verbal images 220
metaphysics 92
meta-questions 250–1
modelling 47, 52–3; geometric 126
modern apprenticeship scheme 52
Molyneux-Hodgson, S. 60
Monaghan, J. 47
Morgan, C. 266
Murphy, Bernard 235

Nabors, W. 114
national curriculum 3, 166; attainment targets 3, 19–20, 23–8; coursework in 260; mathematics in 19–28, 82, 85, 93, 94, 129, 140, 167, 223, 224; programmes of study 19, 20–2; purposes 18–19; teachers and 30–2
national numeracy strategy (NNS) 18, 25, 28–30, 31, 91, 129, 155, 173, 187, 220–1; primary schools and 4, 9, 10, 11, 14, 15
National Vocational Qualifications (NVQs) 52
Newton, D.P. 155, 159
Nicholson, A.R. 181
number lines 12, 95
numeracy 129; arithmetic and 91–2, see also national numeracy strategy (NNS)
Nunes, T. 96

Omar Khayyam 112
open questioning 255–6
Orton, A. 211, 212
Orton, T. 181, 182
Otterburn, M.K. 181
outcome: differentiation by 194

participation: learning as 4–6, 10
Pascal, Blaise 140
Pask, G. 193
patterns 111–12, 160, 263–4
percentages 168–70
Peterson, P.L. 4, 14
physical abilities 193
Piaget model of learning 130, 211, 212
Pimm, David 181, 187
Pinel, Adrian 236
place value 22, 23; cards/charts 13
planning and preparation 275–6; coursework 267–71; for higher education 48–9; progression and 175–7
Plato 92, 113
plausibility shields 188
Plunkett, S. 98
polite numbers 101
Pólya, G. 71
Popper, Karl 73
post-16 mathematics 33–49; changes in 33–4; curriculum and assessment issues 38–48; preparing for higher education 48–9; qualifications 36–8; statistical data on 34–6; vocational education 33, 52–67
Postlethwaite, K. 192, 193, 197, 198
Pozzi, S. 39
Pratt, D. 142, 145
preparation see planning and preparation
Presmeg, N. 225
primary mathematics 3–15
prime factor decomposition 21, 23
probability 140–8; computers and 147–8; large scale experiments 146–7; making sense of random experiments 141–4; purpose and utility 144–5; teaching 144–7; testing personal conjectures 145–6; variation of context 147
problem solving 26–8, 39–40, 100, 262–3
procedural methods of calculation 11, 12
procedural understanding 154, 156–7
programmes of study 19, 20–2
progression 164–78; definition 165–7; developing connections 167–71; differentiation and 194–5; knowledge and skills and 175; planning for teaching 175–7; in proving 71–2; understanding and 171–5

proof 71–86; axioms and assumptions 79–81; by contradiction 82; challenge 77–82; emotion and 73–7; explanations and justifications 77–8; false 80, 81; geometry 125, 131–2; intuition, rigour and argument 81–2; meaning of 72–3; necessary and sufficient conditions 84–5; obviousness 86; problem of 40–3; progression in proving 71–2; purpose 82–6; seeing the point of proving 82–6; theorems 78; visualisation 85–6
psychological differences 192–3
pupils/students: coursework 259–71; differences in see differentiation; emotional involvement 73–7; mathematics and 8, 11–14; questions and responses 248–58; roots of algebra in children's powers 107–10; teacher-pupil relationships 7, 8–10, see also assessment; learning; understanding
Pythagoras 92; Theorem 78, 89–90, 137

qualifications 36–8; vocational education 37–8, 54–8
questions and responses 248–58; cloze technique 248, 250; controlling questions 249–50, 251–2; creation of conjectural atmosphere 253–4; effective use of questions 251–4; formative assessment and 273–8; funnelling 252–3; genuine enquiry 250; genuine interest 254–5; meta-questions 250–1; open and closed questioning 255–6; responding to learners' questions 257; stimulating learners to question 256–7; using attention 254–5; where questions come from 248–9
Quine, W.V. 94

randomness see probability
realistic mathematics movement 158
reasoning 26, 98, 109
rectangles 204–11
Reed, S. 119
relational understanding 154–5, 158–60
resources: for geometry 132–4, 138–9, see also information and communications technology; textbooks
robotics 126
Rogoff, B. 4, 5
Rojano, T. 114
Roper, Tom 269–70
Rowland, T. 96, 185, 188

Sadock, J. M. 189
Savage 137

scaffolding 251, 280
School Mathematics Project (SMP) 33, 228, 230, 231
Seely Brown, J. 53
set theory 95
setting 9, 191, 194
Sfard, A. 4
Shire, B. 181
Shuard, H. 4
Shulman, L.S. 14
Silvester, Becky 243
Simmonds, M. 279
Smith, J.P. 144
Snow, R.E. 193
social constructivist view of learning 224
Socrates 113
Spivak, M. 78
spreadsheets 45, 114–15, 147–8
Standard Assessment Tests (SATs) 24
statistics 47
Stones, E. 164
strategic methods of calculation 11
Stripp, C. 34, 42, 43
students see pupils/students
subject knowledge for student teachers 47–8
Sutherland, R. 39, 60, 114

tables exercises: understanding and 153–5
Tahta, D. 95, 110
Tall, D.O. 281
tallying 94
tasks: differentiation by setting different tasks 194, 197; understanding and 155–6
Tate, Thomas 93
Taverner, S. 38, 39
teachers and teaching: algebra 109–10; coursework 259–71; geometry 129–34; mathematics and 7–8, 14–15; mental mathematics 224–7; orientation towards teaching 6–15, 96–7; questions and responses 248–58; styles of 38–40; subject knowledge for student teachers 47–8; teacher-pupil relationships 7, 8–10; textbooks 228–46; understanding and 153–62; vocational education 59–65, see also national curriculum; progression
textbooks 228–46
Thales of Miletus: theorem of 128, 131
theorems 78; fundamental theorem of arithmetic 21; Pythagoras' Theorem 78, 89–90, 137; Thales' theorem 128, 131
theories of learning 4–6, 10, 130, 161–2, 224
Thompson, I. 95
thought: development of 203–14; exploring the rectangle 204–11; language and 186–7; levels of thinking 203; Thinking Maths

programme 203–4, see also cognitive acceleration
transfer: concept of 53
transformational understanding 155, 160–1
transmission teaching orientation 6, 7, 97
TUNJA sequences 111
Tversky, A. 141, 142

uncertainty: language and 187–9
understanding 153–62; abstract 155, 160–1; contextual 154, 157–8; generalised 155, 160–1; instrumental 154, 156–7; key practices for 162; levels of 153–5; overcoming obstacles 161–2; procedural 154, 156–7; progression and 171–5; relational 154–5, 158–60; strategies for promotion of 156–62; task choice, lesson structure and interaction 155–6; transformational 155, 160–1
university courses 49

van den Heuvel-Panhuizen, M. 158
van der Waerden, B. 112
van Hiele model of learning 130
Viète, François 110
visualisation: geometry 125–6; proof 85–6
vocabulary 180–3

vocational education 33, 52–67; assessment 65–6; qualifications 37–8, 54–8; teaching mathematics to vocational students 59–65; what counts as mathematics 52–3
Vygotsky, Lev 165–6, 186, 188, 203, 251

Wagner, S. 119
Watson, A. 154, 160, 161, 255, 268
Wearne, D. 157
Wells, D. 92, 263–4
Wenger, E. 4
Wheeler, David 240
Whitcombe, A. 92
White, B.Y. 281
whiteboards 11, 13
Whitely, W. 126
Whitt 135
Wiliam, D. 10, 11, 39, 213, 262, 263, 273
Willan, P.T. 3
Willson, W.W. 128
Winter, J. 58
Wood, D. 213, 251
Wood, T. 252
Woodhead, Chris 9
Wray, D. 270

Yeldham, F.A. 92

Zeeman, Christopher 124